INTERNATIONAL MIGRATION RESEARCH

Research in Migration and Ethnic Relations Series

Series Editor:
Maykel Verkuyten, ERCOMER
Utrecht University

The Research in Migration and Ethnic Relations Series is published in association with the European Research Centre on Migration and Ethnic Relations (ERCOMER), Utrecht University, but draws contributions from international scholars in the field. Books in the series will be of interest to students and scholars of migration, nationalism, racism and ethnic relations. The series aims in particular to publish volumes with a comparative European focus, or those nationally-based studies which have a broader relevance to international issues of migration and ethnic relations.

Other titles in the series

Nationalism and Exclusion of Migrants: Cross-National Comparisons
Edited by Mérove Gijsberts, Louk Hagendoorn and Peer Scheepers
ISBN 0 7546 3993 2

Transnational Social Spaces: Agents, Networks and Institutions
Edited by Thomas Faist and Eyüp Özveren
ISBN 0 7546 3291 1

Roma and Gypsy-Travellers in Europe: Modernity, Race, Space and Exclusion
Angus Bancroft
ISBN 0 7546 3921 5

**EUROPEAN RESEARCH CENTRE
ON MIGRATION & ETHNIC RELATIONS**

International Migration Research

Constructions, Omissions and the Promises of Interdisciplinarity

Edited by

MICHAEL BOMMES
University of Osnabrück, Germany

and

EWA MORAWSKA
University of Essex, UK

ASHGATE

Published by
Ashgate Publishing Limited
Gower House
Croft Road
Aldershot
Hants GU11 3HR
England

Ashgate Publishing Company
Suite 420
101 Cherry Street
Burlington, VT 05401-4405
USA

Ashgate website: http://www.ashgate.com

British Library Cataloguing in Publication Data
International migration research : constructions, omissions
   and the promises of interdisciplinarity. - (Research in
   migration and ethnic relations series)
   1.Emigration and immigration - Research 2.Interdisciplinary
   research
   I.Bommes, Michael II.Morawska, Ewa T.
   304.8'2

Library of Congress Cataloging-in-Publication Data
International migration research : constructions, omissions, and the promises of
interdisciplinarity / [edited] by Michael Bommes and Ewa Morawska.
         p. cm. -- (Research in migration and ethnic relations series)
   Includes bibliographical references and index.
   ISBN 0-7546-4219-4
  1. Emigration and immigration--Research. I. Bommes, Michael. II. Morawska, Ewa T.
III. Series.

   JV6013.5.I57 2004
   304.8'072--dc22

                                                                2004022601
ISBN 0 7546 4219 4

Printed and bound in Great Britain by MPG Books Ltd, Bodmin, Cornwall

Contents

List of Contributors

Roland Bank, Chief Legal Adviser, Foundation 'Remembrance, Responsibility and Future' (compensation programme for National Socialist injustice), Berlin, Germany

Michael Bommes, Prof. of Sociology/Methodology of Intercultural and Interdisciplinary Migration Research, University of Osnabrück, Germany

Josef Ehmer, Prof. of Modern History, University of Salzburg, Austria

Adrian Favell, Prof. of Sociology, University of Califormia, Los Angeles, USA

Gary P. Freeman, Prof. of Political Science, University of Texas, Austin, USA

Andrew Geddes, Prof. of Political Science, University of Sheffield, UK

Jost Halfmann, Prof. of Sociology, Technical University of Dresden, Germany

Michael Kearney, Prof. of Anthropology, University of California, Riverside, CA

Sandra Lavenex, Assistant Prof. of Political Science, University of Bern, CH

Dirk Lehmkuhl, Senior Research Fellow in Political Science, University of Zurich, CH

Utz Maas, Prof. of Linguistics, University of Osnabrück, Germany

Leslie Page Moch, Prof. of European History, Michigan State University, USA

Ewa Morawska, Prof. of Sociology, University of Essex, UK

Introduction

Michael Bommes and Ewa Morawska

The enormous expansion of international population flows since the 1980s has been a constitutive component of accelerated globalization processes connecting different regions of the world through trade and labor exchange, international laws and organizations, and rapidly advancing transportation and communication technologies. These swelling international migrations and their diverse consequences for both sender and receiver societies have prompted governments and international organizations to find ways to control these flows either by constraining them (receiver states) or by facilitating the movement (human rights organizations and many sender governments with vested interests in immigrants remittances and their economic investments at home). Increased public concern in Western receiver countries with the influx of immigrants from remote regions of the world and its apparent relationship to globalization have been articulated recently in Huntington's (1991) vision of a 'clash of civilisations', Brimelow's (1995) prediction of 'immigration disaster', or Enzenberger's (1994) fears concerning *Die große Wanderung'* (the big migration).

The recognition of international population flows as the integral component of the globalization processes rather than as a temporary phenomenon has also raised the status of (im)migration research in scholarly disciplines, which has brought new opportunities for funding, employment, and publications, and an increasing number of young scholars interested in pursuing this field of study.[1] This elevation of interest in international migration as an important phenomenon shaping contemporary societal processes has occurred not only in the academic fields that have traditionally focused some (sub-)disciplinary attention on international migration, such as history, sociology, linguistics, or economics, but also in the specializations that have only recently claimed the study of transnational migration as a new field of research, such as the political sciences, anthropology, psychology, medicine and public health. In the United States, a classical immigration society with a long-standing melting-pot ideology, this 'turn' has been a renaissance of the established (if long marginalized) tradition of research on immigration; in Europe and other regions of the world it represents a novel scholarly concern and a quickly growing area of study. (See Kritz et al., 1981; Hui, Bun, and Beng, 1995; Bade and Weiner 1997; Massey et al., 1994, 1998; Castles and Miller, 2003.)

As a process articulating important social transformations at the beginning of a new millennium, transnational migration has been investigated, depending on the disciplinary focuses of its students, in terms of globalization of the economy and the emergence of new structures of inequality through segmented labor markets worldwide (Sassen, 2001; 1996); 'transnationalization' of lifeworlds of millions of people around the globe, unsettling traditional and creating new forms of their economic, political, social, and cultural incorporation into the societies they live in (Glick Schiller, Basch, and Blanc-Szanton, 1995; Portes 1996, 2001; Smith and Guarnizo, 1998; Myers-Scotton, 1997; Vertovec, Cohen 1999; Faist, 2000; Pries 2001); the reshaping of the territorially-bound and legally and politically sovereign nation-state in its classical modern form and of the civic-political loyalties it has engendered (Soysal, 1994; Weber, 1997; Schuck, 1998; Cornelius, Martin, and Hollifield, 1994; Bauböck, 1994; Kleger, 1997; Weiner, 1994; Mackert and Müller, 2000); or challenges to social security and state welfare provisions (Freeman, 1978; Eichenhofer, 1996; Bommes and Halfmann, 1998; Bommes and Geddes, 2000).

This vigorous (im)migration research in several academic disciplines has over the last two decades produced a tremendous amount of empirical knowledge about these issues in different countries and different immigrant groups. But although it has gained recognition as an important research area in several disciplines, international migration has not thus far become integrated into their mainstream agendas, either empirical or theoretical. Yet such mainstream integration is evidently needed when international migration has become the enduring, 'normal' feature of contemporary societies and when it articulates some of the most important transformations of the twenty-first century world.

Because of its central role in major transformations of the contemporary societies, international migration can serve as a base concept-reference in the reconceptualization of the accustomed disciplinary representations of society and its individual and institutional actors in terms of territorially bounded nation-states and its laws and policies; national cultures informed by the presupposition of the settledness of social actors who sustain and reconstitute them through their everyday activities,[2] and exclusive national identities and commitments. It can also serve as a central 'bridging' concept in the formulation of new theoretical frameworks for the analysis of contemporary societal processes in these disciplines. Bringing international migration into mainstream theoretical agendas of the disciplines that now recognize its importance and, thus, augmenting the relevance of this issue of great concern for public interest and public policies in these scholarly fields certainly is not a small but a challenging task for international migration scholars. (Participants in one of the Immigration Section panels held at the 2000 Annual Meetings of the American Sociological Association and attended by one of the editors of this volume expressed a concern that the study of international migration may become a 'mainstream niche' as gender studies have become: recognized as important and visible in the discipline's institutional structures but sidelined as an empirical and theoretical specialization.)

A related challenge for students of international migration is to make their scholarship interdisciplinary. The study of international migration 'naturally' transcends disciplinary divisions and cannot be accomplished comprehensively within a single scholarly discipline such as law, politics, economics, linguistics, or education. During the 1990s a number of studies appeared on international migration assembling (but not interconnecting) contributions from different disciplines (in the United States, e.g., Pedraza and Rumbaut, 1996; Hirschman, Kasinitz, and DeWind, 1999; Foner, Rumbaut and Gold, 2000). The recently published volume, *Migration Theory: Talking Across Disciplines*, edited by Caroline Brettell and James Hollifield (2001) is a deliberately interdisciplinary undertaking informed by an idea of 'bridge building...through the development of interdisciplinary questions' (p. 18) and reflects the growing awareness among international migration scholars of a need for a multidisciplinary approach the subject matter of their studies. Although the Brettell and Hollifield volume provides the necessary first step toward interdisciplinarity in international migration studies, much more remains to be done. However important, letting representatives of different disciplines 'speak' on international migration in their own languages to generate new research questions (the latter postulated rather than delivered in *Migration Theory*), is not the only purpose of interdisciplinarity. In fact, we should not easily assume interdisciplinary work can begin immediately with common questions. Rather than striving for a 'melting pot' that fuses different approaches, interests, and methods into one encompassing theoretical framework and research agenda, interdisciplinary efforts should aim, we believe, at the acquisition, exchange, and expansion of mutual knowledge about particular disciplines' epistemological assumptions, theoretical positions, primary research concerns, and methods of gathering and analysing evidence. This knowledge can then be 'translated' into and in-between disciplines, allowing for well-informed modifications of their accustomed research and analytic strategies and, should anybody so desire, for interdisciplinary projects. Basically, however 'conversant' in many languages, disciplines would retain their distinct profiles and concerns so that the methodologies, theoretical models, and research methods would remain plural.

With its increased visibility as the process articulating major transformations of contemporary societies and its resulting 'empowerment' as a field of research in several scholarly disciplines, international migration, we argue, now has a justified claim to play a central theoretical role in multidisciplinary studies of contemporary societies similar to the one it played, albeit in different historical circumstances, in the founding period of American sociology in the Chicago school.[3] But is the field of (im)migration research prepared to take on such a role? The review of the literature on immigration in North America and Europe, has led Massey et al. (1998) to the conclusion that 'most of this work, unfortunately, is not relevant to the task of evaluating theory. The number of studies that bear directly on theoretical propositions is rather small, and the number that critically compare competing theoretical models is even smaller' (p. 68; for a similar assessment see Portes, 1997). Does, then, international migration research as practiced today in different scholarly disciplines possess the theoretical and methodological capacities to meet the challenges presented by the elevation of its subject matter to a central place in the study of the twenty-first-century world?

This volume has been born of a cautious optimism regarding such potential. But before facing up to the challenge, we should take stock of what migration research has to offer thus far. What theoretical and methodological tools to study migration exist in various disciplines? What are the possible ways of 'talking across' these specializations? The newly recognized significance of international migration in the contemporary world and the promise of an interdisciplinary examination of its relationship with processes transforming global, regional-, state-national, and city economies, politics, and cultures, create a good juncture for a collective reflection on the underlying assumptions and taken-for-granted concerns in international migration research in the disciplines that pursue it.

There is, however, more to these (inter)disciplinary reflections than just good timing. Perhaps because of its unusually prolific growth as an autonomous study area in several academic fields, the study of international migration has been 'out of touch' with some interesting recent developments informing theory and research in social science disciplines. Specifically, increased recognition by social scientists that there is no perfectly 'selfsame' or transparent way to represent the natural or social worlds and that our knowledge of these worlds is inevitably implicated in the linguistic conventions and intellectual schemas characteristic of our multiple sociocultural habitats has resulted in a twofold methodological development.

On the one hand, this heightened epistemological consciousness has produced a number of interesting attempts to account for the artifactual features informing scholarly research and writings in particular fields, and by revealing their pre-suppositions and 'blindspots' making them more open to other, different method-ological and interpretive possibilities, especially those practiced in akin disciplines. On the other hand, this enhanced awareness of the constructed character of social science knowledge has brought to the fore the need for (self-) reflexivity or critical examination of and accounting for the scholar's professional impositions on the course and outcome of the investigation.

The recognition and accounting by researchers of their epistemological positions and their 'creative' impact on the investigated subjects does not under-mine but, to the contrary, enhances scholarly work by making it more trustworthy and, of particular concern here, more amenable to accurate interdisciplinary 'translations' (on the need for self-reflexivity in conceptualizing, executing, and interpreting collected data in historical and anthropological research, see Appleby, Hunt, and Jacob, 1994; Clifford and Marcus, 1986; for coherent methodological arguments on behalf of this position see Van Maanen, 1995; Atkinson, 1990. On the need for, specifically, the sociology-of-knowledge scrutiny of immigration studies, see Rumbaut, 2000; Gans 2000).

Although, given its multidisciplinarity, the study of international migration would seem a natural terrain for such interdisciplinary polylogues and, predicated thereon, collective examination of the premises informing research and interpreta-tions in particular disciplines, neither of these directions has thus far been pursued in this area. This volume presents a collection of such 'self-reflexive' stock-taking accounts of the constructions, omissions, and contextual entanglements of the study of international migration in different disciplines and of the meanings and promises of interdisciplinarity. These exercises in (inter)disciplinary self-reflexivity are intended not only, and not even mainly, to bring international migration research up to date with state-of-the-art developments in historical, cultural, and social science methodologies but also, and primarily, to set down some shared epistemological foundations for the challenge of making international migration a central concept in mainstream research and theory of the disciplines in which it is studied.

The idea for this book emerged during a year-long seminar-and-research Forum sponsored in 1997-98 by the European University Institute in Florence, Italy, and dedicated to 'International Migration: Geography, Politics and Culture in Europe and Beyond'. The Forum provided a unique opportunity for the exchange of ideas and the forging of collaborative projects between European and American migration scholars representing different disciplines. Organized in response to increased concern among government leaders in the European Union (the sponsor of the European University) with the rapid growth of international migration and its consequences for receiver member countries, the program of the Forum expressed high expectations, similar to those we have formulated, regarding the importance and promise of multidisciplinary research on migration.

The Forum fellows met regularly at weekly seminars to listen to presentations and to discuss each other's research projects, and in inter- or separate disciplinary subgroups they also organized several conferences on specific topics related to international migration. Talking across disciplines and at the same time across different national traditions of scholarship and different civic-political cultures was often exasperating, but these exchanges brought forth three questions that inspired this volume: What, if any, innovative theoretical concepts and analytic 'tools' does research on international migration pursued in different disciplines generate? How can they be 'fitted' into the existing theoretical and methodological apparatus of these disciplines? What presuppositions about constructing knowledge and assumed research paradigms specific for different professions and national traditions of 'good science' have informed the study of international migration in different disciplines and should be brought out to make interdisciplinary conversations meaningful and collaborative work possible?

Seven of thirteen contributors to this volume, six Europeans and one American, participated in the Forum, and the remaining six scholars, three Americans and three Europeans come from the disciplines or area studies that deal with international migration but were not represented in the original group. Altogether, they represent eight scholarly fields: law, linguistics, historical demography, anthropology, sociology, history, political science, and gender studies. Self-reflexive examinations of the premises informing (inter)disciplinary research and interpretations in the studies of international migration can be accomplished from different perspectives and, indeed, the authors have approached this task in different ways. Their approaches can be grouped, however, into four categories according to the major issue(s) informing the authors' reflections (in some essays they 'venture' in several directions at once).

In the first group of essays the firmly established epistemological premises, repertoires of theoretical concepts and interpretive frameworks informing the study of international migration and its preferred research methods are scrutinized. These issues are addressed by four contributors: historical demographer Josef Ehmer, political scientist Adrian Favell, anthropologist Michael Kearney, and historian Leslie Page Moch, each of whom considers these accustomed concepts against the actual societal processes and, in particular, transnational population movements having become a constitutive element of the major transformation and global and individual country economies, politics, and culture.

In the second group of essays the role of international migration research as a subfield of different disciplines is considered. What is the position of international migration as a social phenomenon and of research thereon in those disciplines? Are they in the focal theoretical and methodological debates in these fields? Does migration research make any contributions with more general impact on disciplines such as history, sociology, political science, law or linguistics and, if so, what are they? These questions are examined in two essays: one by political scientist Gary Freeman and the other by political sociologist Jost Halfmann.

Essays in the third group examine theoretical and methodological premises and problems of interdisciplinary research on international migration. It is often referred to as a 'natural' terrain for such collaborative work, but can the studies conducted in different disciplines become interdisciplinary without scholars recognizing or 'learning the languages' of their respective epistemological tenets and theoretical paradigms? If they cannot as the authors of contributions gathered in this group believe – it is necessary to try to 'uncover' these foundations before launching joint projects. Two collaborative essays, one by legal scholar Roland Bank and political scientist Dirk Lehmkul and the other by sociologist Michael Bommes and linguist Utz Maas, and the third one by historical sociologist Ewa Morawska address these issues.

In the fourth group of essays the subject of reflexive scrutiny is the interdependency between the scholarly study of international migration and the various social and political contexts in which it is embedded. Migration research has often been conducted as 'applied science' funded by and, as a result, accountable to different state-national and international agencies with vested interests in certain 'solutions' to the rising transnational flow of people. Such extra-scientific entanglements of migration research make it a legitimate subject of the sociology of knowledge and justify the question of to what extent and how this embeddedness influences the conceptual frameworks and problem agendas of scholars who pursue these studies. These inquiries are made in two essays authored by political scientists Sandra Lavenex and Andrew Geddes (and are also addressed in the chapter by Adrian Favell).

We note three important omissions in the volume. First, although we aimed to cover the widest possible spectrum of disciplines in which international migration research is an established subfield, it was obviously impossible to include all of them. Second, the volume contains multidisciplinary reflections on the international migration research of European and American scholars who, although trained in different traditions of professional education, are natives of Western receiver countries and share Western culture[4] and omits representatives of and perspectives from other parts of the world whose populations are highly mobile. Third, although we suggested to the contributors a few possible 'strategies for reflection' and although drafts of the chapters relative to the overall purpose of the volume were discussed at a workshop held at the European University in Florence in the summer of 1999, we made no effort to prescribe modes of scrutiny, leaving it to the authors to choose what they considered relevant in the (inter)disciplinary issues on which they focused. As a result, the volume presents a broad but not exhaustive range of reflexive approaches to the study of international migration. While they are recognized, these omissions do not undermine, we believe, the purpose of this collection of essays as discussed above.

Book Overview

The volume begins with the chapters assigned to the first focus group devoted to the scrutiny of accustomed premises, concepts, and interpretations in the disciplinary studies of migration. Historical demographer *Josef Ehmer* discusses the use in the German history of migration of the persistently vague demographic notions of 'overpopulation' and 'population pressure'. In contrast to the social science theories of international migration which have long since abandoned these abstruse concepts, in German (German and Austrian combined) historical scholarship they continue to (mis)inform explanatory models of cross-border population movements despite evidence from microanalytic studies demonstrating their inadequacy in accounting for the 'flexible and complex' local and regional mechanisms of cross-border population movements. Why, then, asks Ehmer, in view of their deficiency as explanatory factors, have overpopulation and population pressure remained key concepts in German historians' accounts of international migration? The persistence of these notions, he answers, has been the result of their implicit normative denotation of the desired state of things and the embedded history of misuse of these concepts for political purposes by the German/Austrian state and sponsor of the demographic studies (most blatantly the Nazi regimes) that has osmotically permeated tacit understandings in the ostensibly ideologically neutral scholarly research.

Ehmer concludes by calling for the exposure of these implicit premises and their consequences for scholarly analyses among German historians of international migration and for the 'reconciliation' of the micro- and macro- perspectives on this process. The same call, we might add, can also be directed at migration scholars in other social science disciplines in Europe and the United States who unreflexively use demographic concepts in their studies while unaware of the underlying premises that inform them and, thus, of their implications for the research questions and interpretative frameworks guiding their analyses.

In the same focus group, sociologist *Adrian Favell* puts under scrutiny the intellectual roots and analytic strengths and weaknesses of another prominent concept in European (im)migration studies, namely, integration. As the most popular way of conceptualizing the developing relationship between old European nation-states and their growing non-European 'ethnic' populations, it has structured immigration policy debates and policy-focused research in international migration as the most common type of scholarly inquiry into this issue in present-day Western Europe. The discourse about integrating immigrants into West European societies, argues Favell, has been implicitly informed by the deeply embedded paradigm of the nation-state as the basic organizing unit and the fundamental representation of the collective self of modern Western society. Integration is also the key linkage between the conceptualization of society as a bounded, functional whole, and the idea of the state that makes policies to achieve this goal. Thus conceived, the nation-state is attributed the agency to constitute itself a theoretical conundrum that is, arguably, impossible to resolve within the paradigm that posits it and that, most importantly, is no longer appropriate for charting the evolving relationship between present-day immigrants and their host societies. In elaborating these claims Favell examines the impact of the underlying integration paradigm on policy and institutional analyses of immigration and on survey and census-based studies of social mobility and identities of immigrants and ethnic minorities in Western Europe.

Although his point that by examining new forms of transnationalism and multi-culturalism the sociology of (im)migration might well reconsider its accustomed nation state-centered conceptual and interpretive apparatus may be well taken, Favell does not say whether and how it can be accomplished. He demonstrates persuasively that normative presuppositions are deeply inscribed in the analytic tools of the sociology of (im)migration. The question of how to deal with them will undoubtedly be answered in different ways by advocates of different epistemological traditions specific to particular academic fields, but they certainly need to be raised in interdisciplinary conversations.

The approach of anthropologist *Michael Kearney* differs from disciplinary reflections of other authors in the first focus group and, for that matter, from those of all other essays in this volume. He does not examine the 'epistemological pedigree' of the basic concepts informing the anthropological study of international migration and their impact on the research questions asked and the interpretations of findings by the anthropologists of (im)migration. Instead, he takes the empirical case of recent undocumented migrations from Southern Mexico to California to demonstrate the explanatory advantage of the anthropological versus conventional analytic strategies in migration research of disciplines that have traditionally pursued this study. This advantage, in Kearney's opinion, stems from two distinct features of the anthropological approach. First, because it situates the study of migration within the comprehensive ethnography of *trans*national communities and attends to their multiple and interrelated phenomenal levels (from material, technological and economic infrastructures to sociocultural structures of social organization, identity, worldview, etc.), the holistic anthropological approach generates information inaccessible by research strategies informed by more narrow conceptualizations of (im)migration as a basically 'economic', 'political', or 'social' process. Second, because of its historic focus on and identification with 'peripheral' communities, a robust anthropological approach to migration, argues Kearney, seeks theoretical and conceptual 'transnational displacements' from the hegemonic national intellectual-political fields within which international migration issues and theory are typically conceptualized in other disciplines.

If such a self-assured presentation of anthropology's contributions to international migration research stands in a sharp contrast to critically self-reflexive essays by migration scholars from other disciplines, it may well be because as the most recent entrants into this field of study, anthropologists of migration have been preoccupied with carving out in it a distinct place for themselves (see Morawska in this volume), and are not yet ready for such critical scrutiny of their own research. But precisely because the anthropological approach is new in migration studies and brings in distinct epistemological contributions that thus far have not been laid out by its practitioners, the premises of this analytic strategy deserve presentation.

Whereas Ehmer, Favell, and Kearney address causes and effects of theoretical and methodological inadequacy of the prominent concepts or approaches in the study of international migration as 'overpopulation', 'immigrants' integration', and fragmentation of the integral process of transnational migration into particles of disciplinary interests, historian *Leslie Page Moch* examines, instead, the consequences of a specific absence in theories of migration, namely, gender. Like migration, the study of gender cuts across various disciplines. One paradoxical consequence of this situation, according to Moch, is that although it has contributed to theoretical innovations in several disciplines, gender research remains at the periphery in practically all of them. A similar situation obtains in the field of migration studies where vast research on women's migration accumulated during the past twenty-five years has thus far failed to dislodge the established paradigms of transnational population movements.

The obdurate false assumptions of historians and sociologists of migration in Europe and North America that male and female migrations are basically different and that female migration is similar across different (im)migrant groups reveals, argues Moch, the underlying and unproblematized ontological premise that it is biological sex rather than socially constructed and time- and place-variant gender that structures this transnational movement. As a more flexible, more dynamic notion than sex and, very importantly, as a relational concept denoting men *and* women in reciprocal engagements, gender has a much greater theoretical potential for the analysis of transnational migration. Exposing to interdisciplinary scrutiny the implicit assumptions informing mainstream migration research and the epistemic advantages of the concept of gender in accounting for transnational population movements should further, Moch believes, its long-overdue integration into theories of migration.

The second focus group contains essays on the position of migration research within particular social science (sub-)disciplines. Political scientist *Gary Freeman* asks why interest in this issue in his discipline has been so low compared to that in other fields such as sociology or history, especially in view of the fact that international relations is one of the main branches of political science. He attributes this weak position of international migration studies in the internal pecking order of political science to lack of appreciation of a field of research that is practiced by many disciplines but in all of them has until recently remained at the periphery of main empirical and theoretical agendas. Adding to this neglect has been the placement of international migration outside the classical field of 'politics from above' that has defined proper political science interests and (at the empirical level a cause and effect at the same time) the scarcity of reliable and comparable data sets on this issue. As a result, there has been little advance in the political science theory concerning international migration during the last twenty-five years.

The common features of migration research have also contributed, Freeman believes, to this situation, in particular, its mainly descriptive and theoretically un(der)elaborated character, on the one hand, and, on the other, the 'normative bias' of many (im)migration scholars who infuse their research with political-ideological ideas about a 'just society'. In the second part of his essay Freeman demonstrates how, concretely, the two prominent general models in political science, political economy and institutionalism, can be applied to the study of migration. His own, apparently unselfconscious, normative option for the value-free scientistic model of the social sciences notwithstanding, Freeman's chapter raises an interesting question whether the mode of interdisciplinarity practiced by migration scholars may be responsible, in part anyway, for the marginality of this field of study in several social science disciplines? His discussion invites the conclusion that migration research might be best prepared for interdisciplinarity if it is thoroughly familiar with discipline-specific modes of conceptualizing and executing research.

Political sociologist *Jost Halfmann* shares this perspective. He views international migrations as a constitutive component of the emergence of the global world and argues that this development represents a challenge to the established approaches of political sociology and should be taken up as an occasion to rethink the traditional concepts and explanatory models in this discipline. Like Freeman, Halfmann notes that international migration has thus far attracted little attention from political sociologists but he sees a different reason for this neglect, namely, the centrality of the nation-state as the main force of societal integration in political sociology's theoretical and research agenda. World's globalization and the mass international migrations resulting from and contributing to this process reveal and, increasingly, undermine these disciplinary premises as the habituated identification of state and society is confronted with increasingly salient evidence that social realms such as the economy, law, science, or sports are not restricted to territorial borders of the national states, supranational forms of humanitarian and political organizations question states' exclusive sovereignty, and global transnational population movements challenge the unqualified bond of loyalty and care between states and their citizens.

Halfmann suggests political sociology should react to this challenge or effectively alter its theoretical frame of reference by engaging in current debates in social theory, especially the system theory of Niklas Luhmann, which, he believes, offers promising ways to link these two fields of study in the changed situation. For this link to involve political sociology and the study of international migration in a meaningful intellectual exchange, the latter should likewise take stock of its foundational concepts and accepted theories and bring them up to date with the standards of theoretical discussions in the discipline of sociology.

The third section of the book deals with the problems of interdisciplinary research. Migration research has been regarded as a fruitful field for interdisciplinary rapprochement of lawyers and political scientists interested in the processes of internationalization. In a collaborative chapter legal scholar *Roland Bank* and political scientist *Dirk Lehmkuhl* question this assumption. All too often, they argue, the promise of interdisciplinarity is wasted by confusing it either with a crude instrumentalization of knowledge of the other discipline without considering its underlying methodological assumptions, or with the hasty dissolution of disciplinary distinctions. The authors identify three related problem levels in need of (inter)disciplinary reflection. In descending order of generality they include an examination of potential epistemological gains and obstacles in the collaboration of political science and legal studies in migration research, and of a disciplinary practice needed to build up awareness of complementary or compatible concepts and approaches used in both fields; and, at the level of concrete research, the identification of specific issues or areas in the study of international migration where the gains derived from shared interests can be realized in a mutually informed way.

Within the framework of these propositions Bank and Lehmkuhl assess the shortcomings and omissions in the studies lawyers and political scientists claim to be interdisciplinary. This review is followed by general reflections on the risks and advantages of cooperation between these two disciplines. The cross-fertilization of legal studies and political science does not require, the authors argue, the 'fusion' of discipline-specific concerns and approaches. Rather, a 'disciplined interdisciplinarity' should be based on mutual awareness of the involved disciplines' epistemological assumptions and theoretical frameworks and research agendas derived therefrom as the indispensable precondition for reaping benefits from cooperation across disciplinary boundaries.

In another coauthored chapter, linguist *Utz Maas* and sociologist *Michael Bommes* discuss different modes by which their respective disciplines confront the problem of language in the field of migration research. Whereas sociology aims to analyze societal structures and defines the social as the construction of meaning through the interactive process of communication, language as the subject of linguistics does not refer to the social practice of communication, i.e. the production of meaning, but to a set of formal conditions articulating and controlling these social practices. The social as a problem is present in linguistics only in a negative role.

In this context Bommes and Maas argue that without uncovering the different disciplinary modes of constructing an object of study and their implications for the research questions asked and the interpretations of the 'same' evidence by sociologists and linguists, interdisciplinary research limited to the sole aggregation of knowledge assembled in these two fields cannot adequately account for the relationship of language and migration. On this premise the authors identify the issues (and non-issues) in sociological and linguistic research on migration that call for disciplinary self-reflections and interdisciplinary 'translations' before genuine or mutually informed joint research can be undertaken in this area.

In an update of her 1990 review of problem agendas in sociological and historical research on immigration in the United States, historical sociologist *Ewa Morawska* inquires into the major issues and dominant methodological approaches informing these two fields ten years later and assesses the scope of interdisciplinary recognition of these two disciplines. During the 1990s American sociologists and historians of immigration have shown increasing interest in each other's pursuits to a large extent because of the convergence of new concerns with assimilation, transnationalism, and racialization of ethnicity preoccupying scholars in both disciplines. Despite this 'thematic' rapprochement , Morawska argues, most of the current work in the sociology and historiography of immigration, informed by different epistemological traditions, continues to flow in two separate streams, and thus far little has been done to initiate a cross-disciplinary conversation about the research-framing tenets and presuppositions inherent in these disciplinary traditions and about the ways of their reciprocal translation.

A similar situation holds for the relationship between these two disciplines and the most recent addition to the field of migration research, the anthropology of (im)migration. Although each field cites studies of the other two in support of advanced argument, there has been no discussion of the methodological foundations of these respective propositions and their derivative connotations. In the last part of her essay Morawska discusses possible strategies for promoting a meaningful scholarly exchange among historians, sociologists and anthropologists of migration by first highlighting differences among these disciplines and then seeking interconnections and attempting 'translations' in efforts to construct multidisciplinary theories of transnational movement of people

The fourth and concluding section of the book addresses the embeddedness of scholarly research in the broader sociopolitical contexts of its time and place. Thus, political scientist *Sandra Lavenex* opens her chapter with an observation of the 'double contingency' of problem definitions in migration research: the modes of posing problems are usually framed by currently dominant civic-political discourses on this issue, which are, in turn, contingent on the different national contexts (institutional, historical, cultural) in which these debates take place. The author illustrates this observation by comparing two cases, France and Germany, both of which have in the postwar era received large influxes of (im)migrants, generating increased concern in the political establishments of these countries and considerable scholarly interest.

Lavenex's findings confirm her starting observation, but in a surprising manner. In Germany, which is usually presented as the standard-bearer of the ethno-nationalist tradition of citizenship, research on international migration and its consequences has framed these issues mainly in terms of structural integration, treating cultural and ethnic membership not as a precondition but as an implication thereof. In France, migration scholars conceptualize integration primarily as the 'field of tension' between the republican concept of citizenship and civic-political assimilation and the competing concepts of ethnic/national identity and member-ship. These surprising differences in emphases in German and French scholarship on migration, reflect, Lavenex argues, the political and moral devaluation of ethnic/national forms of civic membership in Germany after World War II and the political identity of postwar FRG as a successful welfare state on the one hand and the specific French dilemma – the product of mass immigration – to reconcile the 'particular universalism' of the French notion of citizenship with the political right to ethnic differences on the other.

The chapter of political scientist *Andrew Geddes* is a reflexive analysis in a literal sense: a political-science examination of the developing relationship between his discipline's research on international migration, European integration, and the construction and institutionalization of the 'problems of Europe'. The focus of the discussion is the connection between the development of the European Union's authority over migration-related matters and the expansion of academic research on the EU role in controlling international migration. Geddes examines the 'European-ization' of scholarly agendas in the study of migration as a response to the en-couragements of the EU institutions interested in creating such a 'European research space'. He demonstrates the impact of the EU institutional context for the management of migration-related issues on a range of scholarly ideas about so-called securitization, citizenship, and inclusion/exclusion of immigrants.

While he recognizes the influence of the institutionalization of international migration-related issues as the purview of the European Union on scholarship in this area, Geddes warns against exaggerating its effects. Most of the academic work in the EU member states remains locally (nationally) embedded, and the oppor-tunities for Euro-research are open only to relatively few scholars who usually retain strong links with their national-origin environments. This national embedded-ness imposes institutional and intellectual limits to the Europeanization of migra-tion research and related constructions 'from above' of 'the problems of Europe' that inform scholarly agendas to study these and other problems.

Notes

1   In the year 2000 a total of more than a thousand (im)migration scholars with PhD degrees were employed in American universities, a 300 per cent increase in comparison with twenty five years before (*The Immigration and Ethnic History Newsletter*, May 2000, p. 1). At the American and European Sociology, History, Social History, and Political Science Associations the number of panels dealing with issues of international migration has also been on the increase. An immense and rising volume of scholarly literature on international migration in the United States published since the 1980s and the quickly 'catching up' European studies also witness to the growing popularity of this research topic. Massey's et. al. (1998) found more than 300 references in 25 social science journals in the US and more than 150 scholarly publications in Europe during the decade preceding the publication of their study that dealt just with the question of the generating and sustaining mechanisms of migration leaving aside analyses of immigrants' incorporation into the host societies and of the consequences of international population flows for sender and receiver societies.

2   As documented by several historians, the notion of settledness of pre-modern populations has been more a 'comparative reference myth' of the social scientists of (Western) modernization than an empirical reality (see, for example, Moch and Hoerder, 1992; Bade, 2000).

3   At that time – the beginning of the 20th century – social integration or assimilation of migrants to the receiver national society were seen as the central problem in the sociological study of the American society, but implied in this conceptualization of the international migration was the assumption if its transitoriness and, thus, vanishing relevance for the discipline of sociology, and after World War II it has indeed become marginalized. In the major contemporary social theories of Parsons, Habermas, Luhmann, and also Bourdieu, Giddens, or the American rational choice and social networks schools, international migration of people plays a minor or no role. It should be noted, however, that the structural functionalism of Parsons, has provided a theoretical framework for the important studies of Eisenstadt in Israel (1954, 1985) and of Hoffmann-Nowotny (1970, 1973) in Europe (modified by a theory of power and inequality). In the United States, a reformulated world-system theory of Immanuel Wallerstein (see e.g., Shannon, 1992) and its theoretical applications in urban sociology (Sassen, 2001; see also idem, 1996) have integrated international migration.

4   Ewa Morawska received some of her graduate training in her native Poland, the sender of a large volume of westbound migrants.

References

Appleby, J., Hunt, L., and Jacob, M. (1994), *Telling the Truth About History,* Norton, New York.

Atkinson, P. (1990), *The Ethnographic Imagination,* Routledge, New York.

Bade, K.J. (2000), *Europa in Bewegung. Migration vom späten 18. Jahrhundert bis zur Gegenwart,* C.H. Beck, München.

Bade, K.J. and Weiner, M. (eds.) (1997), *Migration Past , Migration Future. Germany and the United States,* Berghan, Providence, N.J.

Bauböck, R. (1994), *Transnational Citizenship: Membership and Rights in International Migration,* Edward Elgar, Aldershot.

Bommes, M. and Halfmann, J. (eds.) (1998), *Migration in nationalen Wohlfahrtsstaaten. Theoretische und vergleichende Untersuchungen,* Rasch, Osnabrück.

Bommes, M. and Geddes, A. (eds.) (2000), *Welfare and Immigration: Challenging the Borders of the Welfare State,* Routledge, London.

Brettell, C.B. and Hollifield, J. (eds.) (2001), *Migration Theory. Talking across Disciplines,* Routledge, New York.

Brimelow, P. (1995), *Alien Nation: Common Sense about America's Immigration Disaster,* Random House, New York.

Castles, St. and Miller, M. (2003), *The Age of Migration: International Population Movements in the Modern World,* (3rd. edition) Macmillan, London.

Clifford, J. and Marcus, G. (eds.) (1986), *Writing Culture,* Univ. of California Press, Berkeley, CA.

Cornelius, W., Martin, Ph., and Hollifield, J. (1994), *Controlling Immigration: A Global Perspective,* Stanford UP, Stanford.

Eichenhofer, E. (ed.) (1997), *Social Security of Migrants in the European Union of Tomorrow,* Rasch, Osnabrück.

Eisenstadt, S. (1954), *The Absorption of Immigrants,* Routledge & Kegan Paul, London.

Eisenstadt, S. (1985), *The Transformation of Israeli Society: An Essay in Interpretation,* Westview Press, Boulder, CO.

Enzensberger, H.M. (1994), *Die große Wanderung,* Suhrkamp, Frankfurt a.M.

Faist, Th. (2000), *The Volume and Dynamics of International Migration and Transnational Social Spaces,* Oxford UP, Oxford.

Foner, N., Rumbaut, R., and Gold, St. (eds.) (2000), *Immigration Research for a New Century. Multidisciplinary Perspectives,* Russell Sage, New York.

Freeman, G. (1978), 'Immigrant Labor and Working-Class Politics', *Comparative Politics,* 11 (1), pp. 24-41.

Gans, H. (2000), 'Filling In Some Holes: Six Areas of Needed Immigration Research' in Foner, Rumbaut and Gold (eds.), *Immigration Research for a New Century,* pp. 76-92.

Glick Schiller, N., Basch, L., and Blanc-Szanton, Ch. (1995), 'From Immigrant to Transmigrant: Theorizing Transnational Migration', *Anthropological Quarterly,* 68 (3), pp. 48-63.

Hirschman, Ch., DeWind, J., and Kasinitz, Ph. (eds.) (1999), *The Handbook of International Migration: The American Experience,* Russell Sage Foundation, New York.

Hoffmann-Nowotny, H.-J. (1970), *Migration. Ein Beitrag zu einer soziologischen Erklärung,* Enke, Stuttgart.

Hoffmann-Nowotny, H.-J. (1973), *Soziologie des Fremdarbeiterproblems. Eine theoretische und empirische Analyse am Beispiel der Schweiz,* Enke, Stuttgart.

Hui, Ong Jin, Chan Kwok Bun, and Chu Soon Beng (eds.) (1995), *Crossing Borders. Transmigration in Asia Pacific,* Prentice Hall, New York.

Huntington, S. (1991), *The Third Wave,* Univ. of Oklahoma Press, Norman, OK.

Kleger, H. (ed.) (1997), *Transnationale Staatsbürgerschaft,* Campus, Frankfurt a.M. and New York.

Kritz, M. et al. (1981), *Global Trends in Migration: Theory and Research on International Population Movements,* The Center for Migration Studies, New York.

Mackert, J. and Müller, H.-P. (2000), *Citizenship. Soziologie der Staatsbürgerschaft,* Westdeutscher Verlag, Opladen.

Massey, D. et al. (1998), *Worlds in Motion. Understanding International Migration at the End of the Millennium,* Clarendon Press, Oxford and New York.

Massey, D. et al. (1994), 'An Evaluation of International Migration Theory: The North American Case', *Population and Development Review,* 20 (1), pp. 699-751.

Moch, L.P. and Hoerder, D. (eds.) (1992), *Moving Europeans. Migration in Western Europe since 1650,* Indiana UP, Bloomington, IN.

Myers-Scotton, C. (1997), *Duelling Languages. Grammatical Structure in Code-Switching,* Cambridge UP, Cambridge.

Pedraza, S. and Rumbaut, R. (eds.) (1996), *Origins and Destinies. Immigration, Race, and Ethnicity in America,* Wadsworth Publishing Company, Boston.

Portes, A. (1996), 'Transnational Communities: Their Emergence and Significance in the Contemporary World-System', in R.P. Korzniewidcz and W. Smith (eds.), *Latin America in the World Economy,* Greenwood Press, Westport, CT.

Portes, A. (1997), 'Immigration Theory for a New Century: Some Problems and Opportunities', *International Migration Review,* 31 (4), pp. 799-825.

Portes, A. (2001), 'Transnational Entrepreneurs: The Emergence and Determinants of an Alternative Form of Immigrant Economic Adaptation'. ESRC Transnational Communities Research Programme Working Paper WPTC-01-05, Oxford (www.transcomm. ox.ac.uk).

Pries, L., (ed.) (2001), *New Transnational Social Spaces. International Migration and Transnational Companies,* Routledge, London.

Rumbaut, R. (2000), 'Immigration Research in the United States: Social Origins and Future Orientations' in Foner, Rumbaut and Gold (eds), *Immigration Research for a New Century,* Russell Sage, New York. pp. 23-43.

Sassen, S. (2001), *The Global City,* 2nd ed., Princeton UP, Princeton.

Sassen, S. (1996), *Losing Control? Sovereignty in an Age of Globalization,* Columbia UP, New York.

Schuck, P. (1998), *Citizens, Strangers and In-Betweens: Essays on Immigration and Citizenship,* Yale UP, New Haven, CO.

Shannon, Th. (1992), *An Introduction to the World-System Perspective,* Westview Press, Boulder, CO.

Smith, M. and Guarnizo, L. (eds.) (1998), *Transnationalism from Below,* Transaction Publishers, New Brunswick, NJ.

Soysal, Y. (1994), *Limits of Citizenship. Migrants and Postnational Membership in Europe,* University of Chicago Press, Chicago, Il.

Van Maanen, J. (eds.) (1995), *Representation in Ethnography,* Sage Publications, Thousand Oaks, CA.

Vertovec, St. (2001), 'Transnational Social Formations: Towards Conceptual Cross-Fertilization'. Paper presented at the Workshop on 'Transnational Migration: Comparative Perspectives', Princeton University.

Vertovec, St. and Cohen, R. (ed.) (1999), *Migration, Diasporas and Transnationalism,* Edward Elgar, Cheltenham/Northhampton, MA.

Weber, A. (ed.) (1997), *Einwanderungsland Bundesrepublik Deutschland in der europäischen Union,* Rasch, Osnabrück.

Weiner, M. (1994), *The Global Migration Crisis: Challenge to States and Human Rights,* Harper Collins, New York.

PART I
THEORETICAL CONCEPTS
AND INTERPRETATIONS
IN MIGRATION RESEARCH

Chapter 1

Migration and Population in German Historical Thought: Some Critical Reflections[1]

Josef Ehmer

In attempts to seek simple explanations for causes of international migration, demographic arguments play an important role in the way political issues are commonly understood in contemporary societies. The concept of 'overpopulation' – explicitly stated or merely implied – assumes a central position in this line of argumentation. It states that a certain society or region is inhabited by a larger number of human beings than is compatible with the natural or economic resources of this society or region. This disproportion or disequilibrium produces 'population pressure' which results in migration. The most significant – and currently the most frequently encountered – field of application for this hypothesis is the area of migrational relationships between the prosperous north and the impoverished south of our contemporary world. The Third World's rapid population growth and slow economic development are interpreted as 'overpopulation' which is, in turn, construed as the cause of international migrational flows – and even, in some research, presented as a threat to developed societies or to the very future of our planet. Terms such as 'population bomb' and 'population explosion' give expression to such fears and concerns. It seems that demographic arguments are powerfully attractive because they take complex sets of facts and circumstances and trace them back to a single cause – one which is, moreover, seemingly plausible (Sen, 1994).

In contrast to their political use, what role do demographic arguments play in scholarly discussions? As it seems, the situation is a contradictory one. On the one hand, terms like 'overpopulation' belong to the cultural repertoire of the explanation of migration. Göran Rystad, for instance, speaks of the universality of migration in human history, and substantiates this claim with a brief reference to population size: 'When the size of a population becomes overwhelming in relation to the resources which it has access to, a portion will be forced to seek a livelihood elsewhere…' (Rystad, 1992, p. 1172). On the other hand, in the current theoretical debate on the analysis and explanation of migration, demographic arguments either do not play any role at all or have been shifted to the very periphery of interest. Rystad, in the article quoted above, does not use any further demographic arguments in the subsequent elaboration of 'theories of international migration'. A similar example is the essay 'Theories of International Migration: A Review and Appraisal' authored by an international and interdisciplinary 'Committee on South-North Migration' of the International Union for the Scientific Study of Population (IUSSP) and published in the Population and Development Review in 1993 (Massey et al., 1993). This essay claims to explicate and integrate the leading contemporary theories of international migration, with respect to both the initiation of international movements and the persistence of or increase in transnational population flows across space and time. The authors present numerous theories, disseminating a diverse theoretical repertoire of approaches to both empirical investigation and explanation of international migrational movements. It is interesting to note that demographic arguments do not come up at all, neither in the theories which the committee presents nor in its evaluation of them. Terms such as overpopulation or population pressure do not even come in for a single mention. It seems that the foremost social scientific theories of international migration have achieved a degree of complexity which can no longer be reconciled with the obvious simplicity of demographic arguments. Generally, one might say that in neoclassical economic approaches and in simple push-pull-models demographic concepts indeed have their place, usually as part of the explanatory chain overpopulation–poverty/unemployment–migration. As in migration theory, over the last two decades, neoclassical economic approaches have been heavily criticized and replaced by competing approaches, such as the new economics of migration, dual labour market theories, or world system theories; demographic concepts have been regarded as inadequate and left aside. A systematic and fundamental critique of concepts such as overpopulation or population pressure, however, has not been elaborated (cf. Massey et al., 1998; Parnreiter, 2000).

In the field of history the situation is different. Historical works do, as a rule, contain general statements as to the causes, the historical course, and the structure of migrational movements, and these statements certainly do have a theoretical character. Nevertheless, this is, as a rule, not made explicitly clear, but rather is cloaked as 'common sense'. It seems that historical migration research has employed theories in a way that has often been inexplicit and unconscious, and this has fostered the survival of demographic conceptual constructions and explanatory models that have been cast aside in explicit theory formation in the social sciences. This applies particularly, though not exclusively, to research done in German-speaking countries. The following paper examines the use of demographic explanatory models in German historical research on migration and tries to subject them to an empirically-based as well as to a methodological critique.

The Use of Demographic Arguments in German Migration History

In Germany, the explanation of social, economic, and even political phenomena with demographic arguments displays an especially strong intellectual tradition. Its roots go all the way back to the particular central European version of mercantilism known as cameralism (*Kameralismus*) and to the nascent science of demographics in the 17th and 18th centuries, in which the work of Johann Peter Süßmilch assumed particular importance (Birg, 1989; Ehmer 1991, pp. 25-44). A significant influence during the 19th century was the reception given to the theories of Thomas Robert Malthus, whose effect upon political and scholarly thinking can hardly be exaggerated. In the late 19th and early 20th centuries, demographic questions were accorded great importance in the social sciences then undergoing a process of modernization, with this enhanced esteem reaching its peak in the scholarly activities carried on in the Third Reich (Brocke, 1998). 'Historical-sociological demographic theories' in which the subject of migration assumed a central position took shape then (Ehmer, 1992/93). In postwar Germany, population theories stemming from the era of national socialism displayed astounding staying power. Into the 1970s, the few attempts at explicitly historical-sociological demographic theory tied in directly to the line of tradition sketched above (Köllmann, 1975, 1976). But even the modern historical-social scientific migration research that has been emerging since the 1980s has, for the most part, taken an uncritical position towards this tradition. The concepts of 'overpopulation' and 'population pressure' provide many historians with a serviceable framework to explain migrational processes. These terms can be found in encyclopedia articles on social and economic history as well as in specialized monographs and essays, and they are applied to preindustrial societies just as they are to those of the 19th and 20th centuries.

A few examples will serve to illustrate the widespread use of demographic arguments in recent German migration research. With reference to emigration from southwestern Germany, Wolfgang von Hippel (1984) maintained that 'population pressure (had been) increasing dangerously' even in the 16th and early 17th centuries. Mass emigration from Europe in the 18th and 19th centuries was said to have 'decisively contributed to...alleviating the population explosion, in that it eliminated excess population and eased economic and social tensions...' (Hippel, 1984, p. 17). Peter Marschalck argued along similar lines with reference to population growth during the *Vormärz* period prior to the revolution of 1848 that was said to have led to 'overpopulation and social tensions' in Germany. During the second half of the century as well – despite sinking rates of growth – Marschalck maintained that 'population pressure' kept up, 'partly lessened by overseas emigration...' (Marschalck, 1987, p. 20). The same demographic arguments have been used by historians of the German Empire both to account for mass emigration from Germany, as well as mass immigration to Germany and domestic migration from eastern to western Germany. Horst Rössler regards the 'background factor of general population pressure' and 'relative overpopulation' as chief causes of the mass exodus from Germany (Rössler, 1992, p. 148). According to Christoph

Klessmann, the 'pressure of rural overpopulation in the East' in conjunction with the attraction exerted by heavy industry triggered the large-scale domestic migration within Germany (Klessmann, 1992, p. 304). Similarly, Steve Hochstadt also regarded 'rural overpopulation' as the essential explanation for 19th-century German mass migration. He stated that migration is a 'response to population pressure' and 'population density': 'When population density outstrips the capacity of the local economy to provide work and income, migration is the universal demographic response' (Hochstadt, 1996, p. 144).

Klaus J. Bade, who has made the most important contribution to the development of historical-social scientific migration research in Germany, is entirely of the opinion that the process of migration can 'not be explained (with) natural population movements or the mechanistic consequences of "population pressure" and "absorption"' (Bade, 1987b, p. 10; a recent cautious and differentiated discussion is offered in Bade, 2000, pp. 165-8). Nevertheless, in earlier publications for him as well, the 'disequilibrium between population growth and employment opportunities' was the 'key impetus' or the 'most important driving force behind mass migration overseas' during the 19th century (Bade, 1984b, p. 57; 1992c, p. 311). Bade also invoked demographic arguments to explain the migration of specific segments of the population. In his influential paper on tramping by crafts and trades journeymen in Germany during the early modern period, for example, he explained the spread of mandatory tramping in guild crafts and trades during the 16th century as stemming from 'growing competitive pressure' (*Übersetzungsdruck*) in the crafts and trades which resulted from general 'population pressure pushing up against the limits of *Nahrung*' (Bade, 1982 p. 11).

Similar explanatory patterns are employed in texts giving a general historical overview. In their work on 'Social and Economic History of Europe in the 20th Century,' Gerold Ambrosius and William Hubbard come to the conclusion that the 'less industrialized regions with excess population' were the 'source regions of "classic" migrations'. Emigration is said to have constituted an 'outlet to prevent overpopulation' (Ambrosius and Hubbard, 1986, pp. 33-5). They thus repeat an argument which was applied to a whole series of countries and a variety of periods during the 19th and 20th centuries in 'The Fontana Economic History of Europe' published by Carlo Cipolla and Knut Borchardt (Cipolla and Borchardt, 1985/86). This list of examples could be continued. They show that 'overpopulation' and 'population pressure' represent a practically universal means of explaining migration, and one which can be applied to a wide variety of historical situations. Indeed, none of the works cited above made the attempt to operationalize or to test the postulated connection between population and migration. Occasional references to the density or growth of the population in source regions of emigration rather serve to illustrate demographic explanatory models than to seriously testing them empirically. Obviously, many historians – including some particularly innovative and thoughtful representatives of this field – presume that the connection between population and migration is a matter to be taken for granted and which requires no further proof.

Demographic Explanatory Models and the Results of Microhistorical Analysis

Despite this model having become so widespread, doubt and criticism have grown considerably in recent years. This has been voiced primarily by historians who have empirically investigated migrational processes of the 18th and 19th centuries on the local and regional levels and were not able to square their results with prevailing concepts of 'overpopulation' and 'population pressure'. It is precisely those regions that have long served as classic examples of the connection between mass-scale emigration and 'overpopulation' which are well on their way to becoming examples of the revision of this model. The following section will focus on some results generated by this research.[2]

One of the classic emigration areas of early modern central Europe was the German southwest, mainly the provinces surrounding the upper and middle Rhine, the Main and Neckar, and the upper Danube. From the late 17th century and throughout the 18th century, tens of thousands of people emigrated to north America and hundreds of thousands to eastern and southeastern Europe, mainly to Habsburg Hungary. From contemporary observers to present day historians, 'overpopulation' has become the most popular explanation of the mass emigration from this area. For instance, one of the local officials in the village of Steinau in Hesse reported in the early 18th century: 'The general causes of why it looks so bad…are that…the number of inhabitants is too high' (Fertig, 1997, p. 287). In 19th and 20th century historiography of migration, this argument was fully accepted and has become almost common wisdom. The orthodox argument usually starts with the custom of split inheritance in the German southwest, which stimulated uncontrolled growth of the population and led to high population density as well as to the split-up of peasant landholdings, which in turn caused poverty and overpopulation and which finally produced a latent propensity to migrate. Thus, following this argument, migration worked as a safety valve and reestablished the balance between population and land.

Recently, however, some scholars have begun to question this classic line of argumentation. The first issue that must be addressed is which territory the assumption of 'overpopulation' refers to. If what is meant are large territories such as individual states in southwestern Germany, or regions like the upper Rhine area, or the Holy Roman Empire as a whole, then it must be kept in mind that emigration to north America or southeastern Europe in the 18th century was marginal in comparison to domestic migration. For example, Georg Fertig estimates that in the Reich as a whole during the 18th century, at least one third of the population changed its dwelling place, but barely more than one percent emigrated (Fertig, 1997, p. 274). Thus, the vast majority of migrants moved entirely within areas that have been considered 'overpopulated'. It is not until attention is focused on a tiny region or a single village that the viability of the concept of 'overpopulation' can be precisely tested. For instance, a large number of persons did indeed emigrate to north America during the 18th century from the village which Fertig investigated, Göbrichen in Baden. Nevertheless, neither the rate of population growth, nor the ratio of population to available land, nor per capita grain production gives evidence of a connection to the rhythms of migration. Although the inhabitants of this district certainly did eke out an exceedingly meager existence, there is no indication that Göbrichen had reached or even surpassed some sort of population 'ceiling' or 'carrying capacity' over the course of the 18th century (Fertig, 2000, pp. 398ff.). The poverty that was in no short supply was further exacerbated during years of crisis by steep increases in the price of grain; nevertheless, short-term price fluctuations are more simply and plausibly explained by weather influences on the size of the harvest than with reference to the size of the population. Moreover, it were, generally speaking, not the most impoverished persons who emigrated. Detailed investigations of the property of emigrants and non-emigrants have shown that 'agrarian property had virtually no influence on out-migration'. As a rule, emigrants did not come from the most marginalized social strata, but rather from the better-off classes (Fertig, 1997, p. 275; 2000, p. 399; similarly in respect to mid-nineteenth-century Hesse-Cassel, Wegge, 2002).

The microanalysis of the demographic and economic development of an individual village thus shows that 'overpopulation' or 'population pressure' are unsuitable concepts to explain the extent and the rhythms of emigration. But are there alternative interpretations available to explain the actually quite high level of emigration from southwestern Germany? Answering this question would call for intensive comparative research which has only just begun, partly because, in the past, the overpopulation concept seemed to have already provided a general explanation. Initial comparative attempts show that in the southwest, climatic catastrophies, bad harvests, and periods of high grain prices were not more frequent than in other parts of the Empire. Living conditions in southwestern Germany do not seem to have been any worse than in many other parts of central Europe with much less emigration (Fenske, 1980, p. 339).

Efforts to identify the distinguishing characteristics of the classic emigration regions of southwestern Germany have brought other factors to the fore. Hacker (1975), for instance, indeed mentions 'surplus inhabitants' and 'overpopulation' as one of the causes of migration, but then gives chief consideration to 'concrete events related to matters of war, politics, weather and colonization' (Hacker, 1975, pp. 22, 23, 35). Contemporary eyewitnesses brought up the political causes of emigration, and above all increasing nepotism (*'Vetterleswirtschaft'*) during the late 18th and early 19th centuries, whereby there was a tendency toward social closure of village elites who controlled small towns by means of familial networks, and impeded access to political influence and economic resources by those who did not belong to these networks (Sabean, 1998, pp. 37f.; Fertig, 1995, p. 30). What must be continually kept in mind is the high degree of individual liberty and absence of feudal dependency in this region. The emigration policy of the states was quite liberal, so everyone could go as he or she wished, after paying a moderate emigration tax. There was also a highly developed and liquid real estate market in this region. People were used to buying and selling, inheriting and bequeathing pieces of land throughout their lives in order to accumulate wealth; real estate holdings, assets and status actually did vary considerably over the course of an individual's life (Sabean, 1990). Under these circumstances, ownership of land was a flexible category, and the legal, economic and mental ties to a particular parcel seem to have been slight. According to Georg Fertig, among the characteristic features of the migrational behavior of persons from the rural upper Rhine region was the fact that '*Nahrung*, and not homeland' constituted an essential value for them (Fertig, 1992, p. 120).

'*Nahrung*' constituted a flexible and blurry category in the language of the emigrants; it was a term which subsumed a broad spectrum of opportunities in life. The inhabitants of southwestern Germany had a pretty accurate conception of how labor and real estate markets, real wages and land prices in their homeland differed from those in North America. If 'poverty' had played a role in their decision to emigrate, then not in the sense that they had run up against the upper limit of a 'range of *Nahrung*' – however this might be defined – but rather in the sense of difference. It is difficult to empirically establish that the upper Rhine region was 'poor' in absolute terms, and this was obviously not particularly important for the decision to emigrate. To be sure, it was poor compared to Pennsylvania, the 'poor man's best country' (Fertig, 1992, p. 120; 1995, p. 11).

That the inhabitants of southwestern Germany were able to perform such comparisons naturally presupposes an intensive flow of information. One factor that has been repeatedly stressed in more recent migration research, and which also played an essential role in this region, is the 'self-generating character' of migration. As soon as migrational and informational networks were set up between two regions, they began to impact the potential choices and actions of human beings. Every successful migration drew more migration in its wake. Georg Fertig's microanalysis also showed that short-term oscillations in the number of emigrants were much more strongly influenced by the possiblities of a half-way secure transatlantic journey than by the fluctuations of grain prices and mortality rates (Fertig, 1995, p. 8). Fertig arrives at the general conclusion that, as a result of long traditions and wide variety of types of migration, 'socially accepted and well-known forms of spatial mobility were almost universally available in early modern Central Europe'. The existence of 'channels of mobility' was part of the collective knowledge that was available to potential emigrants, and the networks linking emigration and immigration regions developed their own dynamics (Fertig, 1997, pp. 280, 290; Fertig, 2000, p. 399).

Finally, it should not be forgotten that the governments and large land owners of Hungary, Russia, and colonial America who were interested in attracting immigrants concentrated their emigration propoganda on southwestern Germany, perhaps – as Hans Fenske presumes – because they were thoroughly aware of the unique features of this region enumerated above.

Hans Fenske draws the conclusion that even in the case of 'notoriously overpopulated' southwestern Germany, the push-factors had much less influence on the emigrants than the pull-factors which attracted them to new homelands. 'For the most part, the emigrants did not flee an unbearable situation, but followed the promises of the propaganda' (Fenske, 1980).[3]

Methodological Shortcomings of the Concepts of 'Overpopulation' and 'Population Pressure'

The above-cited examples show that the concepts of 'overpopulation' and 'population pressure' are unable to make a meaningful contribution to the explanation of migration processes on the local and regional level. To a much greater extent, they block the development of research strategies that are appropriate to the task of dealing with the complexity of migration. The following are just some of these problem areas.

The very first question that arises is whether it even makes sense to search for general 'causes of migration'. This issue is hardly addressed in current research on migration in the social sciences; rather, the focus has been on rhythms, forms, and consequences of migrations (Morawska, 1990). Frequently hidden behind this question of 'causes' is the assumption that human beings normally settle down and remain immobile, and have to be 'pushed' or 'pulled' in order to develop a willingness to migrate. Many central European governments that were surprised by their subjects' favorable disposition to migration in the late 18th and early 19th centuries proceeded under this assumption. Cameralistic authors above all regarded emigration as an indicator of social evils and improprieties of all kinds such as economic mismanagement, misgovernment, or lack of religious freedom. At the same time, they held the opinion that economic reforms and a 'good' government would prevent migration. Thus, during this period, migration was part of a political discourse and, presumably, the observations and arguments it brought forth say more about the political thinking of that epoch than they do about migrational behavior (Fertig, 1997, p. 287; Sabean, 1998, p. 37).

For the most part, 19th and 20th century historians have concurred with this cameralistic view, and have regarded emigration as symptomatic of economic crises, of social and political evils, or simply of 'overpopulation'. This is especially true with respect to preindustrial and early industrial societies. It is only quite recently that the conception has become established in historical migration research that migration is not to be regarded as the manifestation of crisis or solely as a characteristic of modern societies, but rather as a 'normal and structural element of human societies throughout history,...(or as) part of the general human pattern' (Lucassen and Lucassen, 1997, p. 9; Hochstadt, 1983). With reference to preindustrial Europe, this process has shifted focus onto the diversity of migrational forms: the regular change of domicile in connection with the life course, with education, marriage or profession; the cyclical labor migration on the part of male and female farm hands, apprentices, journeymen, or peddlers; the seasonal movements making up the great European migration systems; or permanent emigration (Lucassen, 1987; Moch, 1992; Beck, 1993; Fontaine, 1996; Oberpenning, 1996). From this perspective, long-distance and transatlantic migration does not seem at all to be extraordinary extensions of the scope of more or less permanent local and regional mobility. A finding that holds true for the Spanish emigration of the 16th century can certainly be applied on a much broader basis. 'In the largest sense the most important connection between internal mobility and transatlantic migration lay in the predisposition of people of practically all levels of society to relocate temporarily or permanently, principally in conjunction with the search for economic opportunity and security...The willingness to move, and the means to do so afforded by networks of communication and personal ties, affected people's decisions...' (Altmann, 1997, p. 260). In contrast to this approach, demographic explanatory models focus on short-term crisis scenarios and ignore the long continuities of spatial mobility.

Furthermore, the concepts of 'overpopulation' and 'population pressure' run the risk of overemphasizing conditions in migrants' regions of origin in comparison to the places to which they migrate, or of considering such source and destination regions in isolation from one another. More recent migration theories, in contrast, stress the systematic interrelationship between migrant's source and destination regions (Morawska, 1990; Hoerder, 1997). The rhythms of migration are, in many cases, less dependent upon business cycle developments in regions of origin than upon those in destination regions. Steve Hochstadt's seminal study of migrational movements in Germany during the 19th and 20th centuries shows very clearly that migration rates are closely associated with business cycles, but not in the way conventional crisis scenarios would suggest. Quite the contrary: 'higher migration rates in good times, lower in recession' (Hochstadt, 1999, p. 246) have prevailed in Germany during the 19th and 20th centuries. Both for rates of migration entirely within Germany as well as for those of immigration from abroad, the German economy's labor requirements were determinative.

To be sure, migration ought not to be regarded as a one-way street. In the past, European migration did not only consist of various circulating movements, such as the migration of agricultural servants, urban journeymen, seasonal labourers and the like. Immigration and emigration were very often strongly interwoven. For example, southwestern Germany in the 18th and early 19th centuries not only sent hundreds of thousands of emigrants to north America and eastern Europe, but also attracted agricultural servants, seasonal stonemasons and bricklayers from the Swiss and Austrian Alps. International migration in the German Empire in the late 19th and early 20th centuries was characterized both by mass emigration to the Americas and mass immigration from Poland and parts of the Habsburg Empire. Germany showed a double character of 'emigration land' and 'labor importer land' (Bade, 1992a; Klessmann, 1992).

In addition, return migration constitutes a considerable part of domestic and international mass migration (Morawska, 1987, pp. 228ff.). It is well-known that between one third and one half of all Europeans who emigrated overseas later returned, and some of them subsequently 're-emigrated' (Morawska, 1990, p. 195). Even the migrational relationships between industrial and agricultural regions were by no means one-way streets well into the late 19th century. Industrial laborers migrated to agricultural areas during the summer season if higher wages beckoned there, and for many of these individuals, returning to the land after reaching the age of 40 or 50 was a normal rite of passage in their life course (Postel-Vinay, 1994; Ehmer, 1994). Migration consists of a wide variety of parallel and opposing, overlapping and contradictory movements. The classic 'overpopulation theory' is conceptually incapable of embracing the fluidity and complexity of migratory movements.[4]

Malthusian Arguments as a Tautological Circle

The main methodological problem goes far beyond the field of migration research. It is inherent in the very concept of 'overpopulation'. The intellectual roots of this concept go back to the English clergyman and economist Thomas Robert Malthus, who has been enormously influential in demographic thought. In his 'Essay on the Principle of Population' (1798) he put forth a 'law of population', according to which population tended to rise much more rapidly than the production of food-stuffs could be increased. As a result, there emerges a surplus and superfluous population which threatens the entire society with poverty and hunger. According to Malthus, there are two possibilities of reestablishing an equilibrium between population and food supply. The first of these – functioning spontaneously and according to natural law – consists of famines and other catastrophes that reduce excess population. Malthus called this a 'positive check'. The second possibility entailed voluntary abstinence as a means of avoiding an increase in population, the so-called 'preventive check'. Whoever was not in a position to provide food for a family should refrain from marriage and reproduction. This second alternative could bring about the establishment of a long-term equilibrium between population and economic resources, and guarantee a state of social harmony. Migration played no particularly significant role in Malthus' work, but it appeared as an additional possibility of adjusting to available foodstuffs for a society whose population had grown too quickly. According to his theory, 'overpopulation' was reached when the population's per capita economic output fell below the subsistence level. A series of catastrophes and a high mortality rate would ensue.

Since Malthus' day, the definition of 'overpopulation' and related concepts like 'optimum population' or 'maximum population' have been further developed and refined (Zimmermann, 1989b). Population has been related to available foodstuffs, to land, jobs, or even to a certain standard of living. The definition of 'overpop-ulation' is thus highly diverse or – to put it another way – arbitrary.

The main methodological shortcoming of the concept of overpopulation is that – however it is defined – it cannot be subject to empirical proof. Overpopulation and related concepts such as population optimum, maximum, or pressure, are sim-ply not measurable.[5] What is accessible to historians are the assumed consequences or the presumed symptoms of 'overpopulation': the division and fragmentation of peasant land holdings, an increase in land and grain prices, the emergence of a class of landless persons, and, finally, migration, emigration, vagabondage and pauperism (Grigg, 1980, pp. 20-8). The clearest manifestations of 'overpopulation' appear, then, to be the major famines and mortality crises in European history, from the crisis of the 14th century to Ireland in the 1840s. This approach leads to a perfect tautological circle: the fact that the assumed symptoms of 'overpopulation' can be observed serves as proof for the proponents of this theory that there actually was 'overpopulation'; and conversely, 'overpopulation' functions as an explanation of the actually observed social crises.

Of course, it is beyond doubt that living conditions in preindustrial and early industrial Europe were wretched, and that hunger and food shortages were very real threats. But this by no means leads to the conclusion that these conditions were attributable to or exacerbated by a population that was too large or grew too fast. The economy of premodern Europe was highly dependent upon nature. Periods of adverse weather or crop failures had a tremendous effect upon the survival chances of human beings. To these circumstances can be added life-threatening social conditions such as wars or the consequences of social redistribution, inequality and exploitation. Would these threats have been any less dangerous if the population had been smaller or had grown less quickly? Would the living conditions in a village, a region, a state, or in Europe as a whole have been more favorable with ten per cent, 50 per cent or 90 per cent fewer inhabitants? There is no evidence supporting this contention. No one can say whether the population has ever run up against a 'ceiling' of production or productivity. Even if there were no doubts as to the existence of such a 'ceiling', it would still be irrelevant to scholarly research since there is not a single concrete historical situation in which it can be proven that such a ceiling had been reached or not. As William Chester Jordan's (1996) book on the famines of the 14th century shows, actual social problems can be better and more plausibly explained with alternative interpretational approaches than with the theory of 'overpopulation'. Furthermore, the relationship between the economy and the population is a highly complex one. In economic history, this is an intensively and extremely hotly disputed issue, whereas it seems that the majority of historians regard population growth and population density less as a threat and rather as an indispensible precondition for economic growth and the intensification of exchange and communication (Livi-Bacci, 1989, p. 106). To sum up, the concepts of 'overpopulation' and 'population pressure' seem to be completely inadequate for guiding us to an understanding of historical and present economic and social processes in general, and of migration in particular.

'Overpopulation' as a Normative Concept

Despite the methodological inadequacies outlined above, the theory of 'overpopulation' has been surprisingly successful in scholarly thought. Its attractivness presumably lies in its ability to explain complex social problems like poverty, hunger, waves of high mortality, as well as social unrest and revolutions in a way that is tantamount to invoking a natural law. In my opinion, the success of the theory of 'overpopulation' has to do with its character as a normative concept. It does not serve to shed light on actual social circumstances, but rather provides an image of the way society ought to be.

The southwestern region of German-speaking Europe can once again serve as an example of the normative character of the concept of 'overpopulation'. During the period of so-called 'pauperism', the population argument played a particularly dominant role as an explanation of real or feared disturbances of the prevailing order. Although the population of southwestern Germany was growing quite slowly during this period, the image of 'overpopulation' dominated the political discourse. The laments and fears were voiced loudest in those very places where population growth was weakest and overseas migration was strongest (Walker, 1967, p. 398). In those regions where villages and small towns had a long tradition of self-government, the state and the local elites introduced a system of legal restrictions on the right to marry and to take up residence which was designed to prevent 'overpopulation'. In his classic study of 'German Home Towns', Mack Walker (1967) attempted to deconstruct the meaning of 'overpopulation' under these circumstances. This concept made only superficial reference to a specific number of human beings or to any quantities at all. To a much greater extent, it was directed at social qualities. 'Overpopulation' referred to the underclasses who did not fit into the predominant image of society. According to Walker, legal restrictions placed on the right to marry and take up residence had the paradoxical effect of actually stemming the growth of the population but – as a result of their exclusionary effect – simultaneously increased the number of outsiders who were characterized by the term 'overpopulation'. 'The protective and exclusive social mechanism of the home towns...operated precisely to that effect of creating "overpopulation" while (at the same time) holding back population growth' (Walker, 1967, p. 398).

The normative character of the concept of 'overpopulation' is shown most convincingly by Elisabeth Mantl (1997) using the example of Tyrol. Tyrol was the German-speaking territory in which legal restrictions of the right to marry most powerfully impacted members of the lower classes and remained in effect longest (until after World War I). 'Overpopulation' was one of the prime arguments used by local elites to deny applications for permission to marry and to keep the entire restrictive legal structure in force. In contrast to their arguments, Tyrol – both before and after the introduction of mandatory official consent to marry – was distinguished by an extraordinarily low rate of population growth, by an extremely high age at marriage and a high proportion of singles, as well as by an extremely small number of paupers subsisting on community support (Mantl, 1997, p. 140). The social reality was diametrically opposed to the image suggested by the complaints of 'overpopulation'. As Elisabeth Mantl shows, these objections had nothing to do with real demographic conditions; rather, their aim was to preserve a traditional system of social inequality.

In the late 19th and early 20th centuries, the demographic discussion underwent a dynamic upturn. Demographic issues were discussed in the context of economics, sociology and history, and demographics was increasingly able to establish itself as an independent scholarly discipline. The first international population conference took place in Geneva in 1927, and led to the formation of the International Union for the Scientific Investigation of Population Problems-IUSIPP (after 1947: International Union for the Scientific Study of Population-IUSSP) (Höhn, 1989). The question of 'overpopulation' or 'underpopulation' – alongside the issues of birth control and international migrations – assumed a central position in this discourse. The new concept which attained preeminence in the discussions of the day was 'optimal population' (Zimmermann, 1989a, p. 4). The term had been introduced in 1908 by Julius Wolf, the German economist and, later, expert in the field of sexual behavior, and quickly achieved wide international acceptance. Among the chief issues treated by the international population conference in Geneva was 'international migration and its control' as well as the topic 'optimal population' (Höhn, 1989). Although the participating experts had no difficulty coming to an agreement on an abstract definition of optimal population, sharply conflicting opinions were expressed when it came to a practical determination of whether a particular land or continent could be said to be 'overpopulated' or 'underpopulated'. The German example provides a good basis for a discussion of the contradictory nature of the results. The advocates of the 'overpopulation hypothesis' maintained that the destruction of capital and markets in World War I exceeded the loss of human lives. They regarded the high unemployment figures as clear proof of the 'overpopulation' of Germany, a nation said to have ten to fifteen million more inhabitants than it actually needed. The proponents of the 'underpopulation hypothesis' argued by citing the declining birth rate, which they supposed to lead to an 'excessive aging' of the population and ultimately to an 'extinction of the *Volk*' (Heim and Schaz, 1996, pp. 15, 19, 27, 33).

Between these positions – which seemed so widely divergent – were a number of areas of agreement. One had to do with international migration. Whereas in the discussion of 'over- and underpopulation' human beings appeared as abstract quantities without concrete characteristics, the migration debate brought into play the 'quality' of human beings. The prevailing opinion among the German experts in population studies – as well as among their colleagues from other countries – was that emigrants were, above all, persons in the prime of their working lives with high qualifications. Therefore, unemployment was not expected to be reduced by emigration. Immigrants, on the other hand, were said to be primarily 'inferior' individuals from the poorest countries of eastern and southern Europe who were economically useless and racially dangerous (Heim and Schaz, 1996, pp. 34, 205). As had already been the case in the pauperism discussion of the early 19th century, the term 'overpopulation' did not merely refer to a number of human beings, but rather served to characterize politically, socially, religiously or ethnically un-desirable groups.

Demographic Models in Nazi Scholarship

The scholarly inadequacy and the normative character of the concept of 'over-population' obviously suit it to an especially high degree to be instrumentalized for political and ideological purposes. This as well has been particularly clear in German migration research. Friedrich Burgdörfer, one of the leading German population scientists from World War I up to the 1960s, published numerous papers in which he postulated a relationship between declining birth rates and immigration, to which he gave a racist interpretation (Brocke, 1998, pp. 88-93; Aly and Roth, 1984). His mechanistic conception of migration processes enriched the concept of 'overpopulation' with meteorological metaphors. A German 'low pressure zone' faced off with an eastern European 'high pressure area' out of which a 'tidal wave of Slavs' or, in general, 'hordes of foreigners exhibiting a low level of culture' would flow into Germany (Burgdörfer, 1917). From the late 19th century on, the concept of 'overpopulation' was charged with racist and anti-Semitic connotations, and, to an ever-greater extent, the immigration of Jews from eastern Europe to Germany became the 'crystalization point of the symbols of crisis' (Gerhard, 1997, p. 49).

Furthermore, the concept of 'overpopulation' and the 'migration pressure' triggered by it played a central role in social sciences as practiced under national socialism. The most important theorist was Gunther Ipsen (1899-1984), Professor of Sociology at the Universities of Leipzig (1926-1933), Königsberg in East Prussia (1933-1939), Vienna (1939-1945), and director of the Office of Social Research at the University of Münster in Dortmund (1951-1961) (Ehmer, 1992/93). I am referring to Ipsen in particular not only because he was one of the most prominent social scientists in Nazi Germany, but also due to the extraordinarily powerful influence he exerted upon German population studies and historical population studies in particular. Even in the 1960s and 1970s, his theories were still being characterized as 'pioneering' a new 'historical-sociological population theory' (cf. Ehmer, 1992/93). Gunther Ipsen can be considered as the originator of the theory of homeostatic demographic regimes in the preindustrial agrarian socie-ties of Europe. According to his view, there arose an 'autoregulative demographic system' between population and natural/economic resources, though only in those parts of Europe which were ruled by Germanic agrarian institutions. In eastern Europe, on the other hand, the peasant population had not significantly increased over the course of centuries; the sole reason for this was said to have been the dominion and control exerted by lords of the manor and feudal noblemen. The peasant emancipation of the 19th century then led to a compulsive sexual behavioral pattern 'of virtually animalistic proportions' and to 'unbridled fertility', the upshot of which was said to be the emergence of a 'host of wretched peasants with dwarf-sized parcels' or, formulated in another way, 'the agrarian overpop-ulation of the Slavic East'. Since, at this same time in Germany, population growth was being restrained through the use of birth control, population pressure emerging 'from the overpopulated region was exerted upon the depopulated one', which

Ipsen interpreted as a '*völkisch*' or 'racial struggle' (Ipsen, 1933, pp. 433, 446). In Ipsen's view the Germans were in danger of being pushed out of their particular *Lebensraum*, the upshot of which was seen as an increase in emigration (Ipsen, 1940, p. 21).

The concepts of overpopulation and migration pressure were widely disseminated in teaching and research under the national socialist system. They were applied above all in the context of so-called 'Ostforschung' (eastern studies) which was aggressively promoted by the national socialist state (Burleigh, 1988; Haar, 1997, 2000; Schönwälder, 1997). This field experienced another burst of growth during the early years of World War II in the German-occupied areas of eastern Europe, producing not only ideologies justifying German aggression in general, but also serving as applied social sciences which were closely allied with population policies and ethnic policies. For German economists, historians and demographics experts, it was a well-established fact that the 'overpopulation' of eastern Europe was the central problem of this region (Heim, 1997: p. 125; Haar, 2000, pp. 280-6). 'Overpopulation' was identified as the cause of the Russian revolutions of 1905 and 1917, and was likewise considered to be the force fomenting the political instability and economic crises of that region. Werner Conze (1910-1986), highly esteemed after 1945 as one of the founders of 'modern German social history', wrote at around 1939 as a young historian: 'In large parts of Eastern Central Europe, rural overpopulation is one of the most serious social and political questions we face…In Russia, it was decisive in bringing about the overthrow of the political order' (Conze, 1940, p. 40).

Thereafter, empirical research focused on differentiating among individual ethnic groups, paying particular attention to the Jewish population, whereby the theory of 'overpopulation' was modified. According to this new approach, agrarian 'overpopulation' would generally lead to migration into cities and thus to urbanization. In eastern Europe, however, cities and, in particular, commerce and the trades were dominated and monopolized by 'the Jews'. This was said to close off the possibility of migrating away from rural areas for the excess population of young peasants. 'The cities were "blocked", as it were, by the Jews' (Seraphim, 1941, p. 45). But since the cities as well were overflowing with impoverished Jews, their ultimate aim for decades had been, according to Seraphim, emigration to Germany. In order to now deter migration pressure on the part of the excess rural population and the Jewish city dwellers being exerted from eastern Europe upon Germany, and to simultaneously break the vicious circle of 'overpopulation' and poverty among the non-Jewish eastern European population, experts in population studies recommended one measure above all to the political and military authorities: namely, an ethnic cleansing directed at Jews, the '*Entjudung* of the cities and small market towns' in eastern Europe, as Werner Conze formulated it in 1940 (Conze, 1940, p. 48; Aly, 1998).

Conclusion

In Germany, modern-day historians of migration are beyond even the slightest suspicion of having anything at all to do with this scholarly logic and its deadly consequences. Quite the contrary: many of them regard their historical research on migration as a contribution to an objective, unbiased, and anti-racist discourse that considers 'spatial movement and cultural confrontation' as a chance for 'complementarity and enrichment' (Bade, 1992b, pp. 9, 15-25). Precisely for this reason, not only the methodological dubiousness of these concepts of 'overpopulation' and 'population pressure' but also their function in national socialist scholarship should serve as a warning.

Notes

1 A first version of this paper was presented for discussion in January 1998 at the European Forum on 'International Migrations: Geography, Politics and Culture in Europe and Beyond' (Josef Ehmer, The Use and Misuse of Demographic Arguments in the Historiography of Migrations: Some Critical Reflections, European University Institute, Seminar Paper MIG/8, 1998). I wish to thank all the participants of the European Forum for their critique and suggestions – in particular Michael Bommes, René Leboutte, Ewa Morawska and Bruno Ramirez. I am grateful to Georg Fertig and Werner Lausecker for their support and critical comments, and to Christof Parnreiter for sharing his unpublished findings with me. An expanded German-language version of this paper appeared in the Tel Aviver Jahrbuch für deutsche Geschichte 1998: 'Migration und Bevölkerung – Zur Kritik eines Erklärungsmodells', *Tel Aviver Jahrbuch für deutsche Geschichte*, XXVII, pp. 5-30. I express my thanks to Melvin Greenwald for his help with the English version.

2 On this topic, see especially the work of Georg Fertig, who combines the microhistorical analysis of emigration to America from a village in Baden with a systematic critique of the overpopulation model.

3 A very similar discussion developed on the subject of two other 'classic' European emigration regions, Ireland and the Alps. The traditional Malthusian interpretation of Irish and Alpine demographic and migration history has come in for increasing criticism of late. In the case of Ireland, many of the established views concerning the demographic behavior of the population were the results of projections of Malthusian ideas onto the Irish society rather than expressions of reality (Guinnane, 1997). In respect to the western Alps, David Siddle (1997) has sought to critically examine the assumption that it was the function of emigration to moderate the 'pressure on the level of subsistence' and to slow down the rate of population growth.

4 New approaches in migration theory, in contrast, such as new economics of migration, network theories, and segmented labor market theories, indeed offer analytical instruments for understanding and explaining the multifaceted character of migration (cf. Hoerder, 2002; Parnreiter, 2000; Massay, 2000). Applications of these new approaches in German-speaking migration history are offered, for example, in Bade, 2002; Fertig, 2000, pp. 20, 49-63; Lubinski, 1997, pp. 14ff., 223-234, 261-6; Steidl, 2003, pp. 30-49; Wegge, 2002).

5 The most detailed and comprehensive discussion of this subject is offered by David Grigg (1980). Grigg himself considers 'overpopulation' and 'population pressure' to be

thoroughly useful concepts. In his book, he undertakes the task of testing their plausibility in various historical situations. At the same time, he is, indeed, completely aware of the methodological problems raised by these concepts. On the problem of measurability, see particularly Grigg, 1980, pp. 16f.

References

Altmann, I. (1997), 'Moving Around and Moving On: Spanish Emigration in the Sixteenth Century', in Lucassen and Lucassen (eds.), *Migration, Migration History, History*, pp. 253-70.

Aly, G. (1998), *'Endlösung'. Völkerverschiebung und der Mord an den europäischen Juden*, Fischer Taschenbuch Verlag, Frankfurt a.M.

Aly, G. and Roth, K.H. (1984), *Die restlose Erfassung. Volkszählen, Identifizieren, Aussondern im Nationalsozialismus*, Rotbuch, Berlin.

Ambrosius, G. and Hubbard, W.H. (1986), *Sozial- und Wirtschaftsgeschichte Europas im 20. Jahrhundert*, C.H. Beck, Munich.

Bade, K.J. (1982), 'Altes Handwerk, Wanderzwang und Gute Policey: Gesellenwanderung zwischen Zunftökonomie und Gewerbereform', *Vierteljahrschrift für Sozial- und Wirtschaftsgeschichte*, 69, pp. 1-37.

Bade, K.J. (ed.) (1984a), *Auswanderer – Wanderarbeiter – Gastarbeiter. Bevölkerung, Arbeitsmarkt und Wanderung in Deutschland seit der Mitte des 19. Jahrhunderts*, Scripta Mercaturae, Ostfildern.

Bade, K.J. (1984b), Einführung: 'Vom Export der Sozialen Frage zur importierten Sozialen Frage: Deutschland im transnationalen Wanderungsgeschehen seit der Mitte des 19. Jahrhunderts', Introduction to Bade (ed.), *Auswanderer – Wanderarbeiter – Gastarbeiter*, pp. 9-72.

Bade, K.J. (ed.) (1987a), *Population, Labour and Migration in 19th- and 20th-Century Germany*, Berg, Leamington Spa.

Bade, K.J. (1987b), 'Population, Labour, Migration. Historical Studies and Issues of Current Debate', Introduction to Bade (ed.), *Population, Labour and Migration in 19th- and 20th Century Germany*, pp. 1-14.

Bade, K.J. (ed.) (1992a), *Deutsche im Ausland – Fremde in Deutschland. Migration in Geschichte und Gegenwart*, C.H. Beck, Munich.

Bade, K.J. (1992b), Vorwort und Einführung: 'Das Eigene und das Fremde – Grenzerfahrungen in Geschichte und Gegenwart'. Foreword and Introduction to Bade (ed.), *Deutsche im Ausland – Fremde in Deutschland*, pp. 9-25.

Bade, K.J. (1992c), '"Billig und willig" – die "ausländischen Wanderarbeiter" im kaiserlichen Deutschland', in Bade (ed.), *Deutsche im Ausland – Fremde in Deutschland*, pp. 311-24.

Bade, K.J. (2000), *Europa in Bewegung. Migration vom späten 18. Jahrhundert bis zur Gegenwart*, C.H. Beck, Munich.

Bade, K.J. (2002), 'Historische Migrationsforschung', *IMIS-Beiträge*, 20, pp. 21-44.

Beck, R. (1993), *Unterfinning. Ländliche Welt vor Anbruch der Moderne*, C.H. Beck, Munich.

Birg, H. (1989), 'Johann Peter Süßmilch and Thomas Robert Malthus. Marksteine der bevölkerungswissenschaftlichen Theorieentwicklung', in Mackensen et al. (eds.), *Bevölkerungsentwicklung und Bevölkerungstheorie*, pp. 53-76.

Brocke, B. vom (1998), *Bevölkerungswissenschaft Quo vadis? Möglichkeiten und Probleme einer Geschichte der Bevölkerungswissenschaft in Deutschland,* Leske + Budrich, Opladen.

Burgdörfer, F. (1917), *Das Bevölkerungsproblem, seine Erfassung durch Familienstatistik und Familienpolitik mit besonderer Bedeutung der deutschen Reformpläne und der französischen Leistungen,* Buchholz, Munich.

Burleigh, M. (1988), *Germany Turns Eastwards. A Study of Ostforschung in the Third Reich,* Cambridge UP, Cambridge.

Canny, N. (ed.) (1994), *Europeans on the Move. Studies on European Migration, 1500-1800,* Oxford UP, Oxford.

Cipolla, C. and Borchardt, K. (eds.) (1985/86), *Europäische Wirtschaftsgeschichte* (The Fontana Economic History of Europe), Vols. 3-5, Fischer, Stuttgart.

Conze, W. (1940), 'Die ländliche Übervölkerung in Polen', in D. Gusti (ed.), *Arbeiten des XIV. Internationalen Soziologen-Kongresses in Bucuresti, Abteilung B - Das Dorf,* I. Vol., Rumänisches Institut für Sozialwissenschaften, Bucuresti, pp. 40-8.

Ehmer, J. (1991), *Heiratsverhalten, Sozialstruktur, ökonomischer Wandel. England und Mitteleuropa in der Formationsperiode des Kapitalismus,* Vandenhoeck & Ruprecht, Göttingen.

Ehmer, J. (1992/93), Eine 'deutsche' Bevölkerungsgeschichte? Gunther Ipsens historisch-soziologische Bevölkerungstheorie, *Demographische Informationen,* pp. 60-70.

Ehmer, J. (1994), *Soziale Traditionen in Zeiten des Wandels. Arbeiter und Handwerker im 19. Jahrhundert,* Campus, Frankfurt a.M.

Engelhardt, U. et al. (eds.) (1976), *Soziale Bewegung und politische Verfassung,* Klett Cotta, Stuttgart.

Fenske, H. (1980), 'International Migration: Germany in the 18th Century', *Central European History,* 13, pp. 332-47.

Fertig, G. (1992), 'Um Anhoffung besserer Nahrung willen.' Der lokale und motivationale Hintergrund von Auswanderung nach Britisch-Nordamerika im 18. Jahrhundert, *Beiträge zur historischen Sozialkunde,* 22 (4), pp. 111-20.

Fertig, G. (1995), 'Does Overpopulation Explain Emigration? The Case of 18th Century Transatlantic Migration from the Rhine Lands'. John F. Kennedy-Institut für Nordamerikastudien der FU Berlin, Abteilung für Geschichte, Working Paper 84, Berlin.

Fertig, G. (1997), 'Eighteenth-Century Transatlantic Migration and Early German Anti-Migration Ideology', in Lucassen and Lucassen (eds.), *Migration, Migration History, History,* pp. 271-90.

Fertig, G. (2000), *Lokales Leben, atlantische Welt. Die Entscheidung zur Auswanderung vom Rhein nach Nordamerika im 18. Jahrhundert,* Universitätsverlag Rasch, Osnabrück.

Fontaine, L. (1996), *History of Pedlars in Europe,* Duke UP, Durham.

Gerhard, U. (1997), 'Flucht und Wanderung in Mediendiskursen und Literatur der Weimarer Republik', in Jung, Wengeler and Böke (eds.), *Die Sprache des Migrationsdiskurses,* pp. 45-57.

Grigg, D. (1980), *Population Growth and Agrarian Change. An Historical Perspective,* Cambridge UP, Cambridge.

Guinnane, T.W. (1997), *The Vanishing Irish. Households, Migration, and the Rural Economy in Ireland, 1850-1914,* Princeton UP, Princeton.

Haar, I. (1997), '"Revisionistische" Historiker und Jugendbewegung: Das Königsberger Beispiel', in Schöttler (ed.), *Geschichtsschreibung als Legitimationswissenschaft 1918-1945,* pp. 52-103.

Haar, I. (2000), *Historiker im Nationalsozialismus. Deutsche Geschichtswissenschaft und der 'Volkstumskampf' im Osten,* Vandenhoeck & Ruprecht, Göttingen.

Hacker, W. (1975), *Auswanderung aus dem südöstlichen Schwarzwald zwischen Hochrhein, Baar und Kinzig insbesondere nach Süosteuropa im 17. und 18. Jahrhundert,* Buchreihe der Südostdeutschen Historischen Kommission, Stuttgart.

Heim, S. (1997), 'Sozialwissenschaftler als Vordenker der Vernichtung?' in H. König et al. (eds.), *Vertuschte Vergangenheit. Der Fall Schwerte und die NS-Vergangenheit der deutschen Hochschulen,* C.H. Beck, Munich, pp. 118-32.

Heim, S. and Schaz, U. (1996), *Berechnung und Beschwörung. Überbevölkerung – Kritik einer Debatte,* Verlag der Buchläden Schwarze Risse – Rote Straße, Berlin.

Hippel, W. von (1984), *Auswanderung aus Südwestdeutschland. Studien zur württembergischen Auswanderung und Auswanderungspolitik im 18. und 19. Jahrhundert,* Klett Cotta, Stuttgart.

Hochstadt, St. (1983), Migration in Preindustrial Germany, *Central European History,* 16, pp. 195-224.

Hochstadt, St. (1996), 'The Socioeconomic Determinants of Increasing Mobility in Nineteenth-Century Germany', in Hoerder and Moch (eds.), *European Migrants,* pp. 141-69.

Hochstadt, St. (1999), *Mobility and Modernity. Migration in Germany, 1820-1989,* University of Michigan Press, Ann Arbor.

Höhn, Ch. (1989), 'Grundsatzfragen in der Entstehungsgeschichte der Internationalen Union für Bevölkerungswissenschaft (IUSSP/IUSIPP)', in Mackensen et al. (eds.), *Bevölkerungsentwicklung und Bevölkerungstheorie,* pp. 233-54.

Hoerder, D. (1997), 'Segmented Macrosystems and Networking Individuals: The Balancing Functions of Migration Processes', in: Lucassen and Lucassen (eds.), *Migration, Migration History, History,* pp. 73-84.

Hoerder, D. (2002), *Cultures in Contact. World Migrations in the Second Millenium,* Duke UP, Durham.

Hoerder, D. and Moch, L.P. (eds.) (1996), *European Migrants. Global and Local Perspectives,* Northeastern UP, Boston.

Husa, K., Parnreiter, Ch. and Stacher, I. (eds.) (2000), *Internationale Migration. Die globale Herausforderung des 21. Jahrhunderts?* Brandes und Apsel, Frankfurt a.M.

Ipsen, G. (1933), 'Bevölkerung', in C. Petersen et al. (eds.), *Handwörterbuch des Grenz- und Auslandsdeutschtums,* Ferdinand Hirt, Breslau, pp. 425-63.

Ipsen, G. (1940), 'Agrarische Bevölkerung', in D. Gusti (ed.) *Arbeiten des XIV. Internationalen Soziologen-Kongresses in Bucuresti, Abteilung B - Das Dorf,* I. Volume, Rumänisches Institut für Sozialwissenschaften, Bucuresti, pp. 8-22.

Jordan, W.Ch. (1996), *The Great Famine: Northern Europe in the Early Fourteenth Century,* Princeton UP, Princeton.

Jung, M., Wengeler, M. and Böke, K. (eds.) (1997), *Die Sprache des Migrationsdiskurses. Das Reden über 'Ausländer' in Medien, Politik und Alltag,* Leske + Budrich, Opladen.

Kaufmann, F.-X. (ed.) (1975), *Bevölkerungsbewegung zwischen Quantität und Qualität. Beiträge zum Problem einer Bevölkerungspolitik in der industriellen Gesellschaft,* Enke, Stuttgart.

Klessmann, Ch. (1992), 'Einwanderungsprobleme im Auswanderungsland: das Beispiel der Ruhrpolen', in Bade (ed.), *Deutsche im Ausland – Fremde in Deutschland,* pp. 303-10.

Köllmann, W. (1975), 'Gesellschaftliche Grundlagen der Bevölkerungsbewegung', in: Kaufmann (ed.), *Bevölkerungsbewegung zwischen Quantität und Qualität,* pp. 20-9.

Köllmann, W. (1976), 'Versuch des Entwurfs einer historisch-soziologischen Wanderungs-theorie', in Engelhardt et al. (eds.), *Soziale Bewegung und politische Verfassung,* pp. 260-69.

Livi-Bacci, M. (1989), *A Concise History of World Population,* Blackwell, Oxford.

Lubinski, A. (1997), *Entlassen aus dem Untertanenverband. Die Amerika-Auswanderung aus Mecklenburg-Strelitz im 19. Jahrhundert,* Universitätsverlag Rasch, Osnabrück.

Lucassen, J. (1987), *Migrant Labour in Europe 1600-1900. The Drift to the North Sea,* Croom Helm, London.

Lucassen, J. and Lucassen, L. (eds.) (1997), *Migration, Migration History, History. Old Paradigms and New Perspectives,* Peter Lang, Bern.

Mackensen, R. et al. (eds.) (1989), *Bevölkerungsentwicklung und Bevölkerungstheorie in Geschichte und Gegenwart,* Campus, Frankfurt a.M.

Mantl, E. (1997), *Heirat als Privileg. Obrigkeitliche Heiratsbeschränkungen in Tirol und Vorarlberg 1820-1920,* Verlag für Geschichte und Politik, Vienna.

Marschalck, P. (1987), 'The Age of Demographic Transition: Mortality and Fertility', in Bade (ed.), *Population, Labour and Migration,* pp. 15-33.

Massey, D.S. et al. (1993), 'Theories of International Migration: A Review and Appraisal', *Population and Development Review,* 19 (3), p. 431-66.

Massey, D.S., Arango, J., Koucouci, A. et al. (1998), *Worlds in Motion: Understanding International Migration at the End of the Millenium,* Clarendon Press, Oxford.

Massey, D.S. (2000), 'Einwanderungspolitik für ein neues Jahrhundert', in Husa, Parnreiter, and Stacher (eds.), *Internationale Migration,* pp. 53-76.

Moch, L.P. (1992), *Moving Europeans. Migration in Western Europe since 1650,* Indiana UP, Bloomington, IN.

Morawska, E. (1987), 'Sociological Ambivalence: The Case of East European Peasant-Immigrant Workers in America, 1880s-1930s', *Qualitative Sociology,* 10 (3), pp. 225-50.

Morawska, E. (1990), 'The Sociology and Historiography of Immigration', in Yans-McLaughlin (ed.), *Immigration Reconsidered,* pp. 187-238.

Oberpenning, H. (1996), *Migration und Fernhandel im 'Tödden-System'. Wanderhändler aus dem nördlichen Münsterland im mittleren und nördlichen Europa des 18. und 19. Jahrhunderts,* Universitätsverlag Rasch, Osnabrück.

Parnreiter, Ch. (2000), 'Theorien und Forschungsansätze zu Migration', in Husa, Parnreiter, and Stacher (eds.), *Internationale Migration,* pp. 25-52.

Postel-Vinay, G. (1994), 'The Disintegration of Traditional Labour Markets in France. From Agriculture and Industry to Agriculture or Industry', in G. Grantham and M. MacKinnon (eds.), *Labour Market Evolution: The Economic History of Market Integration, Wage Flexibility and the Employment Relation,* Routledge, London, pp. 64-83.

Rössler, H. (1992), 'Massenexodus: die Neue Welt des 19. Jahrhunderts', in Bade (ed.), *Deutsche im Ausland – Fremde in Deutschland,* pp. 148-56.

Rystad, G. (1992), 'Immigration History and the Future of International Migration', *International Migration Review,* 26 (4), pp. 1168-99.

Sabean, D.W. (1998), *Kinship in Neckarhausen, 1700-1870,* Cambridge UP, Cambridge.

Sabean, D.W. (1990), *Property, Production and Family in Neckarhausen, 1700-1780,* Cambridge UP, Cambridge.

Schönwälder, K. (1997), '"Lehrmeisterin der Völker und der Jugend." Historiker als politische Kommentatoren, 1933 bis 1945', in Schöttler (ed.), *Geschichtsschreibung als Legitimationswissenschaft,* pp. 128-65.

Schöttler, P. (ed.), (1997), *Geschichtsschreibung als Legitimationswissenschaft 1918-1945*, Suhrkamp, Frankfurt a.M.

Sen, A. (1994), 'Die Menschenbombe. Ein globales Problem – Verblendung und Wirklichkeit', *Lettre International*, 27, pp. 6-13.

Seraphim, P.-H. (1941), 'Bevölkerungs- und Wirtschaftsprobleme einer europäischen Gesamtlösung der Judenfrage', *Weltkampf*, 1 (1/2), p. 45.

Siddle, D.J. (1997), 'Migration as a Strategy of Accumulation: Social and Economic Change in Eighteenth-Century Savoy', *Economic History Review*, 50, pp. 1-20.

Steidl, A. (2003), *Auf nach Wien! Die Mobilität des mitteleuropäischen Handwerks im 18. und 19. Jahrhundert am Beispiel der Haupt- und Residenzstadt*, Verlag für Geschichte und Politik, Vienna.

Walker, M. (1967), *German Home Towns*, Cornell UP, Ithaca.

Wegge, S.A. (2002), 'Occupational Self-Selection of European Emigrants: Evidence from Nineteenth-Century Hesse-Cassel', *European Review of Economic History*, 6, pp. 365-94.

Yans-McLaughlin, V. (ed.) (1990), *Immigration Reconsidered. History, Sociology, and Politics*, Oxford UP, Oxford.

Zimmermann, K.F. (1989a), Optimum Population: An Introduction, in Zimmermann (ed.), *Economic Theory of Optimal Population*, pp. 1-16.

Zimmermann, K.F. (ed.) (1989b), *Economic Theory of Optimal Population*, Springer, Berlin.

Chapter 2

Integration Nations:
The Nation-State and Research
on Immigrants in Western Europe[1]

Adrian Favell

Despite its somewhat old-fashioned, functionalist air, 'integration' is still the most popular way of conceptualizing the developing relationship between old European nation-states and their growing non-European, 'ethnic' immigrant populations. It is also widely used to frame the advocacy of political means for dealing with the consequences of immigration in the post-World War II period. Many similar, difficult-to-define concepts can be used to describe the process of social change that occurs when immigrants are 'integrated' into their new host society. But none occurs with the frequency or all-encompassing scope of the idea of integration across such a broad range of West European countries. This fact continues to decisively structure policy research and policy debate on these subjects in Europe.

The wide and varied ordinary language usages of the term are linked to a deeper association of the concept with a longstanding intellectual *paradigm* at the root of modern western society's conception of itself. This paradigm roots applied social policy thinking in the idea of the 'nation-state' as the principal organizing unit of society, with all the epistemological assumptions and political constraints that this term implies. By using the term, writers continue to conceive of 'society' as a bounded, functional whole, structured by a state which is able to create policies and institutions to achieve this goal. This 'nation-state-society' paradigm may now no longer be the appropriate one for charting the evolving relationship of new immigrants and their host contexts in Europe. In this paper, then, I seek to explore the strengths and weaknesses of 'integration' as the seemingly inevitable framework for discussing issues in policy-directed research on immigration and ethnic relations.[2] After discussing *why* integration is still such a prevalent term in European thinking – despite emerging theoretical challenges associated with globalization and transnationalism – I explore some of the distinct national and supra-national contributions to research in this field. Our comparative under-standing is often distorted by the predominant focus in much research on big and established country cases such as Britain, Germany or France. I also make reference therefore to newer debates surfacing in less central European nations such as Italy, the Netherlands and Denmark, as well as the insights afforded by unusual cases such as Austria and Belgium.

'Integration' in Ordinary Language Usages

What is typically spoken of when academics or policy makers use the term 'integration' to speak of a collective goal regarding the destiny of new immigrants or ethnic minorities? We can, of course, think of a long list of measures designed to deal with the longer term consequences of migration and settlement. These can be distinguished from immigration policies *per se*, such as policies on border control, rights of entry and abode, or of asylum. 'Integration' conceptualizes what happens after, conceiving practical steps in a longer process which invariably includes the projection of *both* deep social change for the country concerned, *and* of fundamental continuity between the past and some idealized social endpoint. Measures concerned with integration include (the list is by no means exhaustive, but indicative): basic legal and social protection; formal naturalization and citizenship (or residency-based) rights; anti-discrimination laws; equal opportunities positive action; the creation of corporatist and associational structures for immigrant or ethnic organizations; the redistribution of targeted socioeconomic funds for minorities in deprived areas; policy on public housing; policy on law and order; multicultural education policy; policies and laws on tolerating cultural practices; cultural funding for ethnic associations or religious organizations; language and cultural courses in the host society's culture, and so on (for similar checklists of policies, see Kymlicka, 1995, pp. 37-8; Soysal, 1994, pp. 79-82; Vertovec, 1997, pp. 61-2).

What is interesting is when and why such measures are packaged together and interlinked within the broader concept of 'integration'. The very difficult-to-define process of social change with historical continuity pictured here, is for sure spoken of using a plethora of other terms: assimilation, absorption, acculturation, accommodation, incorporation, inclusion, participation, cohesion-building, enfranchisement, toleration, anti-discrimination, and so on. Yet other terms on this list are either vaguer (absorption, accommodation, toleration); too technically precise, and hence absorbed within integration (such as incorporation, which specifies a legal process, or anti-discrimination, which only describes one type of practical measure); or are concepts which can be used descriptively without necessarily invoking the active intervention of some political agency (assimilation, or acculturation). In recent years, less loaded terms such as inclusion and participation have had some popularity, but neither can match the technical 'social engineering' quality of the term integration; nor do they invoke a broader vision of an ideal end-goal for society *as a whole*. Visionary academics and pragmatic policy makers all need a descriptive *and* normative umbrella term, that can give coherence and polish to a patchy list of policy measures aiming at something which, on paper, looks extremely difficult and improbable: the (counterfactual) construction of a successful, well-functioning multicultural or multi-racial society. The identification of this conceptual space in progressive-minded practical thinking about the consequences of immigration has – however euphemistic – always been a key part of the term's success.

The other key thing about the list of measures seen to be part of 'integration policy', is that they are all things that a *state* can 'do'. Although for the time being it is rare to come across a specifically designated 'Ministry of Integration', the policy field has emerged as a differentiated area of government, often crossing the competences of different departments. Integration is thus not only an ideal goal for society; it is also something a government sets out to achieve. This assumption is crucial to the nation-state centred conceptualization of social processes that will be found at the core of practical ordinary language usages of the term. Such a use precludes the idea that a society might achieve an integrated state of affairs without the state's intervention.

Sociologically speaking, we can, of course, conceive of integration taking place without the structure-imposing involvement of the state. Immigrants can be 'integrated' into the local labor market as employees or service providers, or they can be 'integrated' into complex inter-community relations at, say, city or district level. Looked at from a bottom-up perspective – where the integration of society as a whole is not assumed as the end goal of interaction between ethnically diverse groups – multicultural relations can be seen to take all kinds of organized and semi-organized forms. These may not at all be encompassed by the top-down, organized structures typical of state thinking on the subject, such as policy frameworks, official channels of participation, or legally circumscribed rights, restrictions and entitlements. Multiculturalism as a descriptive state-of-affairs, in this sense, could be the product of something that never had anything to do with the 'multicultural' policies or institutions of the state. However – as historical theorists of the state would remind us with their vivid terminology – the state has always constituted itself in the way it imposes formal structures and institutionalizes social relations via a systematic 'embracing', 'caging' and/or 'penetrating' of society (Torpey, 2000). This logic of incorporation has invariably in recent history taken a dominant form of collective social power (to borrow the terms of Mann, 1993) that seeks to encompass, contain and bind together the state's domination of society, and all the varied market or community relations inside it. This form is the modern nation state. And, as soon as we begin to think of integration as a collective societal goal which can be achieved through the systematic intervention of collective political agency, we inevitably begin to invoke the nation-state in the production of a different, caged and bounded version of multicultural social relations.

It is very difficult, then, to make much sense of the term integration in practical, applied terms, without bringing back in the nation-state, at least in the European political context. This is not only because the term gets monopolized by nationally-rooted policy makers who, I will suggest, typically link their ideas about integration and their measures for achieving it – even when they are 'multicultural' in inspiration – to historical concerns with nation-building. As I will also go on to explain, it is equally because of a range of epistemological constraints imposed by the practical operationalization of integration as a framework for applied research, whether targeted at questions of policy or at generating knowledge through survey-based studies of immigrants and ethnic minorities.

Looking across Western Europe in the broadest possible way, it is clear that 'integration' has emerged as the most widely used general concept for describing the target of post-immigration policies. This is not to say that every political figure or intellectual in every country likes or uses the term. The synthetic, cross-national pronouncements of international and intergovernmental organizations might be taken as one good indicator of its pervasive acceptance by the end of the 1990s. It is noticeable how, for example, the conclusions of the presidency of the European Council of Ministers at Tampere in October 1999, gestured specifically towards integration as the key term for encompassing the post-immigration processes EU institutions would like to get involved with in this area of rising political significance. Although rarely defined, it is also noticeably foregrounded in the formulations of some of the broadest cross-national programmes instigated by organizations as varied as the Council of Europe, the ILO or the OSCE. The formulations of NGOs in Brussels likewise constantly use the term, as do influential transatlantic policy fora such as the Carnegie Endowment for International Peace or Metropolis.[3]

This success echoes the past and recent history of policy debate in individual nation-states. The case of France here is typical. The emergence of *'intégration'* as the central term of the 'new republican synthesis' of the 1980s, followed a period in which older assimilationist ideas vied with the post-60s inheritance of ideas about cultural difference and the anti-racist struggle (Costa-Lascoux, 1989; Weil, 1991; Haut Conseil à l'Intégration, 1993). Integration became the sensible position for the centre trying to distinguish itself from xenophobic nationalism on the one hand, and radical anti-system discourses on the other. A similar centrist convergence occurred earlier in Britain in the late 1960s, notably in a well remembered quotation from then Home Office minister Roy Jenkins, one of the principal architects of race relations legislation (Rose et al., 1969, Rex, 1991). Although the anti-racist left has always rejected it, the concept has retained a high degree of practical significance for the liberal, cross-party centre. Indeed, with the emergence of new migration questions surrounding the reception of asylum seekers, integration has re-emerged as the most comprehensive term for conceiving resettlement policies, and has been central to recent Home Office consultations on immigration policy (Castles et al., 2002). France and Britain are the paradigmatic early 'integration nations' in Europe: turning post-war, post-colonial policies into a mildly nationalist reaffirmation of the tolerant, cosmopolitan, inclusive nature of their conceptions of nationhood (on this, see Favell, 1998).

Across other European countries, we can find numerous examples of countries converging similarly on integration as the widest frame for discussing post-immigration policies (see Mahnig, 1998). It is used frequently in research in Germany or Belgium, albeit with ambiguity about *what* the immigrant is integrating into, given the federal, city-centred and multi-levelled nature of the process here (Esser, 1999; Blommaert and Verschueren, 1998). It has returned to the fore in the Netherlands and Sweden, after periods of flirtation with more cultural differentialist thinking, as they seek to reconnect the provision of welfare benefits and multicultural policy with conditions about the learning of the national language and culture (Fermin, 1999; Soininen, 1999). It has also been the most obvious frame for 'new' (or self-discovering) countries of immigration – such as Italy, Spain, Denmark or Austria – finally formulating a centrist, more progressive response to their current immigration 'crisis'.[4] Perhaps even more importantly, immigrant and ethnic groups themselves speak of desiring integration, or phrase their criticisms of racism and exclusion as barriers to full or fair integration (see, for example, the frequent use of word in Alibhai-Brown, 2000, a well-known ethnic minority spokesperson in Britain).

Some of these ordinary language usages shadow the well-established American preference for 'assimilation' as the core sociological concept (Alba and Nee, 1997). In terms of recent immigrants, 'integration' is here often used interchangeably with assimilation in the US, when it is gesturing to the functional involvement of new migrant 'ethnic' groups in the society's housing, educational, welfare or employment systems (Edmonston and Passel, 1994). Here, indeed, the term has been moved away from its discredited links with desegregation issues over black/white public relations in the 1960s, to a more European-looking concern with the cultural and social absorption of diverse new populations that have grown dramatically in the US since the opening up of immigration laws in 1965.

Europeans, however, usually shy away from the term assimilation, which in a European context would smack of biological overtones and the nasty cultural intolerance of the past. But the European preference for 'integration' ahead of 'assimilation' is not really the choice of a less loaded or more politically sensitive term over one which implies greater conformist and exclusionary pressures, quite the contrary. It signals, rather, a deeper concern with the fact that the changes brought on by post-war immigration in Europe have raised anew questions over historical continuity – about the substance of nation-building – which echo once again the longer histories of nation-building: the more-or-less coercive absorption of minority populations and regions through centralizing processes of modernization (the classic formulation of this is Gellner, 1983). Integration, then, is about imagining the national institutional forms and structures that can unify a diverse population; hence imagining what the state can actively do to 'nationalize' newcomers and re-constitute the nation-state under conditions of growing cultural diversity. The nation building institutions of European nations are – unlike the US and other continents of immigration – not historically built on immigration and geographical distance from Europe, but on bounded notions of specific territory and the constant self-distinction of 'indigenous', culturally 'unique' populations constrained to live alongside very close, and troublesomely similar neighbours. The essential problematic worrying European policy makers is, then, the difficult and often only partial accommodation of culturally distinct outsiders and foreigners into longstanding social and cultural institutions which were essentially defined historically *within* Europe, and for highly *local* reasons, in quite exclusive and belligerent terms. The fear which thus defines the problematic of immigrant integration is that full assimilation on these conditions is probably never likely to occur.

The everyday popularity of integration as a term may appear peculiar at a time when so-called globalization and, in particular, new forms of migration and mobility are said to have generated all kinds of nation-state-transcending 'transnational' actors and forms of organization (see Faist, 2000; Papastergiadis, 1999). Our unit of society is now routinely said to be something we must look for beyond the nation-state (Cohen and Kennedy, 2000). In the more speculative fancies of social theorists we are invited to think of the trajectory of (post-) modernity as going beyond society itself (for example, Giddens, 1990; Urry, 2000). Under these conditions, migrant groups might be thought of as not following the same westernizing, modernizing integration path into full citizenship, membership and belonging of their new host societies. Pan-national and regional cooperation, as well as the re-emergence of the city as the locus for integration, is also said to have reduced the significance of the nation-state as an exclusive, bounded 'population container' in Europe (Torpey, 2000).

Yet the endurance of 'integration' as the goal of most *practical* policy thought on this question in Europe – including amongst the leading independent academic authorities – gives us a clue to the vested interests and applied imperatives of the older, nation-state building paradigm. As soon as their minds turn to applied policy formulations, these people recognize no 'beyond-the-nation-state' to immigration policy. Europeans continue to speak of the integration of immigrants into bounded, nationally-distinct societal units – focusing attention on typical nation-building questions such as naturalization, access to citizenship, access to the welfare state, participation in political and social institutions, and so on – precisely because anything else threatens the basic political ordering of European cultural and social diversity into state-centred, state-organized social forms. To put it another way, the incentive structures of policy thinking and comparative research on the integration of immigrants in Europe, are still very much set by the imperatives of the singular nation-state-society, which recognizes this and only this as the fundamental problematic at stake here.

Integration as a Paradigm for Policy Research

Unlike in America, academic research on immigrants and integration in Europe is still dominantly structured by its explicit or implicit links to the knowledge demands of specific policy agendas and political discussions in different national contexts (on these, see Favell, 2001). In Europe, the overlap and interpenetration of research and policy making is pervasive at national and, increasingly, international level. Academics are co-opted into politicized roles either through the direct shaping of the research agenda by public and institutional funding opportunities to do 'applied' work; by the invitation to take on the role of public intellectual in media or government work; or by their activist involvement as campaigners, in which their work is used to articulate political positions. This involvement clearly is linked to society's functional need for someone to express political agency, with academics contributing through their research to the construction of both social problems (as they are perceived) and their solution. Insofar as their work also often serves to 'think' for the state, it also helps underwrite dominant nation-building ideologies. Such a role has its costs. The involvement of researchers in activism or the policy process can also diminish the intellectual autonomy and viability of independent academic research outside of more instrumentalized uses.

European nations are obviously at different stages of development in their internal debates, but in most cases academic thinking is now moving beyond purely denunciatory work on the negative consequences of immigration (such as studies of racism) into the conceptualization of practical integration solutions and trajectories of multicultural social change. For example, in Britain, the popular sub-field of more critical anti-racist, Marxist and post-Marxist writers (such as the cultural studies writers inspired by Stuart Hall) – whose work tended to focus on condemning the racism of state institutions and celebrating the 'resistance' of immigrant cultures – have themselves found there is a limit to what can be done with such arguments. More recently, they have begun to more consciously contribute to debates about multicultural citizenship, in relation to mainstream policy formulations (i.e., Gilroy, 2000; Alibhai-Brown, 2000).[5] The desire to make a respectable intervention into the public debate, or to get hired for research by the government or political think-tanks, can thus be a disciplining experience. Such contributions can, as the evolution of anti-racist and multicultural thinking in Britain shows, play a major role in legitimizing in the mainstream a national sense of ease with difference and diversity. In many other countries, a similar evolution can be observed, with discussion about 'integration' playing the central mainstream role as a focus for constructive, pragmatic, policy-related interventions.

National self-sufficiency in policy debates has, however, been the rule. The terms and categories that dominate discussion in different places – for example, 'multiculturalism' and 'race relations' in Britain, or republicanism and *citoyenneté* in France – are the product of often exclusively internal national political dynamics. Notably, they are discourses which reflect and reproduce longer standing narratives of nationhood and national destiny popular in these countries. When references to other countries appear, comparison usually enters as a further self-justificatory strategy for the national ideology. In France, for example, a key move among many public intellectuals involved in producing the 'new republican synthesis' and idea of *intégration* of the 1980s was the contrasting of the 'universalist' French tradition with the 'differentialism' of its European and North American rivals (most dramatically in Schnapper, 1991; Todd, 1994). Over time, however, the prejudices of comparison have softened, especially as policy actors and academics have themselves been increasingly exposed to debates and consultation with other national counterparts. Under these conditions, their national reflection may begin to incorporate more explicit elements of structured comparative knowledge, recognizing the specificities of the other national starting points and the opportunities of cross-national policy learning. The emergence of pan-European structures (both EU and Council of Europe) has added to this imperative, tendering research which, in order to get funded, must be explicitly cross-national in scope and personnel, and policy oriented in its objectives.

The first result of academic cross-national policy comparison was the identification of ideal-type national 'models' of citizenship and integration (Hammar, 1985; Castles, 1995). This Weberian comparative impulse was strongly influenced by North American writers bringing a more autonomous set of interests to the study of immigration in Europe (especially Brubaker 1989, 1992). The models approach was popular because it proved to be such an effective heuristic strategy: reducing the problem of the vague and indefinable object of enquiry – a national 'society' in all its complexity – to a 'model' which captures the key explanatory variables of social change. These were invariably identified as 'path dependent' historical sources of national cultural difference. The most well-known argument linked to the models approach has been the classic distinction between the 'ethnic' and 'civic' nation in citizenship studies, distilled from a reductive (and largely inaccurate) stylization of French and German nationality law as ideal types of *ius soli* and *ius sanguinis* citizenship. It was surely questionable to 'explain' the differences between these two similar cases by reference to national ideologies, themselves produced in the past by nationalist intellectuals and state actors to distinguish one nation from the other (on this see Weil, 1996). Yet even if historically dubious, the power of the contrast here worked to generate effective normative arguments about a *de facto* national convergence across Europe – foreseeing mixed sources of nationality and a limited recognition of *ius soli* for second and third generations – thus helping German policy makers to move towards reforms (Hansen and Weil, 2000).

The deeper explanatory challenge here would be to produce a more reflexive understanding of the ideological modes by which similar European nation-states have justified and reproduced their own models, as culturally distinct projections of collective identity (see Favell, 1998; Alund and Schierup, 1991; Joppke, 1999). More even handed comparison has gone on to recognize that while national policy legacies matter, they cannot be reduced to positive and negative national examples. One response was the move to introduce typologies of incorporation, factoring in modes of state-society relations and multi-levelled constitutional structures, as a more sophisticated reflection of the different factors determining integration. Soysal's work in particular had the virtue of turning the ethnic/civic distinction on its head: highlighting in its arguments about the postnational status of migrant groups such as Turks in Germany, the normative dogma involved in always equating full national citizenship with full integration (Soysal, 1994). Structured case-by-case comparisons along these institutionalist lines have enabled a more fruitful type of cross-national work, particularly those located at sub-national levels such as the city (i.e., Ireland, 1994; Bousetta, 2000).

However, away from these predominantly North American led comparative efforts, more explicitly policy-oriented studies with a comparative range have tended to follow the least sophisticated academic approaches. This has certainly been the case with work produced through the sponsorship of European institutions. For example, the big winner from an intense bidding struggle among academics in this field for money from the Targeted Social and Economic Research (TSER) programme on 'exclusion' was a national models-based study – led by well-known national figures Friedrich Heckmann and Dominique Schnapper – that explicitly structured its investigations around the idea that immigration and ethnic relations in each country are determined by classic policy 'models' rooted in political cultural differences between France, Germany, Britain and so on (Heckmann and Schnapper, 2003). A models-based approach of this kind will often itself reproduce the ideological fictions each nation has of its own and others' immigration politics. Schnapper and associates duly found that minorities and majorities do indeed *talk* about the issues in each country in ways that follow the distinct national ideologies. But little or no *self-reflexive* effort was made to ask how these nation-sustaining ideas about distinct national 'models' have themselves been created and sustained by politicians, the media and the policy academics themselves in each country, precisely in order to foreclose the possibility that external international or transnational influences might begin to affect domestic minority issues and policy considerations.

Practical institutional imperatives also dictate that the policy study packages and presents its findings in a narrowly targeted way, which naturally curtails many of the more interesting lines of enquiry. This has been well-understood by one of the more influential NGOs in this field in Brussels – the Migration Policy Group – who have been involved in two of the most wide ranging funded surveys on integration policies across European society (Vermeulen, 1997; MPG, 1996). In the latter, the 'societal integration project', they set up roundtables in around twenty countries, and listened to the expert opinions of policy makers and policy intellectuals, generating a mass of material about how policy makers talk about the same issues in different places. However, in the end the slim report of highlights and recommendations boiled all this down to a reaffirmation that convergence was the source of future norms on citizenship and integration across Europe. Being limited to the typical state-centric talk and self-justification of policy makers, it was unable to offer any genuine comparative evaluation. Moreover, the freedom of reflection of such a project is naturally cut down by the expectations of the sponsors who lay down the lines of research. By definition, such comparative policy studies produce findings which reinforce the state-centred, top-down formulations familiar at national level. The one difference here – as a product of a supra-national European initiative – is that the conclusions about the inevitability of convergence underline a familiar EU strategy to focus, not on national excep-tionality or uniqueness (as do national level studies) but rather on the narrowing of national differences. In other words, as we might expect given the sponsors involved, these arguments work to narrow down the freedom of agency of individual states, hence their sovereignty. Convergent citizenship criteria become like convergent criteria for monetary union.

To really be able to answer the evaluatory question of which nation-states are doing better on integration than others, we would need some kind of 'integration index': a convertible scale which enabled us to read off across European societies degrees of social segregation in housing, success in schooling or employment, differences in resistance of cultural behaviour, persistence of racist attitudes, relative social mobility, or whatever is argued to be the best set of objective measures. These indicators would then have to be linked to the existence, or the success and failure, of specific national policies or institutions. The inevitable impulse to cross-national evaluation of state policy is not only exceedingly difficult to do, given the cross-national data constraints I will go on to discuss. It also imposes as an assumption an untenable automatic correlation between success on the index and the effectiveness of state policies having achieved their goals by shaping or influencing the behaviour of groups and individuals. This assumption itself is a state-reinforcing one, penalizing any society which is less structured by state intervention, regardless of how well 'integrated' groups or individuals may in fact be.

The one way this kind of approach works is as a comparative shaming strategy directed towards states with less extensive formal rights and entitlements for migrants than others. The most extensive survey of this kind was a six nation Austrian study which did just this, in order to shame the Austrian government into better migration policy and anti-discrimination measures (Çinar et al., 1995; Waldrauch and Hofinger, 1997; Waldrauch, 2001). The extensively documented study broke down all formal rights and entitlements of non-nationals across various European states, rating each one between 0 and 1 as an index to barriers to integration. By definition, the approach foresees a state-centred, state-organized solution to integration, and cannot capture any forms of multiculturalism which are the outcome of more *laissez-faire* style approaches. We end up with the very common conclusion that highly state-organized societies, such as Sweden or the Netherlands, do it best. Yet these are also highly unified national societies, who put high demands of linguistic and cultural assimilation on their inhabitants (something to which the index is blind). They are also societies racked with dilemmas of informal economy, and high degrees of social segregation among their immigrant population. Current discussions on immigration in Denmark provide a good example of the paradoxes here in some of Europe's most enlightened social democracies. Laws and policies ensure excellent access to rights and high rates of formal participation among the so-called 'new Danes'. Yet the many socio-economic problems linked to disadvantaged immigrants are routinely interpreted in political discussion as dysfunctional to the smooth running of the Danish national welfare state, and stigmatized as 'ikke dansk'; i.e., rule-breaking immigrants not behaving in a 'true' Danish manner (on Denmark, see Schierup, 1993).

Rights-based evaluations of integration contrast dramatically with those which focus on different formal indicators. Britain, with its weak constitutional structures and idiosyncratic race relations institutions, does rather badly in the Austrian study, yet this contrasts sharply with how comparative British evaluations of European experiences view the matter. Contrasting its longstanding and successful multicultural practices with the troubled politics and social situations of many continental European societies, the most extensive studies made by British researchers have always found Britain to be far better endowed with anti-discrimination legislation and multicultural policies (Forbes and Mead, 1992; Wrench, 1996). The British state in fact pursues a minimalist style of intervention into the many and diverse forms of multiculturalism that have developed in the country. Yet homegrown studies routinely link these successes to the agency of the British state and its policy legacy: what is perceived by them as the existence of a strong state-centred multicultural race relations framework. Multiculturalism is thus claimed as an achievement of the British state, rather than a consequence of the weak penetration of the state in everyday life in Britain. From this point of view – which is more plausible in a comparative perspective – it could be argued that it is *laissez faire* that has enabled London and a small handful of other cities to develop as multicultural cities, in sharp distinction from the white and intolerant provincial hinterlands.

As more positive visions of multicultural integration become prevalent across Europe, other less 'advanced' integration nations than France or Britain are likely to follow their lead and see their ruling national elites claim the multicultural success in the name of their own tradition of nationhood. For sure, France and Britain look like successful multicultural societies on this score. Yet, it is precisely a country like France which imposes the biggest cultural burdens on newcomers in terms of their adhesion to the particular ways of the nation; or a country like Britain, which buys enlightened race relations as a trade-off for some of the toughest border controls in Europe. These paradoxical results follow from the fact that both countries practice 'multiculturalism-in-one-nation': a multicultural nationalism, that sees no other source of multiculturalism than the miraculously tolerant cosmopolitanism of the home culture. Such countries may then be 'universalist', and yet apparently highly intolerant of specific cultural differences; or they might be highly multicultural and multi-racial, and yet be at the same time extraordinarily xenophobic. There are clear costs involved in the stubborn maintenance of the fiction of exclusive nation-state agency over the multicultural aspects of these locations.

The strong sense of national self-preservation displayed here perhaps explains why the European Union has only been able to gain the weakest influence over immigrant integration policies, jealously guarded at the national level. The EU can get involved to identify good practices, or the best convergent norms across societies; but it cannot begin to constitute itself as a political agency here without taking agency (i.e., sovereignty) away from nation-states, which have used issues of immigrant integration precisely to actually underline and reproduce their own

existence as coherent, bounded, nation-building societies. European integration is
of course itself the search for political agency at a supra-national level; but the fact
that it seems to fail to constitute itself as a state, suggests that this is largely because
the actual boundaries of European society remain very much fixed at the national
level.

Survey and Census Based Work on Integration

It is no surprise that policy-centred studies should inevitably reproduce the state-
centred, nation-building optic in their framing and prescription of ways to achieve
integration. As the preceding discussion has indicated, such studies by definition
can say very little about the kind of less structured social processes that are
characteristic of much multiculturalism to be found in Europe's cities and
metropolitan regions. Rather, where they recognize multiculturalism, policy and
institutional-based studies tend to bolster nationalizing ideologies which affirm the
nation-state as the sole relevant locus of political agency able to shape a 'society'.
They are also, needless to say, the contributions which best chime with the interests
of agents of the state, concerned with maximizing their realm of political influence
by emphasizing the growing importance of top-down immigration and integration
policy.

But what of bottom-up studies: empirical work which focuses on the
experiences, attitudes or social mobility of the immigrants or ethnic minority
members themselves? Policy and institutional-based studies often have very little to
say about actual migrant experiences of integration. Here, more ambitious uses of
survey and census-based work, based on studying their values, discourses and
behaviour, offer a more advanced integration index for measuring and evaluating
what is going on. Clearly, this would be material close to the actual process of
social change going on inside 'multicultural' nation-states; and, it might be thought,
material more likely to reveal evidence of tendencies that are decomposing the
conventional nation-state integration paradigm. For example, it might be expected
to find strong evidence – in those European cities that are significant 'nodes' in the
global economy – of the growing transnationalism characteristic of the social and
cultural forms of migrant groups whose activities are embedded in global economic
networks (see Faist, 2000; Rath, 2000).

Ambitious studies along these lines are now beginning to emerge. The
possibility of doing such work has grown out of an increasing societal thirst for
more systematic knowledge about immigration phenomena as the political salience
of the subject has risen. Governments, policy think tanks, international institutions
and the media, are all beginning to show interest in funding much more large-scale
survey data driven studies of integration issues. The positivistic style of large-scale
survey work offers an interesting counterpoint to the normative leanings of policy
studies and institutional-based works, which have tended to frame their more
journalistic-style methods with the value-laden rhetoric of citizenship and rights.

Survey-based researchers, meanwhile, preserve their credibility, not by shadowing the language and conceptualizations of policy actors, but by the distinct 'scientific' autonomy of their methodology and results. By definition, the kind of work they are doing cannot be mounted by the personnel of governments and newspapers, lacking in the specialist quantitative and qualitative techniques required; such work has to be commissioned, with freedom of research negotiated in advance. This fact creates distinctive material conditions for the kind of work produced. One advantage is that the process of deriving 'policy' directed normative conclusions is (or should be) left to post-hoc interpretation, and not in-built in the normative state-centred conceptualizations which typically measure integration: such as those which rate already institutionalized state policy structures linked to citizenship rights or legal and political channels.

Numerous examples of impressive large-scale survey work do now exist in various countries at the single-case national level (see the discussion in Phalet and Swyngedouw, 1999; examples are Modood et al., 1997; Tribalat et al., 1996; Swyngedouw, Phalet, and Deschouwer, 1999; Phalet et al., 2000; Diehl et al., 1999; Veenman, 1998; Lesthaege, 2000). The new frontier for survey-based research is the possibility of cross-national comparative survey work on the integration of immigrants. However, as was clear from exploratory discussions at a conference in September 1999 on the subject organized by Hartmut Esser – which brought together the European Consortium for Sociological Research, a grouping of the leading quantitative social scientists in Europe – very few of the epistemological problems of doing such work have yet been considered by researchers more familiar with doing cross-national studies on employment, educational mobility or inequality (e.g., Erikson and Goldthorpe, 1992). Cross-national efforts have to be synthesized from the best of the national level data provided on a nation-by-nation basis by governments. The very best of current cross-national efforts in the area of immigration mounted by an international organization, which monitors migration stocks and flows around the developed world – the annual OECD-SOPEMI report – is notoriously hampered by the fact that the expert respondents each report figures for its own country based on different national means of data-gathering (SOPEMI, 1998). Moreover, there is nothing like the systematic quantitative effort on integration questions as there is in the report for basic issues of entry, legality, residence and so on. The report does have a growing section on integration, but it is by far the weakest part of it, reflecting perhaps a lack of sociological expertise among the geographers and economists who make up the immigration specialist panel. The report in fact falls back into a more policy-centred style of analysis: reproducing the same old frameworks about national models and comparative rights indices.

We can imagine perhaps a more concerted attempt to conceptualize the integration questions in a way which escapes this nominalist nation-state centred approach. But the real problem here is that all available data on immigrant or minority numbers basic to the SOPEMI effort, follow the significantly different conventions in each country about collecting population data. There is, in other words, an in-built dependency on nationally-specific research technologies; usually the state apparatus that has been built up around census gathering. The specific methods used to identify populations of immigrant origin in the post-war period vary from country to country, as does the political sensitivity with which this information is released or extrapolated. The technical methods – and the politics surrounding such sensitive state knowledge production – inevitably reflect the national ideology each nation has fashioned for itself as a narrative of nation-building. No matter how insulated the methodology, the broader national policy definition of integration as a social process impacts upon the production of categories and numbers elicited from survey results.

Counting only non-nationals as the immigrant population is still the base-line norm across nearly all European countries except Britain, which has a famously idiosyncratic form of ethnic self-identification in its census. Most comparative tables offer figures for non-nationals by nationality, which works up to point in countries where original nationality remains a distinguishing factor (as, say, in Germany, Italy or Spain; although it runs into problems in Germany, for example, in counting the three million *Aussiedler* from Eastern Europe). This method is clearly a criterion of declining usefulness, however, as increasing numbers of second and third generation immigrant children in fact accede to full national citizenship; it can indeed be simply a crude measure of administrative exclusion. Naturalization rates over time are a second set of figures, which trace the absorption of immigrants over shorter, given periods of time. Other countries may also offer figures which count those people who identify older family members born outside of the country. From this, a great deal can be extrapolated into second and third generation, but a country such as France still maintains barriers for ideological reasons to researchers using this information, which means that some naturalized second or third generation are lost to studies once they leave the immigrant household.

A strong moral prohibition, meanwhile, exists on the classification of people by race or religion across Europe. There is little more distasteful to continental Europeans than anything with a whiff of former Nazi racial classifications, or indeed the common practice in multinational empires such as the Soviet Union or Yugoslavia to brand people permanently on their interior passports with an 'ethnic' nationality (see Brubaker, 1995). However, a more racially heterogeneous population such as the Portuguese avoids these racial classifications for rather different reasons, to do with the cosmopolitan colonial conception of the nation. In Belgium, you are classified by language according to political records after you vote, religion after you choose university. Here, however, the census is banned by law to answer such questions up front. In the Netherlands, meanwhile, there is no national census at all, after a libertarian public revolt in the 1970s. Ethnic statistics here have to be reconstructed from local city and police records or special ministry surveys, something that has contributed significantly to the sense of unease about the numbers of 'undocumented' residents in the country. Other countries, however, such as Denmark and Britain – which in other respects have very different census methods – are prepared under certain circumstances to make available census data to track specified (anonymous) individuals over time between censuses, in order, for example, to analyze spatial mobility or rates of political participation (see Togeby, 1999; Fielding, 1995). Such a babel of census information is a difficult starting point. In talking about integration, *who* are we talking about: 'legally resident foreigners', 'immigrants', 'illegal/undocumented residents', 'third-country nationals', 'ethnic groups', 'racial minorities', new or naturalized 'citizens', or simply formally undistinguishable 'nationals' with a different *de facto* cultural history or skin colour?

The narrow definition of immigrants as resident non-nationals has the virtue of avoiding the integration issue entirely. It offers the normative panacea of equating citizenship with full integration, an idea which has long reassured French republicans on the virtues of a cosmopolitan type of nationhood. A normative dogma such as this makes no sociological sense, of course, once any one is willing to admit that host populations and migrants alike will continue to informally discriminate themselves and each other regardless of which passport they are holding. Once some outsiders become insiders, however, their formal categorization (or 'recognition', in more affirmative terms) itself becomes a part of the integration process. Whether or not they are separated off for official monitoring purposes, and how and where they can be placed on some path towards full integration, becomes a crucial part of the integrative process itself, not least because the separation from one's original nationality may also be a coercive state-enforced act (see Simon, 1997). There is a profound moral truth in the French refusal to actually recognize any French citizen of non-national 'ethnic' origin as such in official statistics, because the recognition itself can indeed be a form of inequality or discrimination. The power of naming does indeed count for something. The French refusal is also a dramatic statement of the nation-state's continued prerogative to nationalize a new citizen as indivisibly French. Yet, on the other hand, no policy can be devised for systematic integration of foreign-origin groups until the nation-state begins to collectively recognize and classify minorities of ethnic origin, with special claims – targeted policies, resources, legal allowances, etc – that follow from this (this is the central problematic of the influential work of Kymlicka, 1995).

There is another side of the classificatory separation, however. Integration cannot be conceived, identified, let alone measured as degrees of inequality and so on, until a control group representative of the national population has been specified. But this raises the question: we are talking about integration into *what*? Here, the logic of classification becomes even more slippery. Are they the indigenous population ('de souche' in French), but if so, what length of time constitutes 'roots'; are they defined culturally, by their family origins, by their length of residence; are they, rather, simply to be identified as the majority 'white' or 'European' population; or, are we in fact speaking of some representative sample or statistical mean of the citizenry as a whole, including all those new and culturally exotic recent additions? Moreover, as Michael Banton points out (2001), it makes little sense to measure the integration of an immigrant or ethnic minority population, until we have some precise measurement of how well the majority population is integrated as a nation. Whatever method is chosen – however the state chooses to classify, count and control its population or define those who are in and those who are out – will again amount to a pre-determined national 'sampling frame', that is very closely linked to the ideological concept of nationhood present. Behind this, of course, lies the normative commitment to integration as societal end-goal, the underlying assumption that holds the nation-state-society unit together. Researchers who thus set out to objectively measure integration, without taking into account how much the nation-state unit has already determined the very quantitative tools they use, will fail to see how much the bounds of what they can discover have already been pre-set for them. If so, they are working no less to underwrite the predominance of the nation-state optic, than policy studies researchers who accept without challenge nation-state centred definitions of 'universal' citizenship or 'cosmopolitan' multiculturalism.

On the whole, however, progressive minded commentators across Europe do not challenge this conceptual recuperation of their very tools of research by a nation-state centred vision of integration. The majority, rather, has been content to push a different, conciliatory line, that squares the circle between the reality of on-going nation-building efforts and the contrasting idealism of cosmopolitan multiculturalism. They argue that European nations have become, or are becoming, 'countries of immigration'. Such arguments have been very much present in those countries whose right wing refuses to recognize the reality of continued immigration and settlement at all. Among those promoting this happier version of Europe's immigrant future, the coercive weight of ever-present nation-building processes is thus lightened by the claim that the integration of immigrants in Europe can be equated with what happens to immigrants in Australia, Canada or the US. The normative inspiration is clear – constitutional universalism, cosmopolitan idealism, the melting pot, open immigration regimes, and so on – but the idea of the old nation-states of Europe metamorphosizing into brand new 'countries of immigration' is a dubious rhetoric on any empirical level, not least from a historical point of view. In Europe, we are talking about tightly bounded and culturally specific nation-states dealing in the post-war period with an unexpected – but still not very large – influx of highly diverse immigrant settlers, at a time when, for other international reasons, their sense of nationhood is insecure or in decline. It is a problematic very different to those faced by the US or Australia, whose histories and sense of nationhood have always been built on immigration. Europe, rather, faces a problematic where the continuity of nation-building is perhaps a much more significant fact than the multicultural hybridity that is sometimes sought for in these other, newer 'model' nations. A great deal of revisionist effort has gone into reconstructing certain European nations as undiscovered immigration nations (e.g., Noiriel, 1991). Although widely accepted, it is an effort which in fact empties significance out of other empirical attempts to problematize integration as a limited process of cultural change, combining multicultural adaptation with national reinvention. Instead, it rather lamely gestures European survey-based researchers back towards the most culturally-neutral model available: that of classic American assimilation research, which charts the progress of different immigrant ethnic groups towards some ideal-typical absorption into the suburban middle class – a process where the pervasively national orientation of American assimilation is never even put into question, and where the nation-building effect here stays invisible (see also Brubaker, 2001). The spectacular resurgence of American patriotism in its crudest forms post '9/11' has at least clarified how deeply nationalistic ideas of American unity and America's global role in fact are.

Operationalizing this particular normative frame for immigrant integration – which recasts European societies as immigration nations in the idealized, immigrant American mould – has been done in distinctive national ways. On the face of it, the French offer the purest instance of a self-styled universalist country of immigration, not least after the assiduous reconstruction of this idea by historians and sociologists in the 1980s. Establishing this as the normative frame for new progressive policies was relatively straightforward. But, in empirical terms, the formal prohibition in official survey data on introducing any sub-categorization of the population by ethnicity (i.e., in the data produced by the national statistics office, INSEE), left grandiose declarations about the continued success of the French republican model bereft of evidence for these claims. For how else could the sociological integration of different cultural groups in France in fact be measured? A study which reintroduced some sub-classification of the population by ethnicity was, in other words, needed to show that ethnicity in fact did not matter. The nation-sustaining argument about integration was in a sense generating its own contradictions, that would then need resolution by a new scientific approach. This, then, was the background to the ambitious study by INED, headed by Michèle Tribalat, that still represents the state-of-the-art in integration research in France (Tribalat, 1995; Tribalat et al., 1996). Sample ethnic groups of different national origin – tracked down by ethnographic investigation, using the census only indirectly – were compared to a control group of non-immigrant origin French on questions of cultural behaviour, language use, housing concentration, political participation, and so on. The strongly French socialization of most groups observed – the Turkish and Chinese being the two outliers – in fact offered strong evidence for continued 'assimilation' in France, as Tribalat preferred to call it. The mere introduction of ethnicity into the survey, however, brought desperately controversial public reactions from other commentators, such as Hervé Le Bras (1998); and this despite the fact that it led to such conventionally 'French' results.

Systematic cross-ethnic comparative work is much more highly developed in Germany, which has strong national surveys of data by national-origin available, such as the socioeconomic panel commissioned annually by the Deutsches Institut für Wirtschaft, which provides data on ethnicity, language, identity questions and participation (an example of such work being Diehl et al., 1999). Progressive researchers here are even more sensitive to the de-categorization of foreigners and the positive idea of Germany as a country of immigration. There have been advantages to such research in the fact it has had to be diverted away from the ideologically dominated discussions on citizenship and naturalization, where progress has been more difficult. German research is thus more likely to concentrate on conceptualizing integration in technical socioeconomic terms: in terms of participation in the welfare state, and in differences between federal or city level contexts. One consequence is the possibility of internal comparisons of integration geographically within the nation, something of which there is no trace in France and Britain. German research, however, does not escape the pervasively nation-centred frame which dominates its political debates. Negative evidence of non-integration – such as ethnic concentration or the failure of second and third generations to speak German – tends to get constructed as evidence of segregation or marginalization, in contrast with more successful state-centred integration or assimilation. These closed typologies of immigrant trajectories – which reinforce the idea of full national integration as the ideal – can be found in research going on in all kinds of countries (Nauck and Schönpflug, 1997; see also the closed scheme of claims-making laid out as an introduction by Koopmans and Statham, 2000).

In Britain, meanwhile, the 'ethnic' self-identification question in its census is clearly out of sync with its European neighbours. It indicates a conceptual history that has always looked for its normative inspiration to American race relations of the 1960s, and has always defined Britain more narrowly as a country of post-colonial immigration only. For all the masses of data provided about the select group of post-colonial racial and national groups recognized in the census, the framework has come to have serious limitations over time. The categories themselves have become highly politicized, putting into practice a variable geometry that has sought to respond to the emerging demands of new and increasingly diverse migrant groups who recognize that the census categories are a fundamental source of recognition, as well as legal coverage and public funding. Basic black and white distinctions, for example, have now fallen away into a broader recognition of Asian groups. Other new migrants in Britain, however, find themselves lost between the generic 'white' and 'other' boxes. Indeed, with Jewish and Irish anti-discrimination campaigners forcing open the pandora's box of whiteness (the all important control group) in the census of 2001, it is quite likely that the sharp 'minority' ethnic groupings that have been the core and inspiration of British race research may in future begin to crumble.

Obviously, the sources of minority data, and the qualitative evidence it also provides about nuances in ethnic self-identification, have created a boon for identities type work in Britain, much of it now pursued under the banner of 'new ethnicities'. There are numerous studies in which individuals are ethnographically studied playing with or resisting (unsurprisingly) their given 'ethnic minority' category (Back, 1995; Anthias and Yuval-Davis, 1993; Modood et al., 1994). Such work can often be an ideal vehicle for articulating ethnic 'voices' themselves. But structural work about the social mobility of such groups is hampered by the crude comparison forced by the data between racially designated ethnic groups and the generic 'white' block of the host population; this, inevitably it seems, leads research to claim ethnic success as rooted in minority group solidarity, but ethnic failure as rooted in majority group racial discrimination. In this frame, too, there is no way of assessing the continued impact of nation-building assimilation – via evidence on cultural behaviour, etc – on ethnic groups, despite the self-evident Britishness of many of these well-established minority groups. Nor is it easy in this frame to cross-check for class, gender or regional factors, particularly if these might lead to the declining salience of race-based explanations. In some of the best recent work on social mobility and ethnic identities, transnational behaviour and sources of social success are still surprisingly downplayed against the interpretation that ethnic minority success is further proof of vibrant British multiculturalism (Modood et al., 1997). Britain celebrates with some pride its longstanding role in Europe as the leading country of post-war immigration; yet has until very recently refused officially to see itself as a country of *new* immigration. Within this paradoxical picture, well-integrated and recognized ethnic minorities have a status and advantage denied to the many other new migrant groups now found in the country.

In the nation-state centred version of integration research in the larger European countries, there is something odd about the fact that the status and success of immigrants gets measured entirely in terms of a social mobility relative to norms of integration into the nation-society, or average national social mobility paths; yet it is increasingly normal to think of elites in the same country becoming increasingly transnational in their roles, networks and trajectories. The exclusive destiny of full integration into host nation states may however not be the norm for immigrants in the future. Already, in other smaller European nations, a rather different picture is emerging. New migration countries such as Italy, Spain, and Portugal are actually going through the process of formulating their own uncertain national conceptions of integration at a very different historical moment compared to larger nations who continue to offer their models. As well as being countries that are more geographically exposed to migration, they are, moreover, countries with weaker state penetration of society or the market. In these less structured situations, the normative imperative of full national integration begins to lessen, if new non-nation-centred structures of social integration begin to emerge. A similar consequence follows from research on integration into a non-unified or multi-levelled state such as Belgium. In seeking to avoid the inevitability of nation-state centred visions of integration apparently forced on research by the kind of data available and the kind of concepts we work with, studying these smaller or newer integration scenarios may indeed offer a way forward out of the current paradigm.

Beyond the Integration Paradigm?

The clear message from the critical survey of current integration research in Europe offered here is that better research would be research that sets out to be more autonomous academically, and more thoroughly comparative in its intent.

Academics need to escape their role of underwriting nation-building efforts directed towards small immigrant populations that have provoked a renewed symbolic effort to imagine (inclusive) western nation-state cultures. A much higher degree of self-consciousness is needed about the way contextual factors determine the intellectual content of research itself.

How might this be done? I will conclude with a discussion of some of the newer insights provided by the way scholars of transnationalism have approached the problem (e.g., Portes, 1996; Basch et al., 1994; Smith and Guarnizo, 1998). Scholars of transnationalism have sought – for exactly the kinds of reasons I spell out in this paper – to expunge 'integration' from their terms of research. By definition, they do not wish to be underwriting the nation-state in a world which they see as increasingly transnational or global. Methodologically, too, their bottom up, ethnographic drive suits a style of work which draws large conclusions from the study of cases likely to be seen as exceptional, or indeed deviant from the conventional integration-focused perspective. For sure, it is this too which may account for the often excessively celebratory tone of transnational studies. Seeking a new kind of liberation, some studies fall into the longstanding problem that has distorted much radical ethnic and racial studies: the transfer of sympathy for the experiences, difficulties, and sometimes plight of migrants and ethnic minorities, into visions of these groups as some sort of heroic new 'proletariat'. Although the 'search for a new world' – and the slogan 'globalization from below' – is the rather romantic packaging chosen in the work of Portes, Castells et al., this should not deflect us from the key insights of their work. Its major advance has been the empirical uncovering of trans-state, trans-nation economic and cultural networks of transactions (and protean forms of social organization) among new and developing migrant groups. These networks are clearly generating sources of collective social power outside of territorial state structures familiar from our conventional understanding of the world of nations. Whereas Portes principally recognizes the source of transnational power as the global market, others might point to Islam or Hispanic culture, or indeed informal ('illegal') sources of these same powers (see Cohen, 1997; Phizacklea, 1998).

The other crucial aspect of Portes' work, however, is its insistence on linking emergent transnational forms with classic integration questions. The exploration of the notion of 'segmented assimilation' in the US, has pointed towards the new structural relationship between the transnational 'survival' strategies resorted to by migrant groups and the unappealing 'downward assimilation' offered to them by the host societies' state and societal structures (Portes, 1995). European examples of this have been the similar emergence of community resilience against the negative socioeconomic conditions they found themselves in, or the strongly assimilatory host reception. The results have been the paradoxical innovations of the informal economy or inner city Islam in many European cities. The integration path may indeed prove to be, in Kloosterman and Rath's terms, 'a long and winding road' (Kloosterman et al., 1998). As the Dutch state, for example, seems ever tighter in its heavily legislated attempt to discover, encompass, regularize and normalize the spontaneous economic activities of new migrants, so there has seemed to be an ever-growing over-flow of undisciplined, self-organized informal activities in the country (Engbersen, 1996). The very best continental European work has focused on precisely this issue of informality or non-institutionalized forms of social organization; often focusing, unsurprisingly, on those groups identified in conventional integration research as the ethnic cases which fit worst into the kinds of automatically integrating schemes set up, for example, by French and British research (Fennema and Tillie, 1999; Bousetta, 1997; Phalet et al., 2000). It is not surprising that this work has invariably focused on either Turkish or Moroccan groups in various countries: two newer, non-colonial migrant groups that have displayed some of the most pronounced 'transnational', non-integrating social trajectories in Europe.

Systematizing these deviant tendencies in research without simply reproducing the nation-state-society as the container unit has proven a lot more difficult. One might point to the Polanyi-inspired way forward in recent work by Faist (2000) or Kesteloot (2000). In this they offer schemes of transnational or local integration in economic and community structures which cross-cut with national, citizenship-centred forms. Empirical anthropologists, too, have provided some of the best recent work about immigrant and ethnic self-organization in urban contexts (Werbner, 1999; Baumann, 1996). Whether it is the bustling migrant markets of old Antwerp or East Amsterdam, or the mosque-centred inner city Islam of Turks and Moroccans in Brussels, there is clearly a need to recognize these city-embedded activities as emergent forms of social organization – and hence social power – largely unstructured or not incorporated (in formal or informal terms) by the state. The somewhat anarchical multiculturalism of some European cities now points towards a new type of multi-ethnic culture in Europe, rather different to the multicultural citizenship shaped by integrating nation-states. It is not egalitarian, it is not anchored in rights, and it is certainly not conflict free; but it is, for better or for worse, much less disciplined by the nation-building pressures hidden in top-down policies of 'integration'.

Interestingly, however, even this kind of multicultural challenge to dominant European nation-state-centred cultures tends to still be anchored in deterritorialized 'nationalities': the persistence of important political and social links with the 'homeland', as both a concrete and symbolic reference. This fact – which is certainly the case with Turks and Moroccans in Europe – indicates a limit to these forms of transnationalism outside of their European context. Viewed from here they are not really transnational at all, but rather examples of deterritorialized nation-state building, familiar perhaps from the older diasporic histories of countries like Ireland, Italy or Greece. What there is precious little evidence of across Europe is the kind of radical diasporic multicultural forms, beloved of British cultural studies writers: the 'black' Atlantic diaspora or 'black' Asian pan-ethnic groups (see Gilroy, 1987; Brah, 1993; Hall, 1988). Such diasporas would indeed constitute a more radical challenge to the present day international system, still fixed upon relations between nation-states in the western and developing world to the south and east. But their absence betrays just how British these writers in fact are; reflecting – in their archetypal radical responses to frustrations encountered in the ethnic categories of the liberal multicultural race relations framework – the everyday activist struggles of British race politics.

As these overwhelmingly national sources for transnational ideas suggest, we should be wary of seeing transnationalism as an end to the integration paradigm. Rather, transnationalism in Europe has to be seen as a growing empirical exception to the familiar nation-centred pattern of integration across the continent. This remains the dominant focus for policy actors and migrant activists alike. Transnationalism points towards the new sources of power accessed by migrant groups when they begin to organize themselves and their activities in ways not already organized for them by an integrating nation state. By setting these forms against the continuity of nation-state centred patterns of integration, we may be able to understand how and why new spaces in the empire of the state are beginning to develop. What transnationalists should not do is leap beyond this into claims of an emerging international or global structure, in which all these nation-state challenging phenomena add up to a new global framework of governance, at which level a new kind of incorporation will be achieved (Soysal's supra-national human rights regime, for example). To do so is to project the same old normative nation-state-building impulses onto an emerging international situation characterized rather by its market and culture led undermining of traditional nation-state powers. It means, in other words, to reinvent the state by the back door at global level. There are, of course, political actors who dream of a postnational state at European, even global level; but the factual capture of this ideal by the far more powerful *realpolitik* of everyday international relations, simply turns these efforts back into a paradoxical 'rescue of the nation-state', to borrow Alan Milward's (1992) famous phrase.

In many ways, the continued focus on integration as the central idea in post-immigration policy debates across Europe, is itself a choice of rhetoric designed explicitly to rescue the nation-state. European policy makers and commentators have begun to formulate more constructive visions of a multicultural future that will be able to contain and structure within the nation-state the many new forms of immigration and multiculturalism beginning to spring up across the continent. As I have argued, these visions – and the academic research which has provided the knowledge to substantiate their claims – have continued to work within a nation-state centred paradigm, even when they claim to be transcending it. An awareness of transnational phenomena, as well as a better consciousness of the pervasive way work has been structured by a nation-state centred epistemology, may enable migration and ethnic studies researchers to escape in their analyses the normative constraints of the integration paradigm. But it is vital in looking for new concepts and tools to describe the changing relations of state and society across the continent, that we also continue to recognize the extraordinary continuity and resilience of the nation-state-society as the dominant principle of social organization in Europe.

Notes

1 Published in 'The multicultural challenge', *Comparative Social Research,* 22, 2003, pp. 13-42, reprinted with permission from Elsevier Ltd.
2 A more extended discussion and survey can be found in Favell (2001). Responding to this piece, Banton (2001) dismisses the use of 'integration' – 'a treacherous mathematical metaphor' – in any sociological studies on the subject. His vision is to purify sociological research on ethnic and race relations of these pervasive ordinary language concepts. Though a valid scientific response to the dilemma of using such terms, it forecloses the possibility in our research of reflexively accounting for *why* such terms are so predominant in policy discussions and academic research alike. See also related discussions in Bommes (1998) and Wimmer and Glick Schiller (2002).
3 The number of quasi-academic policy studies on integration funded by such organizations in recent years has been remarkable. The Council of Europe's Committee on Migration has produced a number of reports on gender and religious issues, labor markets, and social and political participation, as well as an outstanding conceptual framework for research by Bauböck (1994). The ILO has pursued work on integration in labor markets (Doomernik 1998), and the OSCE has been linking minority rights and integration. Among NGOs in Brussels, there is the highly active Migration Policy Group, who have produced major cross-national studies of policies and policy thinking on integration (MPG 1996; Vermeulen 1997). Finally, charitable transatlantic organizations, have also joined the trend. The Carnegie Endowment's massively ambitious 'Comparative Citizenship Project' identified political and social integration as two key areas of concern (Aleinikoff and Klusmeyer, 2002), and the Canadian-led Metropolis project focused on migrants in cities has sponsored several major studies (i.e., Cross and Waldinger, 1997; Vertovec, 1997). These various studies are some of the most ambitious comparative international projects to be found. Here, I mention but a sample.
4 For example, there was the creation by the left wing government of Italy in 1999 of a 'Commissione per l'integrazione' under the leadership of political sociologist Giovanna Zincone. This was explicitly intended to counter the increasingly salient use of negative anti-immigration rhetoric by Berlusconi's right wing coalition. In Denmark, again under pressure from the right, the government passed an 'Act on the Integration of Aliens in Denmark' in July 1998, followed by much public discussion and further reports on continuing integration problems. In Austria, the turn to integration (see Waldrauch and Hofinger, 1997) has been formulated by the opposition as a response to specifically exclusionary government attitudes.
5 In the report of the Commission on Multi-Ethnic Britain (2000), which involved some of these more radical commentators alongside more mainstream figures, 'integration' was the organizing concept that dared not speak its name. However, the Commission's chair, Bhikhu Parekh, has frequently written about the concept in his own work (Parekh, 2000).

References

Alba, R. and Nee, V. (1997), 'Rethinking Assimilation Theory for a New Era of Immigration', *International Migration Review,* 31 (Winter), pp. 826-74.
Aleinikoff, A. and Klusmeyer, D. (2002), *Citizenship Policies for an Age of Migration,* Carnegie Endowment, Washington, DC.
Alibhai-Brown, Y. (2000), *Who Do We Think We Are?* Penguin, London.
Alund, A. and Schierup, C-U. (1991), *Paradoxes of Multiculturalism,* Avebury, Aldershot.

Anthias, F. and Yuval-Davis, N. (1993), *Racialized Boundaries: Race, Nation, Gender, Class and the Anti-Racist Struggle,* Routledge, London.

Back, L. (1995), *New Ethnicities and Urban Culture: Racisms and Multiculture in Young Lives,* UCL Press, London.

Banton, M. (2001), 'National Integration in France and Britain', *Journal of Ethnic and Migration Studies,* 27 (1), pp. 151-68.

Basch, L., Schiller, N.G. and Szanton-Blanc, C. (1994), *Nations Unbound: Transnational Projects, Post-Colonial Predicaments and Deterritorialized Nation-States,* Gordon and Breach, Amsterdam.

Bauböck, R. (1994), *The Integration of Immigrants.* CMDG-Report, The Council of Europe, Strasbourg.

Baumann, G. (1996), *Contesting Culture: Ethnicity and Community in West London,* Cambridge UP, New York.

Blommaert, J. and Verschueren, J. (1998), *Debating Diversity,* Routledge, London.

Bommes, M. (1998), 'Migration, Nation State and Welfare State: A Theoretical Challenge for Sociological Migration Research'. Paper presented to the European Forum on Migration, European University Institute, Florence, 16 February 1998.

Bousetta, H. (1997), 'Citizenship and Political Participation in France and the Netherlands: Reflections on Two Local Cases', *New Community,* 23 (2), pp. 215-32.

Bousetta, H. (2000), 'Political Dynamics in the City. Citizenship, Ethnic Mobilisation and Socio-political Participation: Four Case Studies', in S. Body-Gendrot and M. Martiniello (eds.), *Minorities in European Cities: The Dynamics of Social Integration and Social Exclusion at the Neighbourhood Level,* Macmillan, London.

Brah, A. (1993), *Cartographies of Diaspora: Contesting Identities,* Routledge, London.

Brubaker, R. (ed.) (1989), *Immigration and the Politics of Citizenship in Western Europe,* UP of America, New York.

Brubaker, R. (1992), *Citizenship and Nationhood in France and Germany,* Harvard UP, Cambridge, MA.

Brubaker, R. (1995), *Nationalism Reframed: Nationhood and the National Question in the New Europe,* Cambridge UP, Cambridge.

Brubaker, R. (2001), 'The Return of Assimilation? Changing Perspectives on Immigration and Its Sequels in France, Germany, and the United States', *Ethnic and Racial Studies,* 24 (4), pp. 531-48.

Castles, S. (1995), 'How Nation-States Respond to Immigration and Ethnic Diversity', *New Community,* 21 (3), pp. 293-308.

Castles, S., Korac, M., Vasta, E., and Vertovec, S. (2002), *Integration: Mapping the Field,* Home Office, London.

Çinar, D., Hofinger, C., and Waldrauch, H. (1995), Integrationsindex. Zur rechtlichen Integration von Ausländerinnen in ausgewählten europäischen Ländern (Political Science Series No. 25), Institute for Advanced Study, Vienna.

Cohen, R. (1997), *Global Diasporas,* UCL Press, London.

Cohen, R. and Kennedy, P. (2000), *Global Sociology,* Macmillan, London.

Commission on Multi-Ethnic Britain (2000), *The Future of Multi-Ethnic Britain: The Parekh Report,* Runnymede, London.

Costa-Lascoux, J. (1989), *De l'immigré au citoyen,* La documentation française, Paris.

Cross, M. and Waldinger, R. (1997), 'Economic Integration and Labour Market Change: A Review and a Reappraisal'. Metropolis Discussion Paper, www.international.metropolis.net

Diehl, C., Urbahn, J., and Esser, H. (1999), *Die soziale und politische Partizipation von Zuwanderern in der Bundesrepublik Deutschland,* Forschungsinstitut der Friedrich-Ebert-Stiftung, Bonn.

Doomernik, J. (1998), 'The Effectiveness of Integration Policies Towards Immigrants and Their Descendants in France, Germany and the Netherlands', *International Migration Papers,* 27, International Labour Organisation, Geneva.

Edmonston, B. and Passel, J.S. (eds), (1994), *Immigration and Ethnicity: The Integration of America's Newest Arrivals,* The Urban Institute Press, Washington, DC.

Engbersen, G. (1996), 'The Unknown City', *Berkeley Journal of Sociology,* 40, pp. 87-111.

Erikson, R. and Goldthorpe, J. (1992), *The Constant Flux,* Clarendon, Oxford.

Esser, H. (1999), 'Inklusion, Integration und ethnische Schichtung', *Journal für Konflikt- und Gewaltforschung,* 1 (1), pp. 5-34.

Faist, T. (2000), *The Volume and Dynamics of International Migration and Transnational Social Spaces,* Oxford UP, Oxford.

Favell, A. (1998), *Philosophies of Integration: Immigration and the Idea of Citizenship in France and Britain,* Macmillan, London.

Favell, A. (2001), 'Integration Policy and Integration Research in Europe: A Review and Critique' in A. Aleinikoff and D. Klusmeyer (eds.) *Citizenship Today: Global Perspectives and Practices,* Brookings Institute/Carnegie Endowment for International Peace, Washington DC, pp. 249-99.

Fennema, M. and Tillie, J. (1999), 'Political Participation and Political Trust in Amsterdam: Civic Communities and Ethnic Networks', *Journal of Ethnic and Migration Studies,* 25 (4), pp. 703-26.

Fermin, A. (1999), 'Inburgeringsbeleid en burgerschap', *Migrantenstudien,* 15 (2), pp. 99-112.

Fielding, A.J. (1995), 'Migration and Social Change: A Longitudinal Study of the Social Mobility of "Immigrants" in England and Wales', *European Journal of Population,* 11, pp. 107-21.

Forbes, I. and Mead, G. (1992), *Measure For Measure: A Comparative Analysis of Measure to Combat Racial Discrimination in the Member Countries of the European Community,* Employment Dept., Sheffield.

Gellner, E. (1983), *Nations and Nationalism,* Blackwell, Oxford.

Giddens, A. (1990), *The Consequences of Modernity,* Polity Press, Cambridge.

Gilroy, P. (1987), *There Ain't No Black in the Union Jack,* Hutchinson, London.

Gilroy, P. (2000), *Between Camps: Nation, Culture and the Allure of Race,* Penguin, London.

Hall, S. (1988), 'New ethnicities', in J. Donald and A. Rattansi (eds.), *Race, Culture and Difference,* Sage, London, pp. 252-9.

Hammar, T. (ed.) (1985), *European Immigration Policy: A Comparative Study,* Cambridge UP, Cambridge.

Hansen, R. and Weil, P. (eds.) (2000), *Towards a European Nationality: Citizenship, Immigration and Nationality Law in the EU,* Macmillan, London.

Haut Conseil à l'Intégration (1993), *L'intégration à la française,* La documentation française, Paris.

Heckmann, F. and Schnapper, D. (eds.) (2003), *The Integration of Immigrants in European Societies: National Differences and Trends of Convergence,* Lucius and Lucius, Stuttgart.

Ireland, P. (1994), *The Policy Challenge of Ethnic Diversity,* Harvard UP, Cambridge, MA.

Joppke, C. (1999), *Immigration and the Nation State: The United States, Germany and Great Britain,* Oxford UP, Oxford.

Kesteloot, C. (2000), 'Segregation and Economic Integration of Immigrants in Brussels', in S. Body-Gendrot and M. Martiniello (eds.), *Minorities in European Cities: The Dynamics of Social Integration and Social Exclusion at the Neighbourhood Level,* Macmillan, London.

Kloosterman, R., van der Leun, J., and Rath, J. (1998), 'Across the Border: Immigrants' Economic Opportunities, Social Capital and Informal Business Activities', *Journal of Ethnic and Migration Studies,* 24 (2), pp. 249-68.

Koopmans, R. and Statham, P. (eds.) (2000), *Challenging Immigration and Ethnic Relations Politics: Comparative European Perspectives,* Oxford UP, Oxford.

Kymlicka, W. (1995), *Multicultural Citizenship,* Oxford UP, Oxford.

Le Bras, H. (1998), *Le démon des origins,* L'édition de l'aube, Paris.

Lesthaege, R. (ed.) (2000), *Communities and Generations: Turkish and Moroccan Populations in Belgium,* VUB Press, Brussels.

Mahnig, H. (1998), *Integrationspolitik in Großbritannien, Frankreich, Deutschland und den Niederlanden: Eine vergleichende Analyse,* Forschungsberichte des Schweizer Forums für Migrationstudien, 10, Neuchâtel.

Mann, M. (1993), *The Sources of Social Power* (2 vols), Cambridge UP, Cambridge.

Migration Policy Group (MPG) (1996), *The Comparative Approaches to Societal Integration Project,* Brussels, http://www.migpolgroup.com

Milward, A. (1992), *The European Rescue of the Nation State,* Routledge, London.

Modood, T., Beishon, S., and Virdee, S. (1994), *Changing Ethnic Identities,* Policy Studies Institute, London.

Modood, T. et al. (1997), *Ethnic Minorities in Britain: Diversity and Disadvantage,* Policy Studies Institute, London.

Nauck, B. and Schönpflug, U. (eds.) (1997), *Familien in verschiedenen Kulturen,* Enke, Stuttgart.

Noiriel, G. (1991), *Le creuset français,* Seuil, Paris.

Papastergiadis, N. (1999), *The Turbulence of Migration: Globalization, Deterritorialization and Hybridity,* Polity Press, Cambridge.

Parekh, B. (2000), *Rethinking Multiculturalism: Cultural Diversity and Political Theory,* Macmillan, London.

Phalet, K. and Swyngedouw, M. (1999), 'Integratie ter discussie', in Swyngedouw et al. (eds.), *Minderheden in Brussel,* pp. 19-40.

Phalet, K., van Lotringen, C., and Entzinger, H. (2000), *Islam in de multiculturele samenleving,* ERCOMER, Utrecht.

Phizacklea, A. (1998), 'Migration and Globalization: A Feminist Perspective', in K. Koser and H. Lutz, *The New Migration in Europe: Social Constructions and Social Realities,* Macmillan, London, pp. 21-38.

Portes, A. (ed.) (1995), *The Economic Sociology of Immigration,* Russell Sage Foundation, New York.

Portes, A. (1996), 'Transnational Communities: Their Emergence and Their Significance in the Contemporary World-System', in R.P. Korzeniewicz and W.C. Smith (eds.), *Latin America in the World Economy,* Greenwood Press, Westport, CT, pp. 151-68.

Rath, J. (ed.) 2000, *Immigrant Businesses: The Economic, Political and Social Environment,* Macmillan, London.

Rex, J. (1991), 'The Political Sociology of a Multicultural Society', *European Journal for Intercultural Studies,* 2 (1).

Rose, E.J.B. et al. (1969), *Colour and Citizenship: A Report on British Race Relations,* Oxford UP for the Institute of Race Relations, London.

Schierup, C.-U. (1993), *På Kulturens Slagmark: Mindretal og Størretal om Danmark,* Sydjysk Universitetsforlag, Esbjerg.

Schnapper, D. (1991), *La France de l'intégration,* Gallimard, Paris.

Simon, P. (1997), 'La statistique des origines: l'ethnicité et la 'race' dans les recensements aux Etats-Unis, Canada et Grande-Brétagne', *Sociétés Contemporaines,* 26, pp. 11-44.

Smith, M.P. and Guarnizo, L. (eds) (1998), *Transnationalism from Below,* Transaction publishers, New Brunswick, NJ.

Soininen, M. (1999), 'The "Swedish Model" as an Institutional Framework for Immigrant Membership Rights', *Journal of Ethnic and Migration Studies,* 25 (2), pp. 685-702.

SOPEMI (1998), *Trends in International Migration.* Annual report of continuous reporting system on migration, OECD, Rome.

Soysal, Y. (1994), *Limits of Citizenship: Migrants and Post-National Membership in Europe,* Chicago UP, Chicago.

Swyngedouw, M., Phalet, K., and Deschouwer, K. (eds.) (1999), *Minderheden in Brussel,* VUB Press, Brussels.

Todd, E. (1994), *Le destin des immigrés: assimilation et ségrégation dans les démocraties occidentales,* Seuil, Paris.

Togeby, L. (1999), 'Migrants at the Polls: An Analysis of Immigrant and Refugee Participation in Danish Local Elections', *Journal of Ethnic and Migration Studies,* 25 (4), pp. 665-84.

Torpey, J. (2000), *The Invention of the Passport,* Cambridge UP, Cambridge.

Tribalat, M. (1995), *Faire France: une enquête sur les immigrés et leurs enfants,* La découverte, Paris.

Tribalat, M. et al. (1996), *De l'immigration à l'assimilation: une enquête sur la population étrangère en France,* INED, Paris.

Urry, J. (2000), *Sociology Beyond Societies: Mobilities for the 21st Century,* Routledge, London.

Veenman, J. (1998), *Buitenspel: Over langdurige werkloosheid onder ethnische minderheden,* Assen, Van Gorum.

Vermeulen, H. (ed.) (1997), *Immigrant Policy for a Multicultural Society: A Comparative Study of Integration, Language and Religious Policy in Five Western European Countries,* Migration Policy Group/IMES, Brussels.

Vertovec, S. (1997), 'Social Cohesion and Tolerance', in *Key Issues for Research and Policy on Migrants in Cities.* Metropolis Discussion Paper, www.international.metropolis.net

Waldrauch, H. and Hofinger, C. (1997), 'An Index to Measure the Legal Obstacles to the Integration of Migrants', *New Community,* 23 (2), pp. 271-86.

Waldrauch, H. (ed.) (2001), *Die Integration von Einwanderern: Ein Index der Rechtlichen Diskriminierung,* Campus, Frankfurt.

Weil, P. (1991), *La France et ses étrangers: l'aventure d'une politique de l'immigration,* Calmann-Lévy, Paris.

Weil, P. (1996), 'Nationalities and Citizenships: The Lessons of the French Experience for Germany and Europe', in D. Cesarani and M. Fulbrook (eds.), *Citizenship, Nationality and Migration in Europe,* Routledge, London, pp. 74-87.

Werbner, P. (1999), 'What Colour Success? Distorting Value in Studies of Ethnic Entrepreneurship', *Sociological Review,* 47 (3), pp. 548-79.

Wimmer, A. and Glick Schiller, N. (2002), 'Methodological Nationalism and Beyond: Nation-State Building, Migration and the Social Sciences', *Global Networks,* 2 (4), pp. 301-34.

Wrench, J. (1996), *Preventing Racism at the Workplace,* European Foundation for the Improvement of Living and Working Conditions, Dublin.

Chapter 3

The Anthropology of Transnational Communities and the Reframing of Immigration Research in California: The Mixtec Case

Michael Kearney

Prepared for European University Institute
Migration Form: 'Reflections on Migration Research', Florence, May 1999

As Zolberg (1989, p. 403) observed on the twenty-fifth anniversary of the *International Migration Review*, there is a certain convergence among scholars advancing 'the most stimulating newer approaches' to migration research and theory, and they share four characteristics. These are, (1) historical in attending to 'changing specificities of time and place', (2) 'structural rather than individualistic...with special emphasis on the dynamics of capitalism and the state', (3) globalist in the sense that they attend to how local conditions within nations are affected by transnational processes, and (4) critical in seeking to demystify adverse conditions affecting nations and migrants. Nevertheless, although migration studies have now emerged as a more or less coherent field of theory and research, each of the social sciences that deal with human migration – sociology, economics, political science, demography, history, and anthropology – has a distinctive signature with respect to its definition of research problems, theory, and methods.[1] The general features noted above, when combined with those of anthropology noted below, define the special dispositions that anthropology brings to the study of migration that derive from its unique history and its constitution as a discipline that embraces the natural and social sciences, and the humanities.

Anthropology and the Study of Migration[2]

Within the overall division of labor among the social sciences in Europe and the Americas, anthropology has historically assumed responsibility for the study of those societies that are most different and distant from Western forms. Thus, whereas the other social sciences were devised and institutionalized as part of the construction of the modern Western nation-states, anthropology was born more in colonial domains that were also integral to the construction of these nation-states. Therefore, from its inception, anthropology has been oriented more to the periphery of the modern world system, rather than the core nations. Furthermore, the focus of anthropology in its formative years of the late 19th and early 20th century was on non-industrial, non-agrarian societies in these peripheral areas. This attention to the 'primitive' societies of the world gave anthropology an orientation to the non-western other that was consolidated in its classic period in the first half of the 20th century (Kearney, 1996, pp. 23-30).

A second distinctive and enduring ideal of the classic anthropological approach is to seek holistic ethnographic treatment of total communities, beginning with attention, in Marxist terms, to the infrastructure, consisting of the local natural environment, the technology that enables a people to adapt to and extract nutrients and energy from that environment, and their division of labor. To this infrastructural base is added the ethnography of the less tangible aspects of the communities' superstructure such as social organization, political dynamics, ethnoscience, folklore, ritual, religion, and ideology. And not least, the infra- and superstructural aspects of economy are also of basic concern.

With the widespread demise of hunting and gathering societies by the end of World War II, anthropology turned increasingly to the study of peasants, defined as subsistence level agriculturalists with typically unequal economic relations with non-peasant sectors, which politically dominated them (Kearney, 1996, pp. 30-41). From the beginnings of civilization until the mid-twentieth century, in most parts of the world, peasant societies had been the demographically most prevalent social type and the main sources of food and human and animal labor power for urban economies. Indeed, until modern public health technology of the 20th century, most cities were only able to replace their populations and grow by the in-migration of peasants from the countryside. It was therefore inevitable that anthropologists, who in the 1950s and 1960s were mostly working in rural peasant communities, should follow their migrating subjects into cities and thus take the discipline into the realm of migration research and theory, and begin to analyze their communities in such larger global geo-political contexts.[3] And in doing so they brought anthropological sensibilities to the framing of migration research problems, theory, and methods – especially the disposition to focus on *peripheral* communities and to treat them *holistically*. As for holism, not all anthropological studies of migration attain it – few do. But it is accurate to say that as compared with other disciplines, anthropological approaches to migration in today's post-peasant world (Kearney, 1996) entertain broader ethnographic and analytic concerns that take into account multiple infra- and superstructural aspects of entire communities. Anthropology is also distinguished from the other social science disciplines by its emphasis on long-term intensive participatory ethnographic fieldwork as a basic research method.

Anthropology and Transnational Migration Theory and Research

An anthropological approach to transnational migration implies application of its general methods and perspectives to a migrant community throughout its geographic extension. Thus, anthropology brings to study of migration the same concern with total communities in their historical-structural context. Although, as Zolberg observes (see above), there is a tendency in contemporary research and theory to employ globalist perspectives that situate migration phenomena in international contexts, there remain in sociological, historic, and other non-anthropological approaches to migration research certain bipolar dispositions expressed in the language of *assimilation, incorporation,* and *sending and receiving communities,* etc. These orientations are doubtlessly shaped by the largely immigrant and immigration experiences of the Western nations that have been both the main recipients of *immigrants* in the last two centuries and the sites of the most intense politics about and research on migration.

Because anthropology comes to the study of migration from the periphery, it has a sensibility and dispositions different from those of the other social sciences which are more focused on the core, i.e, on the concerns of the 'receiving' nations, such as, for example, immigrant impact and incorporation research. Also, in contrast to these inherently bipolar, nation-centric orientations toward *international* migration, anthropologists are more disposed to conceptualize migration as *transnational* in the sense that it often opens up and takes place in *transnational social spaces* (Goldring, 1999) that subsume and relativize national spaces – a tendency that is most evident in the case of *transnational communities* (Goldring, 1999; Kearney and Nagengast, 1989).

Identities, Borders, Orders

As for what constitutes migration, a good working definition is that it is a significant human movement across a significant border. This definition in turn requires a specification of *borders*.

In taking cross-border movement as a defining aspect of migration it is again useful to refer to Zolberg (1989, p. 40) who says it is, 'the control which states exercise over borders that defines international migration as a distinctive social process'. A powerful heuristic device for examining this nexus of migration, borders, and states is the conceptual triad of 'Identities, Borders, Orders' (Fig. 3.1).[4] The basic idea underlying this triad is that in any specific case, its elements are mutually self-constituting. Thus, social identity can only be formed by being bordered with respect to contrasting identities in a system of relationships and distinctions – that is ordered by some form of social, political, cultural, legal, or possibly spatial-geographical politics, formally or informally, that construct the border in question. Similarly, identities are changed upon crossing a border because of the classifying power of some order or constellation of orders, be they formal or informal, that construct that border. Said differently, *borders* are classificatory devices imposed by some *order* that defines the *identities* of persons who are within their borders, beyond them, and who cross them (and of course, individuals and groups are also active in the construction of their own identities). Similarly, *orders* are defined by the nature of the borders that circumscribe them and distinguish them from other orders.

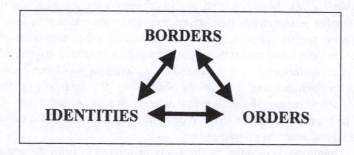

Figure 3.1 The Interactive Triad of Identities, Borders, Orders

The Illegal Immigration Impact Debate

Widespread popular wisdom holds that the arrival of 'illegal immigrants' from Mexico to California negatively impacts the state's economy because they presumably consume more in social services (welfare, medical costs, policing, etc.) than they contribute in taxes and otherwise to the state's economy. This position was strongly advocated by former California Governor Wilson during his term (1991-1999), numerous other policy makers, researchers, and anti-immigrant organizations, and is also widely shared by the general public and manifests as specific policies and legal forms. Of these, the most notable is the 1994 state ballot initiative, Proposition 187, which was approved by 59 per cent of California voters and which sought to deny public education, health care, and financial assistance to undocumented residents in the state. In 1997 a U.S. district court ruled that federal law preempted 'substantially all of the provisions of Proposition 187'.[5]

The thinking underlying such conventional wisdom, viz., that undocumented Mexican migrants consume more in social services and impose more expenses than they pay for with taxes, is flawed. This flaw lies in a basic misconception of the economic relationship between U.S. citizens and the migrants in their midst and between the 'receiving' regions in the United States and the 'sending' regions in Mexico. Indeed, when the issue is reframed within a larger anthropological perspective, the contrary hypothesis seems at least as equally viable, namely that in numerous ways unauthorized Mexican migrants contribute more to the economy of California than they consume in social services, plus other social costs that they impose. In other words, rather than being a drain on the California economy, there may be a net asset to it as pro-immigrant advocates argue. However, at present, the bulk of published data on this bottom line issue seems to support the anti-immigrant position (see below).

Migration and Value: A Case Study

An Identities-Borders-Orders conceptualization of migration as cross-border movement raises the question of why migrants seek to cross borders and also, why orders seek to regulate the cross-border flow of migrants and non-human items and to control their identities. The answer to this query suggested by an anthropological sensibility is that at the heart of border dynamics is a concern with generalized value such that migrants cross borders to better position themselves in fields of value and orders elaborate border policies so as to enhance positive net flows of different forms of value across borders into and out of their territories.[6] This characterization of migration situates it within a broad theorization of general value (see Kearney, 1996, pp. 151-69). From this perspective, *orders* (e.g., states, political parties, special interests groups) seek to shape *borders* so as to affect positive net flows of value into their domains. A robust anthropological sensibility thus theorizes migration within a broader concern with the dynamics of cross-border movement of significant items in general, thus situating cross-border migration theory within a larger theoretical universe that also includes flows of commodities, money, data, and information (see Kearney, 2004; Heyman, 2001).

To illustrate the distinctive qualities of such a robust anthropological approach to migration I should like to present a case study of migration from the Mixteca region in the state of Oaxaca, in Southern Mexico to California.[7] More specifically, I shall use this distinctly anthropological sensibility to recast some basic assumptions that guide current research on the impact of undocumented Mexican migration into California, for indeed, the majority of Mixtecs who enter California do so 'illegally'. In this paper, I do not presume to resolve the debates about the economic impact of 'illegals'. My purpose at this stage is rather to introduce aspects of an anthropological perspective that reframe the basic issues and displace the debates about them into a different transnational conceptual domain apart from the limited national – one is tempted to say nationalist – context that currently defines them. The working assumption here is that such displacement into this transnational and anthropological space will allow some escape from certain theoretical and methodological biases of theory and method inherent in the national perspective.

This anthropological concern with two formally academic and geopolitically distinct areas of study – one, the Mixteca region of Southeastern Mexico, and the other California and other regions of North America – that are now linked by immigration from the former to the latter and circular migration between them requires some basic reconceptualization of the resultant third space, which has popularly become known as *Oaxacalifornia* (Kearney, 1995b; Rivera, 1999a,

1999b). In contrast to a bipolar conceptualization that gives attention to sending and receiving areas, an anthropological sensibility is disposed to conceptualize the migrant community as occupying this third space and to allocate research effort to the exploration of migration and migration related issues within it.

Presently there are large and growing numbers of Mixtec migrant farm workers in California.[8] As such, Mixtec migrants are more or less representative of the so-called 'new immigrants' coming into the state in this post-melting pot era of multi-culturalism and increasing ethnic diversity. To understand why Mixtecs are present in California and the conditions under which they migrate, as well as the immigration politics and debates that swirl around them, some historical background on Oaxaca in the colonial and post colonial periods is necessary.

Oaxaca: Historic Background of Contemporary Migration

In post-conquest Oaxaca in the 16th century there was a specific configuration of this Bordering-Ordering-Identifying whereby Mixtecs were defined as *naturales* as a way of distinguishing them from *Castilians* and other *whites*, i.e., Christian Europeans. In other words, Mixtecs and other indigenous ethnic groups were by degree assigned distinctive and inferior identities within a caste system and, within this legal order, were concentrated into planned communities that were sharply bordered – legally, socially, culturally, spatially – from non-indigenous communities. Once so formed, these indigenous 'closed corporate communities' (Wolf, 1957) served as labor reserves from which enormous wealth was accumulated, much of which was transferred to Spain, as was consistent with colonial policies, informed as they were by mercantilist theories of how colonies were to be sources of wealth for the formation of the emerging nation-states of Europe. In New Spain, this transnational system of accumulation was based on the legal, cultural, and social distinctions – bordering – between indigenous and non-indigenous identities that defined the ways in which the Mixteca was incorporated into the expanding capitalist world system (Wallerstein, 1974; Pastor, 1987).

In the post independence era the legal distinctions of the caste system were swept by the new modern and modernizing Mexican nation-state. The basic biological and social premises underlying the cultural construction of the modern nation was that all the 'races' that formed the basis for the caste system of the colonial period would melt into a single new *mestizo* (mixed) race with a common Mexican national culture and identity. To some large degree this part of the scenario of 'modernization' has happened, but the social inequalities of the former caste system have been transformed into a contemporary class system in which economic inequalities comparable to those of the colonial period are now increasing in the current era of neoliberal restructuring (Barry, 1995). Furthermore, far from disappearing into the Mexican melting pot, indigenous peoples have recently become demographically, culturally, and politically more prominent in Mexico than they were in the colonial period.[9]

The Mixteca region occupies roughly the western third of the state of Oaxaca and bordering areas of Puebla and Guerrero. At the time of the conquest in the early 16th century, the valleys of the Mixteca region were productive corn exporting areas. At present, however, after five centuries of colonial and neo-colonial conditions, much of the Mixteca is a de-developed corn importing region with widespread environmental deterioration. Clearly, now at the end of the 20th century a new regime of bordering-ordering-identifying has come into play, and like the earlier one of the colonial period it too functions within a global political economy so as to effect the transfer of economic value from Mixtec communities.

The colonial period in the Mixteca was a case of classic dependence in which absolute surplus was extracted by tribute, taxation, and other forms of unequal exchange. Now, however, the primary mechanism of such transfer of value is circular migration within Mexico and circular transnational migration to the United States. In other words, the circuits of dependence are now more complex in that the indigenous labor power that lies at the base of the present regimes of accumulation is reproduced primarily not from self-sufficient peasant communities, but from partially proletarianized villages and towns that reproduce via combinations of peasant production and migration to distant sites of wage labor, and participation in the informal economy.

The Cross-Border Flow of Value within the Transnational Community

Central to California's major industry – agribusiness – is an increasing reliance on farm workers from the Mixteca. Elsewhere I and others have written about migration of indigenous peoples from the Mixteca region of Western Oaxaca to Northwestern Mexico and California.[10] Central to the ethnography of Mixtec migration is the presence of transnational communities – TNCs – that span the border and that have created complex patterns of economic, social, cultural, and biological reproduction based on strategies deployed at multiple sites on both sides of the border. In addition to primary communities in Oaxaca, Mixtec TNCs are also comprised of numerous daughter communities in Central and Northwestern Mexico and in the United States, especially in agricultural areas of California, but also in Oregon, Arizona, Florida, North Carolina, and elsewhere. There is considerable movement of households and individuals among such local communities of the greater TNCs.

Since its inception in the late 19th century, large scale corporate agriculture in California has relied heavily on successive waves of migrant workers from throughout the Pacific Basin. Thus a succession of foreign national ethnic groups have cycled through California farm labor system. Today, Mixtecs are but the most significant recent arrivals of the scene, where they are in varying degrees replacing mestizo Mexican migrant workers, who preceded them, as they in turn came after earlier migrations of Filipino, Japanese, Chinese, and other ethnic groups (Kearney, 1986a; Runsten and Kearney, 1994; Zabin et al., 1993).

Our primary concern here is the production and distribution of economic value within Mixtec TNCs and flows of such value between the TNCs and local communities in California, as mediated by migration. A central feature of these TNCs is that they are bisected by the international border. My working hypothesis is that the border functions as a variable filter that affects the flow of persons, information, possessions, and other forms of economic value within the TNC back and forth between Mexico and California. The U.S.-Mexico border effects this process by lying in the vertical zone where the noncapitalist and the capitalist meet and articulate, as depicted in Figure 3.2.[11]

Thus the border is in effect a complex semi-permeable membrane with respect to flows of economic value. As such the border regulates a sort of osmotic process in which more value flows through the TNC from Mexico and into the non-Mixtec California economy than vice versa (see Kearney, 2004). As argued below (see 'The Problem of Limited Domain'), such quanta of value are not taken into account in studies that assess the impact of illegal migrants. It may well be that such positive contributions do not fully offset the net consumption of services by undocumented migrants, but such an assessment cannot be made until such contributions are assessed.

The functioning of the border as a differential filter changes from one historic period to another. At this moment in the wake of the creation of NAFTA (the North American Free Trade Agreement), it is becoming more permeable to capital and commodities, but at the same time it is becoming more restrictive with reference to the northward transborder movement of persons. Until the Great Depression of the 1930s, personal movement across the border was virtually unrestricted (Vélez Ibáñez, 1996, pp. 82-3). It is important to note, however, that while immigration policy currently restricts the movement of persons, it does not entirely prevent such movement. Rather, what border immigration policy – ordering – does by bordering (see Fig. 1) in the case of undocumented workers is to separate labor power from migrant persons, such that ideally their labor power is delivered to sites in California, but they return to Mexico without it (see Kearney, 1991, pp. 55-60).

This basic premise concerning the extra-national economic contribution of illegal immigrants is suggested by dependency theory which posits a net flow of economic value from de-developed 'peripheries' of the world system to developed 'cores', both of which are two sides of the same coin.[12] But for the most part dependency theory focuses on unequal macro economic exchanges between global regions rather than the kind of fine-grain ethnographic analysis required to speak to the issue of the economic impact of transnational individual migrants. A step in that direction was provided by articulation theory, which paid more attention to the dynamics of migration at the level of the household.

Articulation, as in articulation theory, depicts how infrasubsistence peasant households and communities are articulated with distant labor markets via migration (see Kearney, 1996, pp. 81-104). In such systems the labor power delivered to employers is partially reproduced by the production of food and other resources outside of capitalist relations of production, thus articulating capitalist and non-capitalist (peasant) modes of production (see Fig. 3.2).

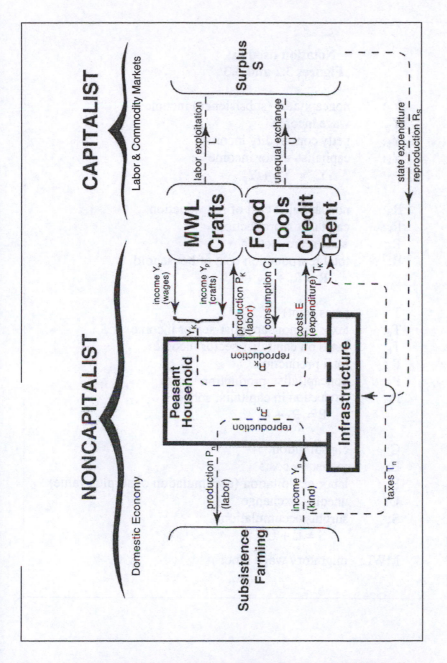

Figure 3.2 The Articulation of the Domestic Economy and Capitalism through Migratory Wage Labor and Petty Commodity Production (from Kearney, 1996, p. 100).

Notation used in
Figures 3.2 and 3.3

Y_n: noncapitalist (subsistence) income
Y_w: wage income
Y_p: petty commodity income
Y_k: capitalist-sector income
$$Y_k = Y_w + Y_p$$

R_n: noncapitalist cost of reproduction
R_k: capitalist reproduction
R_s: state reproduction
R: total reproduction cost of household
$$R = R_n + R_k + R_s$$

T taxes (rent)
T_n: taxes on noncapitalist-sector income
T_k: taxes on capitalist-sector income
P :   total production
P_n: noncapitalist production
P_k: production in capitalist sphere
$$P = P_n + P_k$$

C: consumption
E: monetary costs
L: labor exploitation (accumulation of surplus value)
U: unequal exchange
S: surplus accumulation
$$S = L + U$$

MWL: migratory wage labor

In a situation of articulation the following conditions typically prevail: 1) A rural peasantry lives in a remote region where some combination of demographic pressures and scarcity of good farming land make out-migration in search of wage labor a necessity for survival; i.e., they live in an infrasubsistence local economy.

2) The labor markets that the infrasubistence peasants migrate to are saturated or nearly saturated such that they typically find only seasonal or otherwise partial employment. 3) Because such labor power is partially reproduced with non-wage income (via subsistence farming and the informal economy), it is possible for such workers to accept very low wages and even less than a living wage when they enter labor markets. Said differently, the rate of exploitation, i.e., the accumulation of surplus, of such a work force is potentially higher than from one that is fully proletarianized.[13]

Such an analysis of the articulation of distinct modes of production mediated by migration is well discussed by de Janvry and Garramon (1977). Similarly, and quite relevant for our discussion here, Burawoy (1976) offers a comparable analysis using as case studies the Apartheid system in South Africa and the structuring of Mexican migrant labor in California (see also Wolpe, 1972). Such systems of articulated labor are economically advantageous to the receiving economies not only in that cheap labor delivers itself to them, but also because the costs of the reproduction of that labor are borne by the economy of a different, distant region. In the purest form of this system adult workers migrate at their own expense from their homes, where children and other dependents remain, to sites of employment. From these places of employment they remit earnings that support their dependents who do not have access to public services in the entity where the migrant workers are employed. Then at the end of their work career the workers are retired back to their 'homelands'. If and when migrants begin to settle down in the locals of their wage labor, then the system starts to decay.[14]

The way in which settlement in the receiving areas causes decay in the structural advantages of articulation to such areas over generations is shown in Figure 2b, which is adapted from Meillassoux (1981) who examined labor migration between Senegal and France. Thus, for this system to endure over time there must be some mechanisms that perpetuate a perennial separation of biological reproduction from economic production. In situations of articulation there is, however, typically some settling that is restricted and minimized by an 'immigration policy'. In the case of Apartheid it was the passbook laws; in the Mexico-California case it is the international boundary and the patterned, uneven enforcement of immigration law. Such immigration laws can be seen as functioning to ensure some separation of reproduction from production, so as to perpetuate the economic advantages of this system to the receiving communities. This situation can be seen as a special case of 'segmented assimilation' (Zhou, 1997). Thus, although there is some flow-through, per Fig. 3.3, nevertheless, because of the long-term structuring of articulation of the two regions, the positions left vacant in the lower rungs of the labor markets are filled by new migrants. Thus, the sociocultural and class structure of the TNCs and the articulation of the 'sending' and 'receiving' areas are perpetuated.

NO MIGRATION
$$Yn = \beta B = \alpha (A + B + C)$$
$$L1 = 0$$

CIRCULAR WAGE LABOR, (first generation)
$$Yn < \alpha(A + C), \quad Yw > \alpha\beta$$
$$Yn + Yw = \alpha (A + B + C)$$
$$\beta B = \alpha B + L2 + Mac$$
$$L2 = \beta B - \alpha B - Mac$$
$$L2 > L1$$

IMMIGRATION (second generation)
$$Yw = \alpha (A2 + B) + Mc, \quad Yn \rightarrow \alpha A1$$
$$\beta B = \alpha (A2 + B) + Mc + L4$$
$$L3 = \beta B - \alpha (A + B) - Mc$$
$$L3 < L2$$

IMMIGRATION (third generation)
$$Yw = \alpha (A + B + C)$$
$$\beta B = \alpha (A + B + C) + L4$$
$$L4 = \beta B - \alpha (A + B + C), \quad \alpha C > Mc$$
$$L4 < L3$$

SUMMARY: $L2 > L3 > L4 > L1$

M: remittance
L: labor exploitation (accumulation of surplus value)
    L1-4: generations/phases in L associated with degrees of articulation
        L1:   no articulation
        L2:   articulation, no immigration
        L3:   articulation plus immigration, first generation
        L4:   articulation plus immigration, second generation
Lm: migrant: L = L2
Li: immigrant: L = L3, L4

α, β, A, B, C, per Meillassoux (1981:52):
    A, a: the pre-productive period of childhood
    B, b: the productive period of adulthood
    C, c: the post-productive period of old age
      α: annual consumption per head
      β: annual production per productive individual (in B)

Figure 3.3 Migration and Surplus (from Kearney, 1996, p. 103)

As the newest entrants coming into the bottom of the farm labor markets, the Mixtecs are typically the desired workers from the employers' point of view, since they are recognized as more self-disciplined and productive, as is typical of first generation migrants. It is also important to note that the Mixtecs are now entering California labor markets at a time of widespread anti-'immigrant' sentiments, which are fueled in part by negative impact research. In this climate, compounded by an overabundance of 'illegal' labor, employers and labor contractors can and do use the freshly arriving Mixtecs as a means to discipline more experienced workers, thus getting double mileage out of disciplining the Mixtecs directly.[15]

The Immigration Debate Reframed Anthropologically

This anthropological approach requires an examination of the linkages between research, immigration policy, immigration patterns, and the formation of such identities as 'legals' and 'illegals' (see Fig. 3.1 concerning identities, borders, orders) and, by such application of the anthropological perspective, to go beyond the current debates about immigration facts and policy to examine the structural and categorical features of this binational system. Therefore, with 'binational system' I also mean to include the greater cultural and political forces that shape immigration policy, of which research is also a component. Thus, the anthropological strategy is to displace the vantage point to a position that regards immigration impact research itself as part of the social and political process out of which immigration policy is formed, which in turn can be regarded as a component in the political economy of the State of California to the degree that political interests in the state influence state and federal immigration policy.

Much of this impact research is suspect in that it is commissioned with the explicit intention of collecting data that demonstrate the negative costs of immigrants to different municipal and county governments, and also to the entire state of California so that such data can be used to negotiate reimbursement to local governments from the federal government. The argument for such reimbursements is that the federal government must compensate local governments for costs that they have incurred because of the failure of Washington to adequately enforce the nation's borders from an 'invasion' of 'illegals'.[16]

The main point here is that perceptions of negative impact appear to be integral components of a binational system that actually functions in an inverse manner to such popular descriptions of it. In other words, it is not just that both popular and official perceptions of the 'negative' impact of 'illegals' are quite possibly wrong, but that such perceptions – sustained as they are by much research – are integral features in immigration policy formation that reproduces the conditions whereby 'illegals' who are blamed for taking more than they get, actually might be making positive contributions to those areas and sectors of the California economy into and through which they move. In other words, the current way in which 'immigration' (as opposed to migration) is currently conceptualized is a definition of the problem that is inadequate for accurately making such an assessment.

Thus, the position taken herein is that such research is biased due to the high degree to which it is driven by political objectives and by anti-immigrant public opinion. A stronger version of this hypothesis is that negative impact research is itself an integral part of a binational economic system of asymmetric migration, governed as it is by immigration policy, which is in turn influenced by migration research. The logic of this hypothesis is suggested by a comparable dynamic studied by Jorge Bustamante (1983). Bustamante shows that in times of economic downturn in the U.S. economy, the rate of detentions of undocumented border crossers increases, whereas in times of economic expansion, the rate of detentions goes down (see Fig. 3.4). These data support Cockcroft's (1986) argument that U.S. immigration policy is actually labor policy disguised as immigration policy. In other words, border enforcement appears to function as a valve that controls the flow of Mexican labor into the U.S. economy in accord with need.

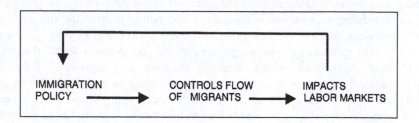

Figure 3.4 Bustamante's Model of the Relationship between Immigration Policy and Labor Markets

Bustamante's study and Cockcroft's observations are incisive and prescient, but do not tell the entire story. In the Mixtec case further anthropological specification of the greater transnational field is necessary that takes into account how the migrants exist outside of the monetized economy when they are in Oaxaca. This peasant dimension of their lives is depicted in Figure 3.5, which combines the basic relationship of articulation, depicted in Figures 3.2 and 3.3 with aspects of Figure 3.4 to demonstrate how articulated migration and the formation of immigration policy concerning migrant farm workers are related.[17]

What I also argue is that there is a similar functional relationship between negative impact research and the migrant labor force. Whereas the Bustamante-Cockcroft model explains how enforcement of immigration border policy is related to the demand for migrant labor in the U.S. economy, i.e., controls the supply (Fig. 3.4), I am proposing that negative impact research functions to promote restrictive immigration policy as a means to discipline and to cheapen the migrant labor force. In other words, negative impact research appears to be not merely a distortion, but an inversion of the actual impacts that undocumented Mexican migrants have on the state's economy, and as such is an integral component of state sponsored labor management policy disguised as U.S. immigration policy (see Fig. 3.6).

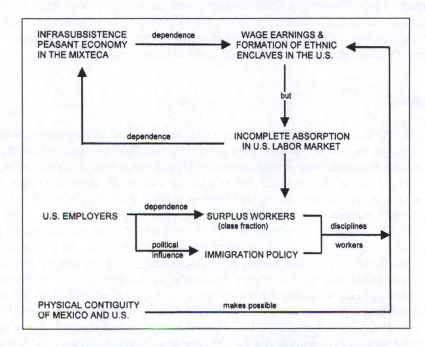

Figure 3.5 Political and Economic Contexts of Articulation of the Mixteca with the U.S. Economy (from Kearney, 1986a, p. 94)

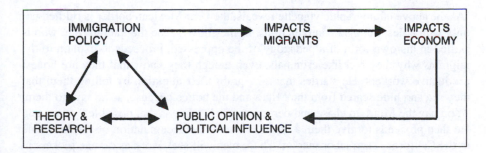

Figure 3.6 The Anthropology of Immigration Research, Policy, and Economics

These two forms of labor management, each disguised as immigration policy, are quite distinct. Whereas the form that Bustamante describes operates mainly by increasing and decreasing the rate of apprehensions of undocumented border crossers, the form that I am describing works mainly by creating a generalized climate of surveillance which serves to drive undocumented workers underground and to generally make them more vulnerable to exploitive labor practices. Such a regime of labor discipline has the double effect of increasing the productivity of migrant workers and decreasing the wages paid to them.

Vignette

Four Mixtec migrants are sitting around a table in the home of anthropologists having their first meal in several days. For the previous four days they have been walking through the rugged mountains of eastern San Diego County. They are exhausted from cold and lack of sleep and food. Part of their trek was through snow; all of them are wearing light cotton clothing and two of them wear tennis shoes. They are talking with a Paraguayan peasant leader now in political exile, who is living in the house and who is astounded at their manner of entry into the United States. They tell him that when they come through these mountains they try to sleep for part of the day and walk at night when it is too cold to sleep. But one night, they say, they became so cold that they had to stop and build a fire. One of them says that he was thinking as they were huddled around the small fire, hoping that it would not attract the attention of the Migra. He was thinking, he says, that he felt like a criminal, like someone who had to hide because they were doing some bad thing. But, he says, he could not understand what bad thing he was doing for he is an honest man who comes to the United States only to work, to leave his sweat and earn some money. He says he is a father and husband and a good worker, and that is why his *patrones* always hire him. They do not think that he is criminal, but he says that he feels like he is a criminal and he cannot understand why. The other men agree that they feel the same when they are exposed to possible apprehension by the Border Patrol or by other police agents.[18]

'As the above ethnographic vignette reveals, the U.S.-Mexican border is riddled not only with holes, but also contradictions. In the above scene the Paraguayan, who is skilled in his own form of a pedagogy of the oppressed, proceeds to explain to the migrants why they feel like criminals, even though they know that they are honest productive workers. He startles them, he grabs their attention by telling them that they run and hide scared from the Migra and the police because, as he says to them, "You pay the Migra to chase and persecute you." "How is that possible?", they ask. He then proceeds to give them a crash course in the accumulation of surplus value in the California farm labor market. These men will seek work as orange pickers in Riverside. The Paraguayan assists them to calculate the approximate unit wage that they are paid for picking a pound of oranges. He then reminds them of the per pound price of oranges in local markets which differs greatly from what they are paid. He then explains how the difference is apportioned into costs of production, taxes, and profits that are paid and earned by the grower. He then calls the men's attention to the taxes that the grower pays and how their taxes go toward the maintenance of the Border Patrol. Thus he proves his point that the migrants pay the Migra to pursue them like criminals. They of course then ask him why things are arranged this way, and by a Socratic questioning he elicits the answer from them: because they run scared all the time and are desperate to get work before they are apprehended and sent back to Mexico, they accept whatever wage is offered and then work like fiends and otherwise do what they can to satisfy their *patrón*. In short, in a lesson that might have been taken from Foucault, he brings them to understand, that the surveillance activities of the Border Patrol are not intended to prevent their entry into the United States to work, but instead are part of a number of ways of disciplining them to work hard and to accept low wages' (Kearney, 1996, p. 61).

A Reformulation of 'Immigration' and 'Impact'

The basic task of this paper is to demonstrate how the assessment of the impact of immigration and the debates around it are reframed by an anthropological approach. In this reconfigured approach to the study of impact, a working assumption is that accurate assessment of impact on local 'receiving' communities can only be made by simultaneously examining how migrants are also situated within domains that include not only the local 'receiving community', but also the migrants communities of origin, as well as other spaces to which they may migrate. Thus, in this alternative approach, 'immigration' is reconfigured to include multidirectional 'migration' that takes place within TNCs (Kearney and Nagengast, 1989). Here it is important to note the structure of this critique. It is not based on an impugning of the integrity of the researchers responsible for the work in question or on the quality of the actual research performed. Instead the critique strikes at two conceptual flaws that inform it and that serve to seriously skew the data collected in favor of the anti-immigrant position. What are these flawed assumptions in standard theory and research? We can refer to them as the problems of *limited domain* and the *categorical errors*.

Subsequent paragraphs outline these flawed assumptions and propose alternative anthropologically informed theory to frame the issues and alternative methods to investigate them.[19] In order to illustrate the limitations of the standard research to depict adequately the impact of undocumented migrants I shall present ethnographic data from my own research on migration within TNCs that are anchored in the Mixteca region of Oaxaca and that are also present in California. The intent here is not to marshal data that disprove the standard model, for in fact such data do not yet exist. Rather, the intent is to outline a characteristically anthropological research plan that overcomes the problems of limited domain and categorical errors.

The Problem of Limited Domain

There are several dimensions to what I refer to as the problem of limited domain. All have to do with a major flaw in impact research which is that its conceptualization of the issue as well as its collection and analysis of data stop at the California-Mexico border. It results in a bias caused by an incomplete collection of data due primarily to the framing of the issue in local terms when it is in reality a transborder phenomenon, as suggested by the above discussion of transnational Mixtec migration.

Early research on migration was conceptualized primarily in terms of 'sending' and 'receiving' communities. In the last decade or so there have been numerous advances beyond such bipolar models, but for the most part these newer approaches to migration have not been employed in impact studies. Thus the impact problem is framed in terms of 'immigrants' who, as it were, drop from the sky into California communities without any biographical antecedents and who come to stay. There are two corollary problems here: one is the definition of 'receiving communities' as bounded and local. Such definition of 'community' as the unit of research is driven by the sociology of typical impact research projects which are commissioned by local governments to assess the impact of undocumented 'immigration' into their jurisdictions. In this conceptualization, 'immigrants' (cf. migrants) are seen as permanently moving from their communities of origin and 'settling' in the 'receiving community'.

The ethnography of Mixtec TNCs reveals that the costs of reproduction and retirement of Mixtec migrants, rather than being concentrated in 'receiving communities', are to a great extent dispersed throughout the TNC, with major fractions of them being borne in Mexico (see Fig. 3.3). As such, what is in reality a binational system of economic production and reproduction of labor power and other forms of human capital is considered only in a fragmentary way by the impact models when applied to such communities.[20] By the same token, not only does impact research fail to take into account the resources that migrants bring with them into local Californian communities, it also fails to assess adequately the ways in which costs are distributed throughout TNCs on both sides of the border. Medical expenses can be taken as an example, for they too are borne in ways that are not captured by impact research (see Bade, 1993, 1994; Martinez, 2004).

First, a common pattern for Mixtec migrants is to return to Mexico when sick or injured such that costs of treatment, rehabilitation, and lost earnings are borne by impaired individuals, their families and communities. Also, there is good evidence that Mixtecs under-utilize Medical services when in the United States and do so for two reasons. One is lack of access, and the other is recourse to traditional (folk) medical care specialists within their communities, both in California and in Mexico (see next section).[21]

The Categorical Errors

In addition to the problem of limited domain, there are other biases built into negative impact research that become apparent with an anthropological concern with cultural categorization. These are the ways in which data are specified and which compound the problem of limited domain. Whereas the problem of limited domain is due to an insufficient collection of data (i.e., limited to California), in a manner that systematically skews results in favor of analyses that demonstrate negative impact, the categorical errors are due to an insufficient definition of what the data are. There are two categorical errors. The first derives from defining economic data in a comparably myopic manner, such that forms of economic value that are essential to a full assessment of transborder impact are not attended to. Such a bias can only be overcome by a robust anthropological economics that attends to both monetized and non-monetized forms of value (see Kearney, 2004).

Thus, the first categorical error is the false assumption that 'economic impact' can be adequately measured in dollar terms, that is, by using standard monetary accounting procedures. But, as I shall argue, a complete assessment of economic impact must take into account forms of value (capital) that are not normally denominated in dollar amounts (cf. Bourdieu, 1986). Thus, there is not only a problem with the framing of the geographical and sociological extent of the problem, there is a serious flaw in the specification of the forms of value that lie at the heart of economic issues. Therefore adequate economic impact research design must attend not only to the way in which the boundary between Mexico and California is disintegrating under the pressure of transnational forces, it must also push to transcend the boundaries that conventional economics draws around its domain. For indeed, the conventional limitation of economics to value forms defined as data denominated in units of currency is one of the critical categorical biases working to inflate negative impact results.

Thus, for example, labor power expended to cultivate corn for self-consumption under 'peasant' conditions in Oaxaca (see Fig. 3.3) is not denominated in monetary units and as such never enters into impact calculations. Nevertheless, corn produced under such domestic conditions outside of capitalist relations of production is consumed by its producers and transformed into labor power which can be cheaply bought under conditions of articulation, say to harvest oranges in California, such that the price of orange juice produced with such labor power is lower than if the oranges were picked with fully proletarianized domestic labor. In such a case, negative impact research fails to appreciate how economic value in Indian corn in effect subsidizes the price of orange juice on breakfast tables in Sacramento.[22]

The second categorical error is that the standard economic dimensions of the problem, which are typically taken uncritically as givens and used as data, are organized and collected in categories that are designed for official administrative purposes and that do not – I am arguing – serve well the task of assessing impact. Furthermore, not only do they not well serve the task of impact assessment, they also strongly bias collection of data and analysis of them towards results that show negative impacts of undocumented Mexican migrants.

What must be realized here is that the categories that state and local governments have established to document data are also categories that are at work in the construction of officially recognized social identities of individual residents of administrative jurisdictions.[23] Clearly, one overt instance of such categorization is the legal distinction of 'citizen' from 'non-citizen', i.e., 'illegal'. What I am proposing is that the standard rubrics for the collection of socio-economic data concerning persons is itself a grid of categories that also define identities in often less overt ways when the data that they contain are activated by being entered into political debates. Thus it is that the data sets used in impact studies have built into them ways of specifying migrants not only as 'immigrants', but immigrants with specific undesirable economic and social characteristics, such as 'unemployment recipient', 'on welfare', etc. The fruit of these categories – the skewed data that they contain – when repackaged as impact studies then enter into the political process as immigration policy and as such plays its part in perpetuating the greater binational system (Fig. 3.6).

We can now, taking Mixtecs as a case study, proceed to an examination of how, contrary to the findings of negative impact studies, undocumented ('illegal') persons might actually make positive economic contributions to communities in California and do so within, and in part because of, a legal and political system that is reinforced by migration impact studies. There are two aspects to this problem. One is the productivity of undocumented Mixtecs while they are in California where they are working under exploitive conditions, which have been documented elsewhere (see Zabin et al., 1993). The exploitation in question is made possible in large part by their undocumented status in the state and just as these workers are undocumented, so are the rates and amounts of the economic value that is extracted from them, and which significantly lower the real wages that they earn.[24] Such data are generally absent from impact research, although there are occasional attempts to approximate them.

Conclusion

The analysis presented herein has taken the negative impact hypothesis as an occasion to demonstrate characteristic features of an anthropological approach to migration theory and research. In doing so it has reframed the assumptions underlying negative impact research by examining them within broader theoretical perspectives and on the basis of not only additional empirical data, but distinctly different data, viz., non-monetized forms of value. In doing so it presents an alternative hypothesis, namely that transnational migration from Mexico into California in the present legal and political context is an integral part of an asymmetric binational system of production in which net economic value is transferred from Mexico to California via migration and other flows of general value through transnational communities. The second related point made herein is that the standard research model, by marshalling spurious data that support the negative impact argument, is an integral part of the reproduction of this binational economic system.

The case study discussed above is also offered as an application of an anthropological approach to migration theory and research that expands the territorial and theoretical fields so as to redefine immigration in terms of the more generic concerns with cross-border flows of value, of which embodied value within migrants is but one form. This case study also demonstrates that a robust theory of migration must attend to and seek to understand the multiple integrated levels of a total social formation's infrastructure and superstructure. The use of such an anthropological perspective thus permits the consideration of both migration and migration theory as historic artefacts within a more phenomenally and transnationally comprehensive frame of reference.

Notes

1 I wish to thank Ewa Morawska for access to a preliminary version of the introduction to this volume, which I have relied on in writing this chapter.
2 For a review and discussion of the rise of migration studies in anthropology, see Kearney (1986b), and for an overview of the growing concern in anthropology with global and transnational features of migrant communities see Kearney (1995a) and Morawska (this vol.). Archaeology, which in the United States is a sub-discipline of general anthropology, deals with migration in prehistoric societies and is outside of the bounds of this paper.
3 Perhaps the best example of this perspective and method is Wolf's (1982) *Europe and the People without History*.
4 I am grateful to Yosef Lapid (2001) for introducing this mutually referential triad of terms. It is possible to foreground any member of this triad and Lapid refers to *identity, borders, orders*, but given my primary concerns in this paper, I emphasize *borders*. Thus, I am focusing on the U.S.-Mexican Border, but do so with a concern with *order*, viz., immigration law, policy and research, and identities, e.g., Mixtecs and 'illegals'. For essential anthropological theory and research on national borders, see Donnan and Wilson (1994), Heyman (1994, 1999), and Wilson and Donnan (1998).
5 *League of United Latin American Citizens v. Wilson*, 997 F. Supp. 1244, 1261 (C.D. Cal. 1997).
6 This theorization of borders as active filters of forms of value is elaborated in Kearney (2004) and Heyman (2001). A basic challenge is to theorize the dynamics and politics of cross border flows of value in an increasingly deterritorialized and transnational world, i.e., one in which borders become less significant barriers to flows of disembodied value. In posing the question of what then become the loci of accumulation, Sassen (1991), for one, points to the role of global cities as such sites.
7 The Mixtec region – *La* Mixteca – comprises the western third of the state of Oaxaca, and adjoining areas of the states of Puebla and Guerrero, which are in the greater cultural area known as Mesoamerica.
8 The number of Mixtecs in California in the summer months is in the range of around 40,000, based on 1994 data (Runsten and Kearney, 1994); by 2004, although firm data are lacking, it is apparent that this number has increased considerably. Many more cycle

in and out of the state. As a group they are a relatively small percentage of the total undocumented population. However, research focused on them as a case study, as suggested herein, is relevant to other undocumented communities in the state and comparable numbers of Zapotecs in the Los Angeles area (Klaver, 1997).

9   The most notable instances of such prominence are the ongoing Zapatista Rebellion in Chiapas (Ross, 1995), a recent amendment of the Mexican constitution to recognize the cultural rights of indigenous peoples, and ongoing movement toward the creation of autonomous regions for indigenous peoples in accord with the language of Resolution 169 of the ILO, which Mexico recently signed.

10 See, e.g., Bade (1993, 1994); Besserer (1999a, 1999b); Kearney (1986a, 1991, 1995b, 1996); Nagengast and Kearney (1990); Nagengast, Stavenhagen, and Kearney (1992); Stuart and Kearney (1981); Velasco (1995, 2002); Wright (1990); for descriptions of the living conditions of Mixtecs in San Diego County, see Chavez (1992). Also, two films about transnational Mixtecs have recently been made: Grieshop and Varese (1993); Ziff (1994). For a review of recent anthropological literature dealing with transnational and global theory and research see Kearney (1995a). For other research relevant to Mexican migration framed transnationally see Kearney (1986b) and for specific studies see Gledhill (1995); Goldring (1999); Mahler (1995); Palerm and Urquiola (1993); Rouse (1988); and Smith (1994).

11 For a detailed discussion of this articulation, see Kearney (1996, pp. 90-105).

12 For a review of the migration research guided by dependency theory see Kearney (1986a); for an assessment of dependency theory in general see Chilcote (1974).

13 Figure 2b shows the effect of increased population in the 'peasant' sector and/or increased taxes on the rate of accumulation of surplus in articulated communities.

14 For extended discussion of the uneven inter-regional exchange of value via articulation, see Kearney (1996, pp. 81-104).

15 For example, it is not uncommon to hear foremen of agricultural work crews exhort their workers to, in so many words, 'Hurry up, work faster and harder or we're going to bring in the Mixtecs to replace you.'

16 There is a body of varied literature consisting of what I refer to as negative impact research. The following are typical examples: Fogel and Martin (1982); Lewis et al. (1994); Parker and Rea (1993); Romero et al. (1994). For examples of research that does not find negative impact see, e.g., Bean et al. (1994) and Muller et al. (1985). I was ably assisted in the review of this literature by Konane Martinez.

17 Case study data on which this analysis is based could only be acquired from intense anthropological ethnographic fieldwork (see Stuart and Kearney, 1981). Regarding the same articulation perspective see also Meillassoux (1981).

18 This scene, observed by the author in 1985, and the following paragraph are taken from Kearney (1991, pp. 60-1).

19 The theoretical premises employed herein resemble those of some of the authors of the Subaltern Studies group of India which has shown how the imposition of official categories are grids that collect data in such ways as to 'silence' other voices and data; see, e.g., Guha (1988) and Chakrabarty (1983).

20 The TNCs consist in large part of articulated households, see Fig. 3.2.

21 See Mines and Kearney (1982), Bade (1993, 1994), and Martinez (2004). Whereas agribusiness is interested only in the labor power embodied in transnational migrants and their dispositions to work, another major corporate interest, namely the health care industry in California, is starting to recognize the value of cultural capital that migrants from 'traditional' communities bring with them. Thus HMOs such as Kaiser Permanente have become interested in Mexican folk medicine as a cost-effective supplement to biomedical care (Diana Carr, personal communication).

22 Note that in this case both the problem of limited domain and a categorical error are operative.

23 This point derives from a more general theory of containment, i.e., the formation of officially defined identities via the interplay between the constructing actions of states and the self-constituting practices of persons (see Kearney, 1996, pp. 61-9, passim).

24 See Zazueta and Zazueta (1980) for such abuses of Mexican undocumented workers in general and Zabin et al. (1993) for such abuses of Mixtecs in farm labor.

References

Bade, B.L. (1993) *Problems Surrounding Health Care Service Utilization for Mixtec Migrant Farmworker Families in Madera, California,* California Institute for Rural Studies, Davis, CA.

Bade, B.L. (1994), *Sweatbaths, Sacrifice, and Surgery: The Practice of Transmedical Healthcare by Mixtec Migrant Families in California,* Ph.D. Dissertation, University of California, Riverside.

Barry, F. (1995), *Zapata's Revenge: Free Trade and the Farm Crisis in Mexico,* South End Press, Boston.

Bean, F. et al. (1994), *Poverty and Welfare Recipiency among Immigrants in California* (prepublication copy), The Tom's Rivera Center, Claremont, CA.

Besserer Alatorre, F. (1999a), *Moisés Cruz: Historia de un transmigrante.* Culiacán: Universidad Autónoma de Sinaloa; Universidad Autónoma Metropolitana, Iztapalapa, Mexico City.

Besserer Alatorre, F. (1999b), 'Remesas y economía en las comunidades transnacionales', in *Coloquio nacional sobre políticas públicas de atención al migrante: Memoria,* Gobierno del Estado de Oaxaca, Oaxaca, pp. 210-18.

Bourdieu, P. (1986), 'The Forms of Capital', in J.B. Richardson (ed.), *Handbook of Theory and Research for the Sociology of Education,* Greenwood Press, New York, pp. 241-58.

Burawoy, M. (1976), 'The Functions and Reproduction of Migrant Labour: Comparative Material from Southern Africa and the United States', *American Journal of Sociology,* 81, pp. 1050-87.

Bustamante, J.A. (1983), 'The Mexicans are Coming: From Ideology to Labor Relations', *International Migration Review,* 17, pp. 323-431.

Chakrabarty, D. (1983), 'Conditions for Knowledge of Working-Class Conditions: Employers, Government and the Jute Workers of Calcutta, 1890-1940', R. Guha (ed.), *Subaltern Studies II, Writings on South Asian History and Society,* Oxford UP, Oxford, pp. 259-310.

Chavez, L.R. (1992), *Shadowed Lives: Undocumented Immigrants in American Society,* Harcourt Brace Jovanovich, Fort Worth, TX.

Chilcote, R.H. (1974), 'A Critical Synthesis of the Dependency Literature', *Latin American Perspectives,* 1 (1), pp. 4-29.

Cockcroft, J. (1986), *Outlaws in the Promised Land: Mexican Immigrant Workers and America's Future,* Grove Press, New York.

De Janvry, A and Garramon C. (1977), 'The Dynamics of Rural Poverty in Latin America', *Journal of Peasant Studies,* 4, pp. 206-16.

Donnan, H. and Wilson, Th.M. (eds.) (1994), *Border Approaches: Anthropological Perspectives on Frontiers,* Univer. Press of America, Lanham, MD.

Fogel, W. and Martin, Ph.L. (1982), *Immigration: California's Economic Stake,* Institute for Governmental Studies, University of California, Berkeley.

Gledhill, J. (1995), *Neoliberalism, Transnationalization and Rural Poverty: A Case Study of Michoacan Mexico,* Westview Press, Boulder, CO.

Goldring, L. (1999), 'Power and Status in Transnational Social Spaces', in L. Pries (ed.), *Migration and Transnational Social Spaces,* Ashgate, Aldershot, pp. 162-86.

Grieshop, J. and Varese, St. (1993), *Invisible Indians: Mixtec Farmworkers in California.* A Film. Applied Behavioral Sciences, University of Califonia at Davis.

Guha, R. (1988), 'The Prose of Counter-Insurgency', in R. Guha and G. Chakravorty Spivak (eds.), *Selected Subaltern Studies,* Oxford UP, Oxford, pp. 44-86.

Heyman, J. (1994), 'The Mexico-United States Border in Anthropology: A Critique and Reformulation', *Journal of Political Ecology,* 1, pp. 43-65. <http://www.library.arizona.edu/ej/jpe/volume_1/ascii-heyman.txt>

Heyman, J. (1999), 'United States surveillance over Mexican Lives at the border: Snapshots of an emerging regime', *Human Organization,* 58 (4), pp. 430-8.

Heyman, J. (2001), 'Class and Classification at the U.S.-Mexico Border', *Human Organization,* 60 (2), pp. 128-40.

Kearney, M. (1986a), 'Integration of the Mixteca and the Western U.S.-Mexican Border Region via Migratory Wage Labor', in I. Rosenthal Urey (ed.), *Regional Impacts of U.S.-Mexican Relations* (Center for U.S.-Mexican Studies, Monograph Series No. 16), University of California, San Diego, pp. 71-102.

Kearney, M. (1986b), 'From the Invisible Hand to Visible Feet: Anthropological Studies of Migration and Development', *Annual Review of Anthropology,* 15, Stanford UP, Stanford, pp. 331-61.

Kearney, M. (1991), 'Borders and Boundaries of State and Self at the End of Empire', *Journal of Historical Sociology,* 4 (1), pp. 52-74.

Kearney, M. (1995a), 'The Local and the Global: The Anthropology of Globalization and Transnationalism', *Annual Review of Anthropology,* 24, pp. 547-65.

Kearney, M. (1995b), 'The Effects of Transnational Culture and Migration on Mixtec Identity in Oaxacalifornia', in M.P. Smith and J.R. Feagin (eds.), *The Bubbling Caldron: Race, Ethnicity and the Urban Crisis,* Univer. of Minn. Press, Minneapolis, pp. 226-43.

Kearney, M. (1996), *Reconceptualizing the Peasantry: Anthropology in Global Perspective,* Westview Press, Boulder, CO.

Kearney, M. (2004), 'The Classificatory and Value-filtering Missions of Borders', *Anthropological Theory,* 4 (2), pp. 131-56.

Kearney, M. and Nagengast, C. (1989), 'Anthropological Perspectives on Transnational Communities in Rural California.' *Working Group on Farm Labor and Rural Poverty, Working Paper No. 3,* California Institute for Rural Studies, Davis, CA.

Klaver, J. (1997), *From the Land of the Sun to the City of Angels: The Migration Process of Zapotec Indians from Oaxaca, Mexico to Los Angeles, California* (Nederlandse Geografische Studies No. 228), University of Amsterdam, Amsterdam.

Lapid, Y. (2001), 'Introduction. Identities, Borders, Orders: Nudging International Relations Theory in a New Direction', in M. Albert, D. Jacobson, and Y. Lapid (eds.), *Identities, Borders, Orders: Rethinking International Relations Theory.* University of Minnesota Press, Minneapolis, pp. 1-20.

Lewis, J.R., Mu, J. and Barnhart, B. (1994), *Summary Report: Assembly Select Committee on Statewide Immigration Impact,* Assembly Publications Office, Sacramento, CA.

Mahler, S.J. (1995), *American Dreaming: Immigrant Life on the Margins,* Princeton UP, Princeton.

Martinez, K. (2004), *Health across Borders: Mixtec Transnational Communities and Clinical Health Care Systems.* Doctoral dissertation, Dept. of Anthropology, University of California, Riverside.

Meillassoux, C. (1981), *Maidens, Meal and Money: Capitalism and the Domestic Economy,* Cambridge UP, Cambridge and New York.

Mines, R. and Kearney, M. (1982), *The Health of Tulare County Farmworkers: A Report of 1981 Survey and Ethnographic Research for the Tulare County Department of Public Health.* State of California Department of Health Services, Rural Health Division and Tulare County Department of Health.

Muller, Th., Espenshade, Th.J., et al. (1985), *The Fourth Wave: California's Newest Immigrants,* Urban Institute Press, Washington, DC.

Nagengast, C. and Kearney, M. (1990), 'Mixtec Ethnicity: Social Identity, Political Consciousness, and Political Activism', *Latin American Research Review,* 25 (2), pp. 61-91.

Nagengast, C., Stavenhagen, R., and Kearney, M. (1992), 'Human Rights and Indigenous Workers: The Mixtecs in Mexico and the United States.' *Center for U.S.-Mexican Studies, Current Issue Brief 4,* University of California, San Diego.

Palerm, J.V. and Urquiola, J.I. (1993), 'A Binational System of Agricultural Production: The Case of the Mexican Bajio and California', in D.G. Aldrich and L. Meyer (eds.), *Mexico and the United States: Neighbors in Crisis,* Borgo Press, San Bernardino, CA, pp. 311-67.

Parker, R.A. and Rea, L.M. (1993), *Illegal Immigration in San Diego County: An Analysis of Costs and Revenues (Prepared for Senator Wm. A. Craven, Chair, Calif. State Senate Special Committee on Border Issues),* Rea & Parker, Inc, San Diego, CA.

Pastor, M. (1987), *Campesinos y reformas: La Mixteca, 1700-1856,* El Colegio de Mexico, Mexico City.

Rivera-Salgado, G. (1999a), 'Welcome to Oaxacalifornia', *Cultural Survival Quarterly,* 23 (1), pp. 59-61.

Rivera-Salgado, G. (1999b), *Migration and Political Activism: Mexican Transnational Indigenous Communities in a Comparative Perspective.* Ph.D. Dissertation, Sociology, University of California, Santa Cruz.

Romero, Ph.J., Chang, A.J., and Parker, Th. (1994), *Shifting the Costs of a Failed Federal Policy: The Net Fiscal Impact of Illegal Immigrants in California,* Governor's Office of Planning and Research, Sacramento.

Ross, J. (1995), *Rebellion from the Roots: Indian Uprising in Chiapas,* Common Courage Press, Monroe, ME.

Rouse, R. (1988), *Mexican Migration to the United States: Family Relations in the Development of a Transnational Migrant Circuit.* Ph.D. Dissertation, Dept. of Anthropology, Stanford University, Stanford, CA.

Runsten, D. and Kearney, M. (1994), *A Survey of Oaxacan Village Networks in California Agriculture,* California Institute for Rural Studies, Davis, CA.

Sassen, S. (1991), *The Global City: New York, London, Tokyo,* Princeton UP, Princeton, N.J.

Smith, R.C. (1994), '*"Los ausentes siempre presentes": The imagining, making, and politics of a transnational community between Ticuani, Puebla, Mexico and New York City.'* Ph.D. Dissertation, Dept. of Political Science, Colombia University, New York.

Stuart, J. and Kearney, M. (1981), 'Causes and Effects of Agricultural Labor Migration from the Mixteca of Oaxaca to California.' *Working Papers in U.S.-Mexican Studies, No. 28,* Program in United States-Mexican Studies, University of California, San Diego.

Velasco Ortiz, Laura (1995), 'Entre el jornal y el terruño: el itinerario de los migrantes mixtecos en el noroeste mexicano', *Nueva Antropología,* 14 (47), pp. 113-30.

Velasco Ortiz, Laura, (2002), *El regreso de la comunidad: migración indígena y agents* *étnicos (los Mixtecos en la frontera México-Estados Unidos),* El Colegio de México, Mexico City.

Vélez Ibáñez, C. (1996), *Border Visions: Mexican Cultures of the Southwest United States,* University of Arizona Press, Tucson, AZ.

Wallerstein I. (1974), *The Modern World-System: Capitalist Agriculture and the Origins of the European World Economy in the Sixteenth Century,* Academic Press, New York.

Wilson, Th.M. and Donnan, H. (1998), *Border Cultures,* Cambridge UP, Cambridge.

Wolf, E.R. (1957), 'Closed Corporate Communities in Mesoamerica and Central Java', *Southwestern Journal of Anthropology,* 13, pp. 1-18.

Wolf, E.R. (1982), *Europe and the People without History,* University of California Press, Berkeley.

Wolpe, H. (1972), 'Capitalism and Cheap Labour-power in South Africa: From Segregation to Apartheid', *Economy and Society,* 1, pp. 425-56.

Wright, A. (1990), *The Death of Ramon Gonzales: The Modern Agricultural Dilemma,* University of Texas Press, Austin, TX.

Zabin, C., Kearney, M., Garcia, A., Runsten, D., and Nagengast, C. (1993), *Mixtec Migrants in California Agriculture,* California Institute for Rural Studies, Davis, California.

Zazueta, Ca. and Zazueta, Cé. (1980), *En las puertas del paraiso: Observaciones hechas en el levantamiento de la primera encuesta a trabajadores mexicanos no documentados devueltos de Los Estados Unidos,* Centro Nacional de Información y Estadísticas del Trabajo, Mexico City.

Ziff, Th. (1994), *Oaxacalifornia.* A film, Citron Nueve Productions, Los Angeles.

Zolberg, A.R. (1989), 'The Next Waves: Migration Theory for a Changing World', *International Migration Review,* 23 (3), pp. 403-30.

Zhou, M. (1997), 'Segmented Assimilation: Issue, Controversies, and Recent Research on the New Second Generation', *International Migration Review,* 31 (4), pp. 975-1008.

Chapter 4

Gender and Migration Research

Leslie Page Moch

Gender is an elusive topic in migration research – at once too general and too narrow for discussion in the way made possible in a disciplinary focus such as political science, sociology or anthropology. This chapter nonetheless explores the research on gender as an issue in international migration to North America and Europe, and internal migration within historical Europe, focusing on studies by historians and sociologists. As an historian of European migration with a sociological perspective, I begin with a familiarity of Western European history and migration since 1650 (Moch, 2003). Here I investigate writing on gender and migration for two thirty-five year periods: the 'age of mass migration' (ca. 1880-1914, when migration to the U.S. and within Europe reached a peak) and that for the recent past (since 1965 policy changes in the U.S. and European developments since the 1960s that encouraged immigration). In assessing the ways that this research has defined and struggled with the issue of gender, I will survey the perspectives and constructions utilized, explore omissions from the research agenda, and reflect on the ways that they may be redressed with future work.

Two factors complicate an assessment of research on gender and migration. First, although history and sociology is each a unique discipline (much concerned, respectively but not exclusively, with change in the past and an understanding of the impact of social structures and norms), the study of migration lends itself to methodological interdisciplinarity. Case study methods of sociologists developed by the Chicago school in the 1920s and 1930s intersect with those of historians; historians fruitfully draw on sociological theory. Moreover, no discipline – especially history and sociology – limits itself to one methodology: consider the diversity within sociological studies of gender and migration, which include analyses of national data sets on country of origin, global studies linking micro and macro causes of migration, national-level studies of immigrant groups, and refined case studies of immigrant groups in a single locale (Castles et al., 1984; Donato, 1992; Morawska, 1985, 1989; Simon and Brettell, 1986). In neither historical nor sociological studies is the investigation of migration linked with a single methodology. This is not to say that historians and sociologists share identical research goals and explanatory strategies, for they do not, as Ewa Morawska has pointed out in her essay in this volume.

Second, what sets the topic of this essay apart from others in this volume is that studies of gender do not represent a single discipline and gender studies are not ordinarily formally organized or conceptualized as a single discipline. University gender studies programs are invariably interdisciplinary. Moreover, the interest and vigorous intellectual excitement produced by studies of gender in several disciplines (anthropology, history, literature, sociology) stem precisely from the pathbreaking mix of disciplinary perspectives adopted by scholars of gender. For example, feminists were among the first historians to attend to the methods of literary criticism with great effect on the practice of history. In 1993 historian William Sewell wrote

> Women's history and feminist studies have been a major site of theoretical struggles in the human sciences....Gender, as feminist scholars and critics have demonstrated, is everywhere – built into not only our families, churches, businesses, and public institutions but also the very language in which we discuss and evaluate our experiences, including the languages of philosophy, art, politics, science, and history. The intellectual project of feminism has consisted largely in bringing to consciousness a vast range of oppressive gender dynamics that existing modes of thought and speaking had rendered invisible. This work of exhuming, of bringing to light, has from the beginning required extensive and explicit theoretical work, a fundamental and ever-vigilant challenging, rethinking, or unthinking of conventional categories....virtually all theoretical perspectives have been drawn, in the very process of critique, into the orbit of feminist discussion (Sewell, 1993, pp. 15f.).

Yet to practitioners in many disciplines, the study of gender remains at the margins and the poststructural models that have been so important to feminist theory have had little impact on migration theory (Phizacklea, 1998, p. 24). For example, the article on sociology and history in this volume mentions the intertwined conceptualizations of ethnicity and class 'and (in special-focus rather than mainstream research) gender...' (Morawska in this volume). Although many historians and sociologists are convinced that gender is a significant topic for historical analysis, many – perhaps most – practitioners remain unconvinced.

Two corollaries of the exclusion of gender research from the mainstream hamper research on migration and gender. There is little conversation, much less sustained dialogue, between feminist scholars and other historians and sociologists of migration. Engaged with distinct research questions and explanatory strategies, feminist and mainstream scholars have been slow to read each other's findings and/or to consider their insights. Partly as a consequence of this, the past twenty years of research on women's migration have failed to dislodge the primary migration paradigms that take the male experience as the norm, despite clear evidence that these paradigms are far from universally applicable. This observation is developed below.

Perspectives/Constructions

In studies of migration, before there was gender, there were women. Indeed, interest in gender began in the early 1980s with the development of the history and sociology of women as part of the turn toward women as a subject of investigation in both fields.[1] Early on came the realization that women had been the majority of immigrants to the U.S. after about 1930 and that they numbered heavily among the contemporary immigrants into Europe – particularly visible among those who entered as dependants of migrant workers when European labor migration was discouraged after 1973 and changes in U.S. law made family relations central to visa approval after 1965. The proportional and numerical import of women migrants continues to be emphasized as researchers correctly insist that assuming the norm of the male migrant misconstrues the immigrant experience and misrepresents the immigrant population (Green, 2002).[2]

Consequently, a flood of studies of women immigrants appeared in the 1980s and early 1990s, focusing both on the historical immigrants to North America and within Europe, as well as on contemporary immigrants to Western Europe and North America. Most studies are compensatory and descriptive, providing extremely valuable information about the hitherto-understudied female migrant. Usually presented as case studies, migration scholarship introduces women's history and sociology to the woman migrant (Diner, 1983; Donato, 1992; Gabaccia, 1994; Harzig, 1997; Nolan, 1989; Weinberg, 1988). Sociological studies of women migrants share the same compensatory and descriptive impulse (Phizacklea, 1983; Morokvasic, 1984). The outcome of this tremendously fruitful research energy has been a set of fascinating case studies, and beyond, more general studies of the themes of women's immigration across nation and ethnic group (Cheng, 1999; Gabaccia, 1994; Pedraza, 1991). Studies of women migrants are an important part of current research; indeed, at the April 2000 European Social Science History Conference, eleven sessions were devoted to female migration.

Most perspectives and constructions of these works on women regard women through two kinds of prisms. One is structuralist – especially regarding the work and labor force participation of immigrant women (both in the 1880-1914 period and today) and the limited options available to women workers. Both case studies and more general observations tend to analyze women's work as part of the segmented labor force. Immigrant women's labor in the informal or secondary sector, then, marked them as the underdog in the world capitalist system, which, as patriarchy, pushed women into the least desirable or remunerative positions. As workers, then, women migrants were subject to double oppression as immigrants and women; triple oppression as immigrants, women, and racial ethnics. The feminist analysis of immigrant women in the labor force came to have a keen understanding of the multiple ways in which social and demographic traits handicap women workers (Anderson, 1993, 1996; Cheng, 1999; Morokvasic, 1991; Potts, 1991). In structural studies, the female immigrant worker's oppression is emphasized and the majority of workers are in the foreground – unskilled industrial laborers and service workers such as domestic servants and sex workers.

At the same time, other less structuralist research emphasizes the non-economic roles and lives of immigrant women, placing them as actors (with varying degrees of agency) in families, communities, clubs, and networks. Here the literature is a vast and rich one, reaching from studies of the migration process and immigrant communities to those of wives (be they picture brides or sweethearts from home) and immigrant marriage (Andall, 1998; Chai, 1992; Fuchs and Moch, 1995; Goodman, 1987; Harzig, 1997; Ortiz, 1996). Such studies perceive the migrant woman as a more complex site for experience than simply a worker, yield valuable insights into the texture of female immigrant life, recognize the agency of the woman migrant, and elucidate the workings of the immigrant community.

The plethora of informed studies of women's migration moved toward refining the guest worker type of model of international migration (Kofman, 1999). This model, accepted by students of history and present-day migrations alike, constats that migration streams begin with male migrants (often temporary workers), then become a more settled community as men send for their wives, sweethearts, and children. Research on women showed multiple exceptions to this pattern (both historical and some present-day) by demonstrating the importance of women in non-dependant roles, the complexities of 'family reunification', and the intricacies of the international marriage market (Chai, 1992; Gabaccia, 1994; Sinke and Gross, 1992, Wilpert, 1988).

Omissions

Although studies of female migration could have served to undermine the so-called traditional understanding of migration histories past and present, they have failed to displace the 'guestworker model' of male and female migration: male migration (sometimes temporary at first) followed by the migration of female dependents. Because studies of female migration have not captured the larger audience of migration researchers in history and sociology, the implications of this crucial work have not been explored. This section elucidates the most serious omissions and their consequences, then turns to the question of gender analysis. The overarching observation is that made by Elinor Kofman: the key failure that has allowed the 'guestworker model' to hold sway is blindness to the diversity of the female experience (Kofman, 1999). As a consequence, the periodization of this standard view has not been questioned, marriage and family reunification have been inadequately considered, and the role of gender in state regulations has been underinvestigated.

The perception that migrations begin with males – with women following – has distorted and overdetermined perceptions of migration histories, and the periodization of group histories. Such a perception may fit such historical groups as Italian men who worked in North America, or Poles who initially came to labor in mines and factories, but it is much less fitting for families of Scandinavian and German farm families in the American Midwest and is unsuited to the Irish, among whom women were important organizers of chain migration and who occasionally outnumbered Irish men. Many migrants in Europe also contradict this model: Breton and other country women who dominated the chains of domestic servants in cities (Paris, in this case, like Germans in Dutch cities) and Polish women who moved independent of men, in harvest teams that dug sugar beets in Denmark and East Prussia (Lucassen, 1987; Moch, 2003; Schrover, 2000).

Many present-day immigrants also fail to fit into this model, such as the Filipina nurses and domestics who travel without their countrymen, to say nothing of the women recruited as sex workers in Western Europe, such as Thais, East Europeans and Russians. Recruited or tricked, these women are neither following a male migration stream nor are they joining a fiancé or husband abroad. Even some recruited guestworkers, such as Turkish women, were invited to Western Europe to work in female groups (Kofman, 1999; Moch, 2003; Perreñas, 2001; Phizacklea, 1998).

For an important group among today's immigrants, the 'guestworker model' is particularly ironic; these are the refugees and asylum-seekers who number 20 million worldwide and who are, in the vast majority (80 per cent), women with dependent children (Phizacklea, 1998, p. 22). From the refugee perspective, the failure of researchers to consider women traveling without countrymen at destination and independent women is especially telling, and the scholar's view that men are producers and women dependents is particularly myopic. Nonetheless, the understanding of temporary migration that gives way to permanent migration, and of male groups that give way to mixed-sex migration streams, remains the general model in migration studies. It would be much more useful for scholars to discard the model than to label cases like the above as exceptions to the rule.

Nonetheless, marriage and family reunification are crucial to female migration. Here, too, however, the dominant understanding of marriage and family reunification is partial and incomplete. Studies of marriage pay inadequate attention to the workings of international marriage markets, where extant research on women suggests that they are not passive dependents or items of exchange. Historically, German brides and Asian picture brides coming to the U.S. to meet husbands had their own ambitions, goals and ideas – and obligations to work – that belie the image of the dependent spouse (Chai, 1992; Sinke and Gross, 1992). Research on city bound Italian women suggests that their own networks and contacts were at play. Investigations of the arranged marriages of Asian Indians in the U.S. show that such marriage arrangements are more complex, multi-faceted, and open to female educational and career plans than is apparent in this so-called traditional matching. Researcher assumptions that marriage with a non-compatriot signals assimilation may be equally misguided (Arru, 1996; Bhalla, 2002; Schrover, 2000). In short, research on women signals that the study of marriage migration and family formation requires the suspension of assumptions about the working man and newly arrived fiancé or wife and considerably more depth than is posited by the standard model.

This image does continue to inform most states, who have the power to regulate migration and, if not to prevent illegal entries, at least to define the individual as a legal or illegal immigrant and thus bestow or deny its imprimatur on relations with police, employers, landlords, and public institutions (Dubois, 2000). The right to live in a family, which is recognized in international conventions, operates with particular norms of family life in the West – usually a nuclear family with a male breadwinner. Research on today's female migrants demonstrates how these powerful norms are gendered, and have important consequences for women. They render married women dependent by definition, and thus it is in many places difficult for them to receive work permits, particularly soon after arrival; they are thus forced into an exacerbated *de facto* dependency or can only work 'off the books' in ill-paid jobs (such as domestic servant or charwoman). More difficult, the immigrant woman who divorces is faced with the threat of deportation with the denial of state aid. This is also the case for a growing category of immigrant wives, who are today's 'picture brides'. They are seen, in short, as actors in the private sphere, not the public sphere. In addition, minority women who petition for family reunification are less likely to be granted such a request than men (Kofman, 1999; Phizacklea, 1998). These gendered dimensions of family reunification policies and operations bear further investigation and articulation.

Migrant women outside the context of a family are subject to similar, but more pernicious, situations. Historically vulnerable to pregnancy out of wedlock and poverty, single women often find work in exploitative occupations such as the sweatshops of southern California, but they are particularly vulnerable if they number among the many illegal immigrants in North America or Europe. Then privatized work – domestic service or sex work – is the norm. Such situations have created, for example, a two-tier system of sex workers in the Netherlands that acts to the disadvantage of illegal immigrants. As with the 'dependent' immigrant woman who leaves marriage, single women who are apprehended are punished, even if, in the case of many sex workers, they were duped into coming and had their passports and return tickets confiscated by the employer (Kofman, 1999; Phizacklea, 1998). As with the dynamics and policies of family reunification, the gendered nature of such female occupations and state responses to them require more analysis.

We have entered the arena of gender and the omission of a gendered perspective. To paraphrase Ewa Morawska's comment on migrant ethnicity scholarship – there are scholars who problematize gender and those who do not (Morawska in this volume). Most migration scholars fail to do so. This is a crucial omission, both from studies of women migrants and from general works. Although gender appeared in many a statement, and even title, the text of articles and books of the 1990s proved to be about women. Historians followed the example of women's studies by researching immigrant women (Gabaccia, 1992, p. xv; Weinberg, 1992), but only a handful had investigated women and men together (ex: Prieto, 1992;

Vikström, 2003). Most sociologists followed a similar pattern, attending both to men and women only in articles based on large data bases (Zlotnik, 1995) or a few very focused case studies (Jones-Correa, 1998; Morawska, 1996; Powers et al., 1998; Thai, 2001, 2003). As crucially informative, and nuanced as studies of women migrants are, gender has not been developed as a central category of analysis in migration studies. Indeed, this is an important part of the reason that studies of women fail to move – to disrupt or displace – migration studies as could a perspective that puts questions and constructions of gender at the center.

Gender is a richer, more critical, and more dynamic concept than sex. A quarter century ago, historian Natalie Zemon Davis wrote that what was interesting was not so much women as the 'significance of the *sexes*', the 'range in sex roles and sexual symbolism'; fellow historian Joan Scott went on to observe that what is important is not sex, but gender – how male and female are constructed, how that construction changes, and how it is experienced subjectively (Scott, 1998, p. 29). Gender, then, has to do with the ways that sexual identity is constructed and identified; this is surely crucial to the study of migrants as they move between cultures, understand their own identity, and are constructed by the host culture. Even more fundamentally, gender is not about women alone; gender addresses the construction and perception of both male and female identity. Gender is a most revelatory concept when it is used as an organizing principle to elucidate the experience of both men and women, as well as the broader assumptions about being female and male. For this reason, gender can be a central construct fruitfully used to interrogate and analyze immigrants and the migration process, using a variety of distinct methodologies.

Promise of Future Work

Several key studies published since the mid-nineties point to promising directions in migration work, to trends that have the potential to problematize gender and thus allow a gendered perspective to realize its potential. These are structural studies, rooted in the society and political economy of the home and/or host society, as well as post-structural analyses rooted in traditions of literary criticism and cultural anthropology. Empirical studies, which have placed women and men – usually separately – in a structural context can be designed to reveal the gendered workings of the migration process. Analyses of identity and assimilation, which draw more on subjective sources, are equally ripe for a focus that includes the experience of both women and men (Beckles, 1995, p. 127; Phizacklea, 1998).

A most interesting line of inquiry has developed in keeping with Anthony Giddens' structuration theory that combines the post-structural insights into the construction of immigrant women, on one hand, while retaining a keen awareness of immigrants' position in the economic and social structure of the host society, on the other (Bryant and Jary, 1991; Giddens, 1984; Goss and Lindquist, 1995; Pooley and Turnbull, 1998, p. 20). Structuration theory provides a middle road between structural approaches and studies of social life that emphasize women's agency, 'collapsing the distinction between agency and structure', thus allowing a way to understand how relatively powerless people like the domestic servants and sex workers among immigrant women carve out spaces for control and influence (Phizacklea, 1998, p. 28).

Research projects suggest that the migration process is gendered at every step. Historical studies have interrogated the sex composition of the migration stream, for example, noting that notions of appropriate work for men and women (as well as available work for men and women at home and abroad) are fundamental to shaping who leaves home (Donato, 1992; Eltis, 1997; Gabaccia, 1994; Hoerder, 1996, 1997; Zlotnik, 1995). Rather than focus on the disabilities to men or to women, they consider that the behavior of both is shaped by notions of appropriate behavior. Indeed, if the process of migration is understood as a gendered one, then every step is available for research on fundamental distinctions between men and women. This has already been suggested explicitly for motivations for departure (Fuchs and Moch, 1990; Hoerder, 1997; Mageean, 1997; Moch, 2003; Lucassen and Lucassen, 1997) and negotiation with family at home (Hoerder, 1997) as well as for work abroad. Studies are now being published of men and women in migration systems that explicitly place distinctions of gender at the center (Thai, 2003; Vikström, 2003). Such enterprises have great potential for unifying the disparate analyses of gender and pushing forward significantly what a 'gendered process' signifies in concrete terms.

An intriguing and decidedly non-structuralist perspective is opened by the consideration in sociological and historical case studies of the different ways in which men and women articulate – and indeed, experience – their lives as immigrants. Researchers who have interviewed their subjects have long reflected on migrants' subjective experience (Berteaux-Wiame, 1979; Berger and Mohr, 1975), but the ways in which men's and women's discourse and lived experience is actually in contrast is a most fruitful, and relatively unexplored, avenue (Chamberlain, 1995, 1997; Hondagneu-Sotelo, 1999; Pessar, 1999; Thai, 2001; Yans-McLaughlin, 1990; Zaboroska, 1995). There is much more work to be done here, listening to the voices of immigrant men and women and interpreting their accounts. For example, if Caribbean men and women in Britain tell – and experience – their personal narratives differently (as Mary Chamberlain has found), do they offer similar contrasts with one another as the accounts of Algerian men and women in France or Turks in Germany? What does this distinction tell us about the gendered nature of the migrant experience?

Personal narratives are closely related to the questions of identity, and trans-national identity in particular, that are animating some work on contemporary immigrants (Kearney in this volume; Morawska in this volume). In this case, because patterns of movement, membership in the polity, and the regulation of residency often vary for men and women, gender is likely to be a fundamental dividing line between the way that immigrants construct and experience an immigrant or trans-national identity (Jones-Correa, 1998; Perreñas, 2001). Likewise, there are abundant indicators from longstanding studies of male immigrants and the more recent literature on women that the 'new old' process of assimilation is experienced differently by men and women for gender and assimilation to be the focus of inquiry (Jones-Correa, 1998; Powers et al., 1998; Hoerder, 1996; Morawska in this volume). Systematic and reflective case studies investigating the experiences of assimilation, rooted in the particulars of male and female experience, can identify with precision just how assimilation and the creation of identity are gendered.

For example, a study of South Asian Indians in a Midwestern state places gender at the center of data and interview analyses. Researcher Vibha Bhalla investigates the history of men's and women's experience and gaps between them in thirty years of migration history – a history of changing sex ratios, a complex and evolving role of arranged marriage, changing norms and practices at home, and shifting possibilities for education and work in the U.S. A history of an understudied but significant group emerges, one that demonstrates the ways in which the evolving experience and significance of international migration varies fundamentally by gender (Bhalla, 2002).

Gendered historical studies of European migrants are drawing on betrothal and marriage records to reconstruct and analyze the movements and networks of women and men. A study of Rome, one of the few predominantly male cities, will capture the emergence of a feminized gender configuration. It is part of the larger project of allowing a view of the ways that women and men enter urban life and will ultimately be compared with similar studies of betrothed women and men in Turin and Naples (Arru, 1996). Another study of rural-born Bretons in the more female city of Paris and male-dominated industrial suburbs will use the records of weddings (including information on witnesses and parents) to investigate the ways in which gender shaped destination, the marriage market, employment, and networks of contact. It will also explore the strikingly different constructions of Breton men and women by Parisians (Moch, 2000).

Indeed, it may be most promising to analyze the importance of gender to the way that immigrants are constructed and perceived by the receiving society. Negative constructions of immigrants in today's North America and Europe (as well as in the past) have shaped the immigrant experience in damaging ways (and, I would argue, injure host societies as well). Gender and sexuality have been central to these 'negative' constructions as they are to all perceptions of foreign newcomers. It is then imperative, if not urgent, that scholars shed light on the formation of perceptions of immigrants; and in this effort, students of gender are particularly well-placed to be productive. Such inquiries can link seemingly disparate elements of immigration such as perceived immigrant sexuality and host nation policies on immigration restrictions. For example, the arrival in the 1960s (and in the earlier period) of migrant groups that were predominantly male produced anxieties on the part of the host society about the sexual danger presented for host society women (for example, Stovall, 1998). How were these anxieties related to the housing and home-return policies for male temporary migrants and guest workers? What is the relationship between these anxieties and the development of family reunification policies and the accepted right of living in a family?

Gender is clearly central to the pernicious constructions of Islamic migrants in France and Germany, as distinct as French and German responses are. Not only are Muslim women perceived to be the carriers of their culture, but also they are seen to be uniformly the site of backwardness, anti-modernity, and traditionalism; this kind of construction exoticizes and homogenizes Muslim women (Kofman, 1999). Gender practices and relations dominate public discourse about Muslims in European societies – as witnessed by the focus on the head scarf, the practice of *purdah,* immigrant gender roles, high fertility rates, and patterns of family authority. Indeed, gender is in many cases at the heart of the most damaging constructions of today's immigrants. The more clearly scholars analyze damaging representations as constructions rooted in host society views of gender and sexuality, the less power such perceptions will have to shape continuing research and discourse.

There is an enormous positive aspect to this observation. Moving gender to the center of migration scholarship has the potential of enriching and deepening the study of human movement and its consequences. Historians and sociologists long have considered women and demographers long have attended to sex ratios. However, if these scholars put gender at the center of research design, they will sharpen the study of the formation, recruitment, perpetuation, and workings of migrant groups; of reception, assimilation, and interactions in the host society. Current studies with a global perspective are beginning to bear the fruit of more flexible and wide-ranging conceptualizations of gender called for by Patricia Pessar in 1999 (Gabaccia and Iacovetta, 2002; Perreñas, 2001; Pessar, 1999, p. 594; Thai, 2003). Interdisciplinarity is essential to such endeavors, which can be best served by combining the structuralist's concern with the obdurate powers of political economies and the state with the historian's eye for agency, representation, and the power of origins.

Notes

1 Women's mobility had been neglected because labor migrants were perceived to be most important, and men were most visible among them; in both the 19th and 20th centuries, men often worked in highly visible construction, extractive, industrial, and harvest teams. Moreover, many of the state documents used by researchers such as military and property records only recorded male behavior (Farcy and Faure, 2003; Lucassen, 1987) and women's name changes at marriage rendered them difficult to trace for researchers using genealogical documents (Rosenthal, 1999, Schrover, 2000).

2 By the end of the 1990s, over half the estimated 100 million people living outside their country of origin worldwide were women (figure for legal immigrants only) (Phizacklea, 1998, p. 22).

References

Andall, J. (1998), 'Catholic and State Constructions of Domestic Workers: The Case of Cape Verdian Women in Rome in the 1970s', in K. Kower and H. Lutz (eds.), *The New Migration in Europe: Social Constructions and Social Realities*, St. Martin's, New York, pp. 124-42.

Anderson, B. (1993), *Britain's Secret Slaves*, Anti-Slavery International, London.

Anderson, B. (1996), 'Overseas Domestic Workers in the European Union', *Report for Stichting Tegen Vrouwendandel*, STV, Utrecht.

Arru, A. (1996), 'Il prezzo della cittadinanza. Strategie di inegrazione nella Roma pontifica', *Quaderni storici*, 91, pp. 157-73.

Beckles, H. (1995), 'Sex and Gender in the Historiography of Caribbean Slavery', in Sheperd et al. (eds.), *Engendering History*, pp. 125-40.

Berger, J., and Mohr, J. (1975), *A Seventh Man: Migrant Workers in Europe*, Viking, New York.

Berteaux-Wiame, I. (1979), 'The Life History Approach to the Study of Internal Migration', *Oral History*, 7, pp. 26-32.

Bhalla, V. (2002), 'American Dreams: Gendered Migrations from India', Ph.D. Dissertation, Michigan State University.

Bryant, C. and Jary, D. (eds.) (1991), *Giddens' Theory of Structuration: a Critical Appreciation*, Routledge, London.

Castles, St., Booth, H., and Wallace, T. (1984), *Here for Good: Western Europe's New Ethnic Minorities*, Pluto, London.

Chai, A.Y. (1992), 'Picture Brides: Feminist Analysis of Life Histories of Hawaii's Early Immigrant Women from Japan, Okinawa, and Korea', in Gabaccia (ed.), *Seeking common Ground*, pp. 123-38.

Chamberlain, M. (1995), 'Gender and Memory: Oral History and Women's History', in Sheperd et al. (eds.), *Engendering History*, pp. 94-110.

Chamberlain, M. (1997), 'Gender and the Narratives of Migration', *History Workshop Journal*, 43, pp. 87-110.

Cheng, S.-J. A. (1999), 'Labor Migration and International Sexual Division of Labor: A Feminist Perspective', in G. Kelson and D. DeLet (eds.), *Gender and Immigration*, New York UP, New York, pp. 38-58.

Diner, H. (1983), *Erin's Daughters in America: Irish Women in the Nineteenth Century*, John Hopkins UP, Baltimore, MD.

Donato, K. (1992), 'Understanding U.S. Immigration: Why Some Countries Send Women and Others Send Men', in Gabaccia (ed.), *Seeking Common Ground*, pp. 159-84.

Dubois, L. (2000). 'Republic at Sea', *Transition: An International Review*, 79, pp. 64-79.

Eltis, D. (1997), 'Seventeenth Century Migration and the Slave Trade: The English Case in Comparative Perspective', in Lucassen and Lucassen (eds.), *Migration, Migration History, History*, pp. 87-109.

Farcy, J.-C. and Faure, A. (2003), *Une génération de français à l'épreuve de la mobilité. Vers et dans Paris: recherche sur la mobilité à la fin du 19e siècle*, INED, Paris.

Fuchs, R.G. and Moch, L.P. (1990), 'Pregnant, Single, and Far from Home: Migrant Women in Nineteenth-Century Paris', *American Historical Review*, 95, pp. 1007-31.

Fuchs, R.G. and Moch, L.P. (1995), 'Invisible Cultures: Poor women's networks and reproductive strategies in nineteenth-century Paris', in S. Greenhalgh (ed.), *Situating Fertility*, Cambridge UP, Cambridge, pp. 86-107.

Gabaccia, D. (ed.) (1992), *Seeking Common Ground: Multidisciplinary Studies of Immigrant Women in the United States,* Greenwood, Westport, CT.

Gabaccia, D. (1992), 'Introduction', in Gabaccia (ed.), *Seeking Common Ground,* pp. xi-xxvi.

Gabaccia, D. (1994), *From the Other Side: Women, Gender and Immigrant Life in the U.S., 1820-1990,* Indiana UP, Bloomington, IN.

Gabaccia, D. and Iacovetti, F. (eds.) (2002), *Women, Gender and Transnational Lives: Italian Workers of the World,* Univ. of Toronto Press, Toronto.

Giddens, A. (1984), *The Constitution of Society: Outline of the Theory of Structuration,* Cambridge UP, Cambridge.

Goodman, Ch. (1987), 'A Day in the Life of a Single Spanish Woman in West Germany', in H. Buechler and J.-M. Buechler (eds.), *Migrants in Europe: The Role of Family, Labor, and Politics,* Greenwood, New York, pp. 207-19.

Goss, J. and Lindquist, B. (1995), 'Conceptualizing International Labor Migration: A Structuration Perspective', *International Migration Review,* 29 (2), pp. 317-51.

Green, N. (2002), 'De l'immigré à l'immigrée', in N.L. Green, *Repenser les migrations,* Presses Universitaires de France, Paris.

Harzig, Ch. (ed.) (1997), *Peasant Maids, City Women: From the European Countryside to Urban America,* Cornell UP, Ithaca, NY.

Hoerder, D. (1996), 'From Migrants to Immigrants: Acculturation in a Societal Framework', in D. Hoerder and L.P. Moch (eds.), *European Migrants: Global and Local Perspectives,* Northeastern UP, Boston, pp. 211-62.

Hoerder, D. (1997), 'Segmented Macrosystems and Networking Individuals: The Balancing Function of the Migration Process', in Lucassen and Lucassen (eds.), *Migration, Migration History, History,* pp. 73-84.

Hondagneu-Sotelo, P. (ed.) (1999), 'Gender and Contemporary U.S. Immigration'. Special issue of *American Behavioral Scientist,* 42, p. 4.

Jones-Correa, M. (1998), 'Different Paths: Gender, Immigration and Political Participation', *International Migration Review,* 32, pp. 326-49.

Kofman, E. (1999), 'Female "Birds of Passage" a Decade Later: Gender and Immigration in the European Union', *International Migration Review,* 33, pp. 269-99.

Lucassen, J. (1987), *Migrant Labour in Europe, 1600-1900,* Croom Helm, London.

Lucassen, J. and Lucassen, L. (eds.) (1997), *Migration, Migration History, History: Old Paradigms and New Perspectives,* Peter Lang, Bern.

Mageean, D. (1997), 'To Be Matched or Move: Irish Women's Prospects in Munster', in Harzig (ed.), *Peasant Maids, City Women,* pp. 57-97.

Moch, L.P. (2000), 'Through a Gendered Lense: Bretons in Paris, 1875-1930'. Paper presented at the Third European Social Science History Conference, Amsterdam, April.

Moch, L.P. (2003), *Moving Europeans: Migration in Western Europe since 1650,* 2nd ed., Indiana UP, Bloomington, IN.

Morawska, E. (1985), *For Bread with Butter: The Life-Worlds of East Central Europeans in Johnstown, Pennsylvania, 1890-1940,* Cambridge UP, Cambridge.

Morawska, E. (1989), 'Labor Migrations of Poles in the Atlantic Economy, 1880-1914', *Comparative Studies in Society and History,* 31, pp. 237-72.

Morawska, E. (1996), *Insecure Prosperity: Small-Town Jews in Industrial America,* Princeton UP, Princeton.

Morokvasic, M. (1984), 'Birds of Passage Are Also Women...', *International Migration Review,* 18, pp. 886-907.

Morokvasic, M. (1991), 'Fortress Europe and Migrant Women', *Feminist Review,* 39, pp. 69-84.

Nolan, J. (1989), *Ourselves Alone: Women's Emigration from Ireland,* UP of Kentucky, Lexington, KY.

Ortiz, V. (1996), 'Migration and Marriage among Puerto Rican Women', *International Migration Review,* 30, pp. 460-84.

Pedraza, S. (1991), 'Women and Migration: The Social Consequences of Gender', *Annual Review of Sociology,* 17, pp. 303-25.

Perreñas, R. (2001), *Servants of Globalization: Women, Migration, and Domestic Work,* Stanford UP, Stanford, CA.

Pessar, P. (1999), 'Engendering Migration Studies: The Case of New Immigrants in the U.S', *American Behavioral Scientist,* 42 (4), pp. 577-600.

Phizacklea, A. (ed.) (1983), *One-Way Ticket: Migration and Female Labour,* Routledge and Kegan Paul, London.

Phizacklea, A. (1998), 'Migration and Globalization: A Feminist Perspective', in K. Kosar and H. Lutz (eds.), *The New Migration in Europe: Social Constructions and Social Realities,* St. Martin's New York, pp. 21-38.

Pooley, C. and Turnbull, J. (1998), *Migration and mobility in Britain since the 18th century,* Univ. College London Press, London.

Potts, L. (1991), *The World Labor Market: A History of Migration,* Zed Books, London.

Powers, M., Seltzer, W., and Shi, J. (1998), 'Gender Differences in the Occupational Status of Undocumented Immigrants in the United States: Experience Before and After Legalization', *International Migration Review,* 32, pp. 1015-46.

Prieto, Y. (1992), 'Cuban Women in New Jersey: Gender Relations and Change', in Gabaccia (ed.), *Seeking Common Ground,* pp. 185-201.

Rosenthal, P.-A. (1999), *Les sentiers invisibles: Espace, families et migrations dans la France du 19e siècle,* Editions de l'Ecole des Hautes Etudes en Sciences Sociales, Paris.

Schrover, M. (2000), 'German Women in the Netherlands, 1850-1912: Marital behaviour and acculturation'. Paper presented at the Third European Social Science History Conference, Amsterdam, April.

Scott, J. (1998), 'Gender: A Useful Category of Historical Analysis', in J. Scott (ed.), *Gender and the Politics of History,* Columbia UP, New York, pp. 28-50.

Sewell, W.H., Jr. (1993), 'Toward a Post-materialist Rhetoric for Labor History', in L. Berlanstein (ed.), *Rethinking Labor History: Essays on Discourse and Class Analysis,* Univ. of Illinois Press, Urbana, IL, pp. 15-38.

Sheperd, V. et al. (eds.) (1995), *Engendering History: Caribbean Women in Historical Perspective,* St. Martin's Press, New York.

Simon, R. and Brettell, C. (eds.) (1986), *International Migration: The Female Experience,* Roman and Allanheld, Totowa, NJ.

Sinke, S. and Gross, St. (1992), 'The International Marriage Market and the Sphere of Social Reproduction: A German Case Study', in Gabaccia (ed.), *Seeking Common Ground,* pp. 67-88.

Stovall, T. (1998), 'The Color Line behind the Lines: Racial Violence in France during the Great War', *American Historical Review,* 103, pp. 737-70.

Thai, H.C. (2001), 'The Two Unmarriageables: College Educated Women in Vietnam and Their Overseas Vietnamese Husbands in Low Wage Work'. Paper delivered at the Social Science History Association, Chicago, November.

Thai, H.C. (2003), 'Clashing Dreams: Highly Educated Overseas Brides and Low-Wage US Husbands', in B. Ehrenreich and A. Hochschild (eds.), *Global Women: Nannies, Maids and Sex Workers in the New Economy,* Metropolitan Books, New York, pp. 230-52.

Vikström, L. (2003), *Gendered Routes and Courses: The Socio-Spatial Mobility of Migrants in Nineteenth-Century Sundsvall, Sweden,* Umeå University, Umeå.

Weinberg, S. (1988), *The World of Our Mothers: The Lives of Jewish Immigrant Women,* Univ. of North Carolina Press, Chapel Hill.

Weinberg, S. (1992), 'The Treatment of Women in Immigration History: A Call for Change', in Gabaccia (ed.), *Seeking Common Ground,* pp. 3-22.

Wilpert, C. (1988), 'The Use of Social Networks in Turkish Migration to Germany', in M. Kritz et al. (eds.), *International Migration Systems: A Global Approach,* Clarendon, Oxford, pp. 177-89.

Yans-McLaughlin, V. (ed.) (1990), *Immigration Reconsidered: History, Sociology, and Politics,* Oxford UP, New York.

Yans-McLaughlin, V. (1990), 'Metaphors of Self in History: Subjectivity, Oral Narrative, and Immigration Studies', in Yans-McLaughlin (ed.), *Immigration Reconsidered,* pp. 254-90.

Zaboroska, M. (1995), *How We Found America: Reading Gender through East European Immigrant Narratives,* Univ. of North Carolina Press, Chapel Hill.

Zlotnik, H. (1995), 'The South-to-North Migration of Women', *International Migration Review,* 29, pp. 229-54.

PART II
MIGRATION RESEARCH
IN DIFFERENT DISCIPLINES

Chapter 5

Political Science
and Comparative Immigration Politics

Gary P. Freeman

Scholars outside political science have largely neglected the political dimensions of migration, even so obvious a topic as state regulation of population flows. Students of politics, for their part, have typically ignored migration altogether. Those political scientists working on migration issues have found audiences mainly among sociologists, anthropologists, and historians and most often have operated in multi-disciplinary settings (Massey et al., 1998). They have scarcely touched political science as a discipline. This may in part reflect the fact that the fledgling political science of immigration has been theoretically weak, focusing on thick description and seat of the pants interpretation, and given to normative posturing and disputation.

Migration into the industrial societies since the 1960s has finally begun to attract the attention of political scientists and new research displays more concern with developing and exploiting theories. Recent surveys of the political science literature on migration reflect these changes (Zolberg, 1999a, 1999b; Bernstein and Weiner, 1999; Hollifield, 2000; Hansen, 2002). Nevertheless, we have a long way to go before we have in hand well-developed and widely-tested theories that purport to explain and predict the role of state regulation of migration, the dynamics of the politics of immigration, the conditions of immigrant political incorporation across a variety of national cases, and the role of migration in international relations.

Although the focus of this volume is how the social sciences can learn from one another and develop cross-disciplinary approaches to migration research, I will argue that the most pressing need in political science is for the mainstream of the profession to bring its own conceptual and theoretical apparatus to bear on a topic left for too long to its sister disciplines.

This chapter begins by considering why political science has been slow to embrace migration as a topic of inquiry. This failing is especially striking with respect to the practitioners of international relations, the sub-field of the discipline with the most obvious interest in transnational phenomena. I also explore the peculiar preoccupations of those political scientists who have dealt with migration issues, especially the normative biases that have, in my judgement, vitiated much political research to date.

I turn, then, to the task ahead: developing theoretically ambitious research on the political dimensions of migration processes. I proceed from the premise that the most promising strategy for students of comparative immigration politics is to apply to their subject theoretical frameworks already well-established in the discipline's work on other subjects. In other words, we do not need a distinctive theory of the politics of immigration but rather we need to view immigration more thoroughly through the analytical lenses of normal political science. I review three theoretical perspectives that have been usefully employed by political scientists in the study of comparative migration politics: these concentrate on interests, rights, and institutions. The concept of interests is central to political economy research. Work in this vein is concerned primarily with determining who wins and who loses from migration and how the experience of these benefits and costs affects the incentives of individuals and states with respect to migrants and migration policy. A second perspective deals primarily with the normative evolution of rights-based liberalism within international regimes and within liberal democratic states. Finally, I review work that concentrates on variations in the institutional characteristics of liberal democracies to account for immigration politics and policy.

Migration Research in Political Science

Migration of persons between national states is, by definition, an international phenomenon and these days an increasingly important aspect of global economics. It is little short of astonishing, therefore, that the literature of international relations and international political economy, the fields of political science with the most plausible interest in migration, all but ignores the subject. The indices of leading books in the field may serve as an indicator of the failure to grapple with the political economy of migration. For example, Robert Gilpin's classic *The Political Economy of International Relations* published in 1987 has no index entries for migration or related terms. When Gilpin brought out his *Challenge of Global Capitalism* thirteen years later in 2000, his lack of curiosity about migration issues was still apparent – again, there are no migration entries in his index. A representative reader in the field edited by William P. Avery and David P. Rapkin (1982) is likewise bereft of a single reference to migration or foreign labor. Stephen D. Krasner's influential collection on *International Regimes* (1983) fails, according to its index, to deal with labor or migration issues and mentions no labor regimes. A decade later things had not improved. The 1996 volume edited by Suzanne Berger and Ronald Dore, *National Diversity and Global Capitalism*, has no index entries for migration, immigration, labor, or manpower, let alone a chapter devoted to the subject. Joan Spero and Jeffrey A. Hart's important text, *The Politics of International Economic Relations* (6th ed., 2002), has no migration-related index entries. The specialized journals are showing some signs of change, however. Amy

Gurowitz (1999, p. 413) notes that the two leading periodicals dealing with international political economy – *World Politics* and *International Organization* – published only two articles on immigration between 1980 and 1995 but five (including her own) between 1995 and 1999. A recent search uncovered two additional articles dealing with immigration published between 2000 and 2003 in these journals.

The situation is not much better in the discipline as a whole. The leading American scholars on immigration are, with a very few exceptions, drawn from outside political science. Any list of luminaries is arbitrary, but if we establish the standard that one must be widely-known and cited outside the migration sub-field for work done on migration, we might include individuals such as George Borjas (economics), Saskia Sassen (urban planning), Rogers Brubaker, Alejandro Portes, David Massey, and Frank D. Bean (all sociologists). Probably the most distinguished political scientists who have written on migration are Aristide Zolberg and the late Myron Weiner. Neither made his original scholarly reputation in the field, however. With the exception of Zolberg's *Escape from Violence* (with Suhrke and Aguayo, 1989), no political science work on migration has achieved significant visibility inside the discipline as a whole. Another indication of the minimal investment in migration research in political science is its treatment by the editors of the profession's main journal. Between September 1981 and June 2003 the *American Political Science Review* published only two articles dealing even tangentially with international migration, a work on citizenship in Israel (Peled, 1992) and a piece of normative political theory on the responsibilities of states for refugees (Gibney, 1999). This is part of a long-established pattern: in its entire history the *Review* has published only seven articles with the terms migration, immigration, diaspora(s), or refugee(s) in their titles, three of those appearing before the end of World War I.[1] The absence of immigration research in the leading journals of political science reflects, most likely, both the lack of salience the subject holds for the discipline's gatekeepers and the failure of political scientists dealing with immigration to produce work of the highest quality.[2]

What accounts for the tendency of American political scientists – whatever their specialties – to ignore international migration? One reason may be that migration falls at the intersection of several disciplines and work on it tends, therefore, to be interdisciplinary. Most of the edited books that have appeared on migration in recent years (and hence the academic conclaves that spawn them) illustrate this fact. Contributors tend to be drawn from a variety of disciplines and many of their names would not be familiar to the general political science reader (eg. Cornelius et al., 1994; Bernstein and Weiner, 1999; Joppke, 1998c; Guiraudon and Joppke, 2001; Freeman and Jupp, 1992; Adelman et al., 1994; Koopmans and Statham, 2000; Brochmann and Hammar, 1999; Joppke and Morawska, 2003; Messina, 2002). The leading journal on migration, the *International Migration Review*, is strongly interdisciplinary and read by relatively few political scientists.[3] Migration, as a topic of inquiry, is not clearly or predominantly within the purview of political science in the way that, for example, political parties, voting and elections, and the legislative process are.

Interdisciplinary work suffers in terms of its prestige in comparison with research more centrally rooted in a single discipline, despite the encouragement of multi-disciplinary collaboration by many leading universities. Scholars working on migration are often better-known outside their disciplines than within them, with predictable negative consequences for their professional careers. The professional incentive structure is such that an article read and cited by just ten political scientists is more valuable professionally than another read and cited by 50 scholars of whom 45 are outside the discipline. Sociologists, anthropologists, and historians do not hire or promote political scientists, nor do they normally referee political science manuscript submissions to journals and presses.

Young scholars seeking to establish their careers and make a name for themselves, especially in years past when migration was truly invisible in political science, might reasonably conclude that migration research carries with it numerous pitfalls and meager promise. To cite a personal example, when a quarter century ago I was casting about for a dissertation topic on European politics the subject of migration was essentially unresearched in political science. The scattering of books and articles dealing with European migration were written by sociologists, demographers, and economists. The little theorizing that existed at the time was either strongly Marxist (Foot, 1965; Castles and Kosack, 1973; Katznelson, 1973) or neo-classical (Institute of Economic Affairs, 1970) in its outlook. Consequently, there was little in the way of guidance in selecting a theoretical framework for a study of comparative policymaking on migration. My dissertation sought to make a virtue out of this deficiency by turning the question of the emergence of migration as a salient political issue into the main research problem.

This pre-theoretical strategy had its uses but the resulting work suffered from a lack of carefully stated and rigorously tested hypotheses (Freeman, 1978, 1979). It also suffered from the fact that it did not engage directly the work of leading political scientists who might have responded to it critically or favorably if it had. No leading political scientists had written anything on immigration at the time. Although the book was well-received in the *American Political Science Review* book section and in other political science journals, and had a modest impact on the emerging sub-field of comparative policy studies, my impression is that it was read mostly by scholars interested in migration rather than in comparative policy studies and most of these were outside political science. Although the book is sometimes referred to as a 'classic' (meaning that it is over 20 years old and is still occasionally referenced) and it may have been groundbreaking in the literal sense that it covered territory previously unexplored by American political scientists, neither it nor the handful of similar works in the period (Miller, 1981) stimulated an immediate flourishing of new work. Although a trickle of books and articles on the politics of migration appeared over the next decade, most scholars apparently decided that migration did not offer the most promising topic for advancing their careers.

According to one authoritative survey, comparative political research in the 1980s displayed five trends: (1) greater attention to the economic aspects of politics, (2) increased interest in the international context of domestic politics and institutions, (3) an altered and sharpened focus on interest groups, especially various forms of corporatism, (4) revival of interest in state structures and their performance, and (5) further work on nationalism and ethnic cleavages (Rogowski, 1993, p. 431). Each of these subjects lends itself to concern with migration processes and migrant behavior; indeed, one would be deliberately obtuse to ignore migration while doing serious work on several of these issues. Yet, it was not until the asylum crisis of the nineties in Europe, and the rise of anti-immigration parties, that migration finally caught the fancy of the political science discipline. At the turn of the century, the state of political science theory and analysis of migration is finally beginning to advance from where it was 25 years earlier.

Finally, it should be noted that one reason political science has paid scant attention to international migration may be the appalling absence of reliable and comparable statistical data sets on population movements. The most sophisticated political economy models require time series data permitting cross-national comparisons. Such data for migration are simply not available. The OECD has not been able to accomplish for migration what it has done for economic data more generally. The organization's Continuous Reporting System for Migration (SOPEMI) is a valiant effort to present in usable form data on population flows and stocks for the OECD member states, but national idiosyncracies in definition of terms, data collection techniques, and reporting standards make life difficult for quantitatively-oriented migration scholars (OECD, 2002). Outside the OECD region migration data are not just unreliable, they are often non-existent. Following the unfortunate pattern in which practitioners of the most advanced analytical techniques select research topics for which amenable data sets are available regardless of their intrinsic interest, migration flows are neglected in favor of more readily quantified economic subjects.

When political scientists do take up the challenge of writing on migration issues, they often import normative preferences that dissipate their energies and stand in the way of intellectual progress. Dispassionate analysis of migration politics is in short supply. Most academic students of migration seem favorably disposed to the process, seeing it as a noble expression of political freedom and the indomitable human spirit and finding most criticisms inexplicable and ill-conceived. This disposition, understandable as it is, often intrudes into research in unfortunate ways, so it may be worth considering its derivation.

Although I know of no reliable data, simple observation suggests that many migration scholars are themselves first or second-generation migrants. Human curiosity seems naturally to turn in upon itself. The history of social science is marked by attempts of scholars belonging to oppressed or marginal groups to draw attention to their plight. Women's studies is dominated by women, minority studies by minorities, etc. Migrant scholars bring with them special insight and commitment and deserve credit for much of the field's growth. They produce some of the best work available. Nevertheless, it would be surprising if persons who have themselves been forced to leave their home countries due to war or persecution or who have benefitted professionally and economically from voluntary migration were not inclined to see the opportunity to migrate as a good in itself and to think that migrants are, on the whole, likely to be valuable contributors to the societies in which they settle. Having gone through the pain and anguish of taking leave of their homelands and adjusting to a new environment, it would be odd if migrant scholars were not especially sensitive to issues of discrimination and xenophobia. That they might see themselves as voices for immigrants against their critics is unsurprising. Indeed, when a migrant scholar raises questions about the wisdom of particular migration policies (as, for example, the Harvard economist and Cuban-American George Borjas [1999] has done), the rarity and incongruity of the situation is ruefully noted and even leads to private accusations of betrayal by some peers.

The Australian sociologist Katharine Betts has explored the social origins of more general academic attitudes toward migration (1988, 1996, 1999). In her view, protagonists on either side of the migration debate in various countries may be divided into cosmopolitans and provincials. Cosmopolitans are likely to be tertiary-educated and to see themselves as having a broader and more sophisticated view of social problems than ordinary folk. For these members of the intelligentsia, or 'new class' as she calls it, support for immigration and multiculturalism is a cultural marker of one's elevated status, distinguishing oneself from the narrow and provincial views of one's less well-educated fellow citizens. The intelligentsia plays a major role in setting the terms of debate over immigration matters and this means that the norms of 'political correctness' must be observed. Migrants may not always be ethnic minorities but it is minority migrants whose presence is the most visible and contentious and who are most often the object of discrimination. They are naturally appealing subjects for middle-class social scientists for whom compassion and tolerance are core values. The admirable impulse to prevent migrants becoming 'scapegoats' in practice means that faults of no sort may be attributed to them.[4] Even when no personal deficiency can be reasonably implied, reporting negative empirical findings may be interpreted as an 'attack' on migrants. For example, a study demonstrating that engineers are over-supplied in country X leading to high rates of unemployment, especially among migrant engineers, might be criticized for implying that the migrant engineers are responsible for their unemployment or that of native engineers. A likely response is that racism or discrimination rather than supply and demand produce the undesirable social outcome.

The upshot of the normative commitments of social scientists studying migration is that certain questions often go unasked and the answers to others are all too often foregone conclusions. Political scientists have been preoccupied, for example, with the causes that propel certain individuals to oppose migration and to be wary of migrants but have largely ignored the related question of why some powerful groups, including the intelligentsia, support migration. Researchers have presumed that mass migration is both desirable and inevitable and that what is problematic and, thus, to be explained is the opposition or resentment it provokes. The literature contains, consequently, an abundance of studies of radical right opposition to migration flows in Western nations, but only a handful of serious studies of the coalitions that support migration in the same countries. American, Australian, and Canadian scholars in particular are prone to generalize from their country's acceptance of mass immigration as the normal experience of a settler society to the presumption that Western European countries that resist such influxes are racist, nationalist, and unacceptably out of tune with contemporary realities. In the same way that social democrats in the United States lament that their country is not more like Sweden, immigration enthusiasts are irked that Germany is not more like the United States in this respect at least. Nonetheless, scholars from the settler societies have a strong propensity to criticize their own countries for nativist responses to immigration now and in the past and for the nastiness of their ethnic politics (see, for example, Massey, Durand, and Malone, 2002, and Castles et al., 1998). The ideological commitments of migration scholars are on display wherever they gather to discuss the topic. Academic fora devoted to questions of migration, which have proliferated in the last decade or so, are often bland exercises in the obvious if all the participants share the underlying normative consensus about the positive characteristics of migration. They may degenerate into heated name-calling and self-righteous screeds if a brave or foolish dissident strays from the accepted line.

To recapitulate, immigration has been mostly ignored by the best minds in political science. As a consequence, the literature tends to be a-theoretical and descriptive, to consist of ad hoc case studies that are difficult to aggregate, and to display a strong normative content with a tendency toward advocacy and celebration rather than rigorous analysis. Immigration research is not all that well-regarded in political science, and, unfortunately, its poor reputation is to a considerable extent deserved. Nevertheless, this parlous state has shown undeniable signs of improvement in recent years. Currently, the problem is less how to persuade young scholars that migration is a suitable subject for scientific study than to ensure that the cohort of dissertation writers now entering the field benefit from theoretical and conceptual guidelines their predecessors lacked. The remainder of this chapter is devoted to a consideration of three broad theoretical developments in recent research on migration politics. Employing a kind of short-hand, I label these as the perspectives of interests, rights, and institutions.

Interests[5]

Political economy, the study of the connections between political and economic life, seems an appropriate approach to migration because migrants are typically factors of production (labor) and migration flows often track labor market conditions and respond to differences in wage levels between sending and receiving countries. Even when migrants are not active in the labor market their presence affects the consumption, production, and fiscal outcomes of the receiving states. Political economy presumes that individuals, as consumers and producers, act on the basis of their interests as they see them. Migrants, in this view, respond to the incentives they confront, as do employers, trade unions, and other members of the host population.

From the perspective of political economy immigration politics and policy is fundamentally about interests. Despite the claims of some immigration advocates that 'everyone' is better off under various liberal immigration regimes, in the real world there are likely to be winners and losers from all social change processes, at least in the short term, and their identification is a key task of social science. Wilson (1980) argues that there are four types of politics depending on whether the benefits and costs of policies are concentrated or diffuse. If both costs and benefits are concentrated, interest group politics should follow. If both costs and benefits are diffuse, majoritarian politics should emerge. If costs are concentrated and benefits are diffuse, Wilson predicts entrepreneurial politics. Finally, if benefits are concentrated and costs diffuse, client politics develops. We would expect interest group and entrepreneurial politics to exhibit high levels of conflict whereas majoritarian and client politics should be marked by relatively mild conflict.

Instances of the diffuse benefits of immigration come readily to mind: economies of scale, a larger domestic market, higher gross domestic product, an enriched and more dynamic cultural stew. Concentrated costs might result from an influx of cheap labor that drives down wages in affected sectors, weakens unions, and competes with natives for scarce housing. On the other hand, examples of the concentrated benefits of migration abound: inexpensive and pliable labor for employers, family reunion for previous migrants, etc. The relatively marginal effect on resource depletion of a population enlarged by migration or increased crowding are examples of diffuse costs.

To employ successfully Wilson's framework to predict the mode of politics that immigration policy should produce, it is necessary to show that one or another of these patterns of benefit/cost allocation is dominant. I have argued elsewhere (1995) that the typical mode of immigration politics in the liberal democracies is client politics in which policy makers interact intensively and often out of public view with groups having direct interests in immigration. Client politics develops, according to the model, because the benefits of immigration tend to be concentrated while its costs are diffuse. This gives those who expect to gain from migration stronger incentives to organize than those who anticipate bearing its costs. This argument had at least two deficiencies. First, it treated immigration policy as a cohesive whole, assuming it would produce a single mode of politics; second, it failed to advance a convincing theoretical rationale for expecting particular benefit/cost allocations. I have addressed the first problem elsewhere (2003); here, I discuss the theoretical issues.

Three theoretical perspectives seem promising for predicting particular patterns of cost/benefit allocation from immigration policy. The first I label the theory of post-industrial change. Work in this vein investigates the effects of processes of social change on particular groups and social strata and has been particularly useful in accounting for mass opinion on migration and the emergence of radical right-wing populist parties to oppose liberal migration policies (Betz, 1994; Betz and Immerfall, 1998). The gist of the argument is that major transformations of the advanced societies are taking place due to the transition from industrialism to post-industrialism and to the accelerating processes of globalization (Sassen, 1988). This transformation puts significant segments of these societies at risk econom-ically, culturally, and politically. Support for right-wing parties and hostility toward immigrants is, in this interpretation, the result of fear and resentment among those adversely affected by these changes (Betz, 1994, p. 85). Variations on this theme can be found in numerous publications (Richmond, 1994; Betts, 1988, 1996, 1999; Bean, 1995; Kitschelt, 1995; Givens, 2002).

A second promising line of theory has been developed by Jeannette Money (1997, 1999a). This work, which Money calls political geography, looks at the way the impact of migration is distributed across space. Money proceeds from the observation that migrants show a pronounced propensity to be concentrated spatially in all receiving countries. From this she develops a model based on the political consequences of migrant concentration in particular electoral constitu-encies. National politicians attend to opinion in local constituencies, she suggests, only if the outcome in those constituencies is critical to the outcome of a national election. When anti-immigrant sentiment develops in swing or marginal districts, the national parties pick up the issue. Money fruitfully applies the model to immigration policy in Great Britain in her 1997 article and extends it to Australia and France in her 1999 book.

The third approach is drawn from models of international trade. As noted earlier, students of international trade have traditionally ignored migration, but recently a few scholars have applied trade theory to migration data in a number of countries. Alan Kessler (1997, 1999) has done the most extensive work, exploiting a wealth of empirical evidence for the United States and more limited data for certain European countries. Kessler hypothesizes that the welfare effects of immigration on domestic factors of production in the receiving states, especially labor, are 'key determinants of a country's migration policy' (Kessler, 1997, p. 1). Where immigrants and domestic workers are substitutes, labor should lobby more aggressively for protection (i.e. immigration restriction). Whether the demand for restriction will be met depends on a country's factor endowments and which factor(s) are predominant in the political process. With respect to the demand for immigration policy, Kessler concludes that where 'migrants and domestic workers are substitutes in production, the relative earnings of domestic landholders (or capitalists) will rise, while those of domestic labor will fall. Consequently, labor has a clear political incentive to lobby for immigration restriction whereas land (or capital) has none' (Kessler, 1997, p. 17).[6]

Each of these three theoretical perspectives needs to be elaborated, critiqued, and further tested. Trade theory has the advantage of drawing on a highly developed and formalized body of postulates developed in economics but significantly transformed through their introduction into political science. Post-industrial change and spatial theory are less theoretically advanced. Post-industrial change theory, in particular, would benefit if someone would work out more specifically how migration processes fit into the macro-economic convulsions taking place in the global economy. Jeannette Money has single-handedly fashioned a spatial approach to migration politics that is ripe for testing in additional national and local contexts. She has herself addressed the anomaly that once migrants become sufficiently numerous in countries where naturalization is readily available and, thus, access to the ballot box, the impact of concentrated immigrant populations in particular electoral constituencies tends to produce positive rather than negative pressures with respect to immigration policies (Money, 1999b).

Armed with these or other theoretical notions, scholars should be in a position to produce testable hypotheses about the cost/benefit consequences of immigration policies and, consequently, the modes of politics likely to emerge. The next step would then be to consider more carefully the implications of various modes of politics for the generation of demands for specific immigration policies.

Rights

While not denying that interests are involved in disputes over immigration, some observers stress the extent to which the individual rights that are at the heart of democratic states displace interests and limit the actions of states. Soysal (1994), for example, argues that the transnational spread of the concept of the basic rights of persons creates pressures on states to confer upon resident aliens most of the benefits previously reserved for citizens. Hollifield (1992, 1998; cf. Jacobson, 1996; DeLaet, 2000) has developed the analysis of the connection between the politics of rights and the politics of immigration most fully. He suggests that migration policies in democratic states reflect the more general 'embedded liberalism' that students of international politics and foreign economic policy argue characterizes Western states in the post-World War II era (Ruggie, 1982). The largely economic and military institutions under American leadership (the International Monetary Fund, the World Bank, the North Atlantic Treaty Organization) that were the organizational framework of the liberal postwar international order appear to lend themselves to support for freer movement of labor, at least freedom of exit, even though they do not address migration of persons directly. Liberal regimes place a premium on individual rights. Migrants, as well as citizens, avail themselves of the language and privileges of rights-based discourses and policies. Moreover, in the period after colonialism, Nazism, and the American civil rights movement the acceptable terms of discussion in the democracies have narrowed to exclude as illegitimate populist appeals to ethnic solidarity or homogeneity (for majority ethnic groups at least). In their place, strong commitments to anti-racism and multiculturalism have emerged. That immigration policy is more open and generous in the liberal democracies than elsewhere lends at least a surface plausibility to the contention that there is something inherent in the structure or culture of the democracies, and the international institutions they create and sustain, that brings these patterns about.

One objection to this approach is that there is no international regime regulating the movement of labor. The United Nations refugee regime is extremely weak and deals only with a narrowly-defined category of involuntary movement. The same criticisms apply to United Nations human rights and related conventions. The International Labor Office may be seen as seeking to establish a fledgling regime through its international covenants such as that dealing with the rights of migrant workers, but it too is feeble and lacks the power to enforce norms. Scholars such as Hollifield are well aware of this problem, indeed it is the starting point of their analysis, but they stress that the domestic political systems of the liberal democracies place a premium on rights and support the evolution of international norms even as these norms lack sufficient institutional mooring in the international arena.

The concept of embedded liberalism suggests that migration policy will display evidence of path dependency, a simple notion with large implications for our understanding of the evolution of policy over time and, particularly differences in policy trajectories across nations (Steinmo et al., 1992; Pierson, 2000). Path dependency draws our attention to the way in which particular episodes, experiences, or decisions taken at a given point in time narrow or enlarge future possible courses of action. Given particular decisions at T1, some choices at T2 are either impossible or highly unlikely. Path dependency seeks to move historical exposition from description to explanation as historically antecedent events become the cause of subsequent developments. Randall Hansen uses this idea to good effect in his reinterpretation of post-war British migration and citizenship policy (Hansen, 2000).

The model of embedded liberalism suggests the hypothesis that once immigrants and asylum seekers are recognized as having specific rights (to making claims, lodging appeals, being joined by family members, etc.) it will be exceedingly difficult to roll them back. Secondly, as Tocqueville teaches us, democracy once installed tends to develop an expansionary logic of its own so that when rights are recognized for one group the pressure to extend the same rights to those not yet under their cover intensifies. Thirdly, in those states in which liberalism is more fully embedded the courts will likely play a more important role in establishing and protecting the status of migrants. Judicial activism should be most prominent with respect to rights of asylum, but also should figure in the efforts of unauthorized migrants to obtain legal status or avoid deportation and of legal migrants pressing such issues as family reunification and access to welfare state protections (Joppke, 1998a, 1998b, 1998c; 1999).

Institutionalism

Although the interests and rights-based models generalize across the Western democracies, states may vary according to the extent to which they are integrated into liberal international structures and to which they adopt thoroughly liberal, rights-based domestic institutions. Both the interests and rights perspectives focus on societal pressures and claims without bringing states directly into the analysis as independent entities. They concentrate on the demand for policies rather than their supply.

Political scientists have devoted relatively little attention to the causal connections between institutional configurations of states and the immigration policies they adopt, yet it seems highly probable that different state structures create divergent inclinations and capacities for the management of borders, immigration, and integration. To the extent that states have been central to immigration studies, they have played in a debate over the continuing viability of sovereign nation states in an era of intensifying globalization. This argument between proponents of globalization (Sassen, 1998; Soysal, 1994; Jacobson, 1996; Faist, 2000) and skeptics who claim that state sovereignty persists (Freeman, 1998; Joppke, 1999) has been entertaining (Guiraudon and Lahav, 2000), but may be distracting us from the more specific exploration of varieties of state structures and their linkages to variants of immigration policy.

The chief assumption underlying the claims of the globalists about the decline of the nation-state and the erosion of political boundaries is that in the matter of international migration political processes are subordinate to the forces of economic interdependence, inequality, market pressures, or long-term cultural transformations. The evidence they can cite in support of their position is striking – unwanted migrations, porous national borders, influxes of asylum seekers, and widespread unauthorized employment in the rich societies; in other words, failed immigration regimes. In general, they see the capacity of states under siege from above (international norms and regimes), from within (a discourse of rights and the emergence of minority and multicultural claims), and from below (trends toward the decentralization and privatization of migration policy).

There is no space here to consider these arguments in detail. They are obviously rooted in real developments. If there was a golden age of state control of population movements, it probably lasted no longer than from about 1918 to 1951, a period bounded at one end by the termination of the First World War and the more or less universal introduction of the passport system (Torpey, 2000) and at the other by the passage of the United Nations Convention on the Status of Refugees. Nevertheless, states are still the most important actors with respect to migratory movements (Zolberg, 1999b), they still decisively shape the possibilities for movement, and, contrary to widespread perceptions of disarray and disintegration, migration control systems in the advanced societies are growing rather than declining in their complexity, technical prowess, extensiveness, and expense.

A significant issue raised by the institutionalist perspective is the relative openness of policymakers to external influence. How far can state decisionmakers act independently of societal forces? For all their similarities, among which are a general accessibility to popular and group pressures and relatively transparent decision processes, democratic states vary significantly in their vulnerability to social pressures and in their capacity to generate and implement ambitious, long-term policies in the national interest that impose losses on discrete groups (Weaver and Rockman, 1992; Ireland, 1994). The locus of decisionmaking for immigration is of particular interest. To what extent is policy shaped by the views of the professional civil servants in the administration, controlled by the cabinet or the minister responsible for immigration, or subject to the interventions of individual parliamentarians? What license have the courts to overturn governmental decisions? How does partisan competition affect agenda-setting and policy outcomes? The answers to these questions do not lead directly to expectations about the direction of policy. In countries where national policy makers are subject to intense pressure from organized groups the sort of policy chosen will depend, obviously, on which groups have access and which policy they prefer (in the terms of the political economy model, how the costs and benefits are distributed). An autonomous state, on the other hand, may enjoy the flexibility to follow a number of different immigration policies. Specifying the degree of independence and identifying the locus of decision making is only the beginning, not the end, of our task.

With respect to administrative autonomy two competing hypotheses emerge. On the one hand, a bureaucratic supply model would anticipate that administrators responsible for immigration would advocate for large numbers because that would guarantee a larger budget and employee base for the agency. On the other hand, a bureaucratic culture model would presume that the immigration bureaucracy would develop norms favoring strict regulation and, other things equal, smaller numbers in order to maintain control in the same way that finance departments develop budgetary efficiency norms.

Conclusion

For a variety of reasons, political science has failed to deal seriously with the phenomenon of international migration until quite recently. Given that a number of younger scholars are now at work on the issue, however, it is important to develop testable propositions embedded in theory. Some potentially useful variants of theory will surely be borrowed from the other social sciences. In fact, each of the three perspectives I discuss as shedding light on the cost/benefit consequences of migration (post-industrial change, spatial, and trade theory) are drawn from sister disciplines. Nevertheless, it seems a sensible course to exploit as far as possible existing theory that has demonstrated its utility in accounting for political data rather than searching for a theory of migration policy, *sui generis*. Recent work suggests that the discipline's most useful contribution will be by means of middle-range hypotheses about the way immigration is formulated as an issue, how interests develop around these issues, and how states and social interests interact in the creation and implementation of policies. In this way political science will be better positioned to make a valuable contribution to the cross-disciplinary discussion of migration phenomena.

The political economy perspective suggests that the politics of immigration will be organized around its costs and benefits and that analysis should be focused on the question of what interests are at play in immigration decision making. The mode of politics will reflect the distribution of costs and benefits, which should be evident in the organized interests seeking to influence policy. Yet it is obvious that immigration is profoundly concerned with questions of individual rights, those of citizens, those of residents, those of asylum seekers, and those of all persons outside the rich countries wanting to come in. To what extent is a liberal politics of rights embedded in the constitutional and institutional characteristics of particular societies? How important are the courts in constraining the more strictly political decision makers? Do rights claims come primarily from domestic sources or are they an indication of the growing importance of international norms of equality and universal personhood? Is immigration policy path dependent so that rights tend to be extended to new groups, new rights get created, and old rights are resistant to erosion? To what extent is immigration policy affected by the independence of decision makers from interest group pressure? In particular, what difference does the locus of decision making make for policy outcomes? A comprehensive explanation will combine political economy approaches that specify what is at stake for specific groups and how rights are established and protected (predictions of the demand for policy) with institutional models that delineate the linkages between groups and authoritative decision makers (predictions about supply).

Notes

1   This information is the result of a jstor title search (cf. www.jstor.com).
    As this article was going to press, the APSR (American Political Science Review) published Christopher Rudolph, 'Security and the Political Economy of International Migration', 97 (4), pp. 603-20.
2   One exception to this general pattern is in the subfield of normative democratic theory. Here there has been an explosion of interest among political theorists in the issues of race, ethnicity, gender and citizenship. This has necessarily led some scholars to explore the ethics immigration regulation and refugee protection. For a comprehensive bibliography see Kymlicka and Norman, 2000, pp. 395-433.
3   A recent attempt to measure the reputations of journals according to the familiarity, evaluations, and impact as seen by political scientists drew up a list of 115 journals. These were identified as likely to be of interest to political scientists and were taken from earlier studies and from suggestions made by the authors' colleagues. The *International Migration Review* is not on the list, nor is any journal dealing primarily with population or demographic issues (Garand and Giles, 2003).

4   The tendency to celebrate immigrant contributions in the academic literature leads some critics of immigration to engage in somewhat silly efforts to re-establish balance. See, for example, the issue of the journal *The Social Contract* 6/1 (1995) entitled 'Infamous Immigrants'.

5   Political economy has taken on a wide variety of meanings in contemporary political science from rational choice to neo-Marxism. To my knowledge no one has attempted to apply formal models of rational decision making to the analysis of migration politics, although some years ago neo-Marxists interpretation of migration were common (Castles and Kosack, 1973; Castells, 1975; cf. The journal *Race and Class*). My use of the term, as stipulated below, is quite broad.

6   This is a highly simplified presentation of the much more elaborate model developed by Kessler in his dissertation (1999). He disaggregates labor into its skilled and unskilled components and tests his hypotheses in regional labor markets, among other innovations.

References

Adelman, H. et al. (eds.) (1994), *Immigration and Refugee Policy: Australia and Canada Compared*, Vols. I and II, University of Toronto Press, Toronto.

Avery, W.P. and Rapkin, D.P. (eds.) (1982), *America in a Changing World Political Economy*, Longman, New York.

Bean, C. (1995), 'Determinants of Attitudes towards Questions of Border Maintenance in Australia', *People and Place*, 3 (3), pp. 32-9.

Berger, S. and Dore, R. (eds.) (1996), *National Diversity and Global Capitalism*, Cornell UP, Ithaca.

Bernstein, A. and Weiner, M. (eds.) (1999), *Migration and Refugee Policies: An Overview*, Pinter, London.

Betts, K. (1988), *Ideology and Immigration: Australia 1976 to 1987*, Melbourne UP, Melbourne.

Betts, K. (1996), 'Immigration and Public Opinion in Australia', *People and Place*, 4 (3), pp. 9-20.

Betts, K. (1999), *The Great Divide*, Duffy and Snellgrove, Sydney.

Betz, H.-G. (1994), *Radical Right-Wing Populism in Western Europe*, St. Martin's Press, New York.

Betz, H.-G. and Immerfall, St. (eds.) (1998), *The New Politics of the Right: Neo-Populist Parties and Movements in Established Democracies*, St. Martin's Press, New York.

Borjas, G.J. (1999), *Heaven's Door: Immigration Policy and the American Economy*, Princeton UP, Princeton.

Brochmann, G. and Hammar, T. (eds.) (1999), *Mechanisms of Immigration Control*, Berg, Oxford.

Castells, M. (1975), 'Immigrant Workers and Class Struggles in Advanced Capitalism: The Western European Experience', *Politics and Society*, 5 (1), pp. 33-66.

Castles, St. and Kosack, G. (1973), *Immigrant Workers and Class Structure in Western Europe*, Oxford UP, Oxford.

Castles, St. et al. (1998), *Mistaken Identity: Multiculturalism and the Demise of Nationalism in Australia*, Pluto Press, London.

Cornelius, W.A., Martin, Ph.L., and Hollifield, J.F. (eds.) (1994), *Controlling Immigration: A Global Perspective*, Stanford UP, Stanford.

DeLaet, D.L. (2000), *U.S. Immigration Policy in an Age of Rights*, Praeger, Westport, CT.

Faist, Th. (2000), *The Volume and Dynamics of International Migration and Transnational Social Spaces,* Oxford UP, New York.

Foot, P. (1965), *Immigration and Race in British Politics,* Penguin, Harmondsworth.

Freeman, G.P. (1978), 'Immigrant Labor and Working-Class Politics', *Comparative Politics,* 11 (1) (October), pp. 24-41.

Freeman, G.P. (1979), *Immigrant Labor and Racial Conflict in Industrial Societies: The French and British Experience, 1945-75,* Princeton UP, Princeton.

Freeman, G.P. (1995), 'Modes of Immigration Politics in Liberal Democratic States', *International Migration Review,* 29 (112), pp. 881-902.

Freeman, G.P. (1998), 'The Decline of Sovereignty? Politics and Immigration Restriction in Liberal States', in Joppke (ed.), *Challenge to the Nation-State,* pp. 86-108.

Freeman, G.P. (2003), 'Political Science and Immigration: Policy Types and Modes of Politics'. Paper presented at the R.H. Harney Lecture Series, University of Toronto, 21 March.

Freeman, G.P. and Jupp, J. (eds.) (1992), *Nations of Immigrants: Australia, the United States and International Migration,* Oxford UP, Melbourne and New York.

Garand, J.C. and Giles, M.W. (2003), 'Journals in the Discipline: A Report on a New Survey of American Political Scientists', *PS: Political Science & Politics,* 36 (2) (April), pp. 293-308.

Gibney, M.J. (1999), 'Liberal Democratic States and Responsibilities to Refugees', *American Political Science Review,* 93 (1) (March), pp. 169-81.

Gilpin, R. (1987), *The Political Economy of International Relations,* Princton UP, Princeton.

Gilpin, R. (2000), *The Challenge of Global Capitalism: The World Economy in the 21st Century,* Princeton UP, Princeton.

Givens, T. (2002), 'The Role of Socio-Economic Factors in the Success of Extreme Right Parties', in M.A. Schain, A. Zolberg, and P. Hossay (eds.), *Shadows Over Europe: The Development and Impact of the Extreme Right in Western Europe,* Palgrave, Houndmills, Basingstoke, pp. 137-58.

Guiraudon, V. and Joppke, Ch. (eds.) (2001), *Controlling a New Migration World,* Routledge, New York.

Guiraudon, V. and Lahav, G. (2000), 'A Reappraisal of the State Sovereignty Debate: The Case of Migration Control', *Comparative Political Studies,* 33 (2), pp. 163-95.

Gurowitz, A. (1999), 'Mobilizing International Norms: Domestic Actors, Immigrants, and the Japanese State', *World Politics,* 51 (April), pp. 413-45.

Hansen, R. (2000), *Citizenship and Immigration in Postwar Britain,* Oxford UP, Oxford.

Hansen, R. (2002), 'Globalization, Embedded Realism, and Path Dependence', *Comparative Political Studies,* 35 (3), pp. 259-83.

Hollifield, J. (1992), *Immigrants, Markets, and States: The Political Economy of Postwar Europe,* Harvard UP, Cambridge, MA.

Hollifield, J. (1998), 'Migration, Trade, and the Nation-State: The Myth of Globalization', *UCLA Journal of Internatonal Law and Foreign Affairs,* 3 (2) (Fall/Winter), pp. 595-636.

Hollifield, J. (2000), 'The Politics of International Migration: How Can We "Bring the State Back In?"' in J. Hollifield and C. Brettell (eds.), *International Migration: Talking Across Disciplines,* Routledge, New York, pp. 137-85.

Institute of Economic Affairs (1970), *Economic Issues in Immigration: An Exploration of the Liberal Approach to Public Policy on Immigration,* London.

Ireland, P. (1994), *The Policy Challenge of Ethnic Diversity: Immigrant Politics in France and Switzerland,* Harvard UP, Cambridge, MA.

Jacobson, D. (1996), *Rights Across Borders: Immigration and the Decline of Citizenship*, Johns Hopkins UP, Baltimore.

Joppke, Ch. (1998a), 'Why Liberal States Accept Unwanted Immigration', *World Politics*, 50 (2), pp. 266-93.

Joppke, Ch. (1998b), 'Asylum and State Sovereignty: A Comparison of the United States, Germany, and Britain', in Joppke (ed.) *Challenge to the Nation-State*, pp. 109-52.

Joppke, Ch. (1998c), *Challenge to the Nation-State: Immigration in Western Europe and the United States*, Oxford UP, Oxford.

Joppke, Ch. (1999), *Immigration and the Nation-State: The United States, Germany, and Great Britain*, Oxford UP, Oxford.

Joppke, Ch. and Morawska, E. (eds.) (2003), *Toward Assimilation and Citizenship*, Palgrave, Houndmills, Basingstoke.

Katznelson, I. (1973), *Black Men, White Cities: Race, Politics, and Migration in the United States, 1900-30 and in Britain, 1948-68*, Oxford UP, London.

Kessler, A. (1997), 'Trade Theory, Political Incentives, and the Political Economy of American Immigration Restriction, 1875-1924'. Presented at the American Political Science Association Annual Meeting.

Kessler, A. (1999), *International Trade, Domestic Coalitions, and the Political Economy of Immigration Control*. Doctoral dissertation, University of California, Los Angeles.

Kitschelt, H. (1995), *The Radical Right in Western Europe: A Comparative Analysis*, University of Michigan Press, Ann Arbor.

Koopmans, R. and Statham, P. (eds.) (2000), *Challenging Immigration and Ethnic Relations Politics: Comparative European Perspectives*, Oxford UP, Oxford.

Krasner, St.D.Ed. (1983), *International Regimes*, Cornell UP, Ithaca, NY.

Kymlicka, W. and Norman, W. (eds.) (2000), *Citizenship in Diverse Societies*, Oxford UP, Oxford.

Massey, D.S. et al. (1998), *Worlds in Motion: Understanding International Migration at the End of the Millennium*, Oxford UP, Oxford.

Massey, D.S., Durand, J., and Malone, N.J. (2002), *Beyond Smoke and Mirrors: Mexican Immigration in an Era of Economic Integration*, Russell Sage Foundation, New York.

Messina, A.M. (ed.) (2002), *West European Immigration and Immigrant Policy in the New Century*, Praeger, Westport, CT.

Miller, Mark J. (1981), *Foreign Workers in Western Europe: An Emerging Political Force*, Praeger, New York.

Money, J. (1997), 'No Vacancy: The Political Geography of Immigration Control in Advanced Industrial Democracies', *International Organization*, 51 (4), pp. 685-720.

Money, J. (1999a), *Fences and Neighbors: The Political Geography of Immigration Control*, Cornell UP, Ithaca.

Money, J. (1999b), 'Xenophobia and Xenophilia: Pauline Hanson and the Counterbalancing of Electoral Incentives in Australia', *People and Place*, 7 (3), pp. 7-18.

OECD (2002), *Trends in International Migration*, Paris.

Peled, Y. (1992), 'Ethnic Democracy and the Legal Construction of Citizenship: Arab Citizens in the Jewish State', *American Political Science Review*, 86 (2) (June), pp. 432-43.

Pierson, P. (2000), 'Increasing Returns, Path Dependence, and the Study of Politics', *American Political Science Review*, 94 (2), pp. 251-68.

Richmond, A. (1994), *Global Apartheid: Refugees, Racism, and the New World Order*, Oxford UP, Toronto.

Rogowski, R. (1993), 'Comparative Politics', in A.W. Finifter (ed.), *Political Science: The State of the Discipline II*, American Political Science Association, Washington, DC, pp. 431-49.

Ruggie, J. (1982), 'International Regimes, Transactions and Change: Embedded Liberalism in the Postwar Economic Order', *International Organization,* 36 (1), pp. 417-55.

Sassen, S. (1988), *The Mobility of Labor and Capital,* Cambridge UP, Cambridge.

Sassen, S. (1998), 'The *de facto* Transnationalizing of Immigration Policy', in Joppke (ed.), *Challenge to the Nation-State*, pp. 49-85.

Soysal, Y. (1994), *Limits of Citizenship: Migrants and Postnational Membership in Europe,* University of Chicago Press, Chicago.

Spero, J.E. and Hart, J.A. (2002), *The Politics of International Economic Relations,* 6th ed., St. Martin's Press, New York.

Steinmo, S. et al. (eds.) (1992), *Structuring Politics: Historical Institutionalism in Comparative Analysis,* Cambridge UP, New York.

Torpey, J. (2000), *The Invention of the Passport: Surveillance, Citizenship and the State,* Cambridge UP, Cambridge.

Weaver, K and Rockman, B. (eds.) (1992), *Do Institutions Matter?* Brookings, Washington, DC.

Wilson, J.Q. (ed.) (1980), *The Politics of Regulation,* Harper, New York.

Zolberg, A. (1999a), 'The Politics of Immigration Policy: An Externalist Perspective', *American Behavioral Scientist,* 42 (9) (June/July), pp. 1276-79.

Zolberg, A. (1999b), 'Matters of State: Theorizing Immigration Policy', in Ch. Hirschman, Ph. Kasinitz, and J. DeWind (eds.), *The Handbook of International Migration: The American Experience,* Russel Sage Foundation, New York, pp. 71-93.

Zolberg, A., Suhrke, A., and Aguayo, S. (1989), *Escape from Violence,* Oxford UP, New York.

Chapter 6

World Society and Migrations: Challenges to Theoretical Concepts of Political Sociology

Jost Halfmann

Introduction

The questions asked in this chapter are whether modern migration changes the outlook and problem framing of political sociology and what the contribution of political sociology might be to the study of migration. Migration research is typically a multidisciplinary enterprise: many studies on migration freely pick from the methodological and theoretical offerings of sociology, history, demography, political economy or political science. The advantage of eclecticism might be that it allows closer proximity to the social problems of migration; the disadvantage of this approach is certainly that it lacks unitary theoretical and methodological standards and risks applying contradictory and often outdated concepts from these diverse disciplines. In this chapter, I will attempt to reformulate the problem focus and the theoretical assumptions of political sociology to adapt it to the challenges of migration in a global context.

I will particularly argue that political sociology needs to broaden its theoretical and conceptual scope in order to grasp fully the implications of migration and of a global polity for the problem of political power and for the most relevant modern organizational form of processing power, the territorial nation-state. By applying advanced concepts of sociological systems theory to the notions of politics and political power the nation-state is conceived as a segmentarily differentiated unit of the political system of modern world society. Nation-states are described as organizations which regulate membership and exercise political authority on the basis of territorial belonging. Migration poses a problem for the nation-state because it indicates that organizations of some social systems such as the economy, but also science, law, education and health show decreasing concern for territoriality. From the perspective of the modern nation-state globalization means that relevant social systems have overcome the territorial marking of inclusion as is characteristic of membership in the political system. This constellation challenges the classic nation-state solution to the problem of concentrating and using political power with respect to all sectors of society (including industry, science or law) within territorial confines. Migration is indicative of a loss of nation-states' sovereignty which ideal-typically would consist in the control not only over access to the territory, but also over the membership criteria in all organizations on the territory. Migration has, therefore, implications for both aspects of the social basis of power: for the modern democratic forms of legitimizing political organizations and for the capacity of these political organizations to exert authority and to intervene in the diverse social systems of society.

In the first part of this chapter I will briefly reconstruct the current thematic focus of political sociology. Then I will examine some presuppositions and the-matic restrictions of the established concept of political sociology and discuss the major societal causes for the need to reconfigure political sociology: the reciprocal effects of the emergent world society and of international migration on the modern nation-state. I will then propose to reformulate certain theoretical presuppositions of political sociology and conclude with some suggestions on the potential use of political sociology for migration research.

Reconstructing Political Sociology

Political sociology is a hybrid of sociology and political science (Stammer and Weingart, 1972). Because of this heritage, political sociology contains traces of the uneasy coexistence between the very different traditions of the two disciplines. As Irving L. Horowitz noted, the political scientist's emphasis is on the state while the sociologist's eye is fixed on society (Horowitz, 1972, similarly Bendix and Lipset, 1966, p. 26). Political sociology represents a compromise between these two disciplines in claiming that its proper subject be the relationships between state and society. What is problematic about this type of conceptual framing is the implicit or explicit reduction of the notion of society to 'civil society' and the attribution of a special 'extra-societal' status to the state. The distinction between civil society and the state emerged in 18th century political philosophy and was codified in 19th century 'state science' (Staatswissenschaft). Illustrated by the contrast between the 'bourgeois' and the 'citoyen', in social theory the distinction was meant to accom-modate the emergence of an independent economic system with its potential for destabilizing the political order, but to safeguard at the same time the integrative role of the polity in society which had been placed at the center of social theorizing since antiquity. In the wake of nation-state consolidation in the 19th century, the notion of civil society acquired, however, a different meaning. It now referred to the persons and (business, educational or welfare) organizations which existed on the territory over which a nation-state claimed authority and which supposedly shared a common national heritage and destiny. From this understanding of civil society stems the tradition of social scientists to equate society with the nation-state (e.g. Giddens, 1985, p. 172).

This problem focus reflects the social philosophical heritage of the study of politics and accentuates the differences of studying society in political science and sociology.While political science can trace its origins to the political reasoning of antique philosophy, sociology is a product of the empirical-historical and positivist orientation of late 19th century human sciences. While sociology perceives of politics as one social system among others in society and of society as the paramount social system, political science focuses on politics proper and its potential for integrating society and takes notice of other societal activities primarily in terms of external conditions or constraints.

The concentration of political science on the polity originated in antique philosophy which equated society with politics. Aristotle reasoned that the political community, the polis, is the essential social context for humans. The political community (koinonia) not only guarantees safety and peace, it is also the only medium for humans to achieve ethical perfection. It is for this reason that politics is not only an art form, embodied in the practice of statecraft, but also a realm of implementing ethical standards. The household, the oikos, was ill fitted to achieve ethical perfection and to allow living a virtuous life although the head of the household needed to apply ruling techniques which were similar to those in politics. Throughout antiquity and the Middle Ages and up until early modernity any notion of the overarching entity of which oikos and polis were elements was lacking. The idea of political society covered this gap by excluding from the realm of an ethically meaningful life all categories of humans (children, women, slaves) and all activities (economics) which were associated with the oikos. The pathos of ethics in political society rested on the idea of human nature which, due to the special position of humans in cosmos, was endowed with reason and capable of striving for perfection in life.The perfect order for humans was political society which became an ethical imperative. During its long journey through the history of state-building the term politics did not lose this early normative meaning before the turn from the 16th to the 17th century (Sellin, 1978).

Toward the end of the 18th century the emerging manufactural and industrial enterprises led to a new description of society as 'commercial society', slowly challenging the traditional notion of 'civil society' as the politically constituted society (Luhmann, 1998). In the 18th and 19th century social theorists like Hegel and Marx attempted to grasp this change by introducing the distinction between state and society. Politics began to lose its function as a medium for ethical perfection. The state designed to concentrate political power came to be acknowledged as the central organization of the political system. In his study on the French civil war from 1848 to 1851 Marx recognized the new role of the state as the central instance for the control of violence in society, but also the modern dependence of the state on external resources (taxes provided by economic actors, legality achieved by adherence to legal norms, loyalty based on the inclusion of the population in the political system) (Marx, 1960). Marx focused on the empirical mechanisms of state intervention which in his view, by pacifying society and counteracting society's inclination toward instability, served the class interest of the bourgeoisie (Perez-Diaz, 1978). Marx opposed Hegel's concept of the state as the primary instance of ethical perfection in a society characterized by conflicting interests and diverging need dispositions (Depew, 1992).

Rather than pointing at the differences between Marx's and Hegel's theory of the state I would stress their similarities: the belief in the integrative role of the state for society, a capacity which these authors attributed to the elevated, extra-societal status of the state. Empirical research on the factual activities of governments and public administrations has, however, revealed that the modern state follows political criteria of decision making while at the same time depending on the resources of its economic, legal or popular environments. It does not make sense any more to view the state as an 'agent' of one particular social class or group as Marx did nor is it very illuminating to speak of the 'relative autonomy' of the state, as the French neo-marxist tradition did (Poulantzas, 1972), nor is it reasonable to depict in reverse-Hegelian fashion the state as an instance which opposes civil society where the latter contains the resources of reason and ethics which the first has lost on the way to becoming a 'power state' (Habermas, 1975).

Political sociology as an identifiable subdiscipline of social science has emerged in the 1920s. By then the new social science discipline recognized that society is not constituted and sufficiently described by politics, but that society is the encompassing social system. Political sociology also departed from the older contrast between politics and household and narrowed the notion of politics down to the capacity of the state for decision-making. Political sociology shared, however, two premises with 19th political philosophy: first, the juxtaposition of state and society where society was now conceived of as economics, and second, the belief that politics can 'integrate' society by regulating and directing a potentially unruly society. This normative reminiscence of the original reflection on politics still resounds in modern political sociology although it has developed into an empirical social science in its own right. The idea that the state is preoccupied with the inherent instability of society, that the authority of the state is permanently constrained and endangered by competing power centers (such as big private enterprises), and that state intervention can indeed improve or worsen some (assumed) societal equilibrium betrays the allegiance to this19th century concept of society as a social system driven by centrifugal forces. At the same time, political sociology refined and systematized the efforts of the 19th century social theorists to study politics empirically as a social system which aims at concentrating and reproducing a particular social medium: power.

In his overview of political sociology, Morris Janowitz, therefore, places power at the center of political sociology. Political sociology refers to the 'social basis of power in all institutional sectors of society' (Janowitz, 1968, p. 298). Power as a social medium which regulates the relations between those who can effectively claim obedience to their demands and those who submit to these demands is a ubiquitous phenomenon in modern society. One of the major themes of any theory of modern society has been the description of the emergence and organization of *political* power. The emergence of a political system as a differentiated social system within society coincides with the evolution of the modern territorial state and the spread of territorial states over the globe (Tilly, 1992; Spruyt, 1994). In its mature form, the political system constitutes a particular form of power relations: between political organizations such as the modern nation-state whose perseverance rests on the successful claim to produce collectively binding decisions and the collectivity of citizens that is the subject of and subject to political power. For many nation-states liberal democracy has become the most stable form of managing this relationship. The tension between the societal ubiquity of power and the social efforts at concentrating power in the political system has become the research premise for most of political sociology (Bendix and Lipset, 1966, p. 22; for a general review of traditions in the theory of power see Scott, 2001). The social basis of power has become constitutive for political sociology in two ways: as the source of political power and as the object of political power.

It is no coincidence, therefore, that the prime topic of political sociology since the 1920s was (the imperfection of) democracy (and its opposite: autocracy or totalitarian rule) and its capacity to reconcile the state with (civil) society. Robert Michels' pathbreaking study on the laws of oligarchy in democratic institutions as well as Pareto's and Mosca's treaties on the role of elites in modern society may well mark the origin of political sociology's preoccupation with the fragility of political order (Michels, 1962; Pareto, 1935; Mosca, 1939; see also Orum, 1988, pp. 400-401). Political sociology maintained its interest in democracy in the 1960s and 1970s when – in the context of the Cold War – the stability of the state order was believed to be dependent on its legitimacy (Lipset, 1963; Bendix, 1964; Habermas, 1975). Political sociology's preoccupation with the stability of modern society focused on the nation-state as the political institution which, by creating the collectivity for which the state makes binding decisions, homogenizes and pacifies society and thus allows to contain its centrifugal forces. 'The free society is in need of a unifying principle which overarches society and state; liberation itself does not yet provide unity and communality. In the old order religion next to historically grown togetherness provided this unifying principle...The nation replaces religion and tradition. The nation as a political community of consciousness and confession becomes the unifying thread and principle of integration' (Böckenförde, 1991, p. 112; translation by the author). In retrospect, the attempted homogenization of society along the idea of a national community has had very ambivalent implications: it has not only meant the establishment of a more or less encompassing welfare state (in the most general sense, that is: state-sponsored programs of creating cultural, educational and material equality and homogeneity within nation-state borders), it has also meant in all possible forms the '(ethnic) cleansing' of groups of people which were deemed not belonging to a nation (Gellner, 1983). But as a general result the association of nation and state created the concept and practice of citizenship, a direct relationship between individuals and the state which through the framing of politics by constitutions led to representative forms of government and democratic procedures of political rule.

The social-democratic variant of nation-state homogenization which became dominant in Western Europe after World War II and which had some appeal to US governments during the 1930s and 1960s fed T.H. Marshall's programmatic belief in the use of political power for reducing social inequality. Marshall became one of the most influential proponents of this reasoning when he placed the need for social policy within the context of societal modernization (Marshall, 1977). To him the social policy of a state should aim at protecting the citizens from the excessive use of power in many 'institutional sectors' of society, especially in the industrial sector. Social policies were understood as creating the societal collectivity as a community of equals which – according to the logic of modern democratic rule – is a prerequisite for serving as a social basis of power. Implicitly, the programs of social policy were understood as a government strategy of wresting power away from social forces (such as industrial enterprises) which the state could not control by its conventional means of law and force. Marshall's reasoning lies at the root of the modern circle of political power: states use political power to create and maintain the collectivity of citizens which in turn serves as the social basis of power. Marshall believed citizenship to be the central legal-political institution which could solve the problem of internal sovereignty of the modern state. Marshall's vision of the good society was a nation-state society which excluded, however, migration as well as supranational institutions – two phenomena which since then have proved to become the main challenges for the sovereignty of the modern state.[1]

World Society and Migration

International migration and the further emergence of world society in the twentieth century disturbed the picture of self-sufficient nation-states and challenged the idea of equating society with the nation-state in two ways. First, cross border migration revealed the inherent option for nation-state closure in the Marshallian ideal of welfare state equality; it implied the claim that only citizens should enjoy the privileges of national welfare policies. Second, the (re)emergence of world society,[2] and with it, of supranational political organizations undermines the status of nation-states as the sole and sovereign instances of authoritative political decision-making in modern society. This then raises new questions about the capacity of nation-states to make binding decisions for a well-defined collectivity of citizens and organizations on a state's territory.

Migration

Over the last decades, much of migration research has indeed been pursued within the Marshallian mould. Migration has been observed as either creating new forms or confirming established forms of social (and particularly: ethnic) stratification which call for integrative and compensatory measures (Castles and Kosack, 1973;

Piore, 1979; Alonso, 1987; Richmond, 1987; Castles and Miller, 1993; Miles and Thränhardt, 1995). Over time, however, migration research departed from the premise which it had shared with political sociology that society is identical with the nation-state. The global character of migration stimulated reflections on the relationships between migration and the nation-state (Joppke, 1998) and on the forms of transnational institutionalization of migrant rights and ways of life (Bauböck, 1994, Soysal, 1994). Migration, like power, is a ubiqitous phenomenon which has global dimensions and is hard to reconcile with the territorial limitations of nation-states (Weiner, 1994). Migration which crosses nation-state borders and which leads to long term residency in the receiving country (sometimes without changing citizenship) temporarily or permanently puts into question the 'nation-statist' premise of inclusion. Migrants challenge the content and the durability of the special relations between nation-states and the citizens which are expressed in the 'Marshallian' social policy programs and which are geared to foster national collectivities of equals (Halfmann, 2000). By restricting itself to questions of equality and justice for migrants, migration research runs the risk of losing sight of the theoretical implications which the tension between the global character of migration and the local character of nation-state integration has.

No doubt, migration as social mobility aiming at inclusion in social systems at a different geographical location (Bommes, 1999) has been closely associated with the nation-state. Migration was a relevant cause and a result of nation-state building, not only in the American colonies, but also in Europe. During the transformative period from feudal empires to territorial nation-states many people were forced into migration when the ties to the estate order loosened and the traditional familial and communal systems of production and care eroded. At the same time, the mass migration movements of the 17th and 18th century created strong incentives for the emerging European nation-states to intensify the external and internal processes of state building. One of the most important steps of self-assertion of the modern states was the establishment of clear membership criteria which emerged from interstate contracts about population on the one hand and binding agreements of states with the cities and estates which still held relevant rights of taxation, jurisdiction and care on the other (for the case of Prussia: Grawert, 1973).

Most visibly in Europe, nation-state building coincided with welfare state building, again to a substantial degree in response to the problems of migration and membership. The migrant poor had opened the eyes of the political elites to the implications of state rule over a population within a territory. In the beginning, the migrant poor were fundamentally excluded from the new order; and it required enormous public efforts concerning regulation, but also education and financial support to turn them not only into citizens (and army recrutes), but also into workers on the expanding labor markets. These early efforts of policing and regulating the poor which were often initiated under the impression of impending revolt eventually grew into the elaborate system of the modern welfare state (Swaan, 1988). By meeting the threats to social inclusion inherent in unemployment, sickness or age the modern welfare state modifies and moderates the membership rules in a variety of social systems such as the economy, education or health.

The emergence of the modern nation-state indicated yet a much deeper social change than just the dissolution of feudal empires: it also reflected the eventual expansion of functional differentiation throughout society (Luhmann, 1982). By centralizing political power in the state supported by an expanding administration and a binding legal system the modern nation-state enhanced the differentiation process of the political system as well as that of other social systems (Luhmann, 1990a). The attempts at distinguishing between nationals and foreigners, for instance, show very clearly how the emergence of a political system changed the criteria for inclusion and exclusion and the relationships between the rulers and the ruled. Premodern forms of rule did not refer primarily to territories, but to persons. Inclusion into the political realm was not dependent on the locus of permanent residence, but on the status in the feudal order. Modern states engage in direct legal and political relationships with their populations (Bendix, 1964), and, therefore, states take a strong interest in controlling access to the territory. This is reflected in measures of coding membership in the political system and in other social systems territorially and nationally. Global migration poses a problem for modern states because it upsets the historically established attribution of populations to territories and the build-up of special relationships between populations and states which are expressed in legal instutions such as citizenship, but also in the concept of nation. Compared to the regional limits of migration in early modernity, migration in the twentieth century has become global due to big international wars and improved communication and transportation techniques of an increasingly interdependent world society (Sassen, 1988).

With respect to their populations as the social basis of power, nation-states tended to be isolationist and parochial. But the 'nationalist' goals of state policies turned out to have international consequences. Against the original intentions, the stimulation of nationally confined market exchange, industrial growth or scientific and technological research under the tutelage of nation-states furthered the emergence of transnational social systems. This is particularly evident in the economy. Although some economic exchanges had acquired international dimensions quite some time before the birth of the modern nation-state (Wallerstein, 1974), international industrial capitalism and global monetary exchanges paradoxically profited enormously from the state protection and support of national economies in the 18th and 19th century. The further increase of national wealth was only to be attained by allowing transborder commerce and investment. The globalization of function systems and their organizations stimulated international social mobility. Eventually, membership criteria for many organizations shed their national marking: by now foreigners can become civil servants even in the formerly tightly closed German civil service. It is against this background that nationally determined membership criteria based on citizenship or legal residence disrupt international interdependencies and mobility patterns. The tradition of 'nationalist' inclusion in social systems turns from an asset of nation-states (which allowed states to establish direct and exclusive political relationships with their citizens) into a problem (of how to safeguard state identity vis-à-vis mass immigration).

Effective control of cross-border migration remains an important indicator of the sovereignty of a state. In a decision of the late 19th century the Supreme Court of the United States of America confirmed '(the) right to exclude or to expel all aliens, or any class of aliens, absolutely or upon certain conditions, in war or in peace, (as) an inherent and inalienable right of every sovereign and independent nation, essential to its safety, its independence and its welfare...' (Fong Yue Ting v. United States, 149 U.S. 698, 711 (1893), quoted in Neuman, 1990, p. 36). In contrast to this bold statement, James Hollifield claims that the extension of liberal practices in the global economy in the wake of the postwar US-American hegemony has opened up many nation-states (particularly in Western Europe) to migration. One of the most significant consequences of this liberalization of the flow of capital and labor was the improvement of civil and social rights of migrants in the receiving countries. In this sense the extended rights of inclusion for migrants worked as 'a constraint on the actions of states to control their borders and as a potential pull factor, creating legal spaces for foreigners' (Hollifield, 1995). The most significant change in the legal status of migrants consists in the detachment of rights of migrants vis-à-vis states from the institution of citizenship (Sassen, 1998, p. 71). Nevertheless, nation-states take up the challenge of migration to their sovereignty by shoring up their borders (Sassen, 1996, pp. 59-99). This follows from the interest of nation-states in upholding exclusive legal and political relationships with their citizenries among the populations on their territories (Halfmann, 2000).

World Society

Empirical evidence for continuous and increasing globalization of economic (Reich, 1991), scientific (Stichweh, 1996), legal (Shapiro, 1993, Teubner, 1997) or political interchanges (Meyer, 1987) is abound. The first evidence for the emergence of world society can be dated back to the beginnings of global trade relations in the 16th century (Wallerstein, 1974). With the exploration of distant continents the perception of time synchronicity all over the world emerged – the first indicator of globalization. Obviously, the boundaries of the economic system are not identical with those of nation-states. Multinational firms hardly have one particular national reference; for some firms 'offshore' activities (and the concomitant tax payments) exceed by far those on the 'home' market (Ruggie, 1993, pp. 141-2). The close co-evolution of functional differentiation and world society is evident also in the remarkable homologies in the organizational structure of the educational or communication systems or of processes of urbanization across nations with diverging levels of wealth or political participation (Meyer, 1987, pp. 47-8; Ramirez and Boli, 1987; Meyer et al., 1992). Also, the scientific system operates on a global scale as the general acceptance of a lingua franca, the international composition of many research projects or the global exchange of scientific knowledge over the world wide web or at international conferences show (Schott, 1993; Stichweh, 1996).

Finally, the development of statehood shows remarkable isomorphies between older and newer states – despite marked differences in the economic power of these peripheral states which do not necessarily close the gap in wealth to the advanced states. 'Peripheral societies shift to modern forms of industrial and service economy activity; to modern state organizations; to modern educational systems; to modern welfare and military systems; in short, to all the institutional apparatus of modern social organization' (Meyer, 1987, p. 48). The modern nation-state was a prime causal factor in the dynamics of world societal evolution: not only in the sense that the spread of nation-states over the globe co-produced the world polity (inter-state relations) first in Europe and then worldwide (Tilly, 1992, pp. 161-91). The modern nation-state furthered functional differentiation of social systems. By establishing a national system of university science, the German nation-state for instance set the stage for the emergence of an autonomous social system of science which eventually superseded the national boundaries and spread across the world (Stichweh, 1996).

Two observations regarding nation-states follow from the concept of world society. First, from the point of view of a functionally differentiated world society, the attempts of nation-states to exert and stabilize influence over national segments of the economic, scientific or legal system appear as a constant and in many respects futile endeavor to uphold control in areas whose primary mechanisms of inclusion do not follow national and territorial criteria.[3] The reform of the asylum law in Germany is a case in point. The right of individual asylum was written into the German constitution under the impression of the flagrant disregard for human rights by the Nazi regime. The restrictive immigration policy of the German state and the liberal reading of the asylum article by German courts had made asylum the only legitimate form of immigration in the 80s and 90s. Despite the tightening of the recognition criteria for asylum seekers in 1993 Germany could not fully stop asylum immigration (Halfmann, 1999). Under the label of 'deregulation' many states eventually retreat from attempts to control fully their national segments of the world economy (Sassen, 1998, p. 51). By participating in the conditions for liberalized trade and production activities states resign to upholding at least some level of sovereignty. States agree for instance to establish 'free trade zones' on their territories which are exempt from some typical prerogatives of nation-states such as taxation. This process of 'de-nationalizing' of national territory does not only take place in developing countries, but also in highly industrialized nations (Sassen, 1996).

Second, states become more dependent on the political system of world society as a whole than on other individual states. This is expressed by the establishment of supranational organizations and inter-state agreements in international law which constrain the sovereignty of nation-states in many ways. Nation-states bind themselves by engaging in supranational organizations such as the European Union or international regimes such as the General Agreement on Trade and Tariffs

(GATT). While participation in international regimes often allows the states to remain 'masters of the treaties', supranational organizations tend to acquire traits of post-national statehood (for the case of the EU see Keohane and Hoffmann, 1991; Schmitter, 1996). Based on the principles of direct effect and supremacy, the European Court's rulings for instance become binding for the EU member states without any further involvement of national courts (Weiler, 1999). Supranational organizations not only constrain the sovereignty of the states which are their voluntary members, but in some cases already of non-member states, too. In 1998, the NATO intervention in Kosovo marked a step beyond any form of self-induced restraint of nation-state sovereignty when NATO air forces stroke out at targets in Serbia and Kosovo without being party to the conflict in Kosovo or having requested consent from Serbia to enter its territory.

Modern society is characterized by functional differentiation as the dominant mode of differentiation. Other forms of differentiation – stratificatory and segmentary differentiation – do play a role as catalysts and barriers for functional differentiation. And particularly the political system of world society is segmentarily differentiated into nation-states. The territorial basis of nation-states, which was and remains the precondition for states to distinguish between their respective collectivities, becomes a liability under conditions of growing world-wide migraion (Halfmann, 2000). The programmatic goal of national welfare states, reflected in Marshall's vision of a societal community of citizens, was the homogenization of life-chances within a nation-state territory. Globalization of inclusion, however, means that inequalities and asynchronicities do not follow territorial borders, but functional demarcations. Processes of differentiation and inclusion are fundamentally different for the educational, economic or political systems. The more access to labor markets is becoming dependent on achievement (rather than on ascriptive attributes) the less likely it is that living conditions will homogenize within territorial borders – not the least as a result of national welfare state policies. As a consequence, processes of income and status homogenization take place across nation-state borders depending on different levels of qualification (and not on national belonging) of the labor force. With functional differentiation establishing itself on a world scale the 'institutionalization of uniform (territorial) borders for all social systems becomes problematic...One can no longer assume that the societal borders for included and excluded persons remain the same when one switches from political activities to scientific communication or economic transactions and love relationships...This implies that the unity of society which embraces all functions can only be conceived as world society' (Luhmann, 1975, p. 60; translation by the author). In other words, unity and homogeneity within state borders become the exception, particularly in those areas of world society which are most strongly affected by processes of globalization.

The globalization of politics as well as of economics or law has changed the relationship between individuals and the state in important ways. In mature nation-states which are well integrated into world society, citizens are less attached to 'their' nations and national pride loses its role as a constitutive element of personhood. This is in part due to migrants who by sharing the welfare state services with the indigenous population devaluate the meaning of the nation for the formerly privileged community of citizens. States acknowledge this fact by the way the transgressing of borders is organized. The regulation of transborder movements is no longer solely dependent on the citizenship status of individuals, but also on the status of legal residency (Zacher, 1993). In addition, refugees are allowed entry on the basis of human rights which states acknowledge as part of their constitutional creed and by which they are willing to bind themselves in many ways (Soysal, 1994). Finally, transborder movements are contingent upon intergovernmental agreements or supranational regimes by which states agree to restrict their sovereignty under the umbrella concept of economic and political integration. The European Union is an often cited example of this kind of managed self-restraint with respect to border controls and the mobility rights of individuals (Brochmann, 1996; Koslowski, 1998; Geddes, 2000).

But nation-states apparently do not simply accept the loss of sovereignty resulting from global mobility of capital, goods and persons. As the identity of nation-states depends on a functioning relationship with 'their' citizens and organizations states are particularly sensitive to the international mobility of people. States attempt to prevent the sovereignty-eroding impact of migration by shoring up their borders, by forcing immigrants to become citizens and by counteracting the business enterprises' tactics of 'shopping around' for best conditions in several nation-states. Prevention on the one hand demands increasing efforts. Member states of the European Union for instance, particularly if they consider themselves non-immigration countries, are very concerned about asylum immigration. Through readmission agreements with their neighbouring states and by implementing the rule of 'safe third countries' EU states try to shift the burden of asylum immigration to the countries of origin or transit (Lavenex, 1999; Angenendt, 1999; Hailbronner, 2000). Integration and assimilation on the other hand require strong national 'creeds' which tend to become the more abstract and meaningless the more culturally diverse immigrants are and the less loyal citizens become. During the 90s, France for instance departed further and further from its originally strong assimilationist stance to become increasingly selective about the kind of immigrants that were deemed to be ready for and capable of assimilation (Wihtol de Wenden, 1998). In a global network of communication, work and exchange market participation is no longer confined to one state territory: those who offer or demand labor are no longer necessarily members of one state only and often do not remain on just one single state territory while working. Modern welfare states, however, provide their services on the basis of one single citizenship or longterm legal residence. Border-crossing individuals pose a problem for the welfare state's claim to mediate inclusion in social systems within their territory. The question is: should these individuals be subject to the social security rules of the sending or the receiving country? Within the European Union for instance the deepened market integration puts severe strains on the individuality of the welfare state systems of the member countries. Originally designed only for their respective citizenries they now have to cope with the deregulatory effects of liberalized EU markets (Scharpf, 1996).

The dilemma of the modern nation-state has become the dilemma of political sociology. As long as political sociology concentrates its efforts on the nation-state and on the relationship between the state and civil society it will have to live with the slow disappearance of its subject matter. To safeguard its research field political sociology will have explicitly to take notice of the new social and political realities and to revise its terminological and theoretical strategies.

Reconfiguring Political Sociology

The decreasing sovereignty of nation-states and the growing importance of supra-national organizations have been noted and debated many times (Krasner, 1988; Thompson and Krasner, 1989; Cable, 1995; Biersteker and Weber, 1996; Freeman, 1998). What is lacking, however, is a convincing theoretical approach which integrates within one conceptual frame the effects of a global economy on politics, the growing interdependence of nation-states and the role of migration for welfare and nation-state inclusion. It is no coincidence that neither migration nor world society are so far considered relevant topics in the authoritative statements on the scope of political sociology (Bendix and Lipset, 1966; Janowitz, 1968; Orum, 1988; Rush, 1992).[4] Modern sociological systems theory offers a theoretical framework which reformulates the established notions of political sociology such that it can successfully address the causes and effects of globalization.

Niklas Luhmann's theory of politics in modern (world) society integrates concepts from evolutionary biology, general systems theory and the sociology of organizations to describe modern society as functionally differentiated world society (Luhmann, 1982, p. 139; for an overview of his theory see Lange and Schimank, 2001).Within sociological systems theory, society is the encompassing social system which contains all social communications and which itself has no social environment; all other types of social systems – function, organization and interaction systems – are social environments for each other (Luhmann, 1995, chapter 10). Sociological systems theory does not follow Parsons' premise in assuming that functions can be derived from structural exigencies of maintaining societal equilibria. The starting point is instead the idea that social order is an improbable evolutionary event and that social systems are forms of order which can sustain the pressure toward decomposition by establishing a structure which allows maintaining a difference between themselves and their environments. This difference functions as a border which helps distinguish between internal and external events of a system. An interaction system such as a family for instance distinguishes between events which belong to the family and those which are part of the outer world by coding communications as either private and intimate or as public and detached. By further differentiating the meaning of privacy and intimacy for an increasing range of issues a family system can attain communicative closure toward other social systems. Social systems develop communicative complexity, comparable to genetic complexity in living systems by increasing the possible interactions of its elements. Complexity in turn is a prerequisite for managing the various events of the environment which have a potential for challenging the structure of a social system. The evolution of society can be reconstructed as the development of such structures (social systems) which withstand evolutionary pressure toward dissolution by establishing sufficiently complex concepts of themselves and their environments.

What distinguishes modern from earlier forms of society is that problems of social order are addressed by way of functional differentiation. Functional differentiation of society means that social systems emerge within society which exclusively address particular problems of social order. Thus, the political system evolves as a social system which is oriented at providing collectively binding decisions, the economic system at satisfying future needs, the legal system at maintaining normative expectations about social behavior. One needs, however, to stress that the treatment of certain general societal problems (such as power, truth, justice) within the context of function systems is justified and valid only for these function systems; it is their raison d'être, but it is one which is not necessarily acknowledged as such by the other function systems. Different from Parsons' concept of the integrative function of the cultural system sociological systems theory does not assume that there is a societal instance which orchestrates the division of labor between the diverse function systems. In other words: the concrete relationships between these realms of societal problem-solving are permanently shifting. The performance of the educational system has a different meaning for judges (legal system), professors of education (science system) and for parents (family of system).

Systems theory distinguishes between the functional reference – the exclusive acquisition and management of societal problems – and the performative reference of function systems – the diverging performances of function systems for other function systems and their organizations. The evolutionary approach to social systems allows to depart from Parsons' 'analytic' AGIL-schematism and its ensuing architectural rigidities. Empirically, there are more than four function systems: apart from economics, politics and law there are the education, art, science or mass media systems; there is, however, no cultural system which would provide an overarching integration of society. And not all 'candidates' such as sports or social work have (yet?) developed into function systems (Luhmann, 1997).

Premised on the concept that society is the ensemble of social communications and actions, politics can be conceptualized as one particular form of societal communication. Politics is that particular form of social communication which claims exclusiveness in producing collectively binding decisions and which organizes this activity by means of power. In framing politics as decision-making which uses power as a medium for implementation Luhmann revives the functionalist tradition in political sociology. This tradition originates in Talcott Parsons' seminal reflections on politics as a functionally differentiated sphere in society and on power as the medium of political exchanges (Parsons, 1967). This functionalist view of politics was further elaborated in David Easton's system analysis of politics. Easton introduced a fruitful definition of the particular function of politics for society: the authoritative allocation of decisions. 'We may describe the political system as that behavior or set of interactions through which authoritative allocations (or binding decicions) are made and implemented for a society' (Easton, 1968, p. 285). To define society and politics on such a level of abstraction avoids equating society with the nation-state and politics with national politics. Luhmann has pointed at the close connection between the theory of functional differentiation and the concept of society as world society (Luhmann, 1990b).

If one wishes to follow the general theoretical premises of advanced sociological systems theory it does not make much sense to distinguish between society and the global system (as in Giddens, 1990). This distinction creates the impression that transnational phenomena such as the Internet for instance are not part of society, that globalization may affect society, but that it somehow takes place outside of the societal confines. But obviously transnational phenomena such as the web communication are also social and can be clearly distinguished from non-social (natural, psychical) phenomena. Communications like e-mail messages can be seperated from the technical infrastructure (servers, end-user computers, telephone cables etc.) that enables this communication: the former is social, the latter physical. Similar to Giddens, most authors in sociology continue to equate society with the nation-state and then try to label phenomena which transcend nation-state boundaries as global (Robertson, 1992; Albrow and King, 1990).

Sociological systems theory offers an exit from this impasse of theorizing in political sociology by devising society as world society and by identifying states as subunits of the world polity. The political system of world society can then be related to its social environments – other function systems which, to varying degrees, are also global in character. This then allows to take a fresh view of two central problems of current globalization research: the relation of states to organizations of other social systems, such as business firms, and the relation of states to other (particularly: supranational) organizations of the world polity. When states are no longer the only relevant organizations in the political system of world society and when organizations of other function systems can effectively disregard to some degree the authority of the state, power can no longer be localized only in the relationship between nation-states and their collectivities and between nation-states and other nation-states. The reflection on the locus and scope of political power needs to be renewed.

Systems theory has developed further the theoretical implications of power as a medium of politics. The Weberian concept of power as the capacity to enforce one's will on someone else's 'leads to a transitive, hierarchical conception of power, excluding the possibility of circular and reciprocal power relations. It sees powerholders' calculations essentially as predicting a causal sequence...that is oriented by fixed needs and by the ability to prevail in cases of conflict' (Luhmann, 1982, p. 159). Power is defined instead as a selection where the powerholder selects the action of the subordinate. 'Power exists whenever a decision maker chooses one specific possibility from among many and when this selection is in turn accepted by others as a premise for their own decision making – even though it obviously is based on a selective decision' (Luhmann, 1982, p. 151). Power is thus a medium which can be brought into a form by decisions. As a medium power remains invisible: it is a means through which decisions can be processed. Power can, however, be made visible by symbolic or instrumental means. Power is the application of a causal scheme to communications, it identifies a cause – the anticipation of obeying an order – and an effect – the factual obedience. This implies that power can be observed only when a change of behavior takes place. Power is most effective when it remains tacit; it can be challenged and lose its causal effectiveness when the demand for obedience and the sanctioning potential (in terms of physical violence) need to be proven.

States remain the central organizations of the political system because the capacity to exert power for the issuing and implementing of binding decisions depends on functioning relations to an identifiable collectivity. For this purpose states need to keep control over their respective collectivities – which not only consist of populations (citizens and aliens), but also of organizations on their territories (firms, universities, hospitals etc.) (Luhmann, 1982; Luhmann, 1990a). The question which needs to be asked in the light of the effects of global mobility of capital, goods and persons is how states can muster (a) enough power and (b) sufficient discriminatory criteria to uphold stable relationships to their collectivities. As to power, nation-states have lost some of their power to supranational organizations. When power means that the capacity of political organizations for making decisions becomes the premise of the decisions of other political organizations, then it becomes evident that there are organizations in the political system of world society which can constrain the decisional capacity of nation-states. Nevertheless, states are still the only instances which can establish enduring relationships with their respective collectivities and, thus, deal with the implications of migration. This has become a latent, but obstinate stumbling stone for the attempts at constituting a common migration policy within the European Union. Despite the emergence of some aspects of post-national stateness (European citizenship, European Courts, supranational governance structures), the European Union has not developed into a state form which enters into direct relationships with a collectivity of citizens (Abromeit, 1998). Consequently, migration policy remains the domain of union member states despite the expressed will of EU member states to establish a union migration policy (Collinson, 1994; Spencer, 2003).

As to the discriminatory capacities of states, similar problems arise. During the period of nation-state building, the collectivity was circumscribed by the concept of the nation; the nation is semantically constituted by reference to 'demos' or 'ethnos', to political or 'cultural' (linguistic or ethnic) definitions of a national community (Francis, 1965). The belief that states should be associated with ethnically homogeneous nations was a product of the late 19th century (Hobsbawm,

1990). The idea of a nation was based on the (counterfactual) trust in the capacity of states for rejecting unwanted immigrants, for allowing 'surplus' populations to emigrate and for assimilating wanted immigrants. Once the process of nation-state building has come to a close the concept of belonging to a nation-wide community of citizens loses its appeal; other mechanisms and addresses for regulating inclusion and soliciting loyalty have emerged (Tambini, Crouch, and Eder, 2001).

The creeping decoupling of states from their established collectivities which results from international migratory mobility and the partial loss of the capacity for exerting power to supranational organizations might become the central questions of future research programs in political sociology.

Conclusion

The self-limitation of traditional political sociology which is inherent in its convention of equating society with the nation-state has led to a rather narrow treatment of migration, if it is perceived as an issue at all. Migration has been dealt with as a problem of inequality and segregation and of how to overcome it. This has certainly stimulated a rich research tradition which allows comparisons between states according to political and non-political constraints imposed on migrants when they attempt to manage inclusion in the diverse social systems of their host country (for recent literature see Faist, 1995; Bade and Weiner, 1997; Santel and Hollifield, 1998). But this view has in many respects neglected the deeper social implications of migration – that modern migration is an indicator of the growing depth and scope of world society. Placing migration, however, in the framework of world society and perceiving of politics as one among several function systems of society allows to take a broader and richer view of migration. Within such a frame, political sociology would conceive of migration as a problem of inclusion in a variety of social systems (economy, education, health) of which the political system with its organizational segments (the nation-states) is of paramount importance. From this perspective, the nation-state appears as an organization which attempts and sometimes struggles to maintain its historical position as gatekeeper for migrants who seek inclusion in social systems. Through the institutions of citizenship and welfare the nation-state had secured itself a pivotal position in regulating access to markets (economic system), knowledge (educational system), justice (legal system) or physical well-being (health system). The growing autonomy of function systems on a global scale has eroded this relatively strong position of the nation-states. Migration is prompted by a variety of causes which stem from the divergent conditions of inclusion and exclusion in the different social systems. The more these social systems become global the more migratory mobility will increase. Nation-states disrupt these global interdependencies because of the territorial marking of their mode of inclusion. Nation-states set limits to political inclusion (and, therefore, to migration); nation-states are bound to pursue restrictive immigration policies because of the constraint built into the function of politics: to produce binding decisions for an identifiable and (possibly) stable collectivity. Thus, migration is a potential threat to the sovereignty of nation-states because, as long as migrants are not citizens, they are not part of the popular base on which the nation-state's power rests. The question arises whether states need to develop alternatives to the territorial marking of political inclusion or whether the exertion of power will shift to some degree from territorial (nation-states) to non-territorial (supranational organizations) forms of rule (Halfmann, 1998).

Through the broadening of its theoretical basis political sociology might take notice of the implications of migration for the modern nation-state in an appropriate way. Political sociology is challenged to reformulate the question of stateness and political power within a global context. The study of migration allows to place the relationship of the modern nation-states to the social basis of power in an international and transnational context and at the same time to examine the transient character of the 'nation-state solution' to the problem of generating and confining political power.

Notes

1 For a critique of Marshall's nation-state parochialism see Halfmann and Bommes, 1998.

2 Which had 'shrunk' in the wake of the two World Wars of the twentieth century. Particularly, the post-WWII period witnessed substantial decreases in international trade and mobility. This provided the breeding ground for 'Keynesianism' and 'Beveridge' plans, the belief that states could steer their national economies and remove social inequality by expanding the welfare state (Scharpf, 1996, p. 16).

3 The observation that political issues are no longer confined to the state sphere and that almost any social issue has become subject to politicization has led the so-called New Political Sociology to believe that the distinction between politics and other social systems no longer makes sense (Nash, 2000). A similar point is made in the debate of international relations theory and comparative politics on private and public governance (Rosenau and Czempiel, 1992; see Kohler-Koch's statement that '(t)he state is no longer an actor in its own right' (Kohler-Koch, 1996, p. 190)). Obviously, these conclusions are based on a confusion of function with organization systems. When states are no longer the only relevant actors in the political system of world society and have to share power with supranational organizations, this means that the political system is further differentiating rather than dissolving. And when due to a history of (welfare) state intervention many more issues than previously can become subject to political conflict, the system of politics and its organizations is confirmed in its operative modes rather than marginalized.

4 Bottomore's second edition of 'Political Sociology' (Bottomore, 1993) contains a chapter entitled 'Global Politics in the Twentieth Century' which contains, however, hardly any explicit reference to the particularly global aspects of politics. Nash claims that the 'Weberian' state as a hierarchical organization had to give way to a much more decentralized, pluralized and globalized form of politics which is better understood by applying post-modernist concepts of political theory in the Foucault tradition (Nash, 2000, similarly: Owen, 2001). The increased politicization of social issues (such as familial, gender oder environmental issues which used to be non-political) almost

always includes the state as arbitrating, regulating or funding instance and indicates the overburdening rather than the disappearance of the state.

References

Abromeit, H. (1998), *Democracy in Europe. Legitimising Politics in a Non-State Polity,* Berghahn Publishers, New York.

Albrow, M. and King, E. (eds.) (1990), *Globalization, Knowledge and Society: Readings from International Sociology,* Russel Sage Foundation, London.

Alonso, W. (ed.) (1987), *Population in an Interacting World,* Harvard UP, Cambridge, MA.

Angenendt, St. (ed.) (1999), *Asylum and Migration Policies in the European Union,* Europa-Union Verlag, Bonn.

Bade, K.J. and Weiner, M. (eds.) (1997), *Migration Past, Migration Future: Germany and the United States,* Berghahn, Oxford.

Bauböck, R. (1994), *Transnational Citizenship: Membership and Right in International Migration,* Edward Elgar, Aldershot.

Bendix, R. (1964), *Nation-Building and Citizenship. Studies of our Changing Social Order,* John Wiley & Sons, New York.

Bendix, R. and Lipset, S.M. (1966), 'The Field of Political Sociology', in L.A. Coser (ed.), *Political Sociology,* Harper & Row, New York, pp. 9-46.

Biersteker, Th.S. and Weber, C. (eds.) (1996), *State Sovereignty as a Social Construction,* Cambridge UP, Cambrige.

Böckenförde, E.-W. (1991), 'Die sozialen und politischen Ordnungsideen der französischen Revolution', in K. Michalski (ed.), *Europa und die Civil Society,* Klett-Cotta, Stuttgart, pp. 103-17.

Bommes, M. and Halfmann, J. (eds.) (1998), *Migration in nationalen Wohlfahrtsstaaten: Theoretische und vergleichende Untersuchungen,* Universitätsverlag Rasch, Osnabrück.

Bommes, M. (1999), *Migration und nationaler Wohlfahrtsstaat. Ein differenzierungstheoretischer Entwurf,* Westdeutscher Verlag, Opladen.

Bottomore, T. (1993), *Political Sociology,* 2nd ed., University of Minnesota Press, Minneapolis.

Brochmann, G. (1996), *European Integration and Immigration from Third Countries,* Scandinavian UP, Oslo.

Cable, V. (1995), 'The Diminished Nation-State: A Study in the Loss of Economic Power', *Daedalus,* 124 (2), pp. 23-53.

Castles, St. and Kosack, G. (1973), *Immigrant Workers and Class Structure in Western Europe,* Oxford UP, London.

Castles, St. and Miller, M. (1993), *The Age of Migration. International Population Movements in the Modern World,* Guilford, New York.

Collinson, S. (1994), *Europe and International Migration,* Pinter, London and New York.

Depew, D.J. (1992), 'The Polis Transfigured: Aristotle's Politics and Marx's Critique of Hegel's 'Philosophy of Right', in G.E. McCarthy (ed.), *Marx and Aristotle,* Rowman & Littlefield, Savage, MD, pp. 37-73.

Easton, D. (1968), 'Political Science', in: D.L. Sills (ed.), *International Encyclopedia of the Social Sciences,* Vol. 11 and 12, Macmillan and Free Press, New York, pp. 282-98.

Faist, Th. (1995), *Social Citzenship for Whom? Young Turks in Germany and Mexican Americans in the United States,* Avebury, Aldershot.

Francis, E. (1965), *Ethnos und Demos: Soziologische Beiträge zur Volkstheorie,* Duncker & Humblot, Berlin.
Freeman, G.P. (1998), 'The Decline of Sovereignty? Politics and Immigration Restrictions in Liberal States', in Ch. Joppke (ed.), *Challenge to the Nation-State,* Oxford UP, Oxford, pp. 86-108.
Geddes, A. (2000), *Immigration and European Integration: Towards Fortress Europe?* Manchester UP, Manchester.
Gellner, E. (1983), *Nations and Nationalism,* Basil Blackwell, Oxford.
Giddens, A. (1985), *The Nation-State and Violence,* Stanford UP, Stanford.
Giddens, A. (1990), *The Consequences of Modernity,* Polity Press, Oxford.
Grawert, R. (1973), *Staat und Staatsangehörigkeit. Verfassungsgeschichtliche Untersuchung zur Entstehung der Staatsangehörigkeit,* Duncker & Humblot, Berlin.
Habermas, J. (1975), *Legitimation Crisis,* Beacon Press, Boston.
Hailbronner, K. (2000), *Immigration and Asylum Law and Policy of the European Union,* Kluwer Law International, The Hague.
Halfmann, J. (1998), 'Citizenship Universalism, Migration and the Risks of Exclusion', *British Journal of Sociology,* 49 (4), pp. 513-33.
Halfmann, J. (1999), 'Two Discourses of Citizenship in Germany. The Difference between Public Debate and Administrative Practice', in J.S. Brady, B. Crawford, and S.E. Wiliarty (eds.), *The Postwar Transformation of Germany: Democracy, Prosperity, and Nationhood,* The University of Michigan Press, Ann Arbor, MI. pp. 378-98.
Halfmann, J. (2000), 'The Welfare State and Territory', in M. Bommes and A. Geddes (eds.), *Migration and the Welfare State in Contemporary Europe,* Routledge, London.
Halfmann, J. and Bommes, M. (1998), 'Staatsbürgerschaft, Inklusionsvermittlung und Migration. Zum Souveränitätsverlust des Wohlfahrtsstaates', in Bommes and Halfmann (eds.), *Migration in nationalen Wohlfahrtsstaaten,* pp. 81-101.
Hobsbawm, E.J. (1990), *Nations and Nationalism since 1780. Programme, Myth, Reality,* Cambridge UP, Cambridge.
Hollifield, J.F. (1995), 'The Migration Crisis in Western Europe: The Search for a National Model', in: K.J. Bade (ed.), *Migration – Ethnizität – Konflikt. Systemfragen und Fallstudien,* Universitätsverlag Rasch, Osnabrück, pp. 367-402.
Horowitz, I.L. (1972), *Foundations of Political Sociology,* Harper & Row, New York.
Janowitz, M. (1968), 'Political Sociology', in D.L. Sills (ed.), *International Encyclopedia of the Social Sciences,* Vol. 11 and 12, Macmillan and Free Press, New York, pp. 298-307.
Joppke, Ch. (1998), *Challenge to the Nation-State,* Oxford, UP, Oxford.
Keohane, R.O. and Hoffmann, St. (1991), 'Institutional Change in Europe in the 1980s', in R.E. Keohane and St. Hoffmann (eds.), *The New European Community: Decision-Making and Institutional Change,* Westview Press, Boulder, pp. 1-39.
Kohler-Koch, B. (1996), 'The Strength of Weakness: The Transformation of Governance in the EU', in: S. Gustavsson and L. Wewin (eds.), *The Future of the Nation-State: Essays on Cultural Pluralism and Political Integration,* Nerenius and Santerus, Stockholm, pp. 160-210.
Koslowski, R. (1998), 'EU Migration Regimes: Established and Emergent', in Ch. Joppke (ed.), *Challenge to the Nation-State: Immigration in Western Europe and the United States,* Oxford UP, Oxford. pp. 153-88.
Krasner, St.D. (1988), 'Sovereignty: An Institutional Perspective', *Comparative Political Studies,* 21 (1), pp. 66-94.

Lange, St. and Schimank, U. (2001), 'A Political Sociology for Complex Societies: Niklas Luhmann', in K. Nash and J. Scott (eds.), *The Blackwell Companion to Political Sociology*, Blackwell, Oxford, pp. 60-70.

Lavenex, S. (1999), *Safe Third Countries. Extending the EU Asylum and Immigration Policies to Central and Eastern Europe*, Central European UP, Budapest.

Lipset, S.M. (1963), *Political Man. The Social Bases of Politics*, Doubleday Anchor Books, Garden City, NY.

Luhmann, N. (1975), 'Die Weltgesellschaft', in N. Luhmann, *Soziologische Aufklärung. Aufsätze zur Theorie der Gesellschaft*, Vol. 2, Westdeutscher Verlag, Opladen, pp. 51-71.

Luhmann, N. (1982), 'Politics as a Social System', in N. Luhmann, *The Differentiation of Society*, Columbia UP, New York, pp. 138-65.

Luhmann, N. (1990a), 'The "State" of the Political System', in N. Luhmann, *Essays on Self-Reference*, Columbia UP, New York, pp. 165-74.

Luhmann, N. (1990b), 'The World Society as a Social System', ibidem, pp. 175-90.

Luhmann, N. (1995), *Social Systems*, Stanford UP, Stanford.

Luhmann, N. (1997), *Die Gesellschaft der Gesellschaft*, Suhrkamp, Frankfurt a.M.

Luhmann, N. (1998), 'Der Staat des politischen Systems', in U. Beck (ed.), *Perspektiven der Weltgesellschaft*, Suhrkamp, Frankfurt a.M., pp. 345-80.

Marshall, Th.H. (1977), *Class, Citizenship, and Social Development*, University of Chicago Press, Chicago and London.

Marx, K. (1960), 'Der 18. Brumaire des Louis Bonaparte', in K. Marx and F. Engels, *Werke*, Vol. 8, Dietz, Berlin, pp. 110-207.

Meyer, J.W. (1987), 'The World Polity and the Authority of the Nation-State', in G.M. Thomas et al. (eds.), *Institutional Structure: Constituting State, Society, and the Individual*, Russel Sage Foundation, Newbury Park, pp. 41-70.

Meyer, J.W. et al. (1992), *School Knowledge for the Masses: World Models and National Primary Curricula Categories in the Twentieth Century*, Falmer, Washington, DC and London.

Michels, R. (1962) (1915), *Political Parties. A Sociological Study of the Oligarchical Tendencies of Modern Democracy*, Collier-Macmillan, New York.

Miles, R. and Thränhardt, D. (eds.) (1995), *Migration and European Integration. The Dynamics of Inclusion and Exclusion*, Pinter Publishers, London.

Mosca, G. (1939) (1896), *The Ruling Class*, McGraw-Hill, New York.

Nash, K. (2000), *Contemporary Political Sociology. Globalization, Politics and Power*, Blackwell, Oxford.

Neuman, G.L. (1990), 'Immigration and Judicial Review in the Federal Republic of Germany', *New York University Journal of International Law*, 23, pp. 35-85.

Orum, A. (1988), 'Political Sociology', in N.J. Smelser (ed.), *Handbook of Sociology*, Russel Sage Foundation, Newbury Park, pp. 393-423.

Owen, D. (2001), '"Postmodern" Sociology', in K. Nash and J. Scott (eds.), The Blackwell Companion to Political Sociology, Blackwell, Oxford, pp. 71-81.

Pareto, V. (1935) (1915-1919), *The Mind and Society*, Vols. I-IV, Jonathan Cape, London.

Parsons, T. (1967), 'On the Concept of Political Power', in T. Parsons, *Sociological Theory and Modern Society*, The Free Press, New York, pp. 297-354.

Perez-Diaz, V. (1978), *State, Bureaucracy and Civil Society. A Critical Discussion of the Political Theory of Karl Marx*, Macmillan, London.

Piore, M. (1979), *Birds of Passage. Migrant Labor and Industrial Societies*, Cambridge UP, Cambridge.

Poulantzas, N. (1972), *Pouvoir politique et classes sociales,* 2 Vols., François Maspero, Paris.

Ramirez, F.O. and Boli, J. (1987), 'Global Patterns of Educational Institutionalization', in G.W. Thomas et al. (eds.), *Institutional Structure. Constituting State, Society, and the Individual,* Russel Sage Foundation, Newbury Park, pp. 150-72.

Reich, R. (1991), *The Work of Nations,* Knopf, New York.

Richmond, A.H. (1987), *Immigration and Ethnic Conflict,* Macmillan, London.

Robertson, R. (1992), *Globalization. Social Theory and Global Culture,* Russel Sage Foundation, London.

Rosenau, J.N. and Czempiel, E.-O. (eds.) (1992), *Governance without Government: Order and Change in World Politics,* Cambridge UP, Cambridge.

Ruggie, J.G. (1993), 'Territoriality and Beyond: Problematizing Modernity in International Relations', *International Organization,* 47 (1), pp. 139-74.

Rush, M. (1992), *Politics and Society. An Introduction to Political Sociology,* Harvester Wheatsheaf, New York.

Santel, B. and Hollifield, J.F. (1998), 'Erfolgreiche Integrationsmodelle? Zur wirtschaftlichen Situation von Einwanderern in Deutschland und den USA', Bommes and Halfmann (eds.), *Migration in nationalen Wohlfahrtsstaaten,* pp. 123-45.

Sassen, S. (1988), *The Mobility of Labor and Capital: A Study in International Investment and Labor Flow,* Cambridge UP, Cambridge.

Sassen, S. (1996), *Losing Control? Sovereignty in an Age of Globalization,* Columbia UP, New York.

Sassen, S. (1998), 'The *de facto* Transnationalizing of Immigration Policy', in Ch. Joppke (ed.), *Challenge to the Nation-State,* Oxford UP, Oxford, pp. 49-85.

Scharpf, F.W. (1996), 'Negative and Positive Integration in the Political Economy of European Welfare States', in G. Marks et al., *Governance in the European Union,* Russel Sage Foundation, London, pp. 15-39.

Schmitter, Ph.C. (1996), 'Imagining the Future of the Euro-Polity with the Help of New Concepts', ibidem, pp. 121-65.

Schott, Th. (1993), 'World Science: Globalization of Institutions and Participation', *Science, Technology and Human Values,* 18, pp. 196-208.

Scott, J. (2001), 'Studying Power', in K. Nash and J. Scott (eds.), *The Blackwell Companion to Political Sociology,* Blackwell, Oxford, pp. 83-91.

Sellin, V. (1978), 'Politik', in O. Brunner et al. (eds.), *Geschichtliche Grundbegriffe,* Vol. 4, Klett-Cotta, Stuttgart, pp. 789-874.

Shapiro, M. (1993), 'The Globalization of Law', in *Indiana Journal of Global Legal Studies,* 1, pp. 37-64.

Soysal, Y. (1994), *Limits of Citizenship. Migrants and Postnational Membership in Europe,* University of Chicago Press, Chicago.

Spencer, S. (ed.) (2003), *The Politics of Migration: Managing Opportunity, Conflict and Change,* Blackwell, Malden, MA.

Spruyt, H. (1994), *The Sovereign State and its Competitors: An Analysis of Systems Change,* Princeton UP, Princeton.

Stammer, O. and Weingart, P. (1972), *Politische Soziologie,* Juventa, München.

Stichweh, R. (1996), 'Science in the System of World Society', *Social Science Information,* 35 (2), pp. 327-40.

Swaan, A. de (1988), *In Care of the State. Health Care, Education and Welfare in Europe and the USA in the Modern Era,* Oxford UP, New York.

Tambini, D., Crouch, C. and Eder, K. (eds.) (2001), *Citizenship, Markets and the State,* Oxford University Press, Oxford.

Teubner, G. (ed.) (1997), *Global Law without a State,* Aldershot, Dartmouth.

Thomson, J. and Krasner, St.D. (1989), 'Global Transactions and the Consolidation of Sovereignty', in E.-O. Czempiel and J. Rosenau (eds.), *Global Changes and Theoretical Challenges. Approaches to World Politics for the 1990s,* Lexington Books, Lexington, MA, pp. 195-219.

Tilly, Ch. (1992), *Coercion, Capital, and European States, AD 990-1992,* Blackwell, Cambridge, MA and Oxford.

Wallerstein, I. (1974), *The Modern World-System I. Capitalist Agriculture and the Origins of the European World-Economy in the Sixteenth Century,* Academic Press, New York.

Weiler, J.H.H. (1999), 'The Transformation of Europe', in J.H.H. Weiler, *The Constitution of Europe,* Cambridge UP, Cambridge, pp. 10-101.

Weiner, M. (1994), *The Global Migration Crisis: Challenges to States and Human Rights,* Harper Collins, New York.

Wihtol de Wenden, C. (1998), 'Einwanderung im Wohlfahrtsstaat: das Beispiel Frankreich', in Bommes and Halfmann (eds.), *Migration in nationalen Wohlfahrtsstaaten,* pp. 223-37.

Zacher, H.F. (1993), 'Grundfragen des internationalen Sozialrechts', in H.F. Zacher, *Abhandlungen zum Sozialrecht,* Müller, Heidelberg, pp. 431-54.

PART III
ISSUES AND DILEMMAS
OF INTERDISCIPLINARITY

Chapter 7

Law and Politics and Migration Research: On the Potential and Limits of Interdisciplinarity

Roland Bank and Dirk Lehmkuhl

Introduction[1]

Given its concern with phenomena of a fundamentally transnational character, migration research may be regarded as a particularly fruitful field for inter-disciplinary approaches which bring together lawyers and political scientists inter-ested in processes of internationalization. In the European context, for instance, lawyers might ask for the input of political scientists because the relative immaturity of the common European legal stock of migration laws requires a certain knowledge of the historical, political and institutional background of national provisions. Indeed, in recent years it has become increasingly fashionable for both lawyers and political scientists to emphasize the interdisciplinary character of their work, in particular in the sub-disciplines of comparative, international and European law on the one hand and comparative politics and international relations on the other.

Yet, notwithstanding that these two disciplines have rediscovered this, all too often the promise of interdisciplinarity is not kept. Rather, interdisciplinarity is confused with either a crude instrumentalization of other disciplines' knowledge while ignoring the underlying methodological assumptions or an oversimplified dissolution of disciplinary distinctions. What is frequently missing is threefold: on a general level, a reflection of the potential gains and the potential risks or obstacles related to the collaboration of the two disciplines; on a more concrete level, an awareness of complementary concepts and approaches; and finally, on the most concrete level, the identification of specific topics in which gains from common interests and cooperation can be realized.

In this chapter we set out to assess the potential as well as possible short-comings of studies by lawyers and political scientists which claim to be inter-disciplinary. Starting from a lawyer's point of view, the argument is that migration research in the European context is a promising topic for the collaboration of lawyers and political scientists. In their efforts to make proposals for European

Community[2] provisions lawyers might find it particularly helpful to make use of the political scientists' capacity to analyze the embeddedness of norms in different societal and institutional situations at the level of the member states. The examples given in the next section are followed by general considerations about the potential gains and risks of cooperation between the two disciplines.

It will be argued that an attempt to achieve the cross-fertilization of law and politics in general – and in the field of migration research in particular – does not require a convergence of the disciplines or even converting scholars from these different disciplines. Rather – and already demanding enough – disciplined interdisciplinarity is based on the mutual awareness of other (sub)disciplines' ontologies, epistemological assumptions and methodologies as an indispensable precondition for reaping the benefits of cooperation across disciplinary boundaries. At a very basic level, such an awareness facilitates communication between lawyers and political scientists. Although not every problem a lawyer faces may be translated into a problem of political science, knowledge of the other discipline's thinking and arguing allows for cooperative work, for instance by providing complementary insights into a specific topic.

Migration Research as a Promising Terrain for Interdisciplinary Approaches

In principle, a lawyer's educational background equips him or her with the methodological tools for analyzing the context of laws on migration in the European Union and its member states *de lege lata*, i.e., the rules existing on the national level and the legal framework set by international law and primary European law. Given a German legal education, for instance, the lawyer's traditional methodology for elucidating the meaning of a certain provision or a legal field includes various forms of interpretation: literal (including grammar), systematical (exploring the position of the provision within the statute or other legal text in question), historical (using the history of the adoption of the text to be derived, for instance, from parliamentary debates) and teleological (reflecting the aim and purpose of the text).[3] In order to analyze the legal situation with a view to potential inconsistencies, gaps, ambiguities and incompatibilities by employing norms incorporated in national constitutions or international treaties, the lawyer usually does not need the assistance of a political scientist. Yet, to answer questions such as why a specific set of rules is interpreted differently in different countries or why there is a gap between a written norm and its implementation, it can be helpful to turn to political scientists,[4] whose answers might help the lawyer to make suggestions for new laws to be adopted (*de lege ferenda*).

In a similar vein, political scientists are well-equipped with elaborated methodological and analytical tools for describing and explaining the dynamics of a specific area or domain with respect to three dimensions: the formal aspect of institutions and rules (polity), the content and output of interactions of political actors (policy), and the procedural and conflictual dimension involving the process of policy making in a certain institutional setting (politics). Yet, in order to fully understand the impact of a court decision, for instance, or the potential extent of and limits for interpreting a certain provision, the political scientist has to rely on the lawyers' aforementioned methodology and their expertise (for instance Bengo-extea et al., 2001).

In the present context, we claim that the policy on migration and asylum in the European Community constitutes a promising terrain for interdisciplinary endeavors. Firstly, although since the middle of the 1980s the European level has increasingly played a role in attempts to collectively deal with migration questions, and despite the fact that the Treaty of Amsterdam has turned the European Community into the main legislative forum in Europe for questions of migration and asylum, the common European stock of migration legislation is still relatively immature when compared to the longstanding tradition of national provisions. For the development of sustainable and pertinent common ground, it seems necessary to account for the diversity of historical, political and institutional embeddedness of national provisions – a task lawyers alone can hardly cope with. Secondly, it is in the very nature of migration to be transnational. This implies border crossing as migrants move from one territory to another. It is trans-jurisdictionally legal as it takes place within a patchwork of national provisions (Albert, 1999, Friedman, 1996). One major implication is that states unilaterally can only adapt to migration flows, but cannot guide them. To be able to purposefully influence or govern migration affairs, coordinated action with other states is required. Multilateral coordination, however, significantly narrows the scope for idiosyncratic inter-pretations of legal provision. Rather, recommendations that promise a successful harmonization of national migration provisions and practices require an under-standing of the background of legal provisions and policies in other countries, which, in turn, approve political scientists' counterpart of lawyers.

In order to arrive at valuable proposals for European solutions that can cope with the challenges arising from migratory flows, lawyers need not only to analyze the legal texts governing the situation at a certain time, they also need sound knowledge of the sociopolitical and socioeconomic background which led to the existing legal situation, both *de jure* and *de facto*. Moreover, in order to identify those factors representing new challenges, the lawyer needs empirical data and analytical information which political scientists by virtue of their professional education are better equipped to provide. Therefore, the task of adopting new legal texts for harmonizing the differing legal and empirical situations across the EU member states provides a particularly interesting field for interdisciplinary research. The potential focal points of interdisciplinary cooperation shall subsequently be illustrated, evoking the example of refugee law.

The Example of the Definition of the Refugee

The central question of asylum law, naturally enough, is who is a refugee? What are the qualifying criteria for asylum status? National authorities grant asylum by applying the national law on asylum. Although, on the basis of the 1951 Geneva Convention, having a 'refugee' status does not guarantee asylum, a great number of countries apply this definition when deciding on asylum applications (Carlier, 1997, p. 695). The interpretations by national authorities and courts differ widely, however, giving rise to comparative studies filling thick folios (for instance Carlier, Vanheule, Hullmann, and Galiano, 1997). A notorious example is the fact that most states view persecution by private actors as constituting a sufficient reason for granting refugee status, whereas particularly Germany and France refuse to do so. It ought to be kept in mind that the definition of 'refugee' enshrined in the Geneva Convention does not specify exact criteria regarding who is to be legally considered the agent of persecution (Bank, 1999, p. 13; Goodwin-Gill, 1996, pp. 70-74; UNHCR, 1995, pp. 28ff.; UNHCR, 1979, para. 65). While the better arguments indeed speak in favor of defining as refugees those persecuted by non-state agents, it may still be difficult to argue that the interpretation of the law by German and French judges is so outrageous as to amount to an arbitrary bending of the law. This observation suggests that legal interpretation provides a lawyer with the possibility to react to certain problems divergently, without formally breaking written law.

The lawyer may be content with having shown that the definition of a refugee does not require persecution by the state under international law and under a comparative perspective. In so doing he or she argues for an interpretation opposing that applied by the German and French courts. Yet, this is only part of the story, for another interesting question comes to mind: what are the reasons for the fact that the term 'refugee' is interpreted by the courts of one state as including persons fearing persecution, regardless of whether this persecution is carried out by state agents, while the courts in another state come to the opposite conclusion? This raises the issue of the borderline between legal interpretation and political decisions. We will come back to this phenomenon later when discussing the understanding of the politics behind a situation *de lege lata*.

The next fact to be considered in the present context is that a binding text more clearly specifying the requirements for an applicant for asylum will be adopted by the European institutions under the EC treaty framework inserted by the Treaty of Amsterdam. When trying to make informed recommendations for adopting new EC legislation, the level of policy making has been reached. It is necessary to find out why certain states are interested in excluding from the definition of a refugee those persecuted by non-state agents, although, given their commitments under the European Convention on Human Rights,[5] they are obliged not to send back such persons, even if the refugee definition under the 1951 Refugee Convention is interpreted restrictively. It is necessary to understand how normative criteria that can be derived from international treaties and national constitutions can gain influence on the decision making process inside European institutions.[6] It is helpful to have a certain amount of knowledge about the characteristics of the policy making process in the multilevel European polity, that is knowledge of how different national and European actors and institutions interact when making provisions. For instance, a question to be answered is why, even though only two out of fifteen member states do not consider non-state agent persecution to be a sufficient criterion for the legal definition of a refugee, these two states may well manage to push through their restrictive interpretation and may finally receive the support of all other states. To answer this kind of question, a lawyer will inevitably fail to cope with an analysis of both the process of decision making at the European level and its embeddedness in domestic politics if using only his or her own toolbox. Rather, help comes from political scientists who have at their disposal analytical concepts such as the theory of intergovernmentalism (Moravcsik, 1998) or the theory of veto points and veto players (Tsebelis, 2002) in order to delineate and interpret these processes and their implication for European and domestic policies.

The Example of Temporary Protection

The discussion on temporary protection provides another example that may serve to elucidate the potential for interdisciplinary research in the field of migration and refugee law. 'Temporary protection' aims at replacing an approach which focuses on persecuted individuals and which leads to permanent status in the receiving country – as is inherent in the present concept of international refugee law – with a generalized approach providing temporary refugee status in situations in which there are massive flows of refugees. Although not aiming at replacing the asylum status in general, the Amsterdam Treaty has proposed that European-wide minimum standards for temporary protection ought to be elaborated and adopted within a five-year period. This indicates that within a few years temporary protection will probably be an increasingly important complement to the traditional asylum approach.

The more the definition of refugee protection becomes a fuzzy concept, the more do the educational capacities of lawyers reach their limits and the more helpful additional information provided by political scientists' analyses might be. The lawyer will analyze the application and interpretation of the refugee definition and determine the differences between countries. Moreover, he or she will be able to observe that a certain set of laws (in particular, the extension of visa requirements) makes it more difficult for potential asylum seekers to enter the country of destination in order to claim asylum or even to submit the asylum application in the country of the applicant's choice (for instance, due to the safe-third-country concept or the distribution of asylum claims among EU member states according to the Dublin Convention). Moreover, the lawyer will ask whether this state of affairs appropriately reflects the idea of protection for refugees as enshrined in international instruments.

In addition, the lawyer will be able to understand the mismatch between the current concept of refugee protection and actual challenges that are linked to changes in the composition of refugee flows. A number of reasons such as decolonization, secession struggles in Africa and Asia, and increasingly civil wars and generalized violence have multiplied the courses of refugee flows from the 1960s onwards. From a legal point of view, an ever smaller proportion of persons seeking asylum in the West is seen to fulfill the criteria of the refugee definition of the Geneva Convention. Political scientists' knowledge might provide additional insights into how the individual approach in refugee protection has largely been circumvented: barriers have been erected or underpinned which prevent people in need of protection from reaching the host country and consequently from being able to submit their applications for asylum (Hathaway, 1997). Or, freedom from persecution is assumed for certain countries by way of a generalized judgement such as in safe third country rules (Lavenex, 1999a).

Also, with a view to arriving at suggestions for a future concept in the European context – in which asylum and temporary protection could be accorded complementary roles –, a thorough analysis of the prevailing legal framework as well as the institutional context and the underpinning social phenomena is required. In particular, the basic tension between the human rights of persons temporarily protected and the interest of host states to avoid factors that foster a situation in which the refugees do not return home must be fully explored before valuable suggestions for a future policy in this area can be made. While human rights requirements might productively be analyzed by a lawyer, the impact that granting certain rights has on the potential for repatriation after a certain time requires the type of careful analysis for which political and social scientists are better equipped. This may even lead to the conclusion that both perspectives – the guarantee of living in human dignity and the aim to prevent integration from leading to a 'non-return' effect – are irreconcilable. Moreover, it is likely that the concept of temporary protection will only work if it is embedded in sound measures providing repatriation aid and the sharing of responsibilities and costs. Again, these aspects are not within the lawyer's sphere but require input from political scientists.[7]

Interdisciplinary Cooperation as a Contribution to a Fuller Understanding of the Law as it Stands

The use of political science methodology when reflecting on how to make more effective certain normative aims inherent in international treaties or national constitutions represents only one potentially fruitful aspect of interdisciplinary approaches to migration research. In the course of a lawyer's analysis further potentially profitable aspects are to be found.

The relationship between the approach of a lawyer and that of a political scientist may be characterized as following: while the lawyer looks at the letter and system of the law and therefore at the visible outcome, the political scientist concentrates on the processes which led there, the politics lying behind it, and how things work in practice, reflecting a large variety of influential factors (ideally including legal ones). This, however, is a simplification since a lawyer may also need to consider aspects from the political scientist's research basis and vice versa. For instance, if it proves necessary to interpret a norm historically, a lawyer may have to take recourse to a political scientist's analysis of the process of drafting a law – including the discussions within the political process of arriving at the final compromise. Also, interpreting a legal text in accordance with its aim and purpose may prove difficult without going back to the political process that led to the adoption of the provision or text in question.

Differing court interpretations of the same term indicate that sometimes the borderline between political science and law is blurred even more since the application of law, by both the national authorities and the courts, is not free from politicization. This is plainly clear when, for example, the term 'refugee' from the 1951 Geneva Convention is interpreted in a different manner in different European states, as in the above-mentioned case. The lesson to learn is that for at least two reasons it is too simple to assume that the analysis of the process of norm creation falls into the realm of political scientists whereas the interpretation of the existing law is the exclusive realm of lawyers. On the one hand, the application of law does not take place in a sterile environment. Law is applied by human beings who are susceptible to external influences and their own convictions, which will both find their way into the judges' decisions. On the other hand, the application of law entails a significant potential for innovation (Okruch, 1999), and processes of norm development or creation in the course of applying existing provisions are the well-established and well-accepted rule rather than the exception (Christensen, 1987, p. 82). In the European context, the enormous importance of judgements of the European Court of Justice for the entire integration process has frequently been emphasized (Burley and Mattli, 1993; Weiler, 1993, 1994). With respect to fundamental rights, it is the courts rather than parliament that decide on the extension of individual rights and on the limits of public intervention.

Concerning the different interpretations of the refugee definition, the deviation of French and German courts from the generally accepted interpretation of the term with regard to the issue of non-state persecution could possibly be explained by referring to the national situations underpinning the decisions. In Germany there is a strong tendency to stem the generally very high number of asylum seekers through restrictive policies, and this may have found its way into the courts' interpretation. And when considering France one cannot fail to notice that it is the main destination for asylum seekers from Algeria, which for its part is one of the countries that produce the largest numbers of individuals fleeing persecution by non-state actors, i.e., fundamentalist terrorists.

As has been emphasized above, while good arguments speak against the interpretation of the German and French courts, the arguments are not strong enough to allow the conclusion that the French and German law courts are engaged in arbitrarily bending the law. Rather, within the interpretive boundaries different interpretations are possible. Therefore courts have to react to a certain extent to social phenomena, without having time to wait for a formal amendment of the law. Confronted with these findings, the lawyer will mainly be interested in the outcome of the process, i.e., in analyzing the pros and cons of the line of argumentation adopted by the courts in reacting to a new phenomenon. In contrast, the political scientist will be more concerned with showing which factors may have influenced this outcome.

Without being underpinned by careful research, explanations may seem plausible, but remain mere speculation. Finding out more about the true reasons would require an interdisciplinary endeavor with a lawyer analyzing the exact argumentation of the courts in the relevant cases and a political scientist trying to shed light on the way political principles find their way into court decisions.

While a lawyer may successfully cope with the challenges of legal interpretation without having the slightest idea of political science analysis, there may be situations in which it may provide elucidating insights to discover the politics underpinning a particularly complicated set of norms. Understanding the politics behind the situation *de lege lata* is not only valuable as such, but may also contribute to reflections on the need for reform that transcend merely legalistic issues, such as conformity with superior norms or achieving consistency within a given legal system.

An example for this is provided by an analysis of the reception of asylum seekers which was carried out for an interdisciplinary conference on 'Migration and the Welfare State' from the point of view of comparative law (Bank, 2000). As a review of the legal rules governing the liberties and social conditions for asylum seekers in four different European states has brought to light, there is a great variety of models with regard to detention and restrictions on free movement and the choice of residence, on the one hand, and working opportunities, housing, social aid and education, on the other. Of course, the differences in legal provisions and entitlements granted to asylum seekers become all the more vivid by contrasting them with each other. However, the large number of details seems more confusing than elucidating as there are almost no international norms that could have provided normative guidance regarding which of the rules are open to criticism. From a purely legalistic point of view there seems to be no pattern in the variety of models applied in the different states, except for the tendency to restrict asylum seekers' rights and entitlements.

Only after an interdisciplinary discussion with lawyers, political scientists and sociologists reflecting on the policies was it possible to reveal not only the obvious aims of deterring potential asylum seekers and limiting the amount of money spent on those who continue to arrive, but also another principle underpinning restrictive measures: the aim of limiting integration and access to economic, social and cultural benefits in order to avoid developments that could hinder the asylum seeker's expulsion if his or her claim was rejected.

These reflections allows us to draw the conclusion that the treatment accorded to asylum seekers has a purpose that runs contrary to the usual intention of welfare benefits. The latter serve to preserve or to foster (re)integration, while the treatment of asylum seekers during the reception phase serves to impede integration. By excluding asylum seekers as far as possible from taking part in the daily life of the host society, states try to ensure that the law enforcement towards rejected asylum seekers is not impaired by irreversible structures of social ties. Therefore, it was possible to show that from the time of their arrival to the final decision on their claim, the treatment of asylum seekers is dominated by the tension between the two opposing goals of reception policies. One goal is to ensure the exclusion of asylum seekers from European societies. The other goal is to ensure that asylum seekers survive with a minimum of human dignity, as is demanded by the values of modern welfare states with their commitment to humanity. Against this background it was possible to show that the main problem to be addressed is not restriction as such but the question of how long restriction may be applied without violating human dignity.

A Broader Conceptual Framework for Interdisciplinary (Migration) Research

The previous section has illustrated that the (inter)disciplinary cooperation between lawyers and political scientists is a fruitful enterprise. Indeed, since scholars of both disciplines deal with the same empirical phenomena, overcoming academic insularity and building bridges has repeatedly been demanded (e.g. Abbott, 1989; Beck et al., 1996; Byers, 2000; Chin and Choi, 1998a, 1998b; Slaughter Burley, 1993; Slaughter, 1995; Slaughter et al., 1998; Young, 1992; International Organization, 2000, vol. 53, no. 3, Zangl and Zürn, 2004). But is it right, for example, for international law and international politics to cohabit the same conceptual space (Slaughter, 1995, p. 503)? Or should there be a division of territories in which different disciplines examine the same phenomenon from different foci with overlapping segments of disciplines spurring a recombination of knowledge in specialized fields (Dogan, 1998, p. 123)?

While it seems promising to put some effort into achieving cross-disciplinary fertilization, the demanding task of interdisciplinary cooperation between law and politics leads to a number of obstacles related to conceptual, methodological and organizational preconditions. Some of these important preconditions will be delineated below by, firstly, considering some aspects in favor of pooling or accumulating knowledge and experience from political science and law, and, secondly, by pointing out hindrances to achieving cooperation across disciplinary boundaries. In a third step we shall elaborate on our idea of disciplined interdisciplinarity.

Interdisciplinary Utopia

A couple of years ago a prominent professor of international law felt so inspired by the natural affinity between law and politics that he forecasted the emergence of a new joint discipline called the 'study of international cooperation' (Abbott, 1992). For him, law and politics in the disciplines of international law and international relations were 'so neatly complementary that they can enrich each other tremendously across a wide range of intellectual activities' (Abbott, 1992, p. 168). At the end of the day, according to his forecast, the new joint discipline would have the potential of transcending its constituents in much the same way as the law and economics movement did (ibid.).

Abbott elaborated on the potential of mutually supportive activities along five dimensions: descriptive, doctrinal, explanatory, normative, and instrumental. First, the importance of *description* in both disciplines is almost self-evident. Nevertheless, there are significant differences in how it is practiced. Political scientists frequently complain that the legal approach to international affairs relies too heavily on textual exegesis and excludes political, economic and other aspects of reality. In this regard, political science, with its strong interests in generalization, has shown that the value of description increases when it is theoretically informed. Neo-institutional and frame-analytical approaches, for example, have been best suited to explain both the manner and the direction in which migration and asylum policy have developed in Europe since the beginning of the 1980s. Transgovernmental working groups have successfully circumvented the scrutiny of national courts and parliaments and, in addition, have managed to frame questions of asylum policies in terms of security rather than humanity (Guiraudon, 2000; Lavenex, 1999b).

Second, the analysis of *doctrine*, i.e., the analysis of norms and their application to the factual situation (Abbott, 1992, p. 168) and the principles underpinning it, is an essential function of law as a professional discipline, while it is largely missing in political science – although the cognitive turn in political science indicates increasing attention paid to the ideas underlying certain policies. Through legal reasoning – understood as the way in which lawyers frame legal arguments and in which other lawyers respond to them – doctrinal analysis may provide insights into central questions of international relations and help to understand whether and how international obligations constrain state behavior. For instance, a subject of international law might be to ask whether and under what circumstances legal doctrine can become so influential as to constitute a factor independent of states.

Third, *explanation*, of course, is an important dimension in both disciplines. However, explanation plays significantly different roles. While for a political scientist explanation is the central category, for a lawyer it is only the first step on his or her way to come to a normative decision. What is more, both disciplines assign different importance to the explanatory value that the other discipline has to offer, and an awareness of mutual prejudices may help to reveal complementary aspects.

On the one hand, from a political science perspective law is often seen as being theoretically uninteresting; it tends to confuse cause with appearance as it focuses predominantly on 'justificatory behavior'. That is, the law is seen as 'conflating the sources of international law with actual state behavior' (Joyner, 1987, p. 387f.). On the other hand, lawyers are either amused or annoyed by political scientists' efforts to properly label dependent and independent variables (Beck, 1996, p. 18). Because political scientists long failed to view international law as either a dependent or independent variable of importance for the conduct of states, lawyers are quick to accuse internationally oriented political scientists of failing to appraise the role of law carefully and of frequently failing to consider where and how international law fits into the calculus of national policy makers or international diplomacy (Joyner, 1987, p. 388). In recent years, however, the collaboration between lawyers and political scientists has become more fruitful. With respect to bargaining and foreign policy decision making, for example, lawyers' historical interpretations have benefited from political scientists' studies of the bargaining process, and have at the same time contributed to political scientists' awareness of the legal arena (Gould, 1987, p. 384). Law is no longer regarded through an instrumentalist lens (Keohane, 1997) but as a variable in its own right (Kratochwil, 2000; Slaughter et al., 1998; Young, 1994).

On a more abstract level, the potential for explanatory methods to benefit from cooperative work between law and politics can be reformulated in the following way. In epistemological terms, law, traditionally as well as today, relies to a certain extent on its own history. This is partly due to the need for coherence that urges the judge to accommodate his or her decision or interpretation of a certain legal text with both precedents and an historical interpretation of the given legal situation. To put it more poignantly, 'in no other branch of learning (except perhaps religion) does perceived wisdom enjoy a preferred position over newly revealed insights' (Knetsch, 1998, p. 19). Yet, the reliance on its own historical knowledge has a significant drawback. The fact that law is principally a discipline from which theories about social reality, societal interest and conflicts are missing, poses a problem when it is dealing with contemporary problems. Law is incomplete and has to borrow from other disciplines' concepts and theories if it wants to describe, analyze and regulate such problems (Joerges, 1974, p. 557; Slaughter et al., 1998, p. 371). This shortcoming can only be remedied to a certain extent by a dynamic interpretation of legal norms; and a dynamic interpretation is all the more difficult the more detailed existing legal rules on a certain question are.

Fourth, it is normally thought that the conduct of *normative* analysis plays an important role in law and politics in both a critical and a prescriptive assessment of norms, practices and institutions. The objective of normative analysis is to critically scrutinize existing arrangements and to suggest alternatives. Yet, as will be discussed in more detail below, the two disciplines weigh this category in a significantly different manner.

Fifth, the quality of the *instrumental* work achieved through the disciplinary cooperation between law and politics is viewed as particularly noteworthy. In this respect, the descriptive and explanatory help by political science is not only supposed to enrich lawyers' studies of the implementation of treaties and other international agreements. On the one hand, the application of law is at the heart of legal studies; but lawyers seldom have scientific knowledge to assess the impact and efficacy of laws in a changing society. On the other hand, the social sciences have a deeper understanding of the political, economic and social changes in society, and developing and testing of hypotheses is at the heart of their scientific interest. Yet, because of the lack of familiarity with legal technicalities, social scientists are not in the position to propose concrete legal and policy changes (Chin and Choi, 1998b, p. 1). Thus the disciplines are complementary in many respects, and cooperation between them should improve the potential for analyzing substantive problems, developing new concepts for particular institutions and framing better legal solutions (Beck, 1996).

In sum, these considerations tend to support the call for interdisciplinary cooperation as an effort to scientifically treat the unavoidable blind spots deriving from disciplinary differentiation and specialization (Bommes and Maas in this volume). What is still missing, however, is the proof that merging the collaborative enterprise into some kind of brave new world of interdisciplinarity is really the ultimate means to this goal. Indeed, in what follows we will discuss some serious obstacles which hamper such enthusiasm, and thus significantly lower expectations about the achievements to be attained by the cooperation of law and politics.

Obstacles for Interdisciplinary Cooperation

At first glance, one might argue that although frequently dealing with the same subjects in the real world, both fields are trapped in the routine approaches of their own discipline. Thus, lawyers and political scientists fall victim to their own rhetoric, and their prejudices become self-fulfilling prophecies. The gap between the disciplines, however, is a deeper one. A closer look at the limits of disciplinary cooperation between law and politics reveals some important structural impediments. In the following, we elaborate on only two of these obstacles: the differentiation in scientific development and the difference between analysis and advocacy.[8]

Differentiation and Specialization in Science Even a very brief glance at the histories of the disciplines at stake confirms that neither law nor political science are exceptions to the general rule of differentiation and specialization characterizing so much of scientific development. Their common background can be seen in the discipline of *Staatswissenschaft* encompassing in a broader sense legal, political and economic affairs. They have, however, developed in different directions, and the disciplinary emancipation from this more encompassing concept occurred not only between the various disciplines, but also within them. It occurs along cultural, historical, geographical, ontological, methodological and epistemological lines. Schools and sects divide disciplines (Almond, 1990), making the domains and interests of social scientists and lawyers thoroughly heterogeneous, thus contributing to an 'epistemological pluralism' (Young, 1992, p. 174). Given the dramatic increase in expertise that accompanies differentiation and specialization within individual disciplines, it is stated to be 'no longer possible for anyone to have thorough knowledge of more than one discipline' (Dogan, 1998, p. 98). This assumption renders illusionary the ability of individual scholars to be familiar with and combine entire disciplines and reveals the individual struggle for interdisciplinarity to 'carry a hint of superficiality and dilettantism' (ibid., p. 99; Chmielewicz, 1994, p. 26).

These considerations suggest that in a strict sense the word interdisciplinarity is inadequate. To be more precise, one would have to speak of efforts to combine fragments of different disciplines or of a recombination of specialized knowledge. While the consequences for the concept of a cooperation between lawyers and political scientists are discussed in more detail below, we now turn to structural points limiting interdisciplinary work. In this regard, two aspects need to be distinguished. Admittedly, there are examples in which a legal scholar with an LL.M. degree in political science or who has done some basic studies in political science may well combine methodologies and theoretical models within one research project with highly inspiring and interesting outcomes (for instance Noll, 1997; Marauhn, 1998). But such interdisciplinary single-handed endeavors will remain the exception rather than the rule. In addition, as science is always a concert of many and progress rests at least as much on cooperation as on the inspiration of the individual (Dahrendorf, 1968, p. 14), individual efforts are not of much help to systematize interdisciplinary research fora.

Cooperation across disciplines is not only hampered by the limited capacities of individual knowledge, but also by professional pillarization. In particular, cooperation is troubled by entrenched practices in the two disciplines: the professions are organized in neatly separated professional associations, and discourse takes place at different conferences; scholars tend to publish (and read?) almost exclusively in the journals of their own disciplines; narrow vocational agendas put more emphasis on uni-disciplinary and technical training and provide only few incentives for acquiring knowledge in other disciplines. Finally, a different disciplinary socialization entails that different languages are internalized, and the same terms are often assigned different connotations, which frequently impedes interdisciplinary communication at a very basic level (Beck, 1996, p. 19f; Drewry, 1998, p. 194; Kirchner, 1991; Young, 1992, p. 175).

Where Science Ceases and Advocacy Begins There are even more factors that hamper the cooperative effort between political science and law. Political scientists frequently have difficulties in following the lawyers' efforts to accurately characterize the substance of the law instead of its causal relationship(s) to specific behavior. Moreover, given the importance that political science scholars traditionally assign to the realities of power in international relations, to them the international law's aspiration for universal justice and moral attainment has a hopelessly utopian character – while lawyers are critical of wholly reducing real-world politics to power considerations or numerical calculations (Joyner, 1987, p. 389). In addition, political science with its concern for theorizing and generalization is seen as being prone to scientism; and this is viewed as hampering pragmatic and inductive research.

But *nota bene*: 'law and politics are not one continuum in the realm of praxis, but radically different domains that have to be kept differently' (Kratochwil, 2000, p. 39). In this regard, the examples clearly indicate the different ends toward which a political and a legal academic education are directed: *analysis* and *advocacy*, respectively (Beck, 1996, p. 18). Roughly speaking, political scientists and lawyers often ask different questions and expect different answers. In an (admittedly) simplistic way, these differences can be presented as follows.

Political scientists are usually interested in positive analysis[9] and 'pursue the grail of explanation and prediction' (Young, 1992, p. 174). By asking, for instance, how institutional constraints empower or restrict consequential actors differently, how collective action problems are solved and what institutional solutions have been created to provide common goods, political scientists are concerned with descriptive and causal inference, i.e., with impediments to action and goods (King et al., 1994, pp. 7f.), as well as with generalizations about polities, politics and policies. To satisfy their interest in interference and generalization, social scientists take different avenues, weighing the relative merits of meta-theories and middle-range theories (Merton, 1996; Benz and Seibel, 1997). To summarize the difference, political scientists try to explain a certain action or observation and try to arrive at general conclusions about regularities of political behavior. In contrast, lawyers start with a given norm under which they try to subsume a certain action in order to evaluate whether this action fulfills the criteria characterizing the norm. Their interest is less in generalization than in either sanctioning behavior not conforming to the norm or making recommendations for law amendments.

The statement that the interest of (mainstream) lawyers differs significantly from that of (mainstream) political scientists can be substantiated in relation to two aspects, namely the purpose of legal reasoning and the gap between law-in-theory and law-in-practice as the central issue for studies about law. With respect to the former, it has already been mentioned that legal reasoning, as the characteristic discourse of the legal community, is very particular. While largely lacking interest in generalizations, this discourse serves to fulfill two functions assigned to law: resolving disputes and actual social conflicts and accommodating the need for maintaining historical continuity, doctrinal consistency and coherence with societal change and evolution. Lawyers are concerned with formulating principles or doctrines and with applying them methodologically to specific cases or factual patterns. The relation between principles and factual patterns is dialectical.

> One wants to use principles to understand cases and fact patterns. How can you understand a case or a fact pattern without making decisions and deploying some principles? And one wants to use cases to derive principles. One wants a constant dialectic between the principles and the case. It is not a matter of constructing more or less powerful generalizations; it is a matter of developing a dialectical process that allows both for the refinement of principles and for the solving of cases, because *cases must be solved* – the dialectic is not just an intellectual exercise (Young, 1992, p. 175; emphasis added by RB/DL).

In short, there is a significant difference between political scientists striving for explanation, prediction and generalization on the one hand and lawyers' concerns for formulating principles and applying them in order to decide concrete cases on the other. To arrive at a generalization for an unlimited number of potential cases, political scientists try to reduce the number of explanatory variables as much as possible. This interest in abstract conclusions stands in stark contrast to the lawyers' methodology of interpretation that aims at contextualizing the inter-pretation of a specific norm and the subsequent decision or judgement to the highest possible degree.

There is a second factor of major concern to legal scholars that frustrates disciplinary cooperation: namely, the interest in the gap between law-in-theory and law-in-practice.[10] In this respect, the issue of compliance with international norms cannot only be taken as an example of successful cooperation between lawyers and political scientists,[11] but may also help to delineate the difference between positive and normative analysis. International lawyers have traditionally emphasized the elaboration of rules that are notionally binding upon states. In doing so, they have built institutions to help shape and interpret those rules (Toope, 2000, p. 92). Frequently, however, they have been frustrated by the lack of state compliance with international provisions. In this respect, regime theory has contributed insights into the formation and influence of both conventional and customary law. This political theory analyzes the institutional factors influencing the effectiveness of different regimes. In this regard, we agree with Abbott's fifth dimension, according to which the combined knowledge of lawyers and political scientists might be used instrumentally and may contribute to the reformulation of a specific legal frame-work.

At the same time, however, the instrumental dimension confronts us with a problem that is probably as old as science itself: the application of scientific results to practical problems (Dahrendorf, 1968). In this respect, the compatibility between law and politics tends to end when positive analysis ends and normative analysis begins. By crossing the positive-normative divide, science frequently ceases and advocacy begins. In the following we want to illustrate these considerations by briefly pointing out the different weight political science and law assign to positive and normative analysis on the one hand and advocacy on the other.

To start with, in the context of policy research the objective of political science and political sociology is to contribute to an understanding of politics and the conditions under which it is able to produce effective and legitimate solutions to policy problems. While this assessment indicates that positive and normative investigations are closely related, the claim remains that the one must not be confused with the other (Scharpf, 1997, p. 13). Indeed, in political science there is a relatively strict distinction between analysis, normative claims and the use of achieved knowledge for the purpose of advice. When normative analysis becomes part of the work of the political scientist, the criteria for its normativity relate to central categories of the discipline such as transparency of decision making for democratic reasons or the relative importance of power in decision making processes. To give an example, from a political science perspective, the actual formulation of asylum legislation in the Central and Eastern European countries would need to be interpreted against the background of enlargement negotiations with the European Union and the power relations inherent in these processes. From this perspective, the candidate countries have been incorporated into a restrictive system of migration control including the negative distribution of asylum seekers in exchange for the perspective of becoming EU member states. In the same way, the fact that in the European context asylum and refugee questions are framed in terms of internal security affairs at the expense of human rights principles of international refugee protection could be explained with reference to domestic interests and the dominance in the intergovernmental decision making process at the European level of civil servants related to the ministries of the interior (Lavenex, 1999a, 1999b).

These examples indicate that in political science a positive analysis of political processes and its measurement against normative criteria is possible. What we want to emphasize here, however, is that in political science the distinction between analysis and the instrumentalization of its reflexive apparatus and its methodology for purposes of advocacy is sharper than it is in law. We like to distinguish between two major legal professions, that of a judge and a legal scholar, in order to elaborate on the argument that law is inherently more prone to normative judgements and that the consequences are not only more important for the behavior of individuals and political institutions than normativity in political science but that law also runs the risk of incorporating value judgements more often.

As already mentioned, a judge is always confronted with a twofold task. On the one hand he or she must subsume a specific action under a respective norm in order to arrive at a judgement that guarantees individual justice. On the other hand, the judge has to ensure that the individual case is in coherence with precedents and, in addition, he or she has to constantly measure reality with normative principles. In case of disparity between legal reality and the ideal or principle, judges frequently bridge this gap either by interpreting the norm according to societal developments or by introducing new elements into the interpretation of a norm. In doing so, however, the judge inadvertently runs the risk of mistaking personal ideals for the society's ideals (Esser, 1970). This is the more critical when 'decisions are thought from the result', thus assuming the character of politicized decisions under the guise of legal judgements (Müller, 1994, p. 11).

In international law in particular the boundary between those applying law and those doing legal research is frequently blurred. Courts look at normative scholary as a source of law, and international law academics tend to see themselves as part of the 'invisible college' devoted to world justice (Goldsmith, 2000, pp. 981f.). In addition, lawyers are trained to use normative arguments and to convince political decision makers to move law in a direction deemed favorable. One has to bear in mind, however, that similar to provisions within domestic constitutions, international treaties are open to diverse interpretations, so that the process of interpretation can become one of advocacy. Advocacy scholarship is not inherently bad or undesirable. But when scholarship is characterized by policy prescriptions that reflect author preferences (Dunhoff and Trachtman, 1999, p. 24), the danger is simply that it jettisons methodological rigor and tends to selectively and tendentiously support normative conclusions (Goldsmith, 2000, p. 982).

In brief, a problem of political science is first of all a problem of descriptive and causal inference and of matching general explanation with reality. In contrast, a legal problem is a problem of contextualization instead of generalization and, moreover, of comparing legal reality with a legal ideal. When it comes to making recommendations to resolve disparities between the two, science very often ceases and advocacy begins. Then a legal problem becomes a problem of value and, is thus, beyond the reach of political science. Thus, the core problem of legal policy-making becomes a problem of value (Black, 1982, p. 1087). In principle, value considerations are irrelevant to any scientific theory of the empirical world. Political science, for instance, rejects them, as 'value judgements are no doubt relevant as foreign policy considerations, [yet] they are obviously highly subjective quantities; consequently, they do not always lend themselves to scientific or rational analysis' (Joyner, 1987, p. 388). To be sure, value-free science is hardly possible. But the fact that scientific statements are influenced by values does not make them value statements (Black, 1982, p. 1095). Hence, put more generally, there is a clear distinction between the indirect intelligence function a positive scientific analysis takes for the policy process and an implicit or explicit normative analysis fuelling advocatory policy recommendations.

Disciplined Interdisciplinarity

So far we have learned that the cooperation between law and political science is a worthwhile undertaking. Potential benefits would be lost if the formal borders between the two disciplines could not be crossed in the one or the other direction. Indeed, both disciplines can benefit from exploring the enormous hinterland of the other. Yet, it has been demonstrated that cross-disciplinary cooperation will not be handed on a plate but requires serious scholarly study. In addition, there are significant obstacles to the realization of an interdisciplinary utopia in which disciplinary distinctions dissolve.

It is not by accident that we have frequently mentioned international law and international relations when referring to either potential gains or hindrances. References to subdisciplines have been informed by the fact that the historical evolution of science in general can be read as a twofold process: fragmentation of formal disciplines and recombination of specialties resulting from fragmentation. Thus, specialization is regarded as a precondition for progress in science (Dogan, 1998, p. 97). Specialization takes place within a formal discipline. It becomes institutionalized and leads to fragmentation. At the same time, specialization occurs at the intersection of monodisciplinary subfields; that is, a recombination of the fragmented specialities can be observed (so-called hybrids). As sociometric studies have shown, it is significantly more important for specialized scholars to interact with colleagues of other disciplines than it is for them to interact with those of their own discipline (Dogan and Pahre, 1989).

What is important in our case is: first, that at least up to some point, disciplinary boundaries are useful for advancing knowledge, because '[e]ach discipline throws light on a set of variables precisely because other factors are assumed to be external' (Sartori, 1969, p. 66); second, innovations in the social sciences most often are the offspring of cooperation between specialized subfields. An important example is the field of political economy, which, without doubt, integrates many cutting-edge scholars from political science and economics, both at the national and international level. Finally, these hybrids do not stand midway between the two sovereign disciplines. Rather, the respective disciplinary background maintains a visible profile (Dogan, 1998, p. 100).

These considerations constitute the basic assumptions that ought to be borne in mind when considering our call for *disciplined interdisciplinarity*. Cooperation across sub-disciplinary boundaries is desirable; it is a worthwhile undertaking since reciprocal influences and opportunities make overcoming mutual ignorance possible. We would contradict those who propose that the specialization and division of labor yields enormous benefits for the production of all goods and services, and that knowledge and its application is no exception (Knetsch, 1998, p. 11). Rather, from our point of view, cooperation across the boundaries of law and political science makes two things possible: first, it allows a more encompassing understanding of societal change in turbulent environments; and second, it leads to recommendations based on sound empirical description and theoretical inter-pretation. There are thus good reasons for an appeal to disciplined inter-disciplinarity. This, however, should not be confused with a call for blending the approaches of lawyers and political scientists. Rather, the idea to engage in disciplined interdisciplinarity means to preserve differences between scientific disciplines. This rather modest approach is due to a number of profoundly different commitments of the two disciplines of which we have discussed only two above. Thus, we are convinced that only both the awareness of one's own educational pedigree *and* a sound knowledge of the other discipline's epistemological assumptions and methodologies allow us to reap the benefits of cooperation between lawyers and political scientists.

Conclusion

As shown by our brief empirical examples, it is fruitful to approach the field of migration research as a cooperative effort of legal and political science. In the first case examined, the lawyer's lens failed to take into view the entire context relevant for a refugee definition in European Community Law that could sufficiently serve us in the future; it thereby limited the potential for making valuable and adequate recommendations for norms to be adopted. Moreover, with legal methodology only, the lawyer could not explain the background informing the diverging interpretations of the same international norm by French and German courts. Similarly, the second case demonstrated that the new concept of temporary protection which is to be adopted by the European Community not only requires an analysis of norms of human rights that limit the possibilities of choice; it also requires well-founded information on the sociopolitical impact of envisaged action to be considered with these norms. Finally, in the third case, only after interdisciplinary discussion was it possible to identify the tension between the two contrary goals that govern the reception policies in some member states of the European Union. In all these cases, two things become apparent. The first general observation is that law has to be contextualized, i.e. that law is best understood within the context of history, and of political and economic forces. The second observation refers to the finding that law is almost always refracted through a political process and that the political dimension needs to be studied carefully (Falk, 1993, p. 399).

We take this positive evaluation of the cooperation between legal and political science to re-emphasize the importance of efforts to cross disciplinary boundaries in research. Yet, such cooperative work can neither be reduced to instrumentalizing other disciplines' knowledge or concepts nor be confused with blurring disciplinary boundaries. Rather, the knowledge of one's own disciplinary pedigree has to be combined with a well-informed understanding of the counter-disciplines' epistemology and methods. From our point of view three aspects are at the heart of the view of disciplined interdisciplinarity as exercised at the inroads of law and political science.

First (conceptually), scholars of each discipline should be aware of conceptualizations and methods of the other discipline to enable them to appreciate, evaluate and utilize what the other discipline has to offer. Potential candidates for such collaboration are, for instance, scholars of international law and international relations, comparative lawyers and comparative governmentalists, private lawyers and political scientists with a particular focus on the role of private actors, and legal and political science scholars studying the process of European integration, etc.

Second (methodologically), when cooperating with specialists from other subdisciplines, positive and normative analysis should be separated; and, even more importantly, science should not be confused with advocacy. Otherwise methodological rigor runs the risk of being sacrificed on the altar of – value loaded, normative – policy recommendation or suggestions *de lege ferenda*.

Third (organizationally), vocational changes need to be brought about by organizational changes, including changes in finance. Vocational changes such as reforms in curricula may prepare the ground for a scholarly awareness of the benefits of cooperating with neighboring subfields. Because of the outpouring of documentary and scholarly material today, individual efforts to bridge the gap between the two fields merely constitute the necessary starting points for cooperation across disciplines. But it is imperative that these efforts narrow the focus of their study. In order to spur on interdisciplinary cooperation it is thus necessary to improve vocations, either by supporting institutionalized cooperation within faculties or proper institutes, or by finding funding opportunities that allow communication costs to be overcome in scholarly cooperation.

Notes

1 For critical and helpful comments comments we are grateful to Tanja A. Börzel, Michael Bommes, Kirsten Dauck, Christoph Engel, Adrienne Héritier, Sandra Lavenex, Leonor Moral Soriano and Stefan Okruch.
2 As the Treaty of Amsterdam has included migration and refugee matters into the 'first' or 'Community' pillar of the European Union, we will use the expression 'European Community' instead of 'European Union' throughout the text.
3 For a more sophisticated approach see Müller, 1997.
4 '...as far as we are, we know more about politics than any other discipline', M. Holden Jr. in his presidential address of the American Political Science Association 1999, (Holden, 2000).
5 The extradition, expulsion and return of persons in danger of being tortured or ill-treated is forbidden under Art. 3 ECHR irrespective of whether the danger emanates from a non-governmental source or from the state. This has been confirmed in several cases by the European Court of Human Rights (*Ahmed v Austria, D. v United Kingdom, H.L.R. v France*).
6 How such normative criteria function and influence national and European policies on refugees is determined to a certain extent, although not exclusively, by legal factors. In order to establish the legal factors, questions arise such as whether a particular state is applying a monistic or a dualistic regime in the adoption of international law or regarding how far certain international norms may be enforced by the courts of the state or even be reviewed by international courts or human rights bodies. This also means that certain international norms may have a more or less direct legal impact whereas others only rely on their appelative character.
7 The concept of temporary protection has been discussed in a most stimulating manner in an interdisciplinary project under the direction of James Hathaway, without, however, suggesting final solutions, cf. Hathaway, 1997.
8 See Goldsmith, 2000, pp. 981-986 for other obstacles that impede a dissolution of boundaries between international law and international relations.
9 A positive analysis presents facts about 'what has happened' or 'what will happen'. In contrast, an analysis is normative when it is based on value judgements involving a pre-established criterion. Statements of 'what ought to be done' are normative.
10 More precisely, there are two distinct versions of the 'gap problem'. One version refers to the gap between legal rules of the state and what people in a community actually do, the second version refers to the gap between legal rules of the state and what legal institutions actually do (Tamanaha, 1995, p. 512). Our interest is in the second version.
11 Neyer, Wolf and Zürn, 1999; Joerges, 2000.

References

Abbott, K. (1989), 'Modern International Relations Theory: A Prospectus for International Lawyers', *Yale Law Journal,* 14, pp. 333-441.
Abbott, K. (1992), 'Elements of a Joint Discipline', *Proceedings of the 86st Annual Meeting of the American Society of International Law,* American Society of International Law, Washington, DC, pp. 167-72.
Albert, M. (1999), 'Entgrenzung und Globalisierung des Rechts', in: R. Voigt (ed.), *Globalisierung des Rechts,* Nomos, Baden-Baden, pp. 115-39.
Almond, G.A. (1990), *A Discipline Divided. Schools and Sects in Political Science,* Sage, Newbury Park.

Bank, R. (1999), 'The Emergent EU Policy on Asylum and Refugees – The New Framework Set by the Treaty of Amsterdam: Landmark or Standstill?', *Nordic Journal of International Law,* 68, pp. 1-29.

Bank, R. (2000), 'Europeanising the Reception of Asylum Seekers: The Opposite of Welfare State Politics', in: M. Bommes and A. Geddes (eds.), *Immigration and Welfare – Challenging the Borders of the Welfare State,* Routledge, London, pp. 148-69.

Beck, R.J., Arend, A.C. and Lugt, R. D.V. (1996), *International Rules. Approaches from Interantional Law and International Relations,* Oxford UP, New York and Oxford.

Beck, R.J. (1996). 'International Law and International Relations: The Prospects for Interdisciplinary Collaboration', in Beck, Arend and Lugt, *International Rules,* pp. 3-33.

Bengoextea, J.R., MacCormick, N., and Moral Soriano, L. (2001), 'Interpretation, Integrity and Integration at the European Court of Justice', G. de Búrca and J.H.H. Weiler (eds.) *The European Court of Justice,* Oxford UP, Oxford, pp. 43-82.

Benz, A. and Seibel, W. (eds.) (1997), *Theorieentwicklung in der Politikwissenschaft. Eine Zwischenbilanz,* Nomos, Baden-Baden.

Black, D.J. (1982), 'The Boundaries of Legal Sociology', *The Yale Law Journal,* 81, pp. 1086-100.

Burley, A.-M. and Mattli, W. (1993), 'Europe before the Court: A Political Theory of Legal Integration', *International Organization,* 47, pp. 41-76.

Byers, M. (ed.) (2000), *The Role of Law in International Politics. Essays in International Relations and International Law,* Oxford UP, Oxford.

Carlier, J.-Y., Vanheule, D. et al. (eds.) (1997), *Who is a Refugee? A Comparative Case Law Study,* Kluwer, The Hague.

Carlier, J.-Y. (1997), 'General Report', in: Carlier, Vanheule et al. (eds.), *Who is a Refugee?,* pp. 245-78.

Chin, A. and Choi, A. (eds.) (1998a) *Law, Social Sciences and Public Policy,* Singapore UP, Singapore.

Chin, A. and Choi, A. (1998b), 'A Tender for Symbiotic Partnership between Law and Social Science', in Chin and Choi (eds.), *Law, Social Sciences and Public Policy,* pp. 1-10.

Chmielewicz, K. (1994), *Forschungskonzeptionen der Wirtschaftswissenschaft,* 3rd. ed., Schäfer-Poeschel, Stuttgart.

Christensen, R.J. (1987), 'Das Problem des Richterrechts aus der Sicht der Strukturierenden Rechtslehre', *Archiv für Rechts- und Sozialforschung,* LXXIII, pp. 75-92.

Dahrendorf, R. (1968), 'Values and Social Science: The Value Dispute in Perspective', *Essays in the Theory of Society,* Stanford UP, Stanford, CA, pp. 1-18.

Dogan, M. and Pahre, R. (1989), 'Fragmentation and Recombination of the Social Science', *Studies in Comparative International Development,* 24 (2), pp. 2-18.

Dogan, M. (1998), 'Political Science and the Other Social Sciences', in R.E. Goodin and H.-D. Klingemann, *A New Handbook of Political Science,* Oxford UP, Oxford, pp. 97-130.

Drewry, G. (1998), 'Political Institutions: Legal Perspectives', in Goodin and Klingemann (eds.), *A New Handbook of Political Science.*

Dunhoff, J.L. and Trachtman, J.P. (1999), 'Economic Analysis of International Law', *The Yale Journal of International Law,* 24, pp. 1-59.

Esser, J. (1970), *Vorverständnis und Methodenwahl in der Rechtsfindung. Rationalitätsgarantien der richterlichen Entscheidungspraxis,* Athenäum, Frankfurt a.M.

Falk, R.A. (1993), *Remarks.* Paper read at Teaching International Relations and International Organization in Internatinal Law Courses: Constructing the State-of-the Art-International Law Course, at Washington, DC.

Friedman, L.M. (1996), 'Borders: On the Emerging Sociology of Law', *Stanford Journal of International Law,* 32, pp. 65-90.

Goldsmith, J. (2000), 'Sovereignty, International Relations Theory and International Law', *Stanford Law Journal,* 52, pp. 959-86.

Goodwin-Gill, G. (1996), *The Refugee in International Law,* 2nd ed., Clarendon Press, Oxford.

Gould, W.L. (1987), 'Remarks', *Proceedings of the 81st Annual Meeting of the American Society of International Law,* American Society of International Law, Washington, DC, pp. 383-5.

Guiraudon, V. (2000), 'European Integration and Migration Policy: Vertical Policy-making as Venue Shopping', *Journal of the Common Market Studies,* 38 (2), pp. 251-71.

Hathaway, J.C. (ed.) (1997), *Reconceiving International Refugee Law,* Nijhoff, The Hague.

Holden, M. Jr. (2000), 'The Competence of Political Science: "Progress in Political Research"' Revisted. Presidential Address, American Political Science Association, 1999, *American Political Science Review,* 94 (1), pp. 1-19.

Joerges, Ch. (1974), 'Das Rechtssystem der transnationalen Handelsschiedsgerichtsbarkeit', *Zeitschrift für das gesamte Handelsrecht und Wirtschaftsrecht,* 138 (5/6), pp. 549-68.

Joerges, Ch. (2000), *Wie sollte das Recht über seine Befolgung denken und aus der Politikwissenschaft lernen?* Paper presented at a Workshop on Compliance at the European University Institute, Florence, February 28/March 1, 2000.

Joyner, Ch.C. (1987), 'Crossing the Great Divide: Views from a Political Scientists Wandering in the World of International Law', *Proceedings of the 81st Annual Meeting of the American Society of International Law (Boston, MA),* American Society of International Law, Washington, DC, pp. 385-91.

Keohane, R.O. (1997), 'International Relations and International Law: Two Optics', *Harvard International Law Journal,* 38 (2), pp. 487-502.

King, G., Keohane, R.O., and Verby, S. (1994), *Designing Social Inquiry: Scientific Inference in Qualitative Reserach,* Princeton UP, Princeton.

Kirchner, C. (1991), 'The Difficult Reception of Law and Economics in Germany', *International Review of Law and Economics,* 11, pp. 277-92.

Knetsch, J.L. (1998), 'Law and Social Sciences: Reciprocal Influences and Opportunities', in Chin and Choi (eds.), *Law, Social Sciences and Public Policy.*

Kratochwil, F.V. (2000), 'How do Norms Matter?' in Byers (ed.), *The Role of Law in International Politics,* pp. 35-68.

Lavenex, S. (1999a), *The Europeanization of Refugee Policy: Between Human Rights and Internal Security,* European University Institute (PhD thesis), Florence.

Lavenex, S. (1999b), *Safe Third Countries. Extending the EU Asylum and Immigration Policies to Central and Eastern Europe,* Central European UP, Budapest.

Marauhn, Th. (1998), 'A European Security and Defence Network – Developing a Framework of Analysis for Multilateral Defence Co-operation in Europe, in: J. Huru, O.-P. Jalonen, and M. Sheehan (eds.), *New Dimensions of Security in Central and Northeastern Europe,* Tampere Peace Research Institute Research Report No. 83, pp. 85-115.

Merton, R.K. (1996), *On Social Structure and Science.* Edited and with an introduction by Piotr Sztompmka, Chicago UP, Chicago.

Moravcsik, A. (1998), *The Choice for Europe: Social Purpose and State Power From Messina to Maastricht,* Cornell UP, Ithaca, NY.

Müller, F. (1997), *Juristische Methodik,* ed. by R. Christensen, 7th rev. ed., Duncker&Humblot, Berlin.

Neyer, J., Wolf, D., and Zürn, M. (1999), *Recht jenseits des Staates,* Zentrum für Europäische Rechtspolitik and der Universität Bremen (ZERP), Bremen.

Noll, G. (1997), 'Prisoner's Dilemma in Fortress Europe: On the Prospects for Equitable Burden Sharing in the European Union', *German Yearbook of International Law,* 40, pp. 405-37.

Okruch, St. (1999), *Innovation und Diffusion von Normen: Grundlagen und Elemente einer evolutorischen Theorie des Institutionenwandels,* Duncker&Humblot, Berlin.

Sartori, G. (1969), 'From Sociology of Politics to Political Sociology', in S.M. Lipset (ed.), *Politics and the Social Science,* Oxford UP, New York, pp. 65-100.

Scharpf, F.W. (1997), *Games Real Actors Can Play. Actor-Centered Institutionalism in Policy-Research,* Westview Press, Boulder, CO.

Slaughter Burley, A.-M. (1993), 'International Law and International Relations Theory: A Dual Agenda', *American Journal of International Law,* 87, pp. 205-39.

Slaughter, A.-M., Tulumello, A.S., and Wood, St. (1998), 'International Law and International Relation Theory: A New Generation of Interdisciplinary Scholarship', *American Journal of International Law,* 92 (3), pp. 367-97.

Slaughter, A.-M. (1995), 'International Law in a World of Liberal States', *European Journal of International Law,* 6, pp. 503-38.

Tamanaha, B.Z. (1995), 'An Analytical Map of Social Scientific Approaches to the Concept of Law', *Oxford Journal of Legal Studies,* 15 (4), pp. 501-35.

Toope, Ph. (2000), 'Emerging Patterns of Governance and International Law', in Byers (ed.), *The Role of Law in International Politics,* pp. 91-108.

Tsebelis, G. (2002), *Veto Players: How Political Institutions Work,* Princeton UP, Princeton.

UNHCR (1979), *Handbook on Procedures and Criteria for Determining Refugee Status,* Geneva.

UNHCR (1995), *An Overview of Protection Issues in Western Europe: Legislative Trends and Positions Taken by UNHCR.* European Series, Vol. 1, No. 3, September, Geneva.

Weiler, J.H.H. (1993), 'Journey to an Unknown Destination: A Retrospective and Prospective of the European Court of Justice in the Arena of Political Integration', *Journal of Common Market Studies,* 31, pp. 417-46.

Weiler, J.H.H. (1994), 'A Quiet Revolution. The European Court of Justice and Its Interlocutors', *Comparative Political Studies,* 26, pp. 510-34.

Young, O. (1992), 'Remarks', *Proceedings of the 86st Annual Meeting of the American Society of International Law,* American Society of International Law, Washington, DC, pp. 172-5.

Young, O. (1994), *International Governance. Protecting the Environment in a Stateless Society,* Cornell UP, Ithaca and London.

Zangl, B. and Zürn, M. (2004), *Prozesse der internationalen Verrechtlichung – Innovative Wege globaler Politikgestaltung,* Dietz, Bonn.

Chapter 8

Interdisciplinarity in Migration Research: On the Relation between Sociology and Linguistics

Michael Bommes and Utz Maas

Introduction: Interdisciplinarity of Migration Research as Applied Science

Migration research is generally seen as a field of research predestined for inter-disciplinary research. An indication of this is the general willingness to provide a considerable amount of resources for the establishment of research centers trans-versal to disciplinary institutions on a national and international level,[1] for national and international conferences, research projects and other forms of collaboration. Large parts of the comparative literature in this field are a result of this (e.g. Bade and Weiner, 1997; Hammar, 1985; Hammar et al., 1996; Joppke, 1998). Inter-disciplinarity of research is generally seen as worth funding, not only in relation to migration research. But it is an undertaking not only sometimes practically difficult to organize but also scientifically challenging. For those reasons we take migration research as a field which provides an excellent occasion to address some of the problems connected with interdisciplinary research.

What exactly is referred to by stressing the value of interdisciplinary research and why should migration research be seen as a preferable area for this type of research? Before we try to answer these questions some observations concerning interdisciplinary migration research need to be discussed here. The immediate plausibility of the necessity for interdisciplinarity in migration research rests fairly often on a deficit of reflection found in migration research itself. The terms 'migration' and 'migrants' seem to suggest that the kinds of problems are obvious and evident which are to be scientifically addressed. Various disciplines claim responsibility: sociology, psychology, economy, political science, education, law, linguistics, health etc. But in many respects 'migration' refers to problems con-stituted rather outside of scientific disciplines, mainly in the fields of politics and nation states. Picked up from here, they are treated in the scientific disciplines participating in migration research as evidently given and science presents itself as applied science. Recurrently the problem of constituting a subject and defining the corresponding problems and questions with the disciplinary means of science is avoided by keeping the pre-scientific constitution of the subject 'migration' latent, based on a framework of analyses which is centred around the problematics of 'integration' and 'inequality'.[2] For reasons of stressing the argument one could say that inter-disciplinarity in migration research fairly often means interdisciplinarity without disciplines.

This state of the art, interdisciplinarity without disciplines, forms the starting ground for some of the main text books of migration research (Treibel, 1990; Nuscheler, 1995; Sassen, 1996; Castles and Miller, 2003), which claim successfully their interdisciplinary usability. For the everyday-business of migration research this creates no major problem. But presumably as a result of this, migration research has never gained a prominent position in any of its key disciplines since it has rarely contributed to their defining theoretical and methodological problems. Migration research has left out scientific chances by orienting itself, its definitions of problems and solutions, to political and organizational concerns (e.g. of the state, social policy, law, education, health) about potential problems of social integration and conflict based in cultural, ethnic and language differences. In this way migration research remains a so-called applied science.[3]

This description of migration research exaggerates to some extent in order to stress the need to clarify some of the meanings of interdisciplinarity, a scientific practice highly valued but seldom adequately reflected. It forces particularly a serious discussion if there are more systematic and substantial reasons why migration research should practice a kind of interdisciplinarity starting from contributions specified in a disciplinary manner.

In this chapter we discuss the implications of interdisciplinarity based on an example. We deal with the relation between linguistics and sociology and the different modes by which they confront the problem of language in the field of migration. In a first step we present the relation between language and migration and the problems connected in a pre-disciplinary way. In a second step we introduce the different disciplinary moulds of sociology and linguistics to conceptualize language. The next section argues that an interdisciplinary research which operates in a mode of aggregation of knowledge, cannot cope adequately with the problem of language and migration. We take this as indication of a need for genuine multidisciplinary research in this area. The concluding section returns to some more general considerations on interdisciplinarity.

Language and Migration – Some Pre-Scientific Observations

Problems of language are evidently a central phenomenon connected with migration processes. Leaving one's place of origin implies coping with new linguistic challenges. Migration may allow to proceed in a heuristic manner on rather familiar terms, if migration happens within the domain of an overarching language or language family – e.g. if somebody from Austria migrates to Northern Germany. But more often migration implies rather bewildering experiences on an unknown and (structurally) distant linguistic territory – e.g. if somebody from Northern Africa, speaking a rural variety of Berber, migrates to Northern Germany. New linguistic demands and the effort to adapt to this new situation are a central part of the experience of migrants. The ways individuals cope with these demands differ. But the linguistic distance between the language resources appropriated biographically by an individual migrant and the language proficiencies asked for in the immigration context proves to be a key factor independent of the individual capacity to cope with cognitive demands.

This is socially reflected by the institutional reactions to migration as can be easily seen from a few examples: Census reports attribute linguistic affiliation to migrants and count them as members of linguistic communities. The allocation of social resources to immigrant communities occasionally depends on the ascription of linguistic attributes distinguishing e.g. Kurds from Turks within the immigrant group of Turkish citizens or Berber from Arabic speaking immigrants within the group of Moroccan citizens. Even immigration and access to a state territory may be regulated by referring to linguistic criteria as e.g. in the case of immigrants coming from the GUS states to Germany claiming to be Ethnic Germans. German language proficiency is defined here legally as one of the decisive preconditions for naturalization. Consequently Ethnic Germans have to pass a linguistic examination testifying the legitimacy of their claim of national belonging.

These modes of attribution evidently apply language designations in ways that refer to socially quite heterogeneous types of linguistic behaviour. E.g. Berber refers to the linguistic behaviour of people living in North African villages as well as to those who moved to Northern Europe. It is a familiar pattern in Europe that these migrants try to recreate their local culture in the 'diaspora' (Cohen, 1997; Maas and Mehlem, 1999). Except for the unavoidable contacts with administrative officials and colleagues at work, they tend to limit their social exchanges to migrants from the same villages of origin and the extended family and arrange for their own mosques with similar restrictions of access.

The official attribute *Berber* includes additionally the children of these migrants, the second and third generations, who grow up with German as the 'matrix language'[4] in their daily relevant peer group at school and in the neighbourhood. But these immigrant children maintain affiliations to their families and claim – sometimes even violently – Berber as their genuine or native language – despite the fact that they eventually no longer actively speak this language and preserve only a kind of passive understanding. There exists of course a huge array of different constellations in between these extremes.

In pre-scientific discourses the term language connotes different meanings, to a large extent still articulated by religious myths. As far as scientific discourses are linked with pre-scientific conceptualizations, they are still articulated by these conceptualizations. We name only two continuously influential strands of thinking reaching back to these religious traditions:

- one on the relation between language and thinking: in accordance with the Myth of Adam languages are seen as a means of identifying things, they ascribe names to the things created by God;
- the other on the relation between language and communication: in accordance with the Myth of Babel language becomes a subject as a means of communication in the case of communicative disturbance – as well as in the case when this disturbance is healed like in the Whitsun-miracle described in the New Testament.

Conceptualizations of the relation between language and thinking focus on language in singular, i.e. language as a competence. Conceptualizations of the relation between language and communication focus on languages in plural, i.e. language diversity. Both strands were pre-eminent in the western tradition. However the way the relation between communication and language has been conceptualized, took a peculiar road in history: The experience of linguistic diversity as an impediment does not necessarily presuppose linguistic homogeneity as a natural state. The presupposition of large linguistically and culturally homogeneous areas was the outcome of a contra-factual ideological construction established during the process of European nation state building starting in Early Modern Times. In former periods the immediate experience of linguistic and cultural diversity did not feed these kinds of imagination – and probably still does not in many parts of the World (Matthes, 1999). Instead individuals were confronted with the necessity and the social expectation to cope with linguistic diversity by becoming multilingual. Among the early Church Fathers an interpretation of the Myth of Babel different from the presently current one still can be found. According to this version the key event was not the emergence of linguistic diversity but the disturbance of the human capacity to understand different languages presupposed as a normal state of affairs – a capacity in the beginning analogous to the capacity of the angels.[5]

Language problems and socially institutionalized imaginations of language are present and gain relevance in all kinds of migratory constellations. In the field of migration language is not just one moment which can be abstracted from or isolated as just one specific topic like e.g. eating habits or wearing a scarf. Quite independent from the scientific approaches preferred in different strands of migration research, language has to be taken into account as long as linguistic data form a constitutive part of the empirical research data as e.g. interviews, letters, autobiographies or written documents.

Language – Disciplinary Accesses in Sociology and Linguistics

In the previous section the term language and some of its pre-scientific meanings have been discussed in a way which must not be taken as any effort to constitute language as a subject of disciplinary research and theory building. The constitution of a subject in each discipline entails necessarily conceptual idealizations[6] built-in

corresponding to the array of accepted procedures and axioms within the disciplinary scientific community. Conceptualizations of a subject can only be extrapolated
from these idealizations – which implies their dynamic character, changing with
scientific conjectures. But to a certain extent language is a common denominator of
all disciplines referred to as humanities – and of even more than these like theology
or law, all of which are disciplines which deal with linguistically codified documents.

One way to understand how different disciplines[7] constitute their specific
subject and approach their problematic is to look at the way they conceptualize
implicitly or explicitly language as a constitutive part of their research subject. In
this section we discuss the different ways in which linguistics and sociology conceptualize language. We argue that the way both disciplines define language is
constitutive for the construction of their disciplinary subject. In the following
section 4 we ask for the relation between and the consequences of these two
different conceptualizations in the field of migration research when migration is
treated either as a sociological or a linguistic subject.

Language in Linguistics

Around the turn of the century when modern linguistics became institutionalized as
a scientific discipline, its subject was initially conceptualized in terms taken from
the sociology of late 19th century.[8] 'Sociology of language' or in German *'Sprach-
soziologie'* was a frequent title for theoretically ambitious studies in the 1920s.
Despite this early orientation however, the common denominator of the disciplinary
processes of professionalization became a largely accepted set of postulates known
as structural linguistics, establishing itself firmly during the large International
Congresses of Linguistics since 1928. This set founded an array of descriptive
procedures that is explicitly based on the abstraction from problems which define
complementary disciplines like the problem of 'verstehen' (interpretation) in
Sociology.

Leaving aside more complicated problems for reasons of clarity it can be
claimed: Language as the subject of linguistic research does not refer to a field of
study related to social practices of interpretation, understanding, communication or
believing etc. but to a set of formal conditions articulating these social practices:
making them possible and restraining them at once to those individuals that have
access to these practices. The social as a problem is present in linguistics only in a
negative mode. Language is seen as a social fact coextensive with a socially defined
group (a language community), but it is studied only in formal terms.

This holds true even for the so-called sociolinguistic tradition that gained some
kind of impact during the 1960s and 1970s represented e.g. by the work of William
Labov and his collaborators and the work of Basil Bernstein in the 'application
oriented' field of education. In this tradition[9] formal linguistic phenomena – so-
called linguistic variables – were statistically correlated with specific social groups
or with structures of social stratification.

Even if these correlations were investigated with respect to their constitutive social role, e.g. the use of certain linguistic forms as social 'acts of identity' (Le Page), linguistic research sticks to the division of scientific labor which restricts linguistics to the investigation of formal structures.

This holds especially true for research in language contact – whether as the result of migration or as a constant moment of social constitution, to be found in most parts of the world. The investigation of these problems, i.e. questions of linguistic adaptation, of acquiring access to bilingual or even multilingual resources or of mixing these resources, circumscribes a rather marginal research area in main stream linguistics. There is however by now a considerable amount of research on so-called code-switching, being emblematic for language contact situations (see Goebl, 1996, 1997).

But even in this field the conceptual barriers mentioned before prove to be prevalent: The kind of problems linked with code-switching are rather seen as marginal phenomena of disturbance relative to the ideal monolingual communication situation seen as the normal case. Modern linguistics became established in the 19th century as a comparative science, reconstructing the development of diversity based on the background assumption of a prehistoric linguistic unity. More empirically orientated minds tried to invoke linguistic contact as the main cause for language development and the origin of diversity – but they did not succeed in convincing the scientific community so that the topic remains to be seen as concerned with epiphenomena.[10]

Systematic misinterpretations of linguistic research are predictable if the conceptual idealizations founding disciplinary linguistic research are ignored. Non-linguists tend to be rather disappointed by research that investigates painstakingly the restrictions for code-switching and tries to prove that code switching happens in a non-random way restricted by certain formal channels paving the way for change in linguistic register. This type of linguistic analysis provides no answer to the question why actual cases of code-switching appear. Linguists restrict their investigations to the identification of those formal conditions which allow for code-switching without explaining its actual appearance.

From a social science point of view the subject of linguistics pertains to the formal prerequisites of social practice – to a certain extent comparable with other cognitive requirements. Correspondingly recent developments have led to a kind of self-conception that affiliates linguistics to psychology and furthers even more its distance from sociology. The dominating currant in linguistics, the Chomskyan direction of the so-called Generative Grammar even claims to be a sub-discipline of psychology, and more and more linguistic departments are renamed or get integrated into institutes for cognitive sciences.

This disciplinary shift of orientation of course did not go without disclaimers. From the 1960s onwards the field of the so-called sociolinguistics has been conceived as a counter-currant to the idealization of a homogeneous speech community, constitutive for the Chomskyan type of research on the linguistic competence of an ideal speaker-hearer. A result of these disclaimers was a certain amount of scientific confusion and the borders between sociological and linguistic research became fuzzy. But despite impressive empirical results this type of research was not successful to establish a new paradigm in linguistics. During the years of the so-called student movement and the university reforms in the late 1960s and 1970s sociolinguistics became synonymous among linguists with critical attitudes towards society. This direction lost its initial force, the pendulum swung back and current linguistics is fairly securely defined again as structural linguistics. Its main stream is led by Chomskyan linguists pleading for a comprehensive cognitive science paradigm.

Meanwhile however there is a new trend to re-valorize the old question of the relation between language and thinking, a question that had formerly lost scientific credit as a result of dubious speculative research activities around the turn of century and the recurrent affiliation of this type of research to racist discourses.[11] Recent linguistic research on the basis of a very comprehensive survey design (e.g. Berman and Slobin, 1994) has shown that certain cognitive settings – e.g. the mode of knitting a narrative structure by means of temporal and causal relations between narrated events motivating the narrated actions – correlate with language structures. These settings are at least acquired on different paces by learners of different languages. This type of research demonstrates that appropriating a linguistic structure implies to acquire a mode of thinking: language to a preliminary extent 'thinks for the speakers' (Slobin). The way this research constructs linguistic typologies inside of the formal frame of the linguistic discipline, eventually opens a window to a conception of language as social kit.

No new paradigm of linguistics is at sight – but at many places we find researchers striving for overcoming the implied barriers of the established conceptualizations, trying to combine an empirical orientation to linguistic diversity with the effort to develop a cognitive model capable to account for this diversity. In the context of these recent developments and their future potential it may be a significant detail that the research efforts of one of the big international centres for cognitive science research, the Max Planck Institute for Psycholinguistics in Nijmegen (NL), include a department for *social* anthropology (directed by Stephen Levinson).

Language in Sociology

The institutionalization of sociology as a discipline was scientifically based on the differentiation of a problem-field through a process of abstraction and idealization. To a large extent this happened when Max Weber defined sociology as the effort to analyse and to explain 'social action' and he argued that explanations in sociology rely on the operation of 'verstehen' (Weber, 1972, p. 1). In his considerations on the methodological foundations of sociology he differentiates sociology from other disciplines through the concept of meaning (Sinn). These starting definitions were productive in the sense that they delineated a field of problems which was able to attract and in this way to constitute disciplinary attention. Among others this was a result of the use he made of these basic concepts: According to Weber 'meaning' is given if actors combine 'a subjective meaning' with their behaviour. But who is the actor who combines (more or less consciously (Weber, 1972, p. 10) meaning with something if meaning is defined by Weber as a concept which does not refer to a psychic phenomenon?[12] Weber left the discipline with major problems behind; one of them to clarify the concept of 'social action' and the other to clarify the methodological foundations of 'verstehen'.

One other founding abstraction and idealization of sociology is represented by the Durkheimian tradition. Durkheim (1893) was interested in the various forms of a 'conscience collective' in different types of society which he saw as a necessary requirement to keep these societies together. The basic assumption is that societies are integrated societies and that this will only be secured if they develop reasonably coherent forms of solidarity securing the unity of society. Starting from this Durkheimian idea main stream sociology is built on the assumption that societies (in plural) are integrated societies based on social coherence. The underlying pre-scientific and political model has been and to a large extent still is the nation state, its political idea of unity and cultural homogeneity and the starting context of sociology is the social fear of the 19th and the early 20th century that this programme might fail (Tenbruck, 1992). Sociology can be seen as a discipline which is based on the pre-scientific assumption of social and cultural coherence and homogeneity as a necessary prerequisite for the safeguard of society quite in a parallel manner as linguistics is based on the assumption of linguistic homogeneity as a natural state and condition for communication.[13]

It was Parsons who addressed both founding problems of sociology: 'social action' and 'social integration', in a way which had a major influence on the development of the discipline. Following Durkheim's identification of social inte-gration as the central problem of modern societies, Parsons assigned the 'nation' a systematic place in modernization theory. In his theory 'the societal community' has the function of integrating modern society. Linked with the concept of 'citizen-ship' which he took from Thomas H. Marshall, Parsons saw the 'nation' as a universalistic form of inclusion into the 'societal community' (see Parsons, 1971, 1973). For him the disentanglement of the nation from ethnic, i.e. particularistic notions of belonging was likely at each place where the differentiation of society and the generalization of values was making progress. Since Parsons the theoretical presupposition that modern societies are national societies, has been a vastly unquestioned base of main stream sociological theorizing until the end of the 1980s.

Parsons' effort to resolve the problems posed by Weber's conceptualizations of social action and meaning – the 'action frame of reference' (Parsons, 1937) as an undissolvable nexus of means, ends, values and norms – proved to be not nearly as stable as his integration of the concept of the nation into sociological theory. Rather sociological directions after Parsons can be differentiated by the way they deal with the difficulties to keep together concepts of action, meaning and consciousness/ motives. Rational-choice-theories interpret action as a psychological concept and try to explain the social as a result of the actions of individual actors trying to maximize their profits.

Social phenomenology, ethnomethodology and conversational analysis, Mead's theory of the constitution of meaning, symbolic interactionism, sociological hermeneutics, Habermas' theory of communication and Luhmann's system theory, these diverse directions have in common that they subscribe in some way or another to a concept of meaning and to the thesis that meaning is social and not psychic. Social meaning is therefore seen as communicative meaning.

In a sociological perspective communication does not mean something like the transfer of information. Instead communication refers to a recursive process in which events are related to each other as utterances in a reflexive manner. An utterance communicating something, an 'illocutionary act', gains social meaning only if a second communication happens and relates with the forerunning communication, interpreting it, i.e. ascribing meaning to it[14] and making it only in this way a communicative event, an action. The same holds true for this second utterance which becomes only a communicative event when it is treated by the next communication as such etc. Social meaning is conceptualized as a result of these recursive processes and sociology tries to identify the conditions under which the reproduction of meaning is possible. This concept of communication does not reduce communication to face to face-communication, i.e. interaction but accounts for different forms of communication, e.g. interaction, written communication or communication per email. Empirically this requires to examine social meaning as a result of recursive communicative events and to ask how communication produces and reproduces social meaning.

The theoretical, methodological and empirical problems implied in the effort to define a sociological concept of meaning, communication and action led especially during the 1960s, 1970s and early 1980s to a vast interest of sociologists in linguistics. The prominence of meaning and communication in sociological analysis implied some realization of the theoretically and empirically central role of language. Theoretical approaches of linguistics and language philosophy, including linguistic structuralism, Chomsky's grammar theory, philosophical and linguistic speech act theory, linguistic pragmatics, theories of meaning, Wittgenstein and ordinary language philosophy, theories of language socialization, all these different theoretical traditions were introduced in sociological discussions. A further outcome of the sociological realization of the eminent relevance of meaning and communication was the insight that the linguistic structure of sociological data needed to be taken methodologically and empirically serious. This led to a growing interest in the relation between linguistic and sociological methods and methodologies like sociolinguistics, language sociology and the analysis of conversations, speech acts, narratives, discourses, uses of arguments etc.

But this sociological interest in linguistics did not dissolve the different meaning of language as a disciplinary subject of study in sociology and linguistics but eventually rather reinforced the reorientation of sociology back to 'its own problems'. To some extent it was the outside orientation especially to linguistics and language philosophy which helped to clarify what 'the own problems' of sociology are about. Sociology aims at the analysis of social structures and defines the social as the communicative production of meaning structures. The analysis of social structures identifies meaning structures as conditions of restriction which limit and open up at once communicative options, i.e. they define areas of contingencies. E.g. interaction or organization define structures of communication – the co-presence of participants (interaction) or the relatedness of communicative events to a recursive network of decisions (organization) – which open up social options by excluding others. Methodologically this implies that sociology describes and demonstrates empirically the structuration of concrete communicative processes through restrictions which are theoretically assumed to be characteristic for society, e.g. interactions, organizations or functional realms like the economy, politics or science.

Generally it can be argued that sociology discusses the role of language related to three dimensions of its own problematic: 1) the aim of sociological analysis, i.e. the description and analysis of social conditions as meaning structures of communication; 2) methodological and methodical problems; 3) the role of linguistic data for sociological analysis. Sociologists certainly do not all the time reflect these dimensions of analysis in their day to day work. Usually there is no need to go into details of grammatical description and a type of school grammar knowledge suffices. Indeed, most sophisticated types of empirical sociological analysis like the hermeneutic work of Oevermann (e.g. 1979, 1983) demonstrates that in many cases this knowledge fulfils to a satisfying extent the requirement to identify the formal characteristics of the empirical data which justify the hermeneutic ascription of meaning.

It has become common sociological knowledge that communication or social action are linguistically articulated. And furthermore sociological directions like ethnomethodology, conversational analysis, language sociology, but also ethnographic methods in sociology and all kinds of social scientific interpretative methods do rely recurrently on more formal methods of language description. But they use these tools in a disciplinary instrumental way aiming to improve the reconstruction of meaning structures and their validity. It is this disciplinary founding aim which explains the wide range of methods and procedures for coding the empirical data in sociology reaching from strict formal procedures like in quantitative social research to subtle techniques of transcription producing protocols of social micro-events like in conversational analyses. The common denominator of these methods is that they are not defined by the effort to describe their data in accordance with a whole set of formal conditions defining a language in terms of linguistics. Language as a subject of sociological study seems to be based on complementary abstractions to the kind of abstractions found in linguistics. Language as a set of formal conditions articulating social practices is only taken into account as far as this proves necessary for the sociological description of meaning structures. The sociological clarification of the role of language serves to reconstruct the disciplinary subject of sociology.

An implicit danger of this complementary disciplinary conceptualization of language in sociology is the production of blind spots already on the level of methods. If linguistic structures defined as a set of formal conditions, articulate social practices there is a tendency in sociological documentation procedures to 'normalize' linguistic data which are ambivalent or non-transparent in terms of meaning by extinguishing formal inconsistencies.[15]

This becomes a problem especially in the field of migration research. The linguistic resources of migrants as we have discussed them earlier, affect the capability of sociology to analyse and describe meaning structures. One basic premise of sociology is the assumption that social reality is an ongoing recursive process of 'making sense'. Analysing this communicative process of making sense, sociology can usually treat the formal linguistic structures dealt with in linguistics as latent structures, i.e. its analysis relies on these structures as necessary formal conditions for the production of meaning without paying specifically detailed attention to them. Migration circumscribes a research field which confronts sociology with the duty to make this relation between formal linguistic structures and the analysis of meaning structures a more explicit topic. The reason for this is precisely the 'unusual' linguistic form of migrant communication. The 'normalizations' of the sociological documentation procedures tend to hide the role of linguistic structures as a condition and a result of 'making sense' processes.

Language and Migration: Promises and Omissions of Interdisciplinary Research

Migration forces people to readapt their cultural resources and to acquire new ones in order to cope with the social requirements under immigrant conditions. Sociology and the related social sciences have accumulated quite a body of knowledge about the conditions of the so-called integration and assimilation of migrants. Generally speaking it is assumed that restructuration processes of the linguistic and cultural capabilities of migrant individuals depend on their social chances to get socially included in the relevant organizations of the different functional realms of modern society, especially the economy, education, health, religion and law, but also politics, sports or the mass media. On the other hand the capability to realize the existent options in these contexts and to participate in the required communicative processes – reaching from interactions and oral communication to various forms of written communication – depends on the structural preconditions of migrant individuals themselves concerning their linguistic and social skills. These skills are a result of their biographic histories of inclusions and engagements in family networks, in economic, educational, religious or political organizations. The biographic background refers to a context where not only skills are appropriated but also perception schemes for social options and limits, for socially defined loyalties and for restrictions of legitimate participation.

Migration in modern society dealt with in migration research is mainly defined as migration transgressing state borders, i.e. migrants moving from one state to another. The social inclusion of migrants and the resulting restructuration processes of the migrants themselves are socially observed and described by varying criteria of success or failure. Migrants and their forms of participation are accompanied by a permanent process of evaluating their 'social integration'. Being more or less successful is defined by criteria of integration, assimilation, second language proficiency etc. These permanent 'reports of social integration' mostly articulate the political traditions of the country where they are produced. They reproduce the traditions of defining social belonging in terms of the national community. The immigrants themselves however may use distinctive criteria of success for describing and evaluating their migration process e.g. taken from their region of origin or created in the immigration context. Such criteria may be the maintenance of cultural identity or language, the timely limited acceptance of social depravation as a channel to social mobility in the village of origin or as a means to care for the future of their children etc.

The social inclusion of migrants, the preconditions and effects connected may be theoretically conceptualized in different ways dependent on the sociological or linguistic approaches preferred in migration research. But these approaches are in one way or another framed by the disciplinary traditions and questions. Sociology may analyse the social consequences of migration in very different respects. This does not necessarily imply a focus on migrants. But as soon as social contexts involving migrants become the subject of empirical research, social and linguistic restructuration processes of competences may become relevant. Taken seriously this implies a need to rethink the relation between sociology and linguistics.

The same holds true the other way around: Empirically linguistics analyses the structures of linguistic data collected empirically from migrants in order to extrapolate coexisting language systems ('competences' in Chomsky's terms) theoretically understood as controlling those linguistic practices which are seen as a result of migration processes. Taken seriously this implies that social conditions, the inclusion of migrants in communicative processes define relevant conditions for linguistic change and the evolution of formal structures.

In both cases disciplinary abstractions concerning social meaning respectively formal linguistic structures need to be revised to a certain extent and in a methodologically controlled manner. We want to address some of the problems implied in these disciplinary revision processes by discussing examples from our own sociological (a) and linguistic (b) work and their interdisciplinary limits. From this we will draw some conclusions for multidisciplinary work in migration research in the final section.

a) Empirical research has to take the basic assumption of sociology methodologically serious: Social events are by definition meaningful events. In the case of migration, research based on interviews or other kinds of linguistic data cannot presuppose recurrently a shared linguistic background of articulating meaning between researchers and migrants. The linguistic structures of communication and their potential of articulating ongoing social processes cannot be taken for granted on the basis of a shared linguistic competence. This requires to clarify the formal linguistic conditions of making sense, i.e. to deal manifestly with what usually remains latent in sociological analysis. Such an extended effort leaves untouched the basic assumption that the analysis aims at the description of meaning events as realizations of social structure. But it requires a much more detailed clarification of the relation between formal linguistic and sociological descriptions.

But sociological and more generally social scientific migration research usually reduces these kinds of complication to a problem of linguistic knowledge or competence. Redefined in this way it can be dealt with by treating it either 1) as another variable for survey research,[16] or 2) as a problem of data production which can be solved by using translations of mother tongue interviews on the basis of the assumption that interviews of this type provide a better chance of articulation for migrants, or 3) as a problem of linguistically deficient data to be repaired and normalized by the analysis justifying its usability for practical reasons.

These modes of handling language in sociological migration research treat linguistic data[17] like a source of information about a reality laying beyond. They assume that this reality can be read from these data quite in the same way as translations of interviews are taken as 1 : 1 transformations of 'the information' communicated. This is common even in a type of research which aims at the analysis of cultural life forms and knowledge or belief systems. This methodological approach is confronted with major problems since:

- it ignores the fact that these data represent a meaningful social reality of itself and that there is no 'real reality' beyond;
- it treats the multilingual reality resulting from migration processes methodologically as a transitional and deficient social state, but not as a structural condition of communication providing a meaning potential of major social importance;
- it defines linguistic competence primarily as a technical competence to transfer information and ignores that even 'deficient' linguistic structures of communication are condensations of the forms of social inclusion and involvement of migrants in the immigrant context.

This last point indicates the central methodological problem of this approach: If the assumption that social reality is a meaningful reality defines the basic principle of sociological research, then any linguistic behaviour of migrants as a part of social reality, i.e. of communicative processes is meaningful – whatever kind of linguistic deficiencies may be observed from the outside. Sociologically this reality needs to be analysed and interpreted – which means neither to 'normalize' speech, i.e. the substitution of conventional for deviant linguistic forms (an abolition of the problem), nor just to identify externally deficiencies but to identify the meaning potential of the structural resources of communication however limited they may be.

Obviously this presupposes some knowledge about formal structures of languages, i.e. the infrastructure of communication which enables and limits the options of making sense without determining them. But the effort to fulfil these requirements in sociological analysis leads to a kind of bricolage since sociologists are usually not well equipped to do both, sociological and linguistic analysis. They can try to push the limits and to include linguistic methods. But the use of linguistic tools remains not only instrumental for sociological analysis and it is not only restricted by the individual capacity of sociological researchers to combine sociological analysis with linguistic insights. It leaves especially open the question how the two types of analysis found in linguistics and sociology, their different disciplinary perspectives and their implications are related to each other. Two examples may illustrate this point.

In the analysis of the linguistic behaviour of Turkish migrant youth as a specific mode of participation and making sense of the conditions of social inclusion in a middle town in Germany, one of the authors (Bommes, 1993) has included quite an amount of linguistic knowledge. A detailed analysis of the linguistic structures of communication made these structures transparent as forms of making sense of the modes of social inclusion in the organizations of the education system, social work and the labor market as they were typical for these Turkish migrant youth. It was possible to demonstrate that communicative contributions even on the basis of a very restricted language proficiency are meaningful events – not just because the analysis treats them as such. The sequences of communicative events which form the empirical corpus of the analysis, treat those contributions as meaningful in the way they link with them.

The effort to identify the formal linguistic structures of these youth communications relied on linguistic tools like language comparisons, analysis of code switching, descriptions of second language acquisition processes or learner grammars. This made it possible to analyze e.g. the case of a young Turkish immigrant in a way demonstrating that his very restricted German language proficiency (see Bommes, 1993, pp. 170) is suitable and part of the mode he arranges with the social conditions as an unemployed Turkish youth living in Germany for about five years and running without success through various training courses. In a surprising manner he reinvents the traditional social relation between father and son of the Turkish village in the German immigration context. Spending his time mainly in a group of Turkish unemployed youth this allows him to subvert the educational, i.e. communicative efforts of his father by demonstrating social respect, i.e. silence, and to avoid at the same time the 'interpellations' (Althusser) of the German educational and social work organizations. A detailed analysis of his grammatically restricted speech shows that these social conditions are articulated by this form of speech. One result of the analysis is the assumption that his linguistic competence can be seen as a result of the history of social inclusion of this Turkish youth and the way he makes sense of it. But this assumption remains speculative to the extent that the linguistic competence has not been described in a strictly linguistic sense, i.e. as a set of formal conditions regulating the production of utterances. The extent to which these formal conditions as the result of a language acquisition process restrict and pave social options, remains excluded from the sociological perspective even if the analysis is linguistically informed.

The same problem holds true for the analysis of the code-switching practices of Turkish youth groups. Again it is possible to demonstrate that code-switching is meaningful and that the use of two (or even more) languages happens neither random nor just as a means of compensation for minor language proficiency.[18] Bilingual or multilingual communication is a social resource for the production of meaning. Code-switching practices are a result of social inclusion under immigrant conditions and the modes of participation of individual migrants in these practices can be reconstructed by their biographical histories of inclusion. But again the limits of this type of analysis remain the same. It is not based on a formal description of code-switching. Its relation to linguistic investigations remains unclear which identifies the formal restrictions for code-switching and demonstrates that code-switching happens in a non-random way restricted by certain formal channels paving the way for change in linguistic register. This leaves open the question how the two types of analysis found in linguistics and sociology, their different disciplinary perspectives and their implications are related to each other.

Generally normal science and its requirements of disciplinary and subdisciplinary specialization do not easily allow for bridging disciplinary disjunctions by individual scientists. We take this as an indication for the need of inter- or rather multidisciplinary research and return to this later.

b) Linguistic scholars involved in the field of migration research tend to rely on a complementary kind of bricolage compared to sociologists. They usually stick to the disciplinary standards as far as the core of their research is concerned. As soon as they try to account for the complexities of the migratory process and the resulting forms of social involvement defining the 'social context' of linguistic change, a similar problem turns up: The status of the sociological knowledge employed in a linguistic frame of analysis remains open and unclarified.

We discuss this again by taking an example from a research project[19] carried out by one of the authors (see Maas and Mehlem, 1999, 2003), dealing with the linguistic situation of Moroccan immigrants in Germany. The core of this research project deals with the collection and analyses of linguistic data employing the usual descriptive procedures of linguistics. The empirically identifiable linguistic forms used by these Morrocan immigrants are partly identical with those observable in their regions of origin in North Africa, partly these forms are neologisms. It is part of a linguist's job to develop an integrating calculus on the basis of collected linguistic data and to extrapolate the coexisting language systems (the 'competences' in Chomsky's terms) controlling the linguistic practice.

The aim of this research is of course not just to add another grammatical description of a new linguistic variety to the stock of already existing varieties, but to learn about the social conditions of these immigrants and their position in the immigration country as the relevant context in which this new variety evolves. A given linguistic form, e.g. an expression in the Berber (Tarifit) dialect, may be the same in structural terms when elicited in a North African village or in a German suburb – but the usage of this form may gain a rather different position in the linguistic structure of the immigrant utterances.

To give an example presupposes to introduce some rudimentary linguistic notions. One of the most salient parameters in linguistic typology is the way utterances are grammatically structured by the predicate. We can distinguish *head-marking* sentence structure, where the predicate is morphologically marked for the core structure of the predication (the scenario and its participants); and a *dependent-marking* mode where the syntactic structure is marked on the nominal complements of the predicate (e.g. by case marking); the predicate itself tends to be morphologically atomic in this case. Corresponding to this, head-marking languages show mostly verb initial word order. Afro-asiatic languages (e.g. Arabic, Berber) are characterized by head-marking and a verb-initial word order. But the attribution of this kind of structural parameters is always a question of degree – languages are dynamic systems with a changing structure. In most languages the pre-verbal slot in sentence construction permits to give a term a specific profile (marking it as topic or focus of the sentence). This holds also true for the Afro-Asiatic languages which allow for a nominal element as a marked sentence initial. The result is a kind of cleft structure – the initial element serving as a reference point for the remaining utterance (cf. spoken English: 'John he came').

Berber has a very complex verb conjugation and also some elements of nominal morphology marking various complement functions. Two examples may illustrate this:

i-	aznd-d	uriaz	tamettutt
3.S-	send-PROX	man.CONST	woman[20]

'The man sent the woman here.'

i-	aznd-d	ariaz
3.S-	send-PROX	man

'He send the man.'

ariaz: 'man' is a noun with a word initial vowel modifiable by ablaut. This initial vowel shows the syntactic function: *uriaz* is the 'subject' of the predicate (here glossed by CONST[RUCT STATE]), in accordance with its inflectional form: *ariaz* it is the object complement. But the subject can be shifted to the focus position of a sentence,[21] where it is not marked for the construct state.

ariaz	i-aznd-d	tamettutt
man	3.S-send-PROX	woman

'The man sent the woman here.' (= It was the man who sent the woman here.)

If we consider the linguistic situation in Western Europe, where migrants from North Africa are placed into, we see major relevant differences: We find a 'language union' ('Sprachbund'; Comrie, 1981, pp. 204) sharing major structural traits as for instance the word order. In these languages the predicate or finite verb holds the second position of the sentence order and leaves the first position free (as e.g. in German) or reserves it for the subject (as e.g. in English, French, Dutch etc.). This structure may become the matrix structure, as we find it in the case of immigrant children growing up with the language of the immigration country. In this case utterances may require a revised interpretation:

  ariaz i-aznd-d tame~~ttutt~~

A form like this is now congruent with the matrix structure and may be no longer interpretable as a marked structure.[22] It seems that social integration is reflected here in a shift of the usage made of formal linguistic resources. There are other linguistic indicators clustering with this phenomenon. E.g. younger children growing up in Europe tend to make no longer a distinction between different nominal forms (loosing the system of vowel change by ablaut to mark the construct state). But the burden of proof for this analysis cannot be shouldered by a structural analysis alone, for systematic reasons it requires complementary ethnographic observations.

The research project tries to meet this requirement by doing ethnographic research in order to supplement the linguistic part of the research by all kinds of socially and culturally relevant data. But this can be taken only as a first step which permits to some extent to present a picture of the options (potentials and blockades) linked with linguistic practices, i.e. communicative practices defining the social conditions of this migrant population. But what is still lacking here is an integrate theory structuring the two types of empirical research. It remains bricolage in the sense that starting from the research perspective of linguistics the relation between linguistic and sociological data remains unclarified. It is still an open question how the involvement of migrants in social communication practices, i.e. in making sense, can be empirically described and made transparent as the relevant context for linguistic structural change. This implies obviously more than just identifying a correlation between linguistic and social structures in the classical sociolinguistic sense.

Linguistic problems resulting from migration urge both disciplines, linguistics and sociology, to revise some of their built-in abstractions and idealizations in a controlled manner. This may be taken as an occasion to enter into an inter- or multidisciplinary dialogue which tries to clarify the relations between their different ways of constructing a subject by using the same or correlated bodies of empirical data.

Some Considerations on Multidisciplinary Research

Disciplinary differences cannot be bridged by individual rsearchers. In this section we discuss some more general conditions and limits of multidisciplinary research and return finally to some conclusions for multidisciplinary research concerning linguistics and sociology in the field of migration.

Our examples show that explicit interdisciplinary research is not the only occasion when scientists develop some interest in the knowledge of other disciplines. They make use of this knowledge as a necessary means to secure and to clarify the premises and the consequences of their central disciplinary perspectives. In this way sociology relies on psychological, linguistic or historical knowledge, psychology on sociological or biological knowledge, linguistics on sociological, historical, neurophysiological or psychological knowledge etc. This cannot be taken as interdisciplinary research in the meaning of scientific communication between heterogeneous disciplines but rather as an instrumental appropriation of scientific knowledge in the perspective and by the means of a discipline – at the risk of accepting knowledge which may be seen as highly problematic in those disciplines where this knowledge is taken from.[23]

We have indicated that individual scientists participating in interdisciplinary research usually do not have the capacity to fully understand the complexity of knowledge of the other disciplines and sub-disciplines involved. Disciplinary definitions of problems[24] are conceptualized on the background of a disciplinary specific knowledge about theoretical and methodological options. The evolution of disciplines implies the disconnection of interdependencies in the science system which cannot be reversed individually. This implies that restricted individual knowledge capacities are a restricting condition of inter- or multidisciplinary research.

The disconnection of interdependencies also forecloses systematically the option to conceptualize interdisciplinarity as the dissolution of disciplinary differences or as integration through hierarchy. There is no hierarchy between disciplines and no master discipline which could control the coordination and regulation of interdisciplinary cooperation and the resulting frictions. No meta-theory or trans-disciplinary theory exists which could reasonably and without competition claim to integrate the various disciplines. Approaches like Rational Choice or System Theory allow for dialogues and they do this as competing general research paradigms. But they presuppose the differentiation of science into disciplines and subdisciplines, they do not aim to reverse this state.

How can interdisciplinarity be organized as communication between disciplines about scientifically defined problems? We have shown how inter- or multidisciplinarity becomes desirable as an effort to make the unavoidable blind spots of disciplinary differentiation treatable by the means of science. But presumably it is not just by accident that interdisciplinarity in most cases is practically organized as timely restricted communication between scientists.[25] The implied 'personalization' of interdisciplinarity allows the reduction of disciplinary complexity by treating the individual scientist (on the basis of his or her membership role in science organizations) as a representative of his or her discipline and its unity.[26] The contributions of single scientists to an interdisciplinary discussion can be treated as sociological, linguistic, psychological, historical etc. statements. Each contribution represents a disciplinary perspective and by the way of ascribing this perspective to the participating individual scientist, disciplines can be directly addressed and confronted with questions, problems and alternatives.[27]

This opens a way of dealing with the potential effects that different disciplinary perspectives may have on others. It provides an occasion to produce the prism of interdisciplinary research. This prism preserves the differences between scientific disciplines but deflects each perspective by confronting it with the constructions and omissions of other disciplines – with the potential effect of modifying the theoretical and methodological treatment of scientific questions. Disciplinary blindness may be repaired to a certain extent and scientific learning processes and new insights may be triggered off.

Interdisciplinarity does not mean any kind of a synthesis of scientific disciplines. For this reason it may be better termed 'multidisciplinarity'. Serious multidisciplinarity can have effects on the theoretical and methodological level of disciplinary research. But this needs to be demonstrated. Fruitful multidisciplinary research obviously depends on the mode in which scientific problems are initially defined. It requires a challenge stimulating a need for the discussion of disciplinary blind spots.

In the former section we have argued that sociological and linguistic research on language problems in the field of migration research provoke discussions of this kind. One further result of this discussion however is a need for a more intensive and continuous multidisciplinary research organized around a common research field in order to clarify the relation between the complementary ways to define the subject of language in both disciplines.

Language acquisition processes of migrants are an appropriate case for further research of this kind. Recent research has documented a rather clear difference between infant, youth and adult immigrants (Perdue, 1993). Adults having to cope with the complexities of social inclusion in order to secure the necessary means for a living, tend to diminish the relevance of acquiring new language structures and to omit their formal complexities. They often fabricate and maintain a reduced pidgin version if it proves to work in those communication processes they are involved in. The situation of children and youth immigrants, many of them included in the education system, is different. They live in a kind of social moratorium providing room for linguistic experimentation. Their language usage is rather characterized by frequent over-generalizations of linguistic structures, a precondition for acquiring the appropriate grammatical restrictions. There is a striking contrast between the fossilized pidgin of adults maintained for twenty or thirty years in the immigration context and the linguistic practice of young immigrants characterized by the effort to learn and to master even stylistic differences of register. Often these young immigrants make fun of the pidgin of their parents.[28] These kinds of pidgin are highly stigmatized in a social context where social careers are channelled by the education system.

Linguistic behaviour is social behaviour in its own terms. Social participants are aware of linguistic differences. This becomes especially relevant when heterogeneous linguistic horizons are inscribed in a social practice as in the case of migration. On this background the relative success of adult immigrants to master the functional requirements of communication gets devalued in a process of social (self-) marginalization by symbolic means. Exempt from the immediate social stress of their parents but more or less affected by these processes of marginalization, young immigrants strive for symbolic recognition in the social world by trying hard to master the linguistic challenges.

Serious multidisciplinary migration research in this field would require continuous collaboration between sociologists and linguists, one discipline interested in the evolving social structures resulting from the consequences of migration, the conditions of social inclusion of migrants and their structural resources of making sense, and the other discipline interested in the linguistic structures evolving from the specific communicative events which define the social situation of migrants. Both disciplines could gain by a kind research which deals with more or less the same events and contexts and which describes and analyses them with the disciplinary specific means as linguistic or social events. Doing sociology and linguistics in a closely related way may open a path to deal with some disciplinary blind spots by approaching answers to the kind of questions discussed in section 4 and which cannot easily be abstracted from in the field of migration: How can the involvement of migrants in social communication practices, i.e. in making sense, be empirically described and made transparent as a relevant context for linguistic structural change? How does the linguistic competence, i.e. a set of formal conditions which regulates the production of utterances and which is the result of a language acquisition processes, restrict and pave social options of migrants?

Migration research in general could be developed into a promising area of recurrent multidisciplinary research. This presupposes that the current practice of interdisciplinarity in migration research is reflected. Migration research does not delineate a scientific discipline. Migration and its consequences affect various disciplines: sociology, psychology, history, linguistics, economy, political science, law, education etc. Any serious research needs to define the problems linked with migration in terms of its discipline i.e. as problems of sociology, psychology, linguistics, history etc. We have argued that it is not 'the reality of migration' – in this case the problem of language as it is discussed in non-scientific discourses – which asks for multidisciplinary research, but the ways scientific disciplines define and treat the research subject 'migration'.[29] To argue for multidisciplinary research requires us to demonstrate that these ways and the blind spots implied, force us to reflect the disciplinary limits and to seek for multidisciplinary collaborations.

Notes

1 In Germany these are for example the Institute for Migration Research and Intercultural Studies (IMIS) in Osnabrück, the Institute for Intercultural and International Studies (InIIS Bremen), the European Forum for Migration Research (EfMS, Bamberg), regular research activities at the Science Centre of Berlin (WZB), the Institute for Inter-disciplinary Research on Conflict and Violence (Bielefeld). Similar institutes can be found in other countries like the CRER in Warwick/GB, IMER in Utrecht/The Nether-lands or the recently founded IMER in Malmö/Sweden, established in different ways depending on the structure of the universities and other scientific organizations.

2 See Bommes 1999; it is interesting to note that this orientation links sociology, education, political sciences, psychology, but also linguistics which claims to describe linguistic structures as a condition and a sign of successful or unsuccessful integration and/or of the equal or disadvantaged social positions of migrants.

3 Correspondent to this the funding of migration rersearch as well as the establishment of migration research institutes was and is rather due to political conjunctures and less to principal decisions about relevant research areas and their scientific importance.

4 See Myers-Scotton (1997) for this term and the related research design.

5 See Klein 1999 for references.

6 Idealization refers to theoretical constructions that allow the analysis of empirical observations. They should be distinguished from abstractions, a term which technically spoken refers to the granularity of e.g. documentations, for instance more or less finely grained transcriptions, reaching from a phonetically close transcription in IPA to a loose, less detailed 'literary' script. A salient example is the difference between the distinction of oral and written documents and orate/literate registers, the latter an idealization (a conceptual distinction) used to analyse both, oral and written texts (see Maas, 1985, 1992).

7 Disciplines can be understood in a preliminary way as 'forms of institutionalization of processes of cognitive differentiation' (Stichweh, 1979), including the following elements: 1) a nexus of communication between researchers; 2) a body of scientific knowledge present in text books, disciplinary codified, accepted and teachable; 3) a set of problems and questions; 4) a set of research methods and theoretical frames; 6) a career structure and modes of socializing and recruiting young scholars. For a historical approach on the relation between disciplines and interdisciplinarity see Swoboda, 1979.

8 This is true for Whitney in the USA and for de Saussure in Europe.

9 See Ammon, 1987, 1988, including extensive bibliographies.

10 For an account taking linguistic diversity as the normal (default) situation and linguistic homogeneity as the case to be explained by special social conditions see Nichols 1992.

11 Saussure was very explicit in his 'Cours' (published posthumous in 1916) on this topic: Whatever could be said in this field, it could eventually only be counted as a personal opinion of a linguist but not as a legitimate part of scientifc linguistic analysis.

12 The ambivalence of this construction becomes obvious in Weber's research when he argues that the 'subjective meaning' is structured by the 'objective meaning' of e.g. the religious and cultural value-ideas of the protestant ethic which cannot be understood as the result of individual actions (Weber, 1976).

13 It is evident that the conceptualization of migration in both disciplines is based on these founding assumptions of social homogeneity as a normal state. We return to this later.

14 E.g. an utterance gains socially the meaning of a question by the answer given.

15 The transcription of interviews or the edition of written materials are typical occasions where those normalization procedures can be observed as the editorial work of social scientists.

16 E.g. as an indicator of social integration; see for example Esser and Friedrich 1990.

17 And most empirical data in social scientific research are (mainly self produced) linguistic data.
18 See again Bommes, 1993, pp. 391, but also Auer 1984 and Gumperz 1982.
19 This project is funded by the German Volkswagen Foundation.
20 The notation reads: 3.S = third person singular; PROX = particle of proximity; CONST = construct state, marking the syntactically dependent position of a noun.
21 We ignore differences of intonation and related phenomena.
22 The situation is actually even more complicated: Apparently there is a drift in all North African varieties of the Afro-Asiatic languages (including Berber and Arabic) affecting the syntactic structure: If the subject is definite, serving as reference point for the discourse, it tends to be put in the initial position without any implications of emphasis.
23 An example for this are the reciprocal irritations aroused by linguists and sociologists talking about the social or language.
24 N. Luhmann (1990) defines 'a problem' conveniently as the description/identification of something in a way that it cannot be assigned to the distinction true/untrue without being treated with the theoretical and methodical means of science. When this assignment becomes possible this means the solution of a problem in science.
25 This seems to be true also in organizational terms. Examples for this are the Centre for Interdisciplinary Research at the University of Bielefeld, the Wissenschaftskolleg in Berlin, the European Forum in Florence etc.
26 Similar simplifications are also well known from other functional areas: For example entrepreneurs are taken as speakers of 'the economy'.
27 A text cannot be questioned in this way. The answers will always be only the interpretations accessible for the reader. These interpretations certainly can be improved but not without reaching soon the limits of capacity mentioned above.
28 Tarzanca ('Tarzan speech', i.e. 'Me Tarzan – you Jane') is a current mock term among young German Turks referring to this pidgin.
29 The common argument that migration includes social, economic, psychological, linguistic aspects can be made about an endless number of social events.

References

Auer, P. (1984), 'On the Meaning of Conversational Code-Switching', in P. Auer and A. di Luzio (eds.), *Interpretive Sociolinguistics. Migrants – Children – Migrants Children*, Gunter Narr, Tübingen, pp. 87-108.

Ammon, U. (ed.) (1987/1988), *Sociolinguistics: An International Handbook of the Science of Language and Society*, 2 Vols., De Gruyter, Berlin.

Bade, K.J. and Weiner, M. (eds.) (1997), *Migration Past, Migration Future. Germany and the United States*, Berghan, Providence and Oxford.

Berman, R.A. and Slobin, D.I. (1994), *Relating Events in Narrative. A Cross-Linguistic Developmental Study*, L. Erlbaum, Hillsdale, NJ.

Bommes, M. (1993), *Migration und Sprachverhalten: Eine ethnographisch-sprachwissenschaftliche Fallstudie*, Deutscher Universitätsverlag, Wiesbaden.

Bommes, M. (1999), *Migration und Nationaler Wohlfahrtsstaat. Ein differenzierungstheoretischer Entwurf*, Westdeutscher Verlag, Opladen and Wiesbaden.

Castles, St. and Miller, M. (2003), *The Age of Migration: International Population Movements in the Modern World*, (3rd. edition) MacMillan, London.

Cohen, R. (1997), *Global Diasporas. An Introduction*, UCL, London.

Comrie, B. (1981), *Language Universals and Linguistic Typology*, Blackwell Publishers, Cambridge.

Durkheim, E. (1893), *De la Division du Travail Social,* Alcan, Paris.

Esser, H. and Friedrichs, J. (eds.) (1990), *Generation und Identität: Theoretische und empirische Beiträge zur Migrationssoziologie,* Westdeutscher Verlag, Opladen.

Goebl, H. (ed.) (1996/1997), *Kontaktlinguistik: Ein internationales Handbuch zeitgenössischer Forschung,* 2 Vols., De Gruyter, Berlin.

Gumperz, J.J. (1982), *Discourse Strategies,* Cambridge UP, Cambridge.

Hammar, T. (ed.) (1985), *European Immigration Policy. A Comparative Study,* Cambridge UP, Cambridge.

Hammar, T. et al. (1996), *Migration Immobility and Development. A Multidisciplinary View,* Berg Publishers, Oxford.

Joppke, Ch. (ed.) (1998), *Challenge to the Nation-State. Immigration in Western Europe and the United States,* Oxford UP, Oxford.

Klein, W.P. (1999), 'Die ursprüngliche Einheit der Sprachen in der philologisch-grammatischen Sicht der Frühen Neuzeit', *Wolfenbütteler Forschungen,* 84, pp. 25-56.

Luhmann, N. (1990), *Die Wissenschaft der Gesellschaft,* Suhrkamp, Frankfurt a.M.

Maas, U. (1985), 'Lesen – Schreiben – Schrift. Die Demotisierung eines professionellen Arkanums in der Frühen Neuzeit', *LiLi. Zeitschrift für Literaturwissenschaft und Linguistik,* 59 (1), pp. 55-81.

Maas, U., (1992), *Grundzüge der deutschen Orthographie,* Niemeyer, Tübingen.

Maas, U. and Mehlem, U. (1999), 'Sprache und Migration in Marokko und in der marokkanischen Diaspora in Deutschland', *IMIS-Beiträge,* (11), pp. 65-105.

Maas, U. and Mehlem, U. (2003), 'Schriftkulturelle Ressourcen und Barrieren bei marokkanischen Kindern in Deutschland, Abschlußbericht des von der VolkswagenStiftung am Institut für Migrationsforschung und Interkulturelle Studien (IMIS) geförderten Forschungsprojektes, Osnabrück.

Matthes, J. (1999), 'Interkulturelle Kompetenz. Ein Konzept und sein Potential', *Deutsche Zeitschrift für Philosophie,* 47 (3), pp. 411-26.

Myers-Scotton, C. (1997), *Duelling Languages. Grammatical Structure in Code-Switching,* Cambridge UP, Cambridge.

Nichols, J. (1992), *Linguistic Diversity in Space and Time,* Chicago UP, Chicago.

Nuscheler, F. (1995), *Internationale Migration. Flucht und Asyl,* Leske und Buderich, Opladen.

Oevermann U. et al. (1979). 'Die Methodologie einer 'Objektiven Hermeneutik' und ihre allgemeine forschungslogische Bedeutung in den Sozialwissenschaften', in H.G. Soeffner (ed.), *Interpretative Verfahren in den Sozial- und Textwissenschaften,* Metzler, Stuttgart, pp. 352-434.

Oevermann U. (1983), 'Zur Sache. Die Bedeutung von Adornos methodologischem Selbstverständnis für die Begründung einer materialen soziologischen Strukturanalyse', in L. v. Friedeburg and J. Habermas (eds.), *Adorno-Konfernz 1983,* Suhrkamp, Frankfurt a.M., pp. 234-89.

Parsons, T. 1968 (1937), *The Structure of Social Action,* The Free Press, New York.

Parsons, T. (1971), *The System of Modern Societies,* Prentice Hall, Englewood Cliffs, NJ.

Parsons, T. (1973), 'Problems of Balancing Rational Efficiency with Communal Solidarity in Modern Society', in Japan Economic Research Institute, *New Problems of Advanced Societies,* Tokio, pp. 9-14.

Perdue, C. (1993), *Adult Language Acquisition: Cross-Linguistic Perspectives,* Cambridge UP, Cambridge.

Sassen, S. (1996), *Migranten, Siedler, Flüchtlinge. Von der Massenauswanderung zur Festung Europa,* Fischer, Frankfurt a.M.

Stichweh, R. (1979), 'Differenzierung der Wissenschaft', *Zeitschrift für Soziologie,* 8 (1), pp. 82-101.

Swoboda, W.W. (1979), 'Disciplines and Interdisciplinarity: A Historical Perspective', in J.J. Kockelmans (ed.), *Interdisciplinarity and Higher Education,* Pennsylvania State UP, University Park, London, pp. 49-92.

Tenbruck, F.H. (1992), 'Was war der Kulturvergleich, ehe es den Kulturvergleich gab?', in J. Matthes (ed.), *Zwischen den Kulturen?* (Soziale Welt Sonderband 8), Schwartz, Göttingen, pp. 13-35.

Treibel, A. (1990), *Migration in modernen Gesellschaften,* Juventa, Weinheim and München.

Weber, M. (1976), *The Protestant Ethic and the Spirit of Capitalism,* Allen and Unwin, London.

Weber, M. (1972), *Wirtschaft und Gesellschaft,* Mohr, Tübingen.

Chapter 9

The Sociology and History of Immigration: Reflections of a Practitioner[*]

Ewa Morawska

A comparative review I wrote more than ten years ago of the main issues that informed the American sociology and history of immigration since the late 1960s (Morawska, 1990) identified two themes-arguments shared by these two disciplines. Combined, they have unsettled the classical paradigms that dominated American studies of immigration and ethnicity from their inception as an academic discipline until the mid-1960s. One of them was the assumption that in modern and, in particular, American society the socioeconomic success and the life course in general of immigrants and their offspring depended mainly on individual value orientations, skills, and motivations. The other, based on the same underlying vision of modern (American) society, was the premise-cum-prescription of assimilation conceived of as the linear progressive weakening and ultimate disappearance of the primordial traits and bonds of ethnicity as succeeding generations adopted the mainstream society's unitary system of cultural values and became absorbed in economic, social, and political networks that are blind to ethnic differences.

Thus, the movement and adaptation (success or failure) of immigrants to the receiving American society was reinterpreted as shaped primarily by broadly conceived (macro)structural determinants and, in particular, global as well as sender and receiver countries' economic welfare and opportunity structures. Within those constraining or enabling structures, immigrants and their families have relied on collectivist (that is, socially embedded and group-sustained, rather than 'self-made' individualistic) strategies of adaptation in the process of which the 'resilient ethnicity' (rather than assimilation) conceived of as primarily situationally generated and instrumental (rather than embedded cultural-psychological) has played the important role. In both sociological and historical studies immigration and ethnicity were conceived of as closely intertwined with class and (in special-focus rather than mainstream research) gender that influenced the immigrants'/ethnics' socioeconomic position and achievement in the receiver society and the group identities and associations they formed, but as distinct from racial minorities. Although it focused on similar issues, sociological and historical research on immigration – I noted in my 1990 report – had been flowing in two separate streams, largely unaware of each other, carried out and discussed in distinct modes reflecting different end-goals and analytic strategies of these two disciplines. Whereas sociologists wanted first to test competing theoretical models for general applicability, historians aimed primarily to specify the configurations of time- and place-specific circumstances under which a given interpretation would best account for the phenomena studied, leaving the social-historical process inherently context-dependent and, thus, underdetermined.

A reappraisal of American immigration research more than one decade later is useful for recording the persistence and changes of the main interests and approaches in these two disciplines. But it is not the primary purpose of this follow-up assessment. Whereas in the earlier report I sought mainly to identify the main themes of research and discussion in the sociology and history of immigration of the 1970s-80s, in this appraisal I attempt a more complex task by addressing simultaneously the *what, how,* and *why,* or the intellectual (intra- and interdisciplinary) generating contexts of the problem agendas and modes of conceptualization and research in these two disciplines as practiced by American immigration specialists during the 1990s and early 2000s. (See, also, introduction to Foner, Rumbaut, and Gold, eds., *Immigration Research for a New Century*, 2000, for a differently conceptualized reassessment of the current immigration research in the United States in three separately treated disciplines: sociology, history, and anthropology.) Because it is intended as 'personal professional' reflections on rather than an exhaustive review of the subject matter, only limited bibliographic references representative of the discussed positions are cited.

Thus, although the concern with the structural, macroeconomic and microsocial contexts and mechanisms of immigration shared by sociologists and historians has not disappeared (see, e.g., Massey et al., 1998), new 'lead' issues-arguments (or, rather, 'old-new' issues that preoccupied American social science in the first half of the twentieth century; see DeWind and Kasinitz, 1997; Gerstle and Mollenkopf, 2001) have emerged – again similar in both disciplines – that have either replaced or reformulated the key problems that occupied immigration scholars during the 1970s-80s. Following the new agenda set by the recognized top-ranking experts, who also hold significant gatekeeping power in the field, three interrelated issues are attracting today the most lively debate and the rapidly increasing research. They include (1) the assimilation of immigrants and their offspring (rather than the resilient ethnicity); (2) the transnationalization of identities and membership of immigrants and their children, and its impact on their adjustment to the host society and on prerogatives of the territorially bound nation-state; and (3) the racialized ethnicity or the intertwining of ethnicity and race with class and (more in a specialty niche than as part of mainstream research) gender, rather than white 'by default' class-ethnicity or 'ethclass' from earlier conceptualizations. The emphasis on the collectivist strategies of immigrants' adaptation, in previous decades applied primarily to the exploration of different patterns of ethnic resilience, has become refocused during the 1990s on the second of the issues identified above that have attracted particular attention of the American immigration sociologists and historians, namely, group transnational loyalties and involvements of the newcomers.

In most of the sociological and historical debates and research on immigration during the 1990s, these shared new issues are still conceptualized and analyzed in different, discipline-specific traditions that informed earlier studies. But whereas the unsettling in the 1970s-80s of the (same) classical paradigms that informed both fields of immigration research since the 1920s did not call for comparisons of past and present immigrant groups, the reemergence in the 1990s of the new-old concerns invites such juxtapositions. In response to this invitation – a new development absent in the previous decade – in both fields 'vocal' minorities of immigration scholars have appeared who are familiar with and use each other's work on the subject, and some collaborative projects have recently been undertaken. A special issue of the *Journal of American Ethnic History* (spring 1999) in which invited sociologists compare and contrast different aspects of the adaptation to the American society of past and present immigrants, and a multidisciplinary conference sponsored by this journal in collaboration with the Social Science Research Council (fall 2003) on ethnicity and incorporation in an age of globalization illustrate this trend. As in the earlier period, however, an interdisciplinary conversation about the epistemological foundations as well as strengths and limitations of the strategies of inquiry typical for these two fields of immigration research has remained absent (see, e.g., recent multidisciplinary volumes on immigration theory and research: Brettell and Hollifield, 2000, and Foner, Rumbaut, and Gold, 2000; Min's 2002 edited collection on mass migration to the United States in classical and contemporary periods, or an exchange in the *Journal of American Ethnic History*, summer 2002, among the historians, anthropologists, and sociologists of immigration on the role of comparison in their disciplines, which focuses almost exclusively on the substantive issues related to so-called two great waves of immigration to America[1]). By and large absent, too, in the sociological and historical immigration studies of the 1990s-early 2000s have been cross-applications of research methods between the two disciplines.

The least confusing way to examine more closely this complex landscape of current immigration research is to consider separately the entanglements of each of the three major themes-concerns common in both disciplines: assimilation, transnationalism, and racialized ethnicity. I conclude this discussion by suggesting ways a closer dialogue between sociology and historiography of immigration could engage the underlying epistemic premises and the analytic stratagems informing each of the two fields of research, and the cognitive gains to be derived from such collaboration.

Assimilation

Why, then, have American immigration scholars returned to the assimilation idea they discarded in the early 1970s and that had since become 'politically incorrect' as implying antipluralist, homogenizing forces imposed from above by the dominant ethclass? The constellations of factors contributing to this revived interest have been different for the sociologists than for the historians of immigration.

For the students of contemporary, so-called 'new' immigrant groups primarily from South America, Asia, and the Caribbean (as opposed to the 'old', turn-of-the-twentieth-century immigrants from South and East Europe), two such conducive circumstances seem evident. First, the first native-born American generation of the descendants of new immigrants, the majority of whom came to the United States after the implementation of the liberalized provisions of the 1965 Hart-Celler Immigration Act, has just entered adulthood. Questions related to their economic, social, and cultural integration into American society have shifted the attention of students of these new groups from immigration to incorporation. Second, and closely related to the question about the modes of incorporation, has been the new immigrants'/ethnics' lived experience of and current public/scholarly discourse in America about multiculturalism on the one hand, and trans- and postnationalism on the other. Can these phenomena be reconciled, 'empirically', in the lives of the social actors and theoretically? The third factor conducive to the shift of scholarly attention to newcomers' assimilation (incorporation) has probably been the 'insider' status (Merton, 1972; see also Rumbaut, 2000; Gans, 2000) of the sociologists of new immigration, many of whom are themselves foreign-born or first-generation native-born descendants of new immigrants, who have made it in mainstream (here, academic) American society and for whom assimilation is a personal and, thus, interesting experience.

Three different claims about assimilation have been advanced in present-day sociological debates/research on immigrant/ethnic incorporation (see Schmitter Heisler, 2000; Kivisto, 2002; Brubaker, 2003 for reviews thereof). The most influential, that is, the most widely reproduced (primarily, it seems, because it has been authored by one of the most powerful figures in the field) has been the 'segmented assimilation' thesis. The essential argument of this refocused derivation of the dual labor market paradigm of the 1970s is that the upward and downward path of assimilation of immigrants and their children depends on their location in specific segments of a three-pronged postindustrial economy consisting of the formal upper (primary) and lower (secondary) and informal labor markets. Those, particularly non-whites, who are entrapped in lower (secondary) and informal sectors move along a downward path of incorporation into inner-city underclass America without prospects of upward mobility.

The effect of this downward incorporation that results from economic restructuring and racial discrimination is the acculturation of immigrants' children into the 'adversarial culture' of the American underclass based on a willful rejection of mainstream sociocultural norms, values, and role models which, in turn, further entraps this generation in the underclass (the culture-structure reciprocity implied here – a new idea in this basically structurally informed approach – is not, however, theoretically elaborated; for a discussion of this neglect see Perlmann, 1998). The way to avoid this downward incorporation, the proponents of the segmented assimilation thesis suggest, is through the retention of ethnicity – now termed 'adhesive assimilation' – that is, for the immigrants' children to remain within the ethnic economic niches and subcultures of their parents that offer better chances of socioeconomic success (for the paradigmatic statements of the segmented assimilation thesis see Portes and Zhou, 1993; Zhou, 1997; for empirical demonstration of this thesis, see Neckerman et al., 1999; Nee and Sanders, 2001; and Portes and Rumbaut, 2001; for a revised formulation of the segmented assimilation thesis based on Dutch data, see Model, 2003; on 'the second generation decline', see Gans, 1992).

The arguments for the replacement of the classical, linear-progressive assimilation theory, which predicted only one – upward – trajectory of assimilation for all immigrants, by the segmented incorporation thesis are referred to by their advocates as historical, that is, based on the contrasting comparison of past and present situations of the social actors in question. Whereas the classical model worked for the offspring of turn-of-the-twentieth-century South-East European immigrants because of the former's white skins and their participation in an industrial economy with stratified but not segmented labor markets, the different racial characteristics of their contemporary successors and the segmented nature of the American postindustrial economy calls for a differentiated treatment of assimilation. Although a few standard, mainly sociological, classics are cited in support of the claim that 'old' immigrants were received and positioned differently than 'new', no contemporary studies of immigration historians that extensively document the dubious 'whiteness' of those newcomers in the eyes of native-born Americans and their prolonged stay in the lower, secondary sector of the industrial economy are apparently familiar to the segmented assimilation thesis' advocates. Why has such an opportunity for an informed historical comparison not been taken up by sociologists? The occupational socialization, of course, has played a role (the segmented assimilation proponents represent the mainstream positivistic tradition in sociology that has stubbornly disregarded the historical one as non-scientific 'story-telling'), but likely also the ethnic/national backgrounds and 'world orientations' of the scholars in question, most of whom are members of non-European groups for whom Europe has no immediate relevance for the parts of the world and the people whose lives they study. (The NASIS 1997-98 survey of the origins of American scholars specializing in immigration/ethnic studies has revealed a high 37 per cent rate of ethnic background/research subject 'coincidence'; for the immigrant and second generations these figures were 58 per cent and 48 per cent, respectively; see Rumbaut, 2000.)

Although the segmented assimilation thesis is predicated on the recognition of the context-dependency of incorporation processes – an innovation vis-à-vis the classical unitary model – this variability is limited to a few possible avenues determined by the economic structure. Another reconceptualization of assimilation presumes social processes to be more underdeterminate and more 'agentic', that is, contingent on the creative (and not only reactive) negotiations by social actors of the circumstances of their incorporation into the host society. Informed by this recognition, assimilation is understood as the interactive, multitrack process of 'bumpy' (Gans, 1992) or non-linear incorporation of immigrants and their offspring into the native society, allowing for variable degrees and aspects of similarity and difference, twists, (re)turns and 'paradoxes' (Rumbaut, 1997; see also Alba and Nee, 2003; Alba, 1999; *International Migration Review*, 2000 for the reassessment by leading American immigration scholars of Nathan Glazer's and Patrick Moynihan's classic, *Beyond the Melting Pot*, 35 years after its publication; Kivisto, 2003).

In part, this shift toward the agency-sensitive and flexible or open-ended conceptualization of adaptation processes has been a reaction to the overly (macro-) structuralist paradigm of mainstream immigration research since the 1970s. The recent entry and already recognized voice in the contemporary urban immigration/ race/ethnic studies of the anthropologists with their traditional interests and research focused on 'the ground' or people's lived experience, by its very nature flexible and contingent (even postmodernistest-oriented anthropologists try hard to relocalize somehow their uprooted subjects), has also influenced this turn. (On the recent shift of anthropological research from sending to receiving societies see Foner 2000b; 2003; Rumbaut et al., 1999; Axel, 2002; cf. also Michael Kearney in this volume). Bibliographic references in these sociological studies and coedited interdisciplinary volumes suggest this influence to have been much greater than the similarly context-and-difference-sensitive work of immigration historians. The primarily anthropological derivation of the 'contextual shift' and the continued absence or near-absence of the concerns of historians and, specifically, their preoccupation with temporal coordinates as constitutive mediums of social life and their impact on the course and outcomes of societal processes orients the attention of immigration sociologists to the variations and contingencies of space rather than to the effects of time on the shifting flows of social life. (On time and causality see, e.g., the excellent studies of Aminzade, 1992; Abbott, 1992, 2001; Griffin, 1992; Sewell, 1992; Bryant, 1994; Isaac, 1997; also Mahoney and Rueschmayer, 2003.)

This open-ended 'flexible' approach has informed two positions putting different emphases on one basically similar thesis regarding the assimilation of new immigrant/ethnic groups. One proposition, formulated in a polemic with the segmented assimilation thesis, argues that not enough time has passed to assess the progress or decline of immigrant offspring in mainstream American society, particularly as measured against the position of South and East European stock Americans reported in the 1940s-50s (the main historical references used by the segmented assimilation advocates), that is, for the advanced second and third generations. Pointing to the dynamic character of the American and global economies, the 'shifting meanings' of race (see below), and the opportunity, unavailable to past immigrants, for effective public protest/action on their behalf by contemporary immigrant/ethnic organizations created by the institutionalization of (previously mainly declared rather than practiced) pluralism, but aware that the 'judgment is still out', the polemicists against the segmented incorporation thesis remain cautiously optimistic regarding the future of assimilation as the 'direction toward similarity', bumpy and multitrack as it may be[2] (on this position see Alba and Nee, 2003, 1997; Perlmann and Waldinger, 1997; Alba, 1999; Espiritu, 2003; Portes and Hao, 2002).

The proposal to reconcile assimilation with pluralism/multiculturalism derives, basically, from the same 'bumpy and multidirectional' conceptualization thereof, but the emphasis here is more on the coexistence (e.g., Gans, 1997) or the mixing-and-blending (e.g., Foner, 1997) of assimilation or the acquiring/cocreating of the common American cultural forms and symbols and economic, social, and political memberships, and ethnicities as retaining/transforming immigrant/ethnic group traditions and lifestyles.

In comparison with the advocates of the segmented assimilation argument, the proponents of 'the road still undetermined' thesis acknowledge the effects of the duration of time and their comparisons with the situation of European immigrants and their children are historically informed (interestingly, all but one of the above-cited studies representative of this position have been either (co)authored by a historian or by a scholar who is a descendant of 'white ethnics'). Still, even these sociologists use the work of immigration historians primarily for the compare-and-contrast empirical evidence rather than to explore the different propositions of reconceptualizing assimilation that inform the current debate in this field or the ways historians contextualize assimilation processes and argue causality (see below), (for well-informed comparative uses of historical evidence see Alba and Nee, 2003, 1997; Alba, 1999; Kivisto, 2003). Neither, apparently, despite the explicit recognition of the need to apply a 'historical approach' to the study of contemporary immigration, are any of the studies of historical sociologists on the modes of history-sensitive sociological research and analysis consulted or, in any case, referred to in the discussion (see the conclusion of this paper for a discussion of this approach).

The proponent (Waldinger, 2003) of the third way to reconceptualize the concept of assimilation rejects the notion of the presumed teleological end-point or mainstream 'core' implicit in the other, especially the (upward-directed) segmented incorporation and change-toward-similarity theses, and proposes instead, should this concept be retained at all, to interpret it merely as the gradual 'convergence around the mean' or the possibility that children of immigrants will attain lifestyles and standards of living that most Americans enjoy, and that this convergence will be closely (though not perfectly) correlated with similar treatment. (Although a committed anti-assimilationist Roger Waldinger would, I am sure, deny it, his conceptualization converges with one important dimension of Gordon's classical model of assimilation without labeling it as such. On assimilation as the 'general direction toward similarity' see also Brubaker, 2003.)

Although it occurred at about the same time, the (re)turn to assimilation in American immigration historiography has been prompted by a different con- figuration of circumstances, some of which have reflected within disciplinary shifts of interests whereas others have been similar to those affecting immigration sociologists. Four such contributing factors seem to have been of greatest con- sequence. Having replaced American historiography's conventional emphasis on national/political consensus with the focus on class conflict and resistance 'from below' of the disempowered groups, social historians of immigration/ethnicity in the 1970s-80s were interested in collectively agentic 'ethnic resilience' and pluralism rather than in assimilation-as-homogenization perceived as the perspec- tive of the dominant class-ethnic groups. The renewed concern with assimilation among immigration historians in the 1990s has been a move away from the overly resilient, and, from the viewpoint of later (third and fourth by the 1980s) generations of South and East European immigrants' offspring, also ahistorical or fixed-in-time representation of ethnic group integration into American society.

Concurrent with the above has been the observation in personal encounters, local and national politics, and in the media of the integration dilemmas of the new immigrants and their native-born American children, a large proportion of whom are non-white, that differ from those encountered by their predecessors in the American industrial economy of the early twentieth century. The public debates and popular fears whether these 'very different' newcomers can be integrated into American society sound similar to the concerns expressed one century ago – and through the 1920s – about the assimilation of South and East Europeans, moving immigration historians to reexamine this process and its facilitators and obstacles. Innovative studies in the early 1990s by immigration historians of the (until then unacknowledged) significance of race in the Americanization of earlier European immigrants and their children have been quickly followed by more publications which, in turn, have further stimulated interest in reexamining the assimilation concept (see the last section of the paper on the historians' discussion of race and ethnicity).

Lastly, as in the case of immigration sociologists, the outsiders-becoming- insiders effect may have played a role in turning historians' interests toward assimilation. As they entered the discipline in the 1960s-70s, in order to carve out a space for themselves in the historical scholarship and, perhaps, to gain personal security, immigration historians, most of whom were members of 'new' ethnic groups not previously represented in American history departments as ethnic specialists, stressed pluralism and ethnic resilience as the legitimate subject of academic study. By the 1990s, these scholars were well established and recognized specialists in a field of study that has its own academic journals, organizations, research fellowships, and regular meetings. It may be that a 'personal time' for the return to assimilation has coincided with broader disciplinary and societal changes.

The return of immigration historians to assimilation has involved primarily a shift in focus predicated on premises about the nature of social in general and, specifically, immigrant adaptation processes similar to those that informed the conceptualization of ethnicity in the previous decade rather than, as in the case of 'converted' sociologists, the reformulation of the theoretical framework of analysis. Already in the 1980s several historical studies had appeared of the ethnicization-as-Americanization processes among ethnic groups of European origins during the early twentieth century, which documented the mixing-and-blending of old-country and American cultural traditions and ways of association whereby over time the American elements constituted the increasing (although not irreversible) proportion (for reviews thereof see Morawska, 1990; Conzen et al., 1992; Kazal, 1995; Gerstle, 1997; Gjerde, 1999; Diner, 2000). The resuscitation of interest in the idea of assimilation in the 1990s has moved immigration historians to replace the ethnicization- with assimilation-as-Americanization and to reexamine this old-new concept.

This reexamination has been informed by three general approaches. The first, classical method of analysis in the discipline traces the concept of assimilation-as-Americanization from its 18th-century roots in what Gary Gerstle (1997) calls 'the Crevecoeurian myth' or project of all immigrant groups 'melted into a new race of men' (Crevecoeur, 1782, p. 43) through its subsequent meanings and applications up to the present by demonstrating how each of them had been shaped by changing historical contexts in which they were (re)interpreted against or alongside earlier understandings (see, e.g., Kazal, 1995; Gerstle, 1997). In this approach, 'why' social and cultural phenomena change or persist, is explained by showing 'how' they do it (Abrams, 1982; see also Ragin, 1987).

In the second approach, the concept of assimilation is reexamined – and revived – by showing the possibilities of its historicization, that is, of making it time- and place-specific and embedded in multidimensional contexts. In this interpretation, assimilation, understood as (reversible) 'direction toward abandonment' (to play on Brubaker's phrase) of home-national/ethnic identities, loyalties, and involvements, would become one of several possible patterns of the incorporation of immigrants and their offspring into mainstream (American) society, contingent on a combination of home- and host-country circumstances and immigrants'/ethnics' socio-economic and residential location therein (see e.g., Morawska, 1994, 2001c; Min, 1999; Alba, 1999; Neckerman et al., 1999; JAEH and SSRC conference, fall 2003).

Although past and current works of immigration sociologists are referred to in both these approaches, it is mainly as illustrations of the context-specific interpretations that compare and contrast immigrants' past and present adaptation to or as negative examples of ahistorical, universal models of the American society and the assimilation to it of its foreign-stock residents. The resolute ahistoricism of mainstream American sociology in general, its immigration subfield included, is indeed difficult for historians to accept. Historians' distance toward sociologists has probably even increased during the 1990s in comparison with the earlier decade as their interest in the sociological, primarily quantitative, methods of data analysis has waned accompanied by a disappointment with the mostly trivial results produced by these methods, and a 'new cultural history' replaced the earlier 'new social history'. This distance may now be diminishing again as the emergent concern (inspired by anthropologists) among some immigration sociologists with the context-contingency of societal processes becomes recognized by immigration historians through collaborative initiatives such as the recent interdisciplinary projects of the prestigious *Journal of American Ethnic History*.

Like their sociologist counterparts who are interested in immigration history, however, even the historians who reach out across disciplinary boundaries have not engaged the sociological immigration research methodologically, despite the availability of the work of historical sociologists that demonstrates various strategies of historicizing time- and place-insensitive sociological explanations and theory building. In the case of immigration sociologists sympathetic toward the historical past of their subject matter, this neglect – most likely from ignorance – reflects the marginal position of the historical sociology in the discipline at large and the absence of scholars working on immigration among its most widely recognized trend-setters. Historians' disinterest probably results from a 'but we know it all' (about historical methods) attitude combined with the memory, transmitted to the next generation via discussions in classrooms and scholarly journals in the 1980s, of the resolute boundary drawing between historical sociology and social history by gatekeeping historical sociologists who barely concealed their sense of 'theoretical superiority' vis-à-vis social historians (see, e.g., Skocpol, 1987; Skocpol and Somers, 1980; Roy, 1992; for a recent attempt at reconciliation on 'neo/postmodernist' grounds between former social/now cultural historians and historical sociologists, see Bonnell and Hunt, 1999).

In a (thus far unique) example of the intellectual engagement with sociology beyond historical (empirical) comparisons of the situations and prospects of past and present immigrants, Elliot Barkan (1999) has proposed a reformulation of Gordon's classical model of assimilation (1964). Accepting his predecessor's idea of the American 'core' (in this case, shared language, cultural practices, objects of popular consumption material and symbolic etc), to make his model historical context-contingent, Barkan has loosened the steps and stages set firm in Gordon's conceptualization and left the space for twists, turns, and loopholes in the road 'toward similarity'. Overall, his model of assimilation resembles the 'bumpy' conceptualizations of sociologists (it would be ironic, though, if just when the latter retreat from model-building toward conceptualizations acknowledging underdeterminacy of social processes, the 'model' idea were to become attractive to historians).

One more approach should be noted here. Although thus far represented by one historian, it has been recognized in 'revivalist' discussions in the field, debated, and compared and contrasted with other similar projects from outside the discipline (cf. Sollors, 1989; Fuchs, 1990; see Gerstle, 1997 for a comparative discussion thereof). David Hollinger's 'return to the roots' in his *Postethnic America* (1995) serves not, as do the historical narratives noted above, to seek to understand the changing meanings of assimilation through the examination of different contexts in which it was conceived, but to bring back to life the foundational American civic project of the freedom to choose and (re)create one's identities and associations.

The quintessence of Americanism/Americanization is, Hollinger argues, precisely its ethnic and racial pluralism. If not for its disregard for the economic, political, and social-cultural constraints of free choice (such as poverty, undocumented status, native prejudice), this interpretation would be akin to the assimilation cum pluralism approach in sociology (on the neglect of 'power issue' in Hollinger's arguments, see Gerstle, 1997). This contingency-less interpretation, rather unusual for a historian, has probably been the result of the fact that, like 'the Crevecoeurian myth' two hundred years ago, Hollinger's project is, underneath, a vision, and a call for, a moral society with social justice and equality for all Americans regardless of their ethnic and, this time, also racial origins.

Transnationalization of Identities and Membership

Transnationalization of immigrant/ethnic identities and engagements and its impact on the prerogatives of territorially bound nation-states has been another recently emerged theme-argument in American immigration research. Perhaps because, unlike assimilation, this concern is indeed new in the sociology of immigration and because it has been strongly influenced by anthropologists who are also experimenting in this area, the treatment of transnationalism reflects more clearly than that of other themes-arguments considered here the field's difficulties associated with conceptualizing and theorizing research subjects.

As bibliographic references in recent sociological articles, disciplinary affiliations of authors of newly published coedited volumes, and sessions held at sociological conferences suggest, this issue has entered the field under the 'transnationalist banner' of the anthropologists rather than via the intradisciplinary debate about the decline v. survival of the nation-state in a globalized world (for the former see Basch, Glick Schiller and Blanc-Szanton, 1994; Glick Schiller, Basch and Blanc-Szanton, 1996; Glick Schiller, 1996; for the latter see, e.g., Soysal, 1994; Mann, 1993; Brubaker, 1996; Bauboeck, 1994; Joppke, 1998). The identification of 'transnational communities' as one of 'the themes for a new century' by one of the most influential scholars in mainstream immigration sociology (Portes, 1996, 1997, 1999) has resulted in the rapid proliferation of such research. Accordingly, interpreted in the language of the 1980s as part of micro-level networks of economic support functioning as alternative or partial remedies to the barriers in home and host macrostructures, assistance in the arrangement of travel to the United States and, upon arrival, in securing housing and employment, and remittances sent home by immigrants to support families left behind have been redefined as a component of immigrants' 'new transnationalism', defying the boundaries of the nation-state in the local-global framework.

Viewed now as displays of transnationalism, remittances sent home to support immigrants' households, together with other expressions of transnational engagements such as intense cross-border communication and travel, the maintenance of group bi- or multinational cultures in formal and informal associations, and the increasingly frequent simultaneous political involvement in home and host countries, have been treated, as already noted, as the loci classici of the collectivist adaptation strategies of immigrants and their children.

(Re)conceptualizing research problems is, of course, integral to the advancement of scholarship. This task has yet to be undertaken in the sociology of immigration regarding the newly appropriated concept of transnationalism. It must be said in fairness that the conceptual confusion in the usage of this vogue term has not been limited to the sociology of immigration or even sociology in general, but spread through several disciplines that have adopted it, from political science, anthropology, international relations, and legal studies to a new field of 'transnational cultural studies' gathered around journals such as *Public Culture, Social Text,* or *Diaspora.* Searching for new disciplinary identity and research space and flirting along the way with postmodernist philosophy and literary studies, as the collective Paters (Maters?) of the 'transnational turn' in immigration sociology, anthropologists have unavoidably added to the usual confusion in sociologists' handling of their concepts. (On the conceptual confusion in the new transnationalism literature and attempts to clarify it see, e.g., Joppke, 1998; Aleinikoff and Rumbaut, 1998; Aleinikoff, 2003; Faist, 2000; Kivisto, 2001, 2003.)

Two different interpretations of the prefix *trans* can be distinguished in the discourse on this subject by immigration sociologists (-anthropologists). In the first interpretation, transnationalism is understood as a *shift beyond* or, as it were, vertically past (rather than horizontally across) or 'post' the accustomed territorial state/national-level memberships and civic-political claims derived therefrom and state-bound national identities toward *more encompassing* ones such as universal humanity/human rights, suprastatal membership/entitlements (e.g., in the European Union), or panreligious solidarities (e.g., Muslim in Western Europe). In the sociology of immigration this understanding has informed intimations (rather than explicit discussions) of the 'decline of the nation-state' or the loss of its controlling and regulatory capacities such as immigration policies and citizenship and more diffuse references, often used interchangeably with the second understanding, to a 'new space' transcending the bounded entity of the nation-state into which escape the identities and politics of contemporary transnational travelers (for the former see, e.g., Jacobson, 1996; Mahler, 1998; for the latter Guarnizo, 1997; Pries, 2001; Cordero-Guzman et al., 2001).[3]

In the second interpretation, transnationalism refers to some combination of plural civic-political memberships, economic involvements, social networks, and cultural identities reaching *across* and *linking* people and institutions in two or more nation-states in diverse, multilayered patterns. International migrants are the main conveyors of these cross-border connections, and the 'new transnational spaces' they create deterritorialize or extrapolate (rather than undermine) the nation-states interlinked by them (see Levitt, 1997, 2001; R. Smith, 1998, 2003; Glick-Schiller and Fouron, 1998; Guarnizo and Smith, 1998; Min, 1999; Foner, 2000a; on second-generation transnationalism, see Levitt and Waters, 2002; R. Smith, 2002; Brettell, 2003). Since it has been officially proclaimed only in 1997 as a novel phenomenon worth further study, a deluge of transnationalism research by mainstream immigration sociologists is still to appear. Should it follow, as do already published studies, the prescriptions for 'the [new] themes for a new century', the problem is likely to remain focused on the investigation of 'transnational communities [as] dense networks across political borders created by immigrants in their quest for economic advancement and social recognition [and driven by the forces promoting economic globalization]' (Portes, 1997, pp. 812-3).

In the era of commodified academic production, launching a research problem as 'novel' has been a well-tested strategy for success. By setting up immigrants' transnationalism as a new and exciting idea, sociologists and anthropologists (the latter perhaps even more so because of a necessity to establish themselves in a new field with a distinct agenda) have reinforced each other's success strategies, removing from their 'cognitive sight' even a suspicion that their novel phenomenon may not be so new at all (such an aperception would be impossible for assimilation because of its recognized foundational presence in American public and scholarly discourse).

In the context-flexible approach to the study of immigration the meanings of transnationalism have shifted more freely (and probably without the authors' notice) between the movement across (more common) and beyond the political and cultural boundaries of nation-states. Context dependence of immigrants' transnationalism (in both directions) has been understood primarily as multiple and changing locations in physical, socioeconomic, and symbolic space rather than time. In this genre of studies immigrant transnationalism is seldom claimed to be novel and historians' work on 'old' immigrants' bi- or transnationalism has been cited to acknowledge this phenomenon's longer-dure existence (although primarily to emphasize the contrasting or novel qualities of this contemporary phenomenon rather than to explore the continuities with the past). (For historically-informed sociological accounts of 'old' immigrants' transnationalism, see, e.g., Guarnizo, 1998, 2001; Gold, 1997; also Hirschman, Kasinitz, and DeWind in their introduction to the *Handbook of International Migration* 1999; Morawska, 2001a; Kivisto, 2002.) As with assimilation, however, those historians' explanatory strategies in presenting their cases appear to be of no interest to sociologists as illustrations of the time contingency of social developments.

Although studies informed by the context-flexible approach link immigrants' transnationalism with the assimilation/incorporation issue, reflecting the paucity of theory in the field deplored by its major practitioners, they, too, leave this relationship by and large untheorized. The transnationalism-assimilation connection has been made in three ways. In the first one, the emergence of 'transnational fields' in immigrants' lives is interpreted as resistance 'from below' to the power of the nation-state via cultural hybridity, multilocal identities, and undocumented border-crossings, which implies (the relationship is not elaborated) the weakening of the host nation-state's role in shaping immigrants' assimilation (see, e.g., Mahler, 1998; Smith, 1997). The second connection attributes the densification of immigrants' transnational connections to the revived interest in assimilation.

Considering that the discussion of transnationalism has focused primarily on foreign-born and that of assimilation on native-born American generations, a proposition linking the two is promising, but, again, unelaborated. The third transnationalism-assimilation connection, untheorized like the first two, has been via the assimilation cum pluralism proposition noted earlier whereby transnationalism is viewed as an expression of ethnic pluralism (for the reviews of these propositions, see Morawska, 2003; Kivisto, 2001, 2003; Waldinger and Fitzgerald, 2002; Levitt, 2003; and Levitt and Waters, 2002 on the second generation).

Influenced by anthropological studies of multiply rooted translocal communities (for reviews see Brettell, 2000, 2003; Foner, 2000b), the emerging sociology of immigrants' transnationalism has energized and expanded the notion of the multi*local* as the arena and mobilizer of political, social, economic, and cultural agency, individual and collective, and the source of 'cosmopolitanisms', or different identifications and meanings (a core element of American sociology in the early twentieth century, urban community studies have since become a marginal field in the discipline; although the concern of immigration research of the 1980s with micro-level social-economic networks recognized their embeddedness in local communities, it was those microstructures rather than the communities and their residents that attracted attention).

Turning sociologists' attention to immigrant transnational communities has been an undeniable contribution of anthropologists to immigration research, but this influence has also focused the analysis on trans*local* spaces as the arenas of contingency-flexibility effects, leaving out, by and large, the conventional sociology domain of multilayered broader contexts between the local and the global. True, the nation-state on both home and host sides of the (im)migration circuit has been frequently mentioned either as challenged from below by immigrants' cross-national identities and engagements or as involved in reappropriating its citizens'/nationals' loyalties (e.g., through legitimation of double citizenship or by attempting to use immigrants for political lobbying of state-national causes – see e.g., R. Smith, 1998; Cordero-Guzman et al., 2001). But even though these interventions have been used as empirical evidence against claims of the demise of the nation-state, its relationship with transnationalism from below has thus far not been theoretically elaborated (for an exceptional attention by an immigration anthropologist to mezzo-level societal institutions, see Hyman, 1991, 1999).

Although they did not call it 'transnationalism', immigration historians have long been aware of and have extensively documented the enduring bi-national identities and involvements of nearly all American immigrant groups in the 19th and early 20th centuries. The announcement and rapid career of 'new transnationalism' in the 1990s in the sociology (and anthropology) of present-day immigration in the United States combined with incorrect claims about the situation of earlier-wave immigrants took historians by surprise ('don't they ever read what we write?'). As a result, their 'transnational turn' has been largely a reactive interest, unlike the renewed concern with assimilation that was triggered by factors in which the shifting intradisciplinary problem agenda played an important role. The major disagreements of historians with social scientists' claims that present-day immigrant transnationalism is a novel phenomenon have been as follows.

First, they have argued, incorrect has been the view that unlike 'multiple, circular, and return migrations' of present-day movements, turn-of-the-twentieth-century international travels (to America) were 'singular great journeys from one sedentary space to another' (Lie, 1995, p. 304; see also Jones, 1992, p. 219 for a similar statement), and second and related, that as one-way transplants earlier migrations were 'permanent ruptures' with home country affairs, irrevocably dividing past and present lives of the (im)migrants, whereas present-day shuttlers' 'networks, activities, patterns of living, and ideologies [...] span their home and the host society' in new transnational spaces (Basch, Glick Schiller and Blanc-Szanton, 1994, pp. 3-4; see also Portes, 1997, pp. 812-3 for a similar proposition. In response to historians' arguments to the contrary, these scholars have since recognized transnational involvements of old immigrants – see Glick Schiller, 1999; Portes, Guarnizo and Landolt, 1999).

Third, unfounded, too, has been a view that the emergence of these new transnational spaces has created a complex 'new sphere of politics' – supposedly nonexistent in the past – whereby political leaders in the home countries and (im)migrants in the transplanted communities abroad engage in a 'new form of nation-building' as they influence each other and the host country establishment on a 'deterritorialized' plane. Fourth and underlying the above, historically inaccurate has also been the new transnationalists' perception that this new transnational quality of (im)migrants' lives and new transnational political spaces have been generated by the accelerated globalization in the late twentieth century, and, in particular, by the constitutive for it 'dependent' incorporation of less developed South-East (SE) regions of the world into the capitalist world-system dominated by its North-West (NW) 'core' combined with revolutions in transportation and communication technologies, and have been sustained by racist attitudes and discrimination – spared the earlier, white European arrivals – against new SE (im)migrants by members and institutions of the white NW host societies that either block or channel these immigrants' assimilation into the isolated and underpriviledged segments of the mainstream society (for immigration historians' critical discussions of the claims made by the advocates of the new transnationalism thesis see e.g., Gerstle, 1997; Morawska, 2001a, 2003; also Guttierez, 1997; Gabaccia, 2000; and – a historically-minded anthropologist – Foner, 1997, 2000a).

While pointing out unrecognized similarities between past and present transnational involvements of immigrants, historians have, nevertheless, acknowledged their differences. Present-day (im)migrants' transnationalism, shaped by the combination of enduring and new elements, differs from that of their predecessors in two major ways. First, it is much more varied or plural in form and content because contemporary (im)migrants themselves are much more diverse in regional origin, racial identification, gender, home-country socioeconomic background and cultural orientation and, in the host society, in their legal status, the sector of the economy in which they are employed, and their mode of acculturation to the dominant society. Second, both the sending and the receiving nation-states are today much more tolerant of such differences than they were in the past. Whereas earlier-wave immigrants and their children were 'closet transnationalists' subject to exclusionary demands from home and host nation-states regarding their national commitments and were unprotected by legal-institutional and civic tolerance for the practice of diversity, legitimate 'public' options are available to their contemporary successors in terms of identities and participation, ranging from global to transnational, national, local, and different combinations thereof. Although the idea of a 'just pluralism' does not equally embrace all communities, especially those of non-whites (who constitute a large proportion of contemporary [im]migrants) these laws and public discourse create institutional channels and a juridico-political 'climate' for groups and individuals either to pursue their grievances or to remain 'other' without fear of opprobrium and accusations of state-national disloyalty (on multiculturalism as a 'politically correct' option for immigrants and, generally, citizens of late-twentieth-century nation-states, especially the United States, see Glazer, 1997; Salins, 1997; Joppke, 1998, Kivisto, 2002; Morawska, 2003; see also Kymlicka, 1995). Historians' assessment of the discontinuities in contemporary immigrants' transnationalism in comparison with that of their turn-of-the-twentieth-century predecessors agrees by and large with those pointed out in historically informed sociological studies that emphasize contrasts over time. It has been a more balanced account of continuity and change in this enduring phenomenon that has distinguished historical from sociological evaluations.

Racialized Ethnicity/Ethnicized Race

Closely related to a reassessment of the assimilation processes has been the emergence in the 1990s of the issue of race as one of the central problems of American immigration research. In this case, too, although sociologists and historians of immigration have shared some concerns and some awareness of each other's positions, the ways in which they have examined and incorporated this issue into the scholarship of their respective fields have been different.

A combination of four contributing factors has made the issue of race one of the leading themes-arguments on the current agenda in immigration sociology. Two of them have been already noted as 'triggers' of the return to assimilation: the largely non-white composition of post-1965 immigration to the United States and concerns with the obstacles to (or facilitators of) the integration of these immigrants' children into the dominant (white) society. In addition, the increasingly visible presence of these new immigrants and their children in American neighborhoods, schools, workplaces, and among the ranks of welfare recipients has revived among the natives (primarily whites, but also African Americans) what George Sanchez (1997) has called an exclusionary 'racialized nativism' underlaid by a sense of the 'decline of the American nation'. Directly tied to the divisive issue of race, the idea of multiculturalism – originally a response of African Americans to persistent racial discrimination calling for the struggle for social equality and the affirmation of cultural, ethnic and racial differences – has been expanded to include other non-white immigrant/ethnic groups and expressed through their involvement in U.S. local and national politics on behalf of racial minorities' interests. (On multi-culturalism's base in racial inequality see Bulmer and Solomos, 1998; Taylor, 1992; Gutmann, 1993; Joppke, 1998; Glazer, 1997; Espiritu, 1999; Smith, 2003; Waldinger and Fitzgerald, 2002.)

The main divide in the conceptualization of race by present-day sociologists of immigration/ethnicity has been between those who conceive it in terms of the bimodal white versus non-white dichotomy without problematizing either of these components and those who understand the meanings and boundaries of this concept and the cultural construction process it represents as flexible and context-contingent (for a good overview of these arguments, see Kivisto, 2002).

The bimodal concept of race/racism has been most typically represented by advocates of the segmented assimilation thesis. Although presumably it has not been devised for this purpose, the undifferentiated notion of whites and non-whites supports in advance, so to speak, the segmented assimilation thesis or, put differently, prejudices the outcome of its empirical application (so, too, for that matter, does the already noted presupposition of the unquestionable whiteness of earlier European immigrants used as the counterpoint for their late-twentieth-century successors). Ironically, because of their intention to undermine the classical assimilation paradigm, by sustaining the white vs. non-white opposition, its proponents locate themselves within the classical tradition of American sociology in which this paradigm was formulated. (On the tradition of bimodal, black-white conceptualizations of race in American social thought see DeWind and Kasinitz, 1997; Sanchez, 1999; Almaguer, 1994; Lowe, 1996; Morawska, 2001b.)

In accord with its proponents' general analytic orientation, in the bimodal representation race(s) and racial effects are treated mainly in structural terms as systematic, patterned obstacles to (non-whites) or facilitators (whites) of socio-economic advancement. In comparison, the context-flexible conceptualization focuses on the culturally constructed character and implications of the socially embedded racial/ethnic perceptions and identifies, the racialization of ethnicity and the ethnicization of race as overlapping processes. 'A race may be, but is not necessarily, at the same time an ethnic group, and an ethnic group may be, but is not necessarily, at the same time a race' (Cornell and Hartmann, 1998, p. XVII; see, also, Sanchez, 1997; Foner, 2001; Bailey, 2001; Light et al., 1994; DeWind and Kasinitz, 1997; Kibria, 1998; Waldinger and Lichter, 2003 for statements of a similar position). In the interpretation whereby the 'may be' and 'not necessarily' of race and/or ethnicity are outcomes of the dynamic ongoing interaction of structure(s) and human agency(-ies), race is conceived not as an opposition of fixed categories but as a multicolored spectrum that under certain situational or enduring conditions may and does polarize into distinct 'color groups' (e.g., black vs. white and/or oriental in situations of actual or perceived discrimination, or 'Asian Ameri-can' as a constructed category for political or scholarly research purposes). (On the problematic bases and implications of the representation of Asian American highly differentiated across and within groups as a racial minority see Kibria, 1998.)

Two kinds of arguments for the conceptualization of race as a (socio-)culturally constructed idea with multiple meanings can be detected in sociological studies of immigration/ethnicity informed by the context-flexible approach. One derives from a critical examination of the specific historical circumstances that from the beginnings of American sociology until recently have kept it Europe-oriented and informed by the problems specific for eastern and midwestern parts of the country, both of which, combined, have sustained the bimodal, white vs. non-white (black) thinking about race (see, e.g., Glazer, 1997; Sanchez, 1999; Vickerman, 1999; Cordero-Guzman et al., 2001; Kasinitz and Vickerman, 2001; Waldinger and Lichter, 2003; for an assessment of race(-ist) biases in Western social thought in general see Cornell and Hartmann, 1998; also Castles and Davidson, 2000). This argument, whereby showing how it happened explains why it did, has been the most genuinely – although probably un-self-consciously – historical mode of analysis among all the cases of sociological discussions considered here.

The other argument for a context-flexible conceptualization of race, more typical of the historically-informed sociological discussion, has used the work of immigration historians showing ambiguous and shifting meanings of the concept of race and racial distinctions as they were applied by the dominant groups to describe and differentiate among European immigrants in 19th and early 20th century America as supportive evidence against the bimodal white vs. non-white representation (see Alba and Nee, 2003, 1997; Alba, 1999; Perlmann and Waldinger, 1997 – the same scholars who have relied on references to historical studies as arguments for an open-ended or 'bumpy' concept of assimilation; see, also, Goldberg, 1992; Waters, 1999a; Espiritu, 1999; Kasinitz and Vickerman, 2001; Rasmussen et al., 2001).

'Looking toward Europe' (Glazer, 1997) from which originated their research subjects has blinded immigration historians to the distinct impact of race (vs. ethnicity) on immigrant/ethnic incorporation into American society no less than it has the sociologists. Three superimposed factors seem to have been most instrumental in bringing the concept and social-cultural operation of race as a leading problem on the agenda of immigration historians in the 1990s. The observation of and reading about largely non-white contemporary immigrants and their children trying to make their lives in America amid the intensified racialized nativism of the dominant society has been an incentive to reexamine experiences of earlier arrivals from the 'perspective of color'. These motives for the increased concern with race immigration historians have shared with sociologists. The particular focus of the former's discussions of the relationship of race and immigration/ethnicity has been the result of another, intra-disciplinary factor.

Historians' revisionist polemic in the 1990s with the interest and explanatory priority accorded to macroeconomic structures and class divisions/inequalities by the *marxisant* social history of the 1970s-80s has raised the issue of race and racism of the American working class in the late 19th and early 20th centuries. In the field of immigration research, this concern has resulted in historical case studies of racialization and, subsequently, deracialization of ethnicity as European working-class immigrants and their children were incorporated into mainstream American society. Because of the regions (East Coast and Midwestern America) and period (industrial) on which these studies focused, these two processes have been understood by immigration historians as the 'blackening' and, then, gradual 'whitening' of immigrants (case studies of this transformation by Roediger, 1991 and Ignatiev, 1995 have already become classics and have stimulated similarly conceptualized research on different immigrant groups in different times/places; see, e.g., Barkan, 1995; McGreevey, 1996; Gerstle, 2001; Barrett and Roediger, 1997; Gutterl, 2001; Gratton, 2002; Carnevale, 2000; Sheridan, 2002; Guglielmo and Salerno, 2003; cf. also Jacobson, 1998; and the contributions to a discussion about the meanings and assignments of 'whiteness' in the American society over time in the special issue on this subject of the *International Labor and Working-Class History*, 2001, fall).

The 1994 editorial in the leading journal of American ethnic history has further sanctioned the black and white representation of race by immigration/ethnic historians who have pioneered in the integration of this issue into the study of Americanization while demonstrating the context dependent, shifting meanings of race in this process. 'Although African American history and American immigration/ethnic history have often been viewed as two separate fields' – it announced to the readers – 'they are really one – a history of the peopling and peoples of the United States' (Bayor, 1994, p. 3). And indeed, whereas articles on African American history have since been regularly published in the journal, research on non-white/non-black Asian and Latino American historians has appeared only sporadically (it should be noted, however, that the existence of independent Asian and Latino American scholarly associations and journals devoted to the study of immigration and ethnicity of 'their own' groups has also weakened their integration into mainstream immigration historiography).

Whereas the historicizing of race by immigration/ethnic sociologists has 'deconstructed' the non-white category by revealing a multicolored spectrum of peoples subsumed under this label, for all the reasons mentioned historians' attention has thus far focused on demonstrating time- and place-contingency of the bimodal, black-white perceptions. Different conceptual tasks are involved in sociologists' and historians' efforts to integrate the race factor into the study of immigrant/ethnic assimilation into American society: for sociologists, imbuing of the presumedly white ethnicity with race, and for historians, separating fused notions of ethnicity and race[4] might have further contributed to the distinct focuses of these two fields of immigration research.

Promises of Interdisciplinarity

Using my earlier review of the main themes-arguments that informed the American sociology and historiography of immigration since the 1960s as a comparative framework, I have identified three major concerns that have become the new foci of these two fields of immigration studies since the 1990s: the assimilation of immigrants and their offspring; the transnationalization of immigrant identities and membership; and the racialization of ethnicity or the close intertwining of ethnicity and race in immigrants' (mal)adaptation to American society. I have also discussed different ways in which these issues have been conceptualized in each of these two disciplines.

As I assessed comparatively the leading issues and arguments in earlier and contemporary American sociology and history of immigration, I pointed out, too, the most important factors within and without these two disciplines that have jointly contributed to the emergence of new concerns since the 1990s. Regarding the shifted interest from resilient ethnicity to assimilation and the new concern with the role of race in this process, these contributing factors included the gradual 'exhaustion' of the ethnicity paradigm in both disciplines, that is, its diminishing ability to generate innovative research and ask new questions; and the maturing and entry into mainstream American society of native-born children of 'new immigrants' – a process that occurs in the public climate of multiculturalism but confronts entrenched discrimination and prejudice against non-white citizens in American institutions.

Fostering sociologists' interest in immigrants' transnational involvements have been, combined, the high-rate cross-border mobility of immigrants in the context of increased civic-political tolerance for heterogeneity/plurality in sender and receiver societies alike, the 'global (postnational) turn' in American social science theorizing, and the recent vocal entry into immigration studies of anthropologists who used transnationalism as their legitimating/recognition agenda. Immigration historians, I have argued, became interested in transnationalism primarily in a reactive way, by contesting sociologists' (and anthropologists') claims of contemporary immigrants' supposedly 'new' transnationalism and by demonstrating a much longer presence of this phenomenon in American ethnic communities. The foreign-born status and racial minority membership of many immigration sociologists, and white-ethnic working-class family backgrounds and recent (first-generation) entries into the professional stratum of a number of immigration historians have most likely contributed, too, to their increased interest in the issues of assimilation, transnational commitments, and racialized ethnicity/ethnicized race.

The sociology of immigration has witnessed other new developments during the 1990s. Anthropologists' joining the investigation of contemporary immigration has influenced not only the problem agenda of this study area but also the focus and methods of research: the micro-level ethnographic examination of different immigrant (trans-)local communities, overshadowed earlier by the dominant macroscopic approach, has gained recognition and produced a crop of studies. As a result, a number of immigration sociologists appreciate the diversity and context-dependency and, thus, flexibility of social-cultural (here: immigrant/ethnic) assimilation/transnationalization/racialization processes. Finally, the major arguments concerning the new issues of concern in the American immigration studies in the 1990s-early 2000s, namely, the distinctive patterns of contemporary immigrant assimilation, the novelty of immigrant transnational bonds and identities, and the new, racialized ethnicity of minority-group (non-white) immigrants and their children, have evoked historical, primarily contrasting comparisons with turn-of-the-twentieth-century immigrant/ethnic groups of South and East European origin. These comparisons, in turn, have increased familiarity with and references to historians' research in sociological studies. Reciprocally, because of the shared (extra-disciplinary) circumstances that instigated the shift of major interests in sociological and historical studies of immigration, and because historians have felt provoked by the claims about the supposed novelty of these lead issues, they, too, have become more aware of the current work of immigration sociologists.

Although during the 1990s immigration scholars in these two fields have become more familiar with each other's studies and use them more frequently in their own research and arguments, neither the sociologists nor the historians of immigration have tried to engage each other in a conversation about the epistemological foundations, purposes of research, and explanatory strategies of their respective disciplines. I have suggested the most likely reasons for this mutual disinteressment. On the part of sociologists, it has been the marginal position of historical orientation in contemporary American sociology and, thus, of a large body of theoretical and empirical work by historical sociologists on the problematic of time- and space-contingency of social processes and their outcomes, and, in particular, the absence of immigration specialists among the few more widely (mainstream) recognized practitioners of this orientation. The withdrawal of historians from a closer engagement with historically-minded sociologists, which in the early 1980s had produced joint scholarly publications and conferences, has resulted in part, I have argued, from displays by historical sociologists of 'superior distance' on such occasions and, in part, from the turn to cultural-textual and away from social-structural interests in the discipline of history in general.

Highlighting differences (as in the debate between historical sociology and social history in the 1980s) is one mode of interdisciplinary communication. Seeking interconnections and attempting 'translations' is another manner of dialogue. Bringing historical research closer to the historical orientation in sociology while 'historicizing' the latter would be one possible means – worth trying, I believe – toward a closer rapprochement between these two fields of immigration studies. Whereas in the 1980s, the recent and not yet institutionalized revival of the historical orientation in sociology (see Abbott, 1994; Smith, 1994) led the followers of this approach to emphasize strongly their theoretical disciplinary allegiances, twenty years later, historical sociology, although still more marginal than mainstream, is well-established and recognized in the discipline. Having by and large abandoned their 'our approach is different and better' positioning, historical sociologists have since created a large number of excellent methodological studies on the how-to of historically sensitive sociological theorizing and research and several studies that effectively apply these skills.

Historical sociologists conceive the subject matter of their discipline, that is, the shaping of action by structure and the transforming of structure by action as processes in time or processes of continuous *becoming*. The conception of changing time and space coordinates of social life as the *constitutive media* of social action, intrinsic to social processes/institutions and, thus, as limiting frames for the latter, makes the work of sociology into the inherently historical undertaking (for the elaborations of this ideas, see, e.g., Abrams, 1982; Abbott, 2001; Aminzade, 1992; Griffin, 1992; Bryant, 1994; Sewell, 1996; Calhoun, 1996; Isaac, 1997; Hall, 1999; Mahoney and Rueschemeyer, 2003). In this approach, questions about when, at what pace, for how long, how regularly, and in which sequence events happen and where they do so are fundamental to a comprehensive understanding of the what, how, and why of the unfolding (re)constitution of social action and societal structures. Rather than trying to escape these temporal and spatial 'variables' of their analysis to make it as generally applicable as possible, historical sociologists embed them into their research design and explanatory strategies. Incorporating time/place conditions of social action and organization into the explanation thereof does not mean, however, as the advocates of general theory-driven sociology have claimed, that historical sociological explanation has 'forsaken theory' altogether (Kiser and Hechter, 1991; see also Goldthorpe, 1991). True, historical sociologists have little trust in general laws because such laws fail to recognize the social world as fundamentally heterogeneous and transitional in constitution. But most of their inquiries are nevertheless systematically theory-informed, and many are theory-driven in an analytically disciplined manner (I will return to this issue shortly).

Theoretically informed and sensitive to temporal and spatial contingencies of social life, the historical orientation in sociology satisfies the important concerns of both disciplines and, in addition, offers each of them the opportunity to ask new questions and to generate new answers. Here are what I believe could be the major contributions of the historical (sociological) approach to immigration sociology and, reciprocally, of the (historical) sociological approach to immigration history.

When recognized by immigration sociologists, context dependence of the assimilation, transnationalism, and racialization of ethnicity processes has been understood primarily in terms of the differential effects of immigrants' location in geographic, socioeconomic, and cultural space rather than in the historical mode *sensu proprio* as the attribute and consequence of the constitutive temporality of their lives. Incorporating into research projects on the currently leading themes in immigration studies (or any other aspects of the experience of immigrants and their offspring) of the concern about the workings and effects of different temporal dimensions of social life as elaborated by historical sociologists – the pace or tempo of events, their duration, rhythm or regularity, and their trajectory or sequence – would make the already recognized contingencies more complex and robust, allowing for more encompassing and nuanced explanations of the investigated phenomena. Thus, for instance, immigrants' assimilation evolves over extended periods through variable but time- and place-constrained sets of sequential developments involving the acquisition of linguistic and other host-country cultural skills and elements of political, economic, and social incorporation. Or, in the intensified transnationalism of immigrants, changing temporal-spatial coordinates of social life and, in particular, rapid advances in communication and transportation technology and high frequency of cross-border travels of large numbers of migrants constitute a major set of explanatory circumstances.

The immigration sociologists who opt for a flexible, context-contingent approach can profit from the scrutiny and elaboration of the theoretical principles guiding sociohistorical inquiry offered by historical sociologists. In his *Cultures of Inquiry* (1999) John Hall distinguishes between the *particularizing* and *generalizing* strategies of explanation in sociohistorical inquiry. The major distinction between particularizing and generalizing modes of historically informed sociological inquiry is the different balancing of analytic emphases: the interpretation/explanation of case(s) in the former, and the fitting/generating theory in the latter.

The particularizing practice of inquiry has three varieties, each of which is theoretically informed in its own way.[5] The first one, which Hall calls 'situational history', has as its primary purpose the explication of the contemporary situation by causally linking it to past events/developments. The researcher (re)constructs this causal chain by testing different interpretative frameworks to assess which of them can best account for the interplay of constraints, possibilities, and outcomes evolving in the past-to-the-present trajectory. Thus, for example, an 'upward assimilation' process of one (or more) immigrant groups could be better explained by the facilitating effects of the sustained economic development combined and the enduring inclusive (pluralistic) civic-political and social climate in the city/region of immigrant settlement (macro-structural circumstances), or by the long-dure persistence of ethnic assistance networks combined with the established presence of group members-pioneers in the mainstream economic and social niches and a quick pace of uninterrupted educational advancement of immigrant/ethnic group's members (micro-structural circumstances).

The second explanatory strategy of the particularizing genre is 'specific history' whose primary purpose is to account for the unfolding of a specific event/ development over a shorter or longer dure of time and in varying spatial scopes. Whereas it can be done, to borrow a useful anthropological distinction, from either *etic* (outsider), *emic* (insider), or combined extrinsic/intrinsic perspectives (see Denzin and Lincoln, 1998; also Merton, 1968), all these approaches engage social theory. The extrinsic account, through inquiry's own relevance framework, is what Skocpol (1984) has called a 'problem-oriented' analysis guided by – or generating – the theoretical concepts that seem useful and valid to make sense of the phenomenon in question (see also Quadagno and Knapp, 1992; Hall, 1999). Informed by the *verstehende* tradition in sociology, the intrinsic account – an explanation with what Florian Znaniecki (1934) called the 'humanistic coefficient'

– narrates the events in terms of the 'relevance structures' or emplotments of everyday lives (Schutz, 1970) as perceived by the social actors themselves. Far from simply descriptive accounts of individual happenings, such narratives contain 'theoretical maps' causally linking the unfolding events into a coherent (meaningful) explanation – an excellent base for an explanatory narrative in a historical sociological project informed by the concept of human agency as instrumental in societal change and aiming at meaningful understanding of the course of particular historical development (see Sewell, 1996; Bonnell and Hunt, 1999).

An application of the 'specific history' explanatory strategy of the extrinsic/etic type in sociological research on immigration would be, for example, the interpretation of the origins and persistence of black New York Carribean immigrants' resistance to the racialization of their ethnic identities as reported in ethnographic studies (see Vickerman, 2001; Waters, 1999b) that are organized around Herbert Blumer's (1958) acclaimed concept of group position or the 'status-ordering' perceptions the dominant (here: white) and subordinate (here: black) groups hold about self and other. An account of, say, New York Haitian immigrants' unfolding American lifeworlds as narrated by the actors themselves in which shared perceptions and displays of separateness from native-American blacks play an important structuring role, would be an illustration of the specific history of the intrinsic/emic genre whereby theoretical insights are derived from the storytellers' own interpretations of their experience that causally link prior and subsequent events into path-dependent trajectories.

The third type of particularizing strategies of sociohistorical inquiry identified by Hall is 'configurational history'. Whereas in specific history the explanatory emphasis is on the interpretation of the unfolding situations as they are meaningful to the actors themselves, in configurational history the interplay of diverse converging historical phenomena is theorized in a way that transcends meaningful connections among these phenomena themselves. Historical sociologists often theorize this evolving configuration by constructing/applying the ideal type of the investigated phenomenon. 'Configurational history', argues Hall, 'makes it possible to investigate broad features of social change without resorting to "evolutionary stage theories" or universal histories. Optimally, configurational history is a practice directed to discerning culturally significant patterns of development on the basis of theoretically informed empirical reasoning... [It] not only identifies a unique configuration and its antecedents, [but] its typological social theory identifies the relevant range of structural possibilities' (Hall, 1999, pp. 217-9; his example of such comprehensive configurational history is Wolfgang Schluchter's [1989] reconstruction of Weber's analysis of rationalization and capitalism).

Although both temporal and spatial scopes of the phenomena investigated by immigration sociologists are more limited than those of the rise of modern Western capitalism examined by Weber and Schluchter, configurational inquiry still offers exciting prospects of explaining social/cultural developments, especially when involving comparative analysis. My own investigation (2001c) of ethnic identity formation among American Jews in six cities during the early twentieth century illustrates this strategy. The comparative configurational analysis of the 'causal operation' of city-specific subsets from among twenty-three circumstances that were identified in the existing (nationwide) studies of the adaptation of Jewish immigrants and their children to American society during that period as affecting this process or suggested by sociological theories of assimilation, generated three distinct patterns that I called the 'assertive', 'resentful', and 'defensive' enhancement of ethnic identity formation among American Jews. Similar comparative-historical configurational inquiries could investigate emerging/ changing patterns of immigrant transnationalism and the (de)racialization of ethnicity.

Trying some of the approaches elaborated by historical sociologists can serve as a medium of interdisciplinary exchange not only for sociologists but also for historians of immigration who tend to leave implicit whatever theoretical premises they use to inform/guide their studies. In particular, it can help to dissipate historians' programmatic distrust of (explicit) 'theory' which, ironically, they generally understand in the positivistic (ahistorical) sociological tradition as universal laws. As noted here, however, the historical orientation in sociology conceives of and uses social theory in ways that do not violate but, instead, build upon presuppositions about the nature of the social processes and the resulting constraints on knowledge about these processes that have traditionally informed the historical discipline. A more explicit, systematic use of theory can help immigration historians to arrange their evidence and to advance their arguments in a more coherent, clearer way, and to put them in the broader comparative framework of other similar/contrasting cases, which, in turn, helps to sharpen the arguments (for a good discussion of the advantages of using theory – the time/place-contingent genre, of course – in guiding historical research and analysis, see Mann, 1993).

Different ways of making theoretical considerations more explicit and more explicitly ordering analysis in particularizing strategies have already been discussed. Although aimed primarily at fellow (mainstream) sociologists to historicize social theory, the generalizing analytic strategies elaborated by the historical sociologists could also aid an effort of interested immigration historians to systematize and clarify their analyses and arguments. Hall distinguishes three such generalizing practices of inquiry. The purpose of the first one, 'the application of social theory to explain case(s)', is to assess the utility of a model according to 'its ability to convincingly order the evidence' (Hall, 1999, p. 189, after Skocpol and Somers, 1980, p. 178). Detailed examinations of case(s) serve as *in situ* testing of the theory rather than to generate their situational or specific history through a meaningful explanation informed by theoretical concepts. Testing of the segmented assimilation model on, for example, black immigrants from Africa residentially segregated from whites and employed in secondary or informal sectors of the New York economy would be an interesting application of this strategy.

The second generalizing strategy, 'analytic generalization', has as its purpose empirical/historical testing of hypotheses about 'transitory regularities' (Joynt and Rescher, 1961; see also Merton, 1972 on 'middle range' theories) or time/place specific causal relations derived from theory or their (inductive) generation from empirical/historical evidence. Provided there is prior clarification of the conceptual confusion noted earlier, regarding the understanding of transnationalism in American immigration studies, an attempt at a more systematic historical-sociological theorizing of this phenomenon would be very timely and useful in guiding further research. Particularly useful would be a theoretical elaboration of the mezzo-level, intermediate structures linking micro- and macroscopic processes that generate and sustain trans (or post) local immigrant identities and participation, and a systematic 'ordering' account for temporal dimensions of this phenomenon, including explanation of the major mechanisms of continuity and change in its operation.

The third generalizing strategy is 'contrast-oriented comparison'. In this case, which often applies the configurational approach as the means of analysis, the purpose of inquiry is to ascertain how unique features affect the workings of a general process. 'Contrast-oriented comparison', argues Hall, 'evidences the possibility of de-emphasizing theory while maintaining a generalizing orientation of inquiry. Instead of developing theory in any detailed or systematic way, a researcher can make a value judgment about the cultural significance of a theoretical issue [...] and use this issue as an orienting theme for theoretical conceptualization. Research then explores the theme in relation to particular objects of inquiry, [comparatively tracing] the concrete time/place circumstances that give play to particular structural outcomes, cultural constellations, or other developments' (Hall, 1999, p. 199). Hall's illustrations of the themes that have been effectively examined by this strategy draw from the classical repertoire of concerns of historical sociologists: modern rational capitalism, nation-state formation, class mobilization and revolutions, the routinization of charisma. In immigration studies where generalizing concepts and theories are common but more systematic comparative research is scarce, a worthy topic to be examined in a contrast-oriented inquiry would be, for example, the process of immigrants' assimilation – in general or of one ethnic/regional group such as Poles or Asians – in the United States and France or Australia. Or, as interesting, the racialization of ethnicity of immigrants in America as compared with that in Great Britain or France.

For the sociologists who prefer quantitative handling of data gathered during situational or configurational history projects, theory testing or contrast-oriented comparisons, methods of statistical analysis exist that account for 'temporally moving covariances' or the impact of the sequence and duration of events on their outcomes and variable-oriented (quantitative) methods of historical-comparative analysis (see Abbott, 1983, 1988; Ragin, 1987; Isaac and Griffin, 1989; Griffin et al., 1997; Isaac and Leicht, 1997; Jensen, 1997). Available also are methods of disciplined logical analysis in constructing historical generalizations and comparative inquiries that use narrative as an explanatory frame (see Skocpol, 1984; Ragin, 1987, 2000; *Social Science History* 1992 – special issue on narrative analysis in social sciences; Griffin, 1992; Calhoun, 1998, Sommers 1999; Sewell, 1996; also Hall, 1999).

Although it has become visible only in the 1990s, the presence of anthropologists in American immigration studies is already well established, and their scholarly influence has been recognized by both sociologists and historians in the field. It is appropriate, then, to conclude by welcoming this disciplinary broadening of immigration studies and by pointing out some possible directions of an intellectually profitable interchange among the now three participants in this inquiry. Some of the benefits to both the sociology and history of immigration from anthropologists joining this area have already been noted. They bring a strong focus on the (trans)*local* as the arena proper of social relations and conceive of this (trans)local in the holistic or multilayered and complex manner rather than (as is common in sociology) as an aspect of the distinct economic, political, or social structures. They conceive of human (immigrant/ethnic) action as imbued with cultural meanings and, thus, bring a welcome balance to the often overly structuralist (culture-less) approaches of immigration sociology or, for that matter, also social history of immigration. They also have perfected the narrative as a mode of at once rhetoric and explanation, which immigration sociologists and historians interested in this kind of analytic strategies can find very useful.

Immigration anthropologists, in turn, can profit from the sociologists' mezzo-level institutional analyses linking the local and the global. And the work of historical sociologists, specifically, can furnish the rationale and the know-how of different, particularizing and generalizing strategies of theoretically informed explanation – the propositions that may be of particular interest to anthropologists in times of a 'theoretical identity crisis' of their discipline (on this predicament, see Clifford and Marcus, 1996; Brightman, 1995). The 'historical turn' in anthropology, that is, the acknowledgment of the historicity of cultural forms that the disciplinary paradigms until recently held to be patterned by universal principles, has already gained advocates among the outstanding practitioners in this field (see, e.g., Sahlins, 1991; Dirks, 1996; also Sewell, 1999 for a review). It may be of interest to immigration anthropologists to consider their arguments and the contributions of historical orientation to the anthropological study of transnationalism, assimilation, and racialization of ethnicity, as well as other issues relevant to the lives of immigrants in their 'glocal' worlds.

Notes

*   I wish to thank my colleagues: sociologists, historians, and anthropologists, for sharing with me their reflections on the current problem agendas and analytical strategies in their respective fields of immigration/ethnic studies (their names are listed alphabetically): Richard Alba, Elliott Barkan, Ronald Bayor, Rogers Brubaker, John Bukowczyk, Stephen Collins, Kathleen Conzen, Hasia Diner, Nancy Foner, Gary Gerstle, Luis Guarnizo, Grace Kao, Philip Kasinitz, Russell Kazal, Michael Kearney, Peter Kivisto, Peggy Levitt, Ivan Light, Leslie Moch, Pyong Min, Silvia Pedraza, Joel Perlmann, Ruben Rumbaut, Marta Tienda, Roger Waldinger.

1   Although this particular focus was justified by the special occasion of the discussion – the publication of Nancy Foner's comparative-historical study, *From Ellis Island to JFK* (2000a) – an opportunity to broaden its scope by considering theoretical and epistemological grounding of comparative analyses in different disciplines was missed.

2   If workshops organized in-between major conferences at which the leading specialists in the field present their current work can be treated as 'trendsetters' for the research agenda in this area study, a mini-conference on *Transcending Borders: Migration, Ethnicity, and Incorporation in an Age of Globalism,* organized by the Immigration History Society and New York University, October 31-November 2, 2003, indicates a possibility of the emergence of a new theme in the social science immigration research, namely, the relationship between immigrants' religion and their incorporation to the host society, which is conceptualized in a multi-pattern, context-dependent framework characteristic of this approach to assimilation.

3   The 'new' or 'third' space proposition has been most typically represented among the anthropologists – see, e.g., Holston and Appadurai, 1996; also Kearney, 1995. In the literature not identified with the new transnationalism paradigm there exists as well another, third understanding of the concept of transnationalism, and referring to the connections that stretch beyond state borders of one country into another(s) and link members of national/ethnic diasporas outside of their native countries into *single* symbolic deterritorialized national/ethnic communities based on nearly-*exclusive* (rather than inclusive and plural as in the first here identified interpretation) identities and commitments, and, in the case of departed members of sovereign nation-states, often also civic membership. Studies informed by this interpretation have been authored by political scientists and international relations specialists as well as political and cultural sociologists, and have dealt with diasporas worldwide (see Cohen, 1997 for an overview of diaspora literature, and Clifford, 1997 for a critique of the enclosure/non-mixing assumption underlying some of the latter).

4   Since it has been documented beyond doubt in the sources and, thus, obvious to immigration historians that many of 19th and early 20th century immigrant groups were not perceived as 'white' by the representatives of the dominant, native-born American society, considering that until recently immigration history research has primarily focused on the immigrant generation, the fusion of ethnicity and race appeared 'natural' to them and not requiring analytic distinctions (on the race-ethnicity fusion by American immigration historians see Sanchez, 1999).

5   I have reduced Hall's typology of sociohistorical strategies of inquiry by eliminating 'historicism' from the particularizing and 'universal history' from generalizing categories, because the former does not contribute to interdisciplinary rapprochement and the latter has no practical application in immigration studies. For discussion of these omitted strategies, see Hall, 1999, pp. 181-8, 220-8.

References

Abbott, A. (1983), 'Sequences of Social Events: Concepts and Methods for the Analysis of Order in Social Processes', *Historical Methods,* 16 (4), pp. 129-47.

Abbott, A. (1988), 'Transcending General Linear Reality', *Sociological Theory,* 6, Fall, pp. 169-86.

Abbott, A. (1992) 'From Causes to Events: Notes on Narrative Positivism', *Sociological Methods and Research,* 20, pp. 428-55.

Abbott, A. (1994), 'History and Sociology: The Lost Synthesis', *Social Science History,* 15 (2), pp. 201-32.

Abbott, A. (2001), *Time Matters. On Theory and Method,* University of Chicago Press, Chicago.

Abrams, Philip (1982), *Historical Sociology,* Cornell UP, Ithaca, NY.

Alba, R. and Nee, V. (1997), 'Rethinking Assimilation: Theory for a New Era of Immigration', *International Migration Review,* 31 (4), pp. 826-74.

Alba, R. (1999), 'Immigration and the American Realities of Assimilation and Multiculturalism', *Sociological Forum,* 14 (1), pp. 3-25.

Alba, R. and Nee, V. (2003), *Remaking the American Mainstream. Assimilation and Contemporary Immigration,* Harvard UP, Cambridge, MA.

Aleinikoff, A. and Rumbaut, R. (1998), 'Terms of Belonging: Are Models of Membership Self-Fulfilling Prophecies?' Paper presented at the Social Science Research Council Conference on Immigrant Political Incorporation in Europe and the United States, 15-17 May, Berlin.

Aleinikoff, A. (2003), 'Between National and Postnational: Membership in the United States', in Joppke and Morawska (eds.), *Toward Assimilation and Citizenship,* pp. 110-30.

Almaguer, T. (1994), *Racial Fault Lines: The Historical Origins of White Supremacy in California,* University of California Press, Berkeley, CA.

Aminzade, R. (1992), 'Historical Sociology and Time', *Sociological Methods and Research,* 20 (4), pp. 456-80.

Axel, B.K. (ed.) (2002), *From the Margins: Historical Anthropology and Its Futures,* Duke UP, Durham.

Bailey, B. (2001), 'Dominican-American Ethnic/Racial Identities and United States Social Categories', *International Migration Review,* 35 (3), pp. 677-708.

Barkan, E. (1995), 'Race, Religion, and Nationality in American Society: A Model of Ethnicity – From Contact to Assimilation', *Journal of American Ethnic History,* 14 (2), pp. 38-75.

Barkan, E. (1999), 'Something Old, Something New, and Some Things Really for the Future: Recent Work on American Immigration and Ethnicity', *Reviews in American History,* 27, pp. 318-33.

Barrett, J. and Roediger, D. (1997), 'Inbetween Peoples: Race, Nationality, and the "New Immigrant" Working Class', *Journal of American Ethnic History,* 16 (3), pp. 3-45.

Basch, L., Glick Schiller, N. and Blanc-Szanton, C. (eds.) (1994), *Nations Unbound: Transnational Projects, Postcolonial Predicaments, and Deterritorialized Nation-States,* Gordeon & Breach, Amsterdam.

Bauboeck, R. (1994), *Transnational Citizenship,* Edward Elgar, Aldershot.

Bayor, R. (1994), 'Foreword to a Special Issue on African Americans', *Journal of American Ethnic History,* 14 (1), pp. 3-5.

Blumer, H. (1958), 'Race Prejudice as a Sense of Group Position', *Pacific Sociological Review,* 1, pp. 3-7.

Bonnell, V. and Hunt, L. (eds.) (1999), *Beyond the Cultural Turn. New Directions in the Study of Society and Culture,* University of California Press, Berkeley, CA.

Brettell, C. (2000), 'Theorizing Migration in Anthropology', in Brettell and Hollifield (eds.), *Migration Theory,* pp. 97-136.

Brettell, C. and Hollifield, J. (eds.) (2000), *Migration Theory. Talking Across Disciplines,* Routledge, New York.

Brettell, C. (2003), *Anthropology and Migration. Essays on Transnationalism, Ethnicity, and Identity,* Altamira Press, Walnut Creek, CA.

Brightman, R. (1995), 'Forget Culture: Replacement, Transcendence, Reflexification', *Cultural Anthropology,* 10, pp. 509-46.

Brubaker, R. (1996), *Nationalism Reframed,* Cambridge UP, New York.

Brubaker, R. (2003), 'The Return of Assimilation? Changing Perspectives on Immigration and Its Sequels in France, Germany, and the United States', in Joppke and Morawska (eds.), *Toward Assimilation and Citizenship,* pp. 39-58.

Bryant, J. (1994), 'John Goldthorpe and the Relics of Sociology', *British Journal of Sociology,* 45 (1), pp. 3-20.

Bulmer, M. and Solomos, J. (1998), 'Introduction: Re-thinking Ethnic and Racial Studies', *Ethnic and Racial Studies,* 21 (5), pp. 89-137.

Calhoun, C. (1996), 'The Rise and Domestication of Historical Sociology', in McDonald (ed.), *The Historic Turn in the Human Sciences,* pp. 305-38.

Calhoun, C. (1998), 'Explanation in Historical Sociology: Narrative, General Theory, and Historically Specific Theory', *American Journal of Sociology,* 104 (3), pp. 846-71.

Carnevale, N. (2000), 'Language, Race, and the New Immigrants: The Example of Southern Italians', in Foner, Rumbaut, and Gold (eds.), *Immigration Research for a New Century,* pp. 409-22.

Castles, St. and Davidson, A. (2000), *Citizenship and Migration. Globalization and the Politics of Belonging,* Routledge, New York.

Clifford, J. (1997), 'Diasporas', in M.M. Guibernau and J. Rex (eds.), *The Ethnicity Reader,* Polity Press, Oxford, pp. 283-90.

Clifford, J. and Marcus, G. (eds.) (1996), *Writing Culture: The Poetics and Politics of Ethnography,* University of California Press, Berkeley.

Cohen, R. (1997), 'Diasporas, the Nation-State, and Globalisation', in W. Gungwu (ed.), *Global History and Migrations,* Westview Press, Boulder, CO, pp. 117-44.

Conzen, K. et al. (1992), 'The Invention of Ethnicity: A Perspective from the U.S.A.', *Journal of American Ethnic History,* 12 (1), pp. 3-41.

Cordero-Guzman, H., Smith, R. and Grosfoguel, R. (eds.) (2001), *Migration, Transnationalization, and Race in a Changing New York,* Temple UP, Philadelphia.

Cornell, St. and Hartmann, D. (1998), *Ethnicity and Race: Making Identities in a Changing World,* Pine Forge Press, Thousand Oaks, CA.

Crevecoeur, Hector St. John de, *Letters from an American Farmer,* 1782, E.P. Dutton & Co, New York (1912).

Denzin, N. and Lincoln, Y. (eds.) (1998), *Strategies of Qualitative Inquiry,* Sage Publications, Thousand Oaks, CA.

DeWind, J. and Kasinitz, Ph. (1997), 'Everything Old is New Again? Processes and Theories of Immigrant Incorporation', *International Migration Review,* 31 (4), pp. 1096-111.

Diner, H. (2000), 'History and the Study of Immigration', in Brettell and Hollifield (eds.), *Migration Theory,* pp. 27-42.

Dirks, M. (1996), 'Is Vice Versa? Anthropologies and Anthropological Histories', in McDonald (ed.), *The Historic Turn in the Human Sciences,* pp. 17-52.

Espiritu, Y.L. (1999), 'Disciplines Unbound: Notes on Sociology and Ethnic Studies', *Contemporary Sociology,* 98 (5), pp. 510-3.

Espiritu, Y.L. (2003), *Home Bound: Filipino American Lives Across Cultures, Communities, and Countries,* University of California Press, Berkeley, CA.

Faist, T. (2000), 'Transnationalization in International Migration: Implications for the Study of Citizenship and Culture', *Ethnic and Racial Studies,* 23 (2), pp. 189-222.

Foner, N. (1997), 'What's New About Transnationalism? New York Immigrants Today and at the Turn of the Century', *Diaspora,* 6 (3), pp. 355-75.

Foner, N. (2000a), *From Ellis Island to JFK. New York's Two Great Waves of Immigration,* Yale UP, New Haven, CT.

Foner, N. (2000b), 'Anthropology and the Study of Immigration', in Foner, Rumbaut, and Gold (eds.), *Immigration Research for a New Century,* pp. 49-53.

Foner, N., Rumbaut, R., and Gold, St. (eds.) (2000), *Immigration Research for a New Century. Multidisciplinary Perspectives,* Russell Sage Foundation, New York.

Foner, N. (ed.) (2001), *Islands in The City. West Indian Migration To New York,* University of California Press, Berkeley.

Foner, N. (ed.) (2003), *American Arrivals. Anthropology Engages the New Immigrants,* School of American Research Press Santa Fe, NM.

Fuchs, L. (1990), *The American Kaleidoscope: Race, Ethnicity and the Civic Culture,* Wesleyan UP, Middletown, CT.

Gabaccia, D. (2000), *Italy's Many Diasporas,* University of Washington Press, Seattle.

Gans, H. (1992), 'Second Generation Decline: Scenarios for the Economic and Ethnic Futures of Post-1965 American Immigrants', *Ethnic and Racial Studies,* 15 (2), pp. 173-92.

Gans, H. (1997), 'Toward a Reconciliation of "Assimilation" and "Pluralism": The Interplay of Acculturation and Ethnic Retention', *International Migration Review,* 31 (4), pp. 875-93.

Gans, H. (2000), 'Filling in Some Holes: Six Areas of Needed Immigration Research', *American Behavioral Scientist,* June-July, 42 (9), pp. 1302-14.

Gerstle, G. (1997), 'Liberty, Coercion, and the Making of Americans', *Journal of American History,* September, pp. 525-58.

Gerstle, G. (2001), *American Crucible: Race and Nation in the Twentieth Century,* Princeton UP, Princeton.

Gerstle, G. and Mollenkopf, J. (eds.) (2001), *E Pluribus Unum? Contemporary and Historical Perspectives on Immigrant Political Incorporation,* Russell Sage Foundation, New York.

Gjerde, J. (1999), 'New Growth on Old Vines: The State of the Field: The Social History of Immigration to and Ethnicity in the United States', *Journal of American Ethnic History,* 18 (4), pp. 40-66.

Glazer, N. (1997), *We Are All Multiculturalists Now,* Harvard UP, Cambridge, MA.

Glick Schiller, N. (1996), 'Who Are Those Guys? A Transnational Reading of the U.S. Immigrant Experience'. Paper presented at the conference 'Becoming American/ America becoming: International Migration to the United States', Social Science Research Council, Sanibel Island, Florida, 18-21 January.

Glick-Schiller, N., Basch, L., and Blanc-Szanton, C. (1996), 'From Immigrant to Transmigrants: Theorizing Transnational Migration', *Anthropological Quarterly,* 68 (1), pp. 48-63.

Glick Schiller, N. and Fouron, G. (1998), 'Transnational Lives and National Identities: The Identity Politics of Haitian Immigrants', in: Guarnizo and Smith (eds.), *Transnationalism from below,* pp. 130-64.

Glick Schiller, N. (1999), 'Transmigrants and Nation-States: Something Old and Something New in the U.S. Immigrant Experience', in Hirschman, Kasinitz, and DeWind (eds.), *The Handbook of International Migration,* pp. 94-119.

Gold, St. (1997), 'Transnationalism and Vocabularies of Motive in International Migration: The Case of Israelis in the United States', *Sociological Perspectives,* 40 (3), pp. 409-27.

Goldberg, B. (1992), 'Historical Reflections on Transnationalism, Race, and the American Immigrant Saga', in N. Glick Schiller et al. (eds.), *Towards a Transnational Perspective on Migration,* New York Academy of Sciences, New York, pp. 201-16.

Goldthorpe, J. (1991), 'The Uses of History in Sociology: Reflections on Some Recent Tendencies', *British Journal of Sociology*, 42 (2), pp. 208-39.

Gordon, M. (1964), *Assimilation in American Life*, Oxford UP, New York.

Gratton, B. (2002), 'Race, the Children of Immigrants, and Social Science Theory', *Journal of American Ethnic History*, 21 (4), pp. 74-84.

Griffin, L. (1992), 'Temporality, Events, and Explanation in Historical Sociology', *Sociological Methods and Research*, 20 (4), pp. 403-27.

Griffin, L. et al. (1997), 'Comparative-Historical Analysis and Scientific Inference: Disfranchisement in the U.S. South as a Test Case', *Historical Methods*, 30 (1), pp. 13-27.

Guarnizo, L.E. (1997), 'The Emergence of a Transnational Social Formation and the Mirage of Return Migration among Dominican Transmigrants', *Identities*, 4 (2), pp. 281-322.

Guarnizo, L.E. (1998), 'The Rose of Transnational Social Formations: Mexican and Dominican State Responses to Transnational Migration', *Political Power and Social Theory*, 12 (1), pp. 45-94.

Guarnizo, L.E. and Smith, M. (eds.) (1998), *Transnationalism from below*, Transaction Publishers, New Brunswick, NJ.

Guarnizo, L.E. (2001), 'On the Political Participation of Transnational Migrants: Old Practices and New Trends', in Gerstle and Mollenkopf (eds.), *E Pluribus Unum?*, pp. 213-67.

Guglielmo, J. and Salerno, S. (eds.) (2003), *Are Italians White? How Race is Made in America*, Routledge, New York.

Gutterl, M.P. (2001), *The Color of Race in America, 1900-1940*, Harvard UP, Cambridge, MA.

Guttierez, D. (1997), 'Transnationalism and Ethnic Politics in the United States: Reflections on Recent History'. Paper presented at a conference on Immigrants, Civic Culture, and Modes of Political Incorporation, Social Science Research Council, Santa Fe, 2-4 May.

Gutmann, A. (1993), 'The Challenge of Multiculturalism in Political Ethics', *Philosophy and Public Affairs*, 22 (3), pp. 171-206.

Hall, J.R. (1999), *Cultures of Inquiry. From Epistemology to Discourse in Sociohistorical Research*, Cambridge UP, New York.

Hirschman, Ch., Kasinitz, Ph., and DeWind, J. (eds.) (1999), *The Handbook of Transnational Migration: The American Experience*, Russell Sage Foundation, New York.

Hollinger, D. (1995), *Postethnic America: Beyond Multiculturalism*, Basic Books, New York.

Holston, J. and Appadurai, A. (1996), 'Cities and Citizenship', *Public Culture*, 8 (2), pp. 187-204.

Hyman, J. (1991), *Life and Labor on the Border: Working People of Northeastern Sonora, Mexico, 1886-1986*, University of Arizona Press, Tucson.

Hyman, J. (1999), *States and Illegal Practices*, Berg, New York.

Ignatiev, N. (1995), *How the Irish Became White*, Routledge, New York.

International Labor and Working Class History (2001). Special Issue on the Meanings and Assignments of 'Whiteness' in the American Working-Class History, 61 (4).

Isaac, L. and Griffin, L. (1989), 'Ahistoricism of Time-Series Analyses of Historical Process: Critique, Reformulation, and Illustrations from U.S. Labor History', *American Sociological Review*, 54 (4), pp. 873-90.

Isaac, L. (1997), 'Transforming Localities: Reflections on Time, Causality, and Narrative in Contemporary Historical Sociology', *Historical Methods*. Special Issue on Research in Historical Sociology, 30 (1), pp. 4-13.

Isaac, L. and Leicht, K. (1997), 'Regimes of Power and the Power of Analytic Regimes: Explaining U.S. Military Procurement Keynesianism as Historical Process', *Historical Methods,* 30 (1), pp. 28-45.

Jacobson, D. (1996), *Rights Across Borders: Immigration and the Decline of Citizenship,* The Johns Hopkins UP, Baltimore, MD.

Jacobson, M.F. (1998), *Whiteness of a Different Color. European Immigrants and the Alchemy of Race,* Harvard UP, Cambridge, MA.

Jensen, G. (1997), 'Time and Social History: Problems of Atemporality in Historical Analyses with Illustrations from Research on Early Modern Witch Hunts', *Historical Methods,* 30, pp. 46-57.

Jones, D. (1992), 'Which Migrants? Temporary or Permanent?', *Annals of the New York Academy of Sciences,* 645, July, pp. 217-230.

Joppke, Ch. (ed.) (1998), *Challenge to the Nation-State. Immigration in Western Europe and the United States,* Oxford UP, Oxford.

Joppke, Ch. and Morawska, E. (eds.) (2003), *Toward Assimilation and Citizenship. Immigrants in Liberal Nation-States,* Palgrave Macmillan, Houndmills, Basingstoke.

Journal of American Ethnic History (1999), Special Issue on The Classical and Contemporary Mass Migration Periods: Similarities and Differences, 18 (3).

Journal of American Ethnic History (2002), Interdisciplinary discussion about Nancy Foner's book, *From Ellis Island To JFK* (2000), 21 (4).

Joynt, C. and Rescher, N. (1961), 'The Problem of Uniqueness in History', *History and Theory,* 1 (1), pp. 150-62.

Kasinitz, Ph. (1992), *Caribbean New York: Black Immigrants and the Politics of Race,* Cornell University Press, Ithaca, NY.

Kasinitz, Ph. and Vickerman, M. (2001), 'Ethnic Niches and Racial Traps: Jamaicans in the New York Regional Economy', in Cordero-Guzman, Smith, and Grosfoguel (eds.), *Migration, Transnationalization, and Race,* pp. 191-211.

Kazal, R. (1995), 'Revisiting Assimilation: The Rise, Fall, and Reappraisal of a Concept in American Ethnic History', *American Historical Review,* 100, pp. 437-72.

Kearney, M. (1995), 'The Local and the Global: The Anthropology of Globalization and Transnationalism', *Annual Review of Anthropology,* 24 (2), pp. 547-65.

Kibria, N. (1998), 'The Contested Meanings of "Asian American": Racial Dilemmas in the Contemporary US', *Ethnic and Racial Studies,* 21 (5), pp. 938-58.

Kiser, E. and Hechter, M. (1991), 'The Role of General Theory in Comparative Historical Sociology', *American Journal of Sociology,* 97, pp. 1-30.

Kivisto, P. (2001), 'Theorizing Transnational Immigration: A Critical Review of Current Efforts', *Ethnic and Racial Studies,* 24 (4), pp. 549-77.

Kivisto, P. (2002), *Multiculturalism in a Global Society,* Blackwell Publishing, Malden, MA.

Kivisto, P. (2003), 'Social Space, Transnational Immigrant Communities, and the Politics of Incorporation', *Ethnicities,* 3 (1), pp. 5-28.

Kymlicka, W. (1995), *Multicultural Citizenship,* Clarendon Press, Oxford.

Levitt, P. (1997), 'Transnational Community Development: The Case of Boston and the Dominican Republic', *Nonprofit and Voluntary Sector Quarterly,* 26 (3), pp. 509-26.

Levitt, P. (2001), *The Transnational Villagers,* California UP, Berkeley, CA

Levitt, P. and Waters, M. (eds.) (2002), *The Changing Face of Home. The Transnational Lives of Second Generation,* Russell Sage Foundation, New York.

Levitt, P. (2003), 'Keeping Feet in Both Worlds: Transnational Practices and Immigrant Incorporation in the United States', in Joppke and Morawska (eds.), *Toward Assimilation and Citizenship,* pp. 177-94.

Lie, J. (1995), 'From International Migration to Transnational Diaspora', *Contemporary Sociology,* 24, pp. 303-6.

Light, I., Char-Chwi, H. and Kann, K. (1994), 'Black/Korean Conflict in Los Angeles', in S. Dunn (ed.), *Managing Divided Cities,* Ryburn Publishing, London, pp. 72-88.

Lowe, L. (1996), *Immigrant Acts: On Asian American Cultural Politics,* Duke UP, Durham, NC.

Mahler, S. (1998), 'Theoretical and Empirical Contributions Toward a Research Agenda on Transnationalism', in Guarnizo and Smith (eds.), *Transnationalism from below,* pp. 64-102.

Mahoney, J. and Rueschmeyer, D. (eds.) (2003), *Comparative Historical Analysis in the Social Sciences,* Harvard UP, Cambridge, MA.

Mann, M. (1993), 'Nation-States in Europe and Other Continents: Diversifying, Developing, Not Dying', *Daedalus,* 122 (3), pp. 115-40.

Massey, D. et al. (1998), *Worlds in Motion. Understanding International Migration at the End of the Millenium,* Clarendon Press, Oxford.

McDonald, T. (ed.) (1996), *The Historic Turn in the Human Sciences,* University of Michigan Press, Ann Arbor, MI.

McGreevey, J. (1996), *Parish Boundaries: The Catholic Encounter with Race in the Twentieth-Century Urban North,* University of Chicago Press, Chicago.

Merton, R. (1968), 'Middle-Range Social Theories', in Idem, *Social Theory and Social Structure: Toward the Codification of Theory and Research,* The Free Press, New York, pp. 60-91.

Merton, R. (1972), 'Insiders and Outsiders: A Chapter in the Sociology of Knowledge', *American Journal of Sociology,* 78 (1), pp. 8-47.

Min, P.G. (1999), 'A Comparison of Post-1965 and Turn-of-the-Century Immigrants in Intergenerational Mobility and Cultural Transmission', *Journal of American Ethnic History,* 18 (3), pp. 65-94.

Min, P.G. (ed.) (2002), *Mass Migration to the United States. Classical and Contemporary Periods,* Altamira Press, Walnut Creek, CA.

Model, S. (2003), 'Immigrants in the Netherlands: A Review Essay', *Contemporary Sociology,* 32 (3), pp. 277-82.

Morawska, E. (1990), 'The Sociology and Historiography of Immigration', in V. Yans-McLaughlin (ed.), *Immigration Reconsidered: History, Sociology, and Politics,* Oxford UP, New York, pp. 187-238.

Morawska, E. (1994), 'In Defense of the Assimilation Model', *Journal of American Ethnic History,* Winter, pp. 76-87.

Morawska, E. (2001a), 'The New-Old Transmigrants, Their Transnational Lives, and Ethnicization: A Comparison of the 19th/20th and 20th/21st C. Situations', in Gerstle and Mollenkopf (eds.), *E Pluribus Unum,* pp.175-212.

Morawska, E. (2001b), 'Immigrant-Black Dissensions in American Cities: An Argument for Multiple Explanations', in D. Massey and E. Anderson (eds.), *Problem of the Century: Racial Stratification in the United States,* Russell Sage Foundation, New York, pp. 47-96.

Morawska, E. (2001c), 'Becoming Ethnic, Becoming American: Different Patterns and Configurations of the Assimilation of American Jews, 1890-1940', in D. Moore and I. Troen (eds.), *Divergent Centers: Shaping Jewish Cultures in Israel and America,* Yale UP, New Haven, CT, pp. 277-303.

Morawska, E. (2003), 'Immigrant Transnationalism and Assimilation: A Variety of Combinations and a Theoretical Model They Suggest', in Joppke and Morawska (eds.), *Toward Assimilation and Citizenship,* pp. 122-76.

Neckerman, K., Carter, P., and Lee, J. (1999), 'Segmented Assimilation and Minority Cultures of Mobility', *Ethnic and Racial Studies,* 22 (6), pp. 945-65.

Nee, V. and Sanders, J. (2001), 'Understanding the Diversity of Immigrant Incorporation: A Forms-of-Capital Model', *Ethnic and Racial Studies,* 24 (3), pp. 386-411.

Perlmann, J. and Waldinger, R. (1997), 'Second Generation Decline?: Children of Immigrants, Past and Present: A Reconsideration', *International Migration Review,* 31 (4), pp. 893-923.

Perlmann, J. (1998), 'The Place of Cultural Explanation and Historical Specificity in Discussions of Modes of Incorporation and Segmented Assimilation', Levy Working Paper No. 240, July.

Portes, A. and Zhou, M. (1993), 'The New Second Generation: Segmented Assimilation and Its Variants', *Annals of the American Academy of Political and Social Sciences,* 530, pp. 74-96.

Portes, A. (1996), 'Transnational Communities: Their Emergence and Significance in the Contemporary World-System', in R. Korzeniewicz and W. Smith (eds.), *Latin America in the World Economy,* Greenwood Press, Westport, CT, pp. 151-68.

Portes, A. (1997), 'Immigration Theory for a New Century: Some Problems and Opportunities', *International Migration Review,* 31 (4), pp. 799-825.

Portes, A. (1999), 'Conclusion: Toward a New World – The Origins and Effects of Transnational Action', *Ethnic and Racial Studies,* 22 (2), pp. 463-77.

Portes, A., Guarnizo, L. and Landolt, P. (1999), 'The Study of Transnationalism: Pitfalls and Promise of an Emergent Research Field', *Ethnic and Racial Studies,* 22 (2), pp. 217-37.

Portes, A. and Rumbaut, R. (2001), *Legacies. The Story of the Immigrant Second Generation,* Russell Sage Foundation, New York.

Portes, A. and Hao, L. (2002), 'The Price of Uniformity: Language, Family, and Personality Adjustment in the Immigrant Second Generation', *Ethnic and Racial Studies,* 25 (6), pp. 889-912.

Pries, L. (ed.) (2001), *New Transnational Social Spaces,* Routledge, London.

Quadagno, J. and Knapp, St. (1992), 'Have Historical Sociologists Forsaken Theory? Thoughts on the History/Theory Relationship', *Sociological Methods and Research,* 20, pp. 481-507.

Ragin, Ch. (1987), *The Comparative Method. Moving Beyond Qualitative and Quantitative Strategies,* University of California Press, Berkeley, CA.

Ragin, Ch. (2000), *Fuzzy-Set Social Science,* University of Chicago Press, Chicago.

Rasmussen, B.B. et al. (eds.) (2001), *The Making and Unmaking of Whiteness,* Duke UP, Durham, NC.

Roediger, D. (1991), *The Wages of Whiteness: Race and the Making of the American Working Class,* Verso, New York.

Roy, W. (1992), 'Time, Place, and People in History and Sociology: Boundary Definitions and the Logic of Inquiry', *Social Science History,* 11 (1), pp. 53-62.

Rumbaut, R. (1997), 'Assimilation and Its Discontents: Between Rhetoric and Reality', Russell Sage Foundation, New York, Working Paper No. 117.

Rumbaut, R. et al. (1999), 'Immigration and Immigration Research in the United States', *The American Behavioral Scientists,* 42 (9), pp. 1285-302.

Rumbaut, R. (2000), 'Immigration Research in the United States: Social Origins and Future Orientations', in Foner, Rumbaut and Gold (eds.), *Immigration Research for a New Century*, pp. 23-43.

Sahlins, M. (1991), 'The Return of the Event, Again: With Reflections on the Beginnings of the Great Fijian War of 1843 to 1855 Between the Kingdoms of Bau and Rewa', in A.

Biersack (ed.), *Clio in Oceania: Toward a Historical Anthropology,* Smithsonian Institution Press, Washington, DC, pp. 37-100.

Salins, P. (1997), *Assimilation American Style,* Basic Books, New York.

Sanchez, G. (1997), 'Face the Nation: Race, Immigration, and the Rise of Nativism in Late Twentieth Century America', *International Migration Review,* 31 (4), pp. 1009-30.

Sanchez, G. (1999), 'Race and Immigration History', *The American Behavioral Scientist,* 42 (9), pp. 1271-6.

Schluchter, W. (1989), *Rationalism, Religion, and Dominance: A Weberian Perspective,* University of California Press, Berkeley.

Schmitter Heisler, B. (2000), 'The Sociology of Immigration', in Brettell and Hollifield (eds.), *Migration Theory,* pp. 77-96.

Schutz, A. (1970), *On Phenomenology and Social Relations,* University of Chicago Press, Chicago.

Sewell, W. (1992), 'Narratives and Social Identities', *Social Science History,* 16 (3), pp. 479-88.

Sewell, W. (1996), 'Three Temporalities: Toward an Eventful Sociology', in McDonald (ed.), *The Historic Turn in the Human Sciences,* pp. 245-80.

Sewell, W. (1999), 'The Concept(s) of Culture', in V. Bonnell and L. Hunt (eds.), *Beyond the Cultural Turn,* University of California Press, Berkeley, CA, pp. 35-61.

Sheridan, C. (2002), 'Contested Citizenship: National Identity and the Mexican Immigration debates of the 1920s', *Journal of American Ethnic History,* 21 (3), pp. 3-35.

Skocpol, Th. and Somers, M. (1980), 'The Uses of Comparative History in Macro-Social Inquiry', *Comparative Studies in Society and History,* 22, pp. 174-97.

Skocpol, Th. (1984), 'Emerging Agendas and Recurrent Strategies in Historical Sociology', in Th. Skocpol (ed.), *Vision and Method in Historical Sociology,* Cambridge UP, New York, pp. 356-86.

Skocpol, Th. (1987), 'Social History and Historical Sociology: Contrasts and Complementarities', *Social Science History,* 11 (1), pp. 17-30.

Smith, D. (1994), *The Rise of Historical Sociology,* Temple UP, Philadelphia.

Smith, R. (1997), 'Transnational Migration, Assimilation, and Political Economy', in M. Crahan and A. Vourvoulias-Bush (eds.), *The City and the World: New York City in Global Context,* Council on Foreign Relations, New York, pp. 110-32.

Smith, R. (1998), 'Transnational Localities: Community, Technology, and the Political Membership within the Context of Mexico and U.S. Migration', in Guarnizo and Smith (eds.), *Transnationalism from below,* pp.196-240.

Smith, R. (2002), 'Assimilation, Life Course, and Generation as Factors Shaping Second-Generation Transnational Life', in Levitt and Waters (eds.), *The Changing Face of Home,* pp. 145-67.

Smith, R. (2003), *Mexican New York: Transnational Lives of New Immigrants,* University of California Press, Berkeley.

Social Science History (1992), Special Issue on Narrative Analysis in Social Science, Fall-Winter.

Sollors, W. (ed.) (1989), *The Invention of Ethnicity,* Oxford UP, New York.

Somers, M. (1999), 'The Privatization of Citizenship: How to Unthink a Knowledge Culture', in Bonnell and Hunt (eds.), *Beyond the Cultural Turn,* pp. 121-64.

Soysal, Y.N. (1994), *Limits of Citizenship. Migrants and Postnational Membership in Europe,* University of Chicago Press, Chicago.

Taylor, Ch. (1992), *Multiculturalism and 'The Politics of Recognition',* Princeton UP, Princeton.

Vickerman, M. (1999), *Crosscurrents: West Indian Immigrants and Race,* Oxford UP, New York.

Vickerman, M. (2001), 'Tweaking a Monolith: The West Indian Immigrant Encounter with "Blackness"', in Foner (ed.), *Islands in the City,* pp. 237-56.

Waldinger, R. and Fitzgerald, D. (2002), 'Transnationalism in Question'. Unpublished ms.

Waldinger, R. (2003), 'The Sociology of Immigration: Second Thoughts and Reconsiderations', in J. Reitz (ed.), Host Societies and the Reception of Immigrants, Center for Comparative Immigration Research, San Diego, pp. 21-44.

Waldinger, R. and Lichter, M. (2003), *How the Other Half Works. Immigration and the Social Organization of Labor,* University of California Press, Berkeley.

Waters, M. (1999a), 'Sociology and the Study of Immigration', *The American Behavioral Scientist,* 9 (42), pp. 1264-68.

Waters, M. (1999b), *Black Identities. West Indian Dreams and American Realities,* Russell Sage Foundation, New York.

Zhou, Min (1997), 'Segmented Assimilation: Issue, Controversies, and Recent Research on the New Second Generation', *International Migration Review,* 31 (4), pp. 975-1008.

Znaniecki, F. (1934), *The Method of Sociology,* University of Chicago Press, Chicago.

PART IV
INTERDEPENDENCE
OF MIGRATION RESEARCH
AND ITS
SOCIOPOLITICAL CONTEXTS

Chapter 10

National Frames in Migration Research: The Tacit Political Agenda

Sandra Lavenex

[Sociologists, SL] should not satisfy themselves of simple denunciation and should not refrain from historisizing and relativating their own critique while remaining prisoners, without even noticing, of the norms of modern society (Schnapper, 1998, p. 21).[1]

Introduction

A commonly held view among migration scholars and the wider public is that Germany and France represent two fundamentally opposed models of 'integration' structuring the relation between the state and foreign nationals: an ethno-national, pre-political model based on *ius sanguinis* in Germany, and a universalist, republican model based on *ius soli* in France (Brubaker, 1992). Looking at the frames of reference guiding migration research in the two countries since the 1980s, this chapter introduces the opposed view. It is shown that, ironically, ethno-cultural concerns relating to 'assimilation' and 'integration' in the republican nation state are much stronger in the French literature, while German scholars have largely circumvented culture-based arguments and have framed the 'integration' question in much more universalist terms as a question of socio-economic insertion in the social welfare state.

Reconstructing the historical and political context of migration research in the two countries, this chapter argues that migration research often pursues a tacit political agenda. Failing to make abstraction from implicit normative positions, migration studies have often become part of the migration discourses in which they are embedded. In an attempt to specify one of the ways in which migration scholars remain 'prisoners of the norms of modern society' (op. cit.), this chapter argues that a great deal of migration research is caught in specific national normative and discursive traditions, thus replicating the dominant images of the migration 'problem' carried in domestic public and political debates.

Apart from posing a challenge to the development of an abstract, theoretical perspective on problems related to the presence of foreigners, the critical value of these implicit frames of reference arises in a transnational perspective in the attempt to compare migration problems in different nation states. The underlying assumption is that the implicit, unreflected presence of specific national understandings in migration research may lead to a congruence of scientific and political discourses which impede the observation of similarities and differences across cases and countries. On the one hand, implicit national frames of reference may influence the kind of questions that are asked and the kind of social phenomena that are analyzed. On the other hand, such implicit understandings usually also carry normative assumptions about what is good and what is bad, thus yielding divergent conclusions as to the chances and challenges facing modern, differentiated and differential societies. The role of such particular domestic frames in migration research is exemplified for two European countries with a large presence of immigrants, Germany and France.

After a brief reflection on the discursive embeddedness of migration research, section two argues that immigration in Germany and France and political responses to it have moved towards increasing convergence over the last decades. Notwithstanding this progressive approximation of the object of inquiry, it will be shown that its academic reception in social science research differs significantly. Based on a review of a representative sample of the academic literature produced in the two countries, it is argued that migration research is embedded in nationally specific discursive traditions. Reflective of the respective public discourses in the two countries, these national frames in migration research not only limit the scope for comparative insights but, by transporting specific normative understandings, may also carry a tacit political agenda.

'Text and Context' or the Discursive Embeddedness of Migration Research

The reflection on the normative embeddedness of research raises the question of the objectivity of knowledge and the capacity of social scientists to textualize reality. It links up with Potter's belief that 'reality enters into human practices by way of the categories and descriptions that are part of those practices....It is *constituted* in one way or another as people talk it, write it and argue it' (Potter, 1996, p. 98; emphasis original). This relationship between the researcher's text and his or her social context (Shapiro, 1982) is particularly tangible in the field of migration research, which is directly linked to understandings about the ties between the individuals, the society and the state, and thus with questions of national, cultural or ethnic identity. The strong normative values inherent in questions of social and political inclusion and exclusion and their strong politicization in Western publics just add to this sensitivity of the field.

Whereas in the discipline of anthropology awareness of ethnocentrism developed relatively early – referring to the observation of foreign behavior or realities through one's own cultural lenses and values – no comparable epistemological reflection has occurred in sociological or political science migration research (Schnapper, 1998)[2] nor in the study of ethnic relations (Lloyd, 1995). How do our own cultural or national understandings about the social fabric of state-society relations influence the way in which we approach the question of immigration? And how do these national lenses influence our sensitivity towards particular phenomena or aspects of the same phenomena, while leading us to neglect others? These questions shall be addressed by discussing a number of recent studies on immigration and the nation state in Germany and France. Without claiming to be comprehensive or significantly representative, this exercise seeks to present an indicative interpretation of such tacit, because implicit and taken for granted national frames. These frames can be taken as elements of a broader kind of underlying consensus, or, as Adrian Favell has put it, '"public philosophy" – founded on a set of consensual ideas and linguistic terms held across party political lines' and across national academics (Favell, 1998, p. 2). Indeed, this chapter confirms Favell's assertion that 'the vast majority of secondary works in fact simply confirms and reproduces the nationally bounded perspectives on the policy questions at stake' (ibid., p. 6). The unveiling of these implicit assumptions and cognitive frames in migration research highlights some of the fundamental semantics about the unity and order of the nation and thereby helps to identify the impact of public myths and traditions not only in public and political, but also academic discourses.[3]

The relevance of such an exercise is not only the potential to make us more sensitive towards specific national constellations and histories, but also to point at the challenges posed for comparative research. Reflexivity challenges the positivist claim of those comparativists who claim that 'social science research, including comparative inquiry, should and can lead to general statements about social phenomena' (Przeworski and Teune, 1970, p. 4) because this assumption would in fact imply that 'human or social behaviour can be explained in terms of general laws established by observations' (ibid.). National frames indicate that the key variables identified may be difficult to compare, due to different meanings attached to them in different social or historical contexts, such as 'race', 'citizenship', 'welfare', or 'membership'. In this line, it has been argued that the concept of 'race' in the British and US literature cannot be directly applied to the experience of many minority groups in other European countries, since it has largely emerged from the colonial experience and the way in which the discrimination and anti-discrimination movements have evolved in the host societies (Lloyd, 1995; Miles, 1994).

The interest in taken-for-granted templates in social science research resonates with the notion of cognitive frames in sociological discourse analysis (Goffman, 1974; Gamson, 1988). Accordingly, frames refer to social interpretation schemes which organize the experience of a situation. The concept offers a tool for a systematic analysis of knowledge. A frame is 'a central organizing idea or story line that provides meaning to an unfolding strip of events' (Gamson and Modigliani, 1987, p. 143) which, being an unintentional phenomenon, gains the uncontested status of social fact (Eder, 1992, p. 7f.). The knowledge included in a frame comprises factual devices, referring to the presentation of empirical, observable facts, and normative devices, referring to the sphere of moral responsibilities and providing the values against which reality is assessed.[4] Thus, cognitive frames not only organize the interpretation of an underlying problem but also carry guideposts for action which may, in certain cases, be seen as a tacit political agenda. In the following, this chapter identifies national frames structuring the perception of the migration 'problem' using important publications by French and German migration scholars as part of a broader immigration discourse. This shall complement the focus of this volume on the chances and challenges of interdisciplinarity by high-lighting the role of reflexivity and, more precisely, the impact of national dis-courses about the state, the citizen and forms of belonging on migration research.

A Country of Immigration and a 'Non-Immigration' Country Moving towards Convergence

In contrast to France, which has received important flows of immigrants since the second half of the nineteenth century, Germany did not, until recently, consider itself an immigration country.[5] Despite these contrary approaches, the overall structure of immigration has increasingly moved towards convergence, in particular after the stop to the active recruitment of labor migration in 1973 and 1974. This section sketches very briefly the main lines of these convergent developments.

In the post-World War II period, both countries experienced large waves of immigration. In Germany, this influx consisted in the first place of refugees or displaced persons of German origin coming from the GDR or further East. An estimate number of 12 million ethnic Germans were successfully integrated in the new Federal Republic. A second phase started in the mid-1950s with the recovering of the German economy. Realizing that the increasing demand for labor could not be sufficiently supplied by the domestic labor force, the West German government started to conclude bilateral guest worker contracts with Italy and, later on, with Greece, Spain, Turkey, Morocco, Tunisia, Portugal, and Yugoslavia. This phase officially ended with the immigration stop in 1973; however, it soon turned out that many of the former guest workers decided to settle and to be joined by their families. The third phase of immigration began in the late 1970s with the increasing arrival of immigrants and refugees from so-called Third World countries, paralleled by the rising numbers of ethnic Germans coming from Central and Eastern Europe (Bade, 1992). After the opening up of the Eastern Bloc in 1989, one can speak of a fourth phase of immigration in Germany, due principally to a marked acceleration in the immigration flows from the countries of Central and Eastern Europe.

In France, the large arrivals of foreign workers in the 1950s linked up with a long tradition of immigration mainly from European countries. The new wave of non-European immigrants arriving from the former French colonies of North Africa starting in the mid-1960s also looked back on earlier 'internal' movements from Algeria in particular. The colonial history of France granted these persons special access to citizenship provisions, so that many were turned into French citizens (Noiriel, 1988). While one can thus say that in contrast to Germany, France had a longer tradition in the reception of non-European immigrants, the general patterns of immigration followed comparable developments.

Before the mid-1970s, immigration occurred predominantly through actively promoted or at least tolerated recruitment policies. After the general ban on labor migration, the major source of immigration became family reunification, thus expressing the permanent nature of these movements. A second major source of migration were the special links with particular groups or former colonies such as the 'German' *Aussiedler* in Central and Eastern Europe or Algerian citizens. The third major group of immigrants, which became the dominant source during the 1980s, were asylum-seekers in Germany and, especially in France, also undocumented immigrants. According to Angenendt (1992, pp. 308ff.) the immigrant population in Germany and France today is largely comparable concerning ethnic structure, demographic development, socio-geographical distribution and its situation on the labor market. Another point that the two countries have in common is the dominance of one country or region of origin, namely Turkey in Germany, and the Maghreb in France (Manfrass, 1991).[6]

This approximation in the phenomenon of immigration is also salient at the level of policy developments. Although taking partly different paths in the 1980s, immigration policies in France and Germany have moved towards increasing convergence in the last decade.

As mentioned in the introduction, the two countries followed historically very different approaches towards immigration. This is reflected in the general constitutional principles structuring the modes of inclusion and exclusion, where the traditional German particularistic, ethno-cultural conceptions of citizenship and nationhood contrast with the declared expansive, civic and universalistic conception of nationhood in the French constitution (Brubaker, 1992).[7] These divergent conceptions found their expression in the implementation of the principle of *ius sanguinis* in Germany with the nationality act of 1913, attributing citizenship by descent, and a mixture of *ius sanguinis* with the principle of *ius soli* in France which goes back to the nationality law of 1889, allowing for the acquisition of citizenship by birth on the state territory. The ethno-cultural orientation of the German citizenship provisions is replicated in the expansive definition of the German people in the Basic Law (Article 116), which recognizes as Germans also former citizens from the GDR and *Vertriebene*, that is persons who were 'driven out' of Eastern Europe and the Soviet Union because of their German descent in the aftermath of World War II. In contrast, second-generation and even third-generation immigrants of non-German descent could, until January 2000, acquire German citizenship only through naturalization which was basically a discretionary act of the state. After first revisions in 1990 and 1993, this exclusionary stance was significantly relaxed by the new ruling coalition of social democrats and the Greens with a bill introducing the notion of *ius soli* for children born in Germany of foreign parents and requesting them to choose between their old and the German citizenship at the age of 23.[8] This reform was surrounded by a short but highly polemical debate spurred by the conservative opposition, which tried to fight it through a signature campaign among the German population. The arguments presented against the reform took up many elements known from the long-lasting debates on citizenship and nationhood which have dominated the French immigration discourse since the 1980s (see below). In a nutshell, these concerns centered on the cultural requirements of 'integration', in particular language, but also the identification with the German nation, and the civic requirements of loyalty to the state, reflected in the respect for the pillars of the constitution and the 'liberal democratic order' (*freiheitliche demokratische Grundordnung*) of the Federal Republic.

This development towards a more expansive definition of citizenship in Germany was mirrored by a move towards more exclusive citizenship in France, again relaxed by the Jospin government after coming to power in 1998. Announced already by the Chirac government in 1986, a bill which made the attribution of French citizenship based on birth contingent on a formal declaration of intent by the person concerned was passed by Charles Pasqua during his second term in office in 1993. This regulation was the preliminary end of a long and very intensive debate on nationality, citizenship and the state which started in the early 1980s and still dominates the French discourse on immigration – and, as we will see, also academic writings. This debate arose with the endeavors of the first Mitterrand government (1980-1983) to soften centralist structures in the French polity and in particular the affirmation of the '*droit à la différence*' (the right to be different). These endeavors where soon instrumentalized by Jean-Marie Le Pen's emerging National Front which, coining the slogan of the '*non-assimilables*', redefined immigration into a threat to the unity of the French nation, French society and the republican model of state-society relations. Reacting to these concerns, the conservative government of Jacques Chirac announced a reform of the nationality law which would have made the hitherto automatic application of *ius soli* contingent on an '*acte de volonté*', that is an explicit declaration of the will to be French on part of the person concerned. Shelved due to heavy public protests, these controversies were followed up in an extraordinary *Commission de la Nationalité* under the lead of Marceau Long and, from then on, dominated not only the partisan debates but also the alternating governments' political agendas and the academic discourse. Aware of the polarizing impact of these debates which went straight to the conception of the state, its citizenry, and French national identity, the Jospin government declared as one of its first priorities the aim to put an end to the polemics and return to the common 'republican' consensus.[9]

In contrast to this late and still only partial approximation of citizenship regulations, the development of 'integration' and immigration control measures in Germany and France reveal a strong degree of convergence since the 1980s. This convergence relies on a compromise between the major political parties in the two countries which consists in the double aim to combat new entries and enhance the 'integration' of those foreigners who are already present in the country (Manfrass, 1991; Weil, 1995b). This approximation started with the general ban on labor migration in 1973 and 1974 and the attempts starting in the mid-1970s to foster the return of immigrants in France and guest-workers in Germany. The shift regarding the major source of immigration from labor recruitment to family reunification in the second half of the 1970s and the transformation of the former guest-workers into permanent residents induced a wave of 'integration' policies which mainly consisted in the expansion of social rights to immigrant residents (Soysal, 1994). This included the right to equal representation of foreign workers in firms and unions, the freedom of association, and a variety of equal treatment provisions relating to health, schooling and professional training.

Both countries restricted their provisions regarding family reunification, tightened their visa policies, stepped up their entry conditions, strengthened expulsion procedures, introduced carrier sanctions and tightened their asylum laws. Since the mid-1980s, these immigration control policies have increasingly been coordinated at the European level and through the Schengen-framework and are now part of the EU acquis in immigration and asylum matters. Still, this convergence merely concerns the question of admission to the territory. The general approach towards economic immigration, access to the domestic labor markets, policies towards undocumented immigrants, who, in France, have developed into a social movement ('les sans-papiers') and have repeatedly been regularized, or towards regulations regarding family reunification and substantive refugee law have not been approximated and continue to follow specific national criteria.

National Frames in Migration Research

Against the background of a broad convergence of problem structures and public policies in Germany and France, this final section extends the comparative perspective to the field of migration research and reflects on the scholarly reception of the French and German experience with the presence of foreigners. Concentrating on more recent publications in the social sciences, this section explores whether these studies reflect particular national understandings of the immigration 'problem' and of the challenge of integrating immigrants into the host society. The link between these studies and specific national understandings about state-society relations is then recapitulated in the conclusion to this chapter which seeks to expound on the reflexive potential of such comparative perspectives. Of course, the differences highlighted in this chapter are only tendencies observable in a representative number of works, they shall not be interpreted as general features of the disciplines.

Generally speaking, the question of 'integration' into host societies can be approached in cultural, political or socio-economic terms.[10] In modern liberal democracies, host societies can offer opportunities for participation and inclusion at the cultural level of their morals and customs, religion and religious practices, every day habits, language, symbolic uses or historical consciousness. In terms of *demos*, participation and inclusion can also occur at the level of the political constituency with regard to civil rights and obligations and the legal 'integration' into the democratic political body. Finally, a third approach to 'integration' resides at the socio-economic level and refers to participation in education systems, professional training, the labor market and social policy institutions. Starting from these three different approaches to the question of immigrant 'integration', the following discussion concentrates on the manner in which the conditions for the successful 'integration' of immigrants into the host societies are framed in German and French migration research. Throughout, the underlying question is how far these perspectives reflect particular social contexts in Germany and France.

The hypothesis presented here is that while in Germany, immigration research has mainly handled immigrant policies in terms of socio-economic inclusion in the welfare state, research in France has concentrated much more on ethnic and civic dimensions of immigrant 'integration', centering around the questions of assimilation and nationhood in the republican nation state. Although this contrast describes more an overall tendency than a constant feature of German and French migration research, it is argued that these findings reflect underlying differences in the political discourses structuring the ties between state, nation and people.

Germany: The Frame of the Welfare State

In a recent article on transnationalism and migration, Thomas Faist identifies two potential challenges resulting from the granting of double citizenship in receiving states: firstly, the problem of loyalty towards the state, that is the respect for the law and constitution, and secondly, the potential weakening of the conditions for social policy and redistribution in the welfare state (Faist, 2000, pp. 112). In an earlier comparative study of immigration in Germany and the US, the same author concluded that differences and similarities in the 'integration' of young Turks in Germany and young Mexican Americans in the US were a function of their access to education and the labor market as organized by public policies and immigrant entrepreneurship (Faist, 1995). These findings confirmed the basic assumption according to which 'access to training and placement into jobs is of utmost importance if we want to understand the condition of citizenship in advanced Western welfare states' (Faist, 1995, p. 3).

The work by Thomas Faist is indicative of the dominant approach in German writings on immigrant 'integration' which, focusing on socio-economic factors, concentrate mainly on the welfare state context of immigrant inclusion. Accordingly, the successful 'integration' of non-nationals in Germany is discussed as a function of their participation in the social and economic institutions of the welfare state, including in particular schools, professional training, and the labor market. The ethnic dimension of 'integration', in contrast, is rarely stressed. In these writings, the notion of the welfare state describes the constitutive pillars of the receiving society (Germany) and incorporates the criteria for social inclusion and exclusion.

This socio-economic frame of reference has a long tradition in German migration research and can be traced back to the first macro-sociological attempts to provide a theoretical explanation of migration in the early 1970s. One of the most influential works was the structure-functional approach developed by Hoffmann-Nowotny which focused on the role of 'power' and 'prestige' in the creation of inequality and migration (Hoffmann-Nowotny, 1970). In explaining the macro-sociological causes of migration through the context of concepts of inequality, inclusion and exclusion, this theory laid the ground for an interpretation of the migration 'problem' more in terms of socially constructed opportunities for participation than of culturally based conditions for assimilation. Although the concepts of 'structural' and 'anomic' tensions could be applied to both the explanation of the causes and of the consequences of migration in host societies, including questions of inter-ethnic relations and minority groups (Hoffmann-Nowotny, 1973), these factors were not treated in terms of primordial characteristics but rather as consequences of socio-economic failure (in particular insertion in the labor market).[11] In other words, the structure-functional approach was not premised on the question of migration as a given form of inequality but could also be applied to other societal phenomena of inclusion and exclusion. A similar attempt to develop a general framework for the explanation of societal processes was made by Hartmut Esser on the basis of methodological individualism and rational choice theory (Esser, 1980). Accordingly, migration processes could be explained by the interaction between the rational interest of the migrant and the constraints and opportunities created by overarching social structures. A third early example for the socio-economic orientation of German migration research is the application of the approach developed by the Chicago School of Sociology in the US on immigration in Germany by Friedrich Heckmann in 1981 (Heckmann, 1981).

These early sociological works laid the ground for a particular perspective on the migration 'problem' which continues to shape the frames of reference of much of the contemporary migration research in Germany. In an attempt to define an objective theoretical approach for migration research, Michael Bommes defines migration as 'a form of geographic mobility for the realization of chances of inclusion in functional systems and their organizations' (Bommes, 1999, p. 14). The welfare state optic of this system-theoretical approach becomes clear in the discussion of the relevant functional subsystems structuring the (differential) 'integration' of immigrants, as they were the economy, the law, the political system, health, education, or sciences. A system of 'culture' as such is not mentioned.[12] Starting from the observation that the German nation state emerged hand in hand with the organization of welfare (ibid., p. 133), this theory situates the conditions for inclusion and exclusion in the different functional subsystems of the welfare state. It is the exclusionary impact of these functional systems of social, political, or economic inclusion which constructs migration as a political problem (ibid., p. 136).

Contrary to the common picture of an 'ethnic' citizenship in Germany, German academic writings do not focus on 'blood' or culture as the basis of immigrant 'integration', but on the institutionalization of equality and inequality in the national welfare state (Stichweh, 1998, p. 51). Welfare states define the modes of 'solidarity' among their members as a 'form of protection against the imponderabilities of market-dependence' (Heinelt, 1993, p. 80). The constitutive elements of the welfare state establish the 'generally valid principles of social balance (or of...redistribution)' and draw the boundary lines to 'those "outside"' (ibid.). Immigrant 'integration' then becomes the successful creation and guaranteeing of possibilities for social participation such as profession, income, education, legal status, and housing (Hoffmann-Nowotny and Hondrich, 1982, p. 590). In this line of reasoning, the main normative claim of this realm of research becomes the attribution of secure legal status to the immigrant that is meant to ensure successful 'integration' by providing legal protection, work permit, residence permit and access to social benefits. 'Granting immigrants legal rights puts them on a par with the native population and opens up the equality of opportunity and enables individuals to seek support and selective preferential treatment....Failing to grant such rights would erode established patterns of protecting people against the general risks of living, and thus erode the welfare state' (Heinelt, 1993, p. 82). Thus, unsuccessful 'integration' may result in a threat to the basic integrative pillars of the receiving society and ultimately lead to segregation.

Interestingly, this argument is a mirror of public xenophobic discourses, which these authors criticize as 'welfare-chauvinist rhetoric' (Kurthen and Minkenberg, 1995). In the 'context of new economic uncertainties and deepening class inequalities' (ibid., p. 183), public discourse is seen as handling immigrants as scapegoats 'exploiting' welfare provisions and social security entitlements, such as unemployment benefits, old age pensions, medical and housing subsidies (e.g. Faist, 1994; Fijalkowski, 1993; Heinelt, 1993; Kurthen and Minkenberg, 1995; Räthzel, 1995). Thus, xenophobia itself is defined as a function of the welfare state, or better as a consequence of the failure of welfare state policies under the influence of modernization and globalization.

In this framing of immigrant 'integration' in terms of successful welfare state policies, the anti-image or counter-model of immigrant policies becomes the US-American system of political liberalism. In the absence of active social policies, immigration would first lead to internal exclusion with regard to – otherwise – generally valid social rights and, in a second step, to the worsening of working conditions, levels of incomes earned and other statutory regulations in society at large. Coupled with competition for housing, this would ultimately set in motion social segregation, which may affect every group of the population – and thus undermine its social fabric (Heinelt, 1993, p. 83).

Although these authors agree that ethnicity 'introduces at least one other important cleavage line in contemporary welfare states' (Faist, 1995, p. 17), they underline at the same time that they do not want to enter 'a debate on the relative importance of ethnicity' (ibid.). The reflection about the ethnic challenges of a 'multicultural society' is openly rejected, as it would 'lead us into the arena of ideological struggles and/or to a kaleidoscope of horror pictures and idealized images of the society'[13] (Heinelt and Lohmann, 1992, p. 243, more moderately also Bade, 1996, p. 13). This omission to focus on ethnic characteristics in analyzing and explaining processes of immigrant 'integration' has created criticism inside the scientific community itself. German migration research would conceive of 'integration' as an 'individual process'; 'collective aspects', such as ethnic structures, would not find enough attention and would be set aside (Kontos, 1994, p. 90). However, while the comparative perspective in particular with French migration research does confirm this weaker focus on ethnic characteristics in terms of morals, customs, religion and religious practices, cultural factors are included in most German analyses, but with a focus on their relevance for 'integration' into the welfare state rather than 'integration' into a national community of values and habits. According to Bommes, criteria like descent, origin, race, ethnicity, and friendship are in principle irrelevant to the functional conditions for inclusion in the subsystems of society (Bommes, 1999, p. 45). In this perspective, categories like ethnicity and nation become part of a semantic or self-description, whose function is little more but the aggregation and mobilization of individuals in a society (ibid., pp. 109ff.). This semantic may be used for exclusionary interests; it has, however, no independent impact on the definition of the conditions for inclusion and exclusion in the modern 'welfare' state.

France: The Frame of the Nation State

A nice example of the significant differences between the German and the French scholarly approaches to immigration and 'integration' is a chapter by Catherine Wihtol de Wenden in a book edited by two German scholars with the title 'Migration in national welfare states. Theoretical and comparative analyses' (Bommes and Halfmann, 1998). Asked by the editors to elaborate on the challenges posed by immigration to the French welfare state, Wihtol de Wenden put the emphasis on the changes introduced to French citizenship law and the tensions between an expansive definition of French citizenship and social exclusion based on ethnic difference. The centrality of questions of national identity is most salient in her conclusions. Acknowledging that in France, 'the understanding of citizenship is more linked to loyalties and bonds than with the welfare state', with the perception of Islam as 'a new transnational challenge', Wihtol de Wenden concludes that welfare cannot exist without 'the assumption of French identity' (Wihtol de Wenden 1998, p. 237).

Thus, whereas German writings tend to treat ethnic categories as epiphenomenal to the question of 'integration' in the welfare state, these categories usually constitute the central unit of concern in the French literature on immigration and 'integration'. The overarching frame of immigrant 'integration' is the nation state both in its ethno-national and civic-republican forms. In short, the central theme in contemporary French 'integration' research is the tension between the republican ideal of individual membership on the basis of universal rules and the place of group-specific, ethno-cultural understandings and identities in the social and political 'integration' of immigrants.

The emergence of this central theme coincided with developments in the overarching political and public discourse about immigrants in France. Both discourses reached their first peak in 1984 after the launch of the debates on the *droit à la différence* with the publication of two books by politicians from the central-right. These books, which were soon to set the terms of reference in the immigration discourse, questioned the capacity of immigrants, in particular of Maghreb origin, to integrate in the French culture and society. Close to the argumentation of the *Nouvelle Droite*, Alain Griotteray (1984) argued in favor of restrictive immigration policies. His argumentation was based on an allegedly subversive influence of cultural diversity and in particular the Islamic religion and culture on the French laicistic and unitary state, and he denied the ability of Muslim immigrants to become part of the French society. The book by Bernard Stasi (1984), in contrast, stressed the positive contribution of immigrants to the French economy and advocated the mixture of races (the *'métissage'*) and the tolerance of religious and cultural difference in a universalistic perspective.[14] These studies coincided with general public debates on the value of 'assimilation' versus 'insertion' and the 'right to be different' which were initiated with the coming into force of the Socialist government in 1981. This period marks the point of departure from earlier approaches to the study of immigration in France which, closer to the German tradition, focused from a more empirical perspective on the socio-economic conditions for successful immigrant insertion at the level of workplace, schools and housing (compare e.g. Dupeux, 1980, pp. 23ff.; Granotier 1976).

Launched in the early 1980s, these debates on the dilemma between universal principles and group identities continue to dominate much of the scholarly research in the fields of political science and sociology until today. French migration research has moved away from the original consensus that in France political and social institutions *'à vocation universelle'* have historically transformed immigrants into Frenchmen. At the core of these debates are the notions of citizenship and national identity and the reflection about the validity of the republican ideal of individual-based 'integration' in social reality. In these terms, the latest book by Dominique Schnapper opens with the question how one should interpret the discrepancy between the 'proclaimed norms and values' of modern democratic nations and the concrete forms of social behavior (Schnapper, 1998, p. 13). This discrepancy describes the observation that citizenship as a concept of universal judicial equality no longer effectively controls or organizes society (ibid.). Rather, society tends to be structured by 'interethnic relations' (ibid., p. 15) or, more abstractly, 'historical collectivities', which contradict the ideational foundations of legitimate public order based on 'color-blind', universal human rights incorporated in the notion of citizenship (ibid., pp. 73ff.). Schnapper's critique of universal 'myths' extends to the enlightenment philosophy as such and includes the beliefs of the 'scientific and technical society' which ignore the frontiers of race and peoples (ibid., p. 74).

In this literature as in French public discourse, one can distinguish between two axes of the 'integration' debates: a civic one and an ethno-cultural one. The civic dimension links up with what has been referred to as the more political dimension of immigrant politics and deals with the participation of immigrants in the *demos* as political body. In contrast to the republican ideal of a homogeneous people constituted of equal individuals, French migration research emphasizes the factual political mobilization of immigrants along ethnic lines and their action as direct intermediaries through institutions *à vocation universelle* such as unions and political parties (Noiriel, 1988; Wihtol de Wenden, 1988, 1994a and 1994b). From a more juridical and historical point of view, a similar critique has been formulated by Patrick Weil with regard to the representation of the ideal of *ius soli* in the French immigration discourse. Objecting the often wholesale juxtaposition of the French 'extensive' model of citizenship based on the principle of *ius soli* in particular with the German ethno-cultural notion of *ius sanguinis*, Weil shows the perseverance of particularist elements of citizenship by descent in the history and present of immigration in France (Weil, 1995a, 1996).

In the culturalist critique of the republican ideal, the question of immigrant 'integration' is presented as one of identity politics. There seems to be a bottom line in much of French migration research that 'the debate on immigration reveals another, perhaps more fundamental problem – the question of national identity' (Schnapper, 1994, p. 129). This may be seen as a direct reflection of the terms of public and political discourse in France, in which the question of immigration has been gradually transformed from an originally economic issue into a threat to national identity and cohesion (Silverman, 1992). The basic divide in this line of argument is between the assimilationist ideal of the republican model – according to which the immigrant is integrated on the basis of individual, universal characteristics which are beyond ethnic or group characteristics such as religion, race, customs – on the one hand and the more liberal ideas of a 'right to be different', of openness and tolerance towards 'other' modes of behavior on the other. For Patrick Weil, this dilemma is linked to the republican concept of citizenship based on the free will of the individual. Given the openness or universalism of French citizenship, the grant of citizenship provides no answer to the question 'who am I' (Weil, 1995b, p. 296); to be a French citizen says nothing about the personal or social identity of the person (see also Costa-Lascoux, 1989, pp. 118ff.). These arguments are closely linked to the reasoning of the Marceau Long Commission of the late 1980s which, recommending that citizenship be revalued through a voluntarist conception, asked for a strengthening of the civic and cultural aspects of French nationhood (Long, 1988).

Thus, granting political citizenship is not sufficient for successful 'integration' – rather, the republican separation of public and private spheres should be coupled with the implementation of local (ethnic) identities (Weil, 1991, p. 98). According to Sami Nair, the ideals of universalism and equality in communal life would have to give way to a 'new concept' which is centered on the individual subject and 'prioritises liberty over equality and opens up the public space to the clash of cultural particularism' (Nair, 1992, pp. 44f.). Indeed, most French migration scholars agree that the model of 'color blind' assimilation has never been a reality in France and criticize an 'integration' policy based on formal, individual and universal factors such as education, housing, and social protection. This approach would threaten to lose the 'real, political meaning' of citizenship and 'only create[s] a "formal" rather than a "real" level of integration' (Schnapper, 1994, pp. 134f.). In spite of its theoretically inclusionary aspect, the assimilationist argument would espouse a hostility to all 'differences' which are seen as being co-substantial to the reality of immigration (Balibar, 1991 and Targuieff, 1987).

Notwithstanding this critique of the assimilationist rhetoric, however, these same authors warn of the use of 'minority policies', which aim at promoting the social position of particular ethnic groups, as this 'would break with a long tradition of national integration in France and weaken (and perhaps even dissolve) the social fabric' (Schnapper, 1994, p. 134; see also Costa-Lascoux, 1989, p. 144). Similarly, while arguing in favor of ethnic elements at the level of local identities, Patrick Weil immediately proposes that such solutions should not occur through universal institutions such as schools where e.g. 'native classes for foreigners during which pupils follow religious instructions' would 'reinforce ghetto mechanisms' (Weil, 1991, p. 98). The anti-model of immigrant 'integration' criticized in these writings is the Anglo-American, pluralist model of multiculturalism and minority rights, which, by promoting a cultural 'melting pot', is seen to cause societal segregation and to dissolve the sense of national identity (Désir, 1991; Targuieff, 1991a).[15]

Although from a totally different perspective, these concerns about the Anglo-American model of 'integration' meet with the German fears of liberal individualism, leading to a downgrading of living and working conditions. The fundamental value in need of protection is however not the welfare state, as in the German writings, but the nation state and the sentimental ties of a common identity as a product of republican assimilation that binds society together.

Conclusion

This chapter has shown that culturalist arguments play a much greater role in French than in German migration research which has mainly framed the question of 'integration' in socio-economic terms as a question of participation in the institutions of the welfare state. This leads to the conclusion that ironically, the more expansive and inclusive model of state-society relations leads to stricter and more particularist positions with regard to the conditions for the 'integration' of immigrants than the exclusive, ethno-cultural system of *ius sanguinis* in Germany. How can these differences be explained, considering the growing convergence of immigration structures in the two countries? This conclusion argues that these differences highlight the structuring impact of public discourses and national frames on the choice of questions posed by migration scholars and the manner in which these questions are addressed. In this sense, migration research is both a reflection and a constitutive element of public discourses linked to specific national histories and the public myths describing the constitutive principles of the state and the fabric of national identity.

In the case of Germany, four observations seem to be particularly important in explaining the manner in which the questions of immigration and 'integration' have been framed in migration research: the pre-political origins of the German nation; the exclusive definition of citizenship; the experience of national socialism; and the self-description of the Federal Republic as a successful welfare state. In contrast to France, where French national identity was imposed from 'above' through the central state, the idea of a German nation emerged prior to the establishment of a German state and was defined exclusively in pre-political terms. The political identity of a German *Staatsvolk* or *demos* and the national identity of the German people were always split: historically, the German people has participated in several, territorially distinct processes of state formation. At the same time, the modern German nation state has tended to equate the notions of *'ethnos'* and *'demos'* by implementing the principle of *ius sanguinis* and extending the definition of the German people to ethnic Germans outside the federal territory (Article 116 German Constitution). This particular ethno-cultural definition of the German nation excluded a priori the question of cultural assimilation, since a German could – until recently – only be born as a German. This exclusive definition of 'German-ness' implied a unitary vision of the foreigner which allowed only for little differentiation along cultural or religious lines. The experience of national socialism has exacerbated this tendency by turning the reflection about the cultural, ethnic or racial challenges of immigration into a moral taboo. Not only has the exclusive definition of German identity and citizenship a priori excluded the question of assimilation, but the consideration of cultural, racial or religious differences has lost its legitimacy with the crimes committed under the Third Reich. Against this background, it is the re-definition of the German state after World War II which has set the terms of the 'integration' debates in Germany. In public discourse and official reasoning, the history of the Federal Republic has been framed as a success story of the welfare state, reconciling liberty and equality, wealth and justice. A dynamic economy, accompanied by a dense web of social policies became the central motors of 'integration' both inside in the relations between state and society and outside in the relations of the Federal Republic to the society of states and in particular to the European integration project.

If one believes in the interdependence of public and academic discourses, recent developments point at a possible modification of the hitherto dominant frame of the welfare state, with greater attention to cultural or ethno-national factors in migration research. At least, these factors have played an increasing role in public debates since the coming into power of the coalition government between the social democrats and the Greens, fuelled by the polemics of the conservative parties against the possibility of double citizenship and the introduction of *ius soli* in the new citizenship law. With their focus on the cultural requirements for granting German citizenship, the arguments of the conservative opposition may increase sensibilities for other forms of membership and community than socio-economic participation in the welfare state, thus leading to an increased preoccupation among migration scholars with the identity basis of being German. Such a development might also find support in the dynamics of German unification and the experiences made with the admission of *Aussiedler*. The result could be a heightened sense of 'national' identity and hence the stimulation of academic concern with the ethno-cultural fabric of German society.

In France, ironically, the clash between the high aspirations of an a priori universal notion of citizenship, equal to the concept of 'nation', and the factual need to define conditions for acquiring this citizenship has led to an obsession with ethno-cultural criteria, ultimately leading to the reaffirmation of the republican model of 'assimilation' (Noiriel, 1988; Guiraudon, 1996). Three factors seem particularly important in explaining the dominant frame in French migration research: the universal definition of French citizenship as a free act of will; the tension between this universal definition and the reality of immigration from the former colonies; and the early politicization of these questions through the career of Le Pen's national front. Carrying the ideals of the Revolution, France developed the 'purest' version of a modern nation state model where nation, state and culture were designed to coincide perfectly around the tenets of Enlightenment universalism and where the citizen was to become the symbol of abstract egalitarianism. In this celebration of universalism, the very idea of a distinct French *'ethnos'* is a priori denied, and ethnicity is not accepted as a constitutive factor of the French people. In this line of reasoning, the recognition of cultural difference in the public sphere automatically acquires negative connotations and appears as antithetical to the French tradition and, more generally, social cohesion. The dilemma with this philosophical position is that it treats the universal as being homogeneous, or the homogeneous as being universal, without providing for the possibility of accommodating difference. This dilemma has come to dominate both public and scientific debates on immigrant 'integration' in France today, struggling with the perpetual tension between universal aspirations and the cultural understanding of assimilation applied in particular with regard to the large Muslim communities of immigrants from the former colonies. Thus, the French focus on culture and religion as crucial elements in the process of 'integration' may be interpreted as the very product of the tension between republican, laic and universalist notions of citizenship and the unitary and static understanding of the French nation. In this perspective, multiculturalism and the protection of minority rights gain a threatening quality since they would lead to the fragmentation of a unified public space and a subsequent clash of cultural particularisms. These fears were successfully mobilized by Le Pen's right-wing extremist party, the National Front, which coined the slogan *'être français, ça ce mérite'*.[16] These controversies, which came up in the early 1980s and soon became one of the focal points of partisan debates, penetrated into the academic sphere and created a new field of research which moved the conception of the immigration 'issue' away from the more socio-economic idea of *'insertion'* during the 1960s and 1970s towards the more culture based notion of *'intégration'*.

To conclude, this chapter has shown the constitutive impact of specific historical contexts and public discourses on migration research and in particular the manner in which the question of 'integration' is conceived. Historical contexts and public discourses find reflection in national frames which concentrate the attention of migration scholars on particular aspects of a given problem, while neglecting others. Apart from defining the representation of the 'integration' problem, however, such national frames also carry implicit normative assumptions about the desirability or undesirability of particular 'integration' measures, thus becoming an integral part of the political immigration discourse. Awareness of such specific historical and discursive contexts not only helps to abstract from these often implicit orientations, but also opens the way for a truly comparative perspective that is able to state commonalities and differences beyond the limited perspective of one's own discursive embeddedness. With the unfolding process of European integration, such a reflexive comparative perspective becomes more and more important, as it points at some of the deeper implications of developing European citizenship, a Charter of Fundamental Rights, or the efforts to develop a common approach towards what have now become the 'third country nationals'.

Notes

1 The original text reads: 'Ils [les sociologues, SL] ne devraient pas se satisfaire de la seule dénonciation et se dispenser d'historiciser et de relativiser leur propre critique en restant prisonniers, sans même s'en rendre compte, des normes de la société moderne.'
2 For an important exception see Adrian Favell's study of 'philosophies of integration' in France and Britain, Favell, 1998. Although less explicitly, the comparative work on the practice of integration in France and Britain by Lapeyronnie (1993) also reflects on the role of 'national models' of 'integration'.
3 A useful complement to such a perspective would be the analysis of the involvement of academics in political counseling and in policy reform committees and the links between the sponsoring of academic research by state institutions and the contents of this research. For such an analysis see Favell, 2000.
4 Sometimes a third cognitive order is distinguished which refers to the affective dimension including the totality of subjective experiences of the actor as expressed in his emotions and wishes (Habermas, 1981, p. 137). Although certainly useful for analyzing the subjective motivation of particular migration scholars in their research, this dimension is not included in this study which focuses less on individual than inter-subjective, society-wide predispositions.
5 See the principles of (West-)German policy towards immigrants and non-Germans laid down by the Joint Commission of the Federal Government and the States of 1977. With the coming into power of the Social Democrats and the Greens in 1998, this position has been softened. In summer 2000, an expert commission was set up to elaborate an immigration law for Germany.

6 Today, ca. 38 per cent of foreign population in France are of North-African origin, in Germany 28.5 per cent are of Turkish origin (SOPEMI, 1999, p. 40).
7 Brubaker explains the evolution of ethno-cultural understanding of citizenship in Germany with the German *Sonderweg,* that is the fact that the German nation emerged before the establishment of the nation state and that thus, the idea of a nation was originally not political nor linked to an abstract idea of citizenship but pre-political and organic in the sense of cultural, linguistic or racial belonging.
8 The new citizenship and nationality law passed the two chambers of parliament in May 1999 and entered into force as of 1 January 2000.
9 See his discourse given before the National Assembly on 19.6.1997, printed in *Libération* of 20.6.1997. The Jospin government also abolished the amendments of the Nationality Act introducing the mandatory declaration of will which had been passed under the second *cohabitation* in 1993.
10 This distinction between cultural, political and social-economic 'integration' is used in a heuristic manner as a means to highlight various analytical dimensions of 'integration'. This is however only an analytical distinction, while in reality these various dimensions often overlap.
11 For a more culture-based critique of multinationalism see however Hoffmann-Nowotny, 1992.
12 Here, it should be mentioned that Luhmann's system theory itself does not provide for 'culture' as a sub-system. However, already the choice to apply this theory to migration issues reflects the relatively small importance attributed to ethno-cultural factors.
13 The original text reads 'Eine Auseinandersetzung mit Kontroversen um und Konzepten über eine "multikulturelle Gesellschaft" ... würde uns in die Arena ideologischer Streitigkeiten und/oder vor ein Kaleidoskop sowohl mit Schreckensbildern als auch mit gesellschaftlichen Idealbildern führen...'.
14 In addition, Stasi argued that such a consequent 'integration' of Islamic-northern African immigrants would allow an intensification of the links with their countries of origin which, in accordance to the colonial tradition in French foreign policy, offered an alternative to American dominance and European integration.
15 For an excellent comparison of French and British 'Philosophies of Integration' see Favell, 1998.
16 'To be French must be deserved.'

References

Angenendt, St. (1992), *Ausländerforschung in Frankreich und der Bundesrepublik Deutschland,* Campus, Frankfurt a.M. and New York.
Bade, K.J. (ed.) (1992), *Deutsche im Ausland, Fremde in Deutschland: Migration in Geschichte und Gegenwart,* Beck, München.
Bade, K.J. (ed.) (1996), *Die multikulturelle Herausforderung. Menschen über Grenzen – Grenzen über Menschen,* Beck, München.
Balibar, E. (1991), *Sujets ou citoyens? Pour l'égalité, in: Les frontières de la démocracie,* La Découverte, Paris.
Bommes, M. (1999), *Migration und nationaler Wohlfahrtsstaat. Ein differenzierungs-theoretischer Entwurf,* Westdeutscher Verlag, Opladen.
Bommes, M. and Halfmann, J. (eds.) (1998), *Migration in nationalen Wohlfahrtsstaaten. Theoretische und vergleichende Untersuchungen,* Universitätsverlag Rasch, Osnabrück.
Brubaker, R. (1992), Citizenship and Nationhood in France and Germany, Harvard UP, Cambridge, MA.

Costa-Lascoux, J. (1989), *De l'immigré au citoyen,* La Documentation Française, Paris.

Désir, H. (1991), 'Pour l'intégration: conditions et instruments', in P.-A. Targuieff (ed.), *Face au racisme,* vol. 1, pp. 106-19.

Dupeux, G. (1980), 'L'immigration en France de la fin du XVIIIème siècle à nos jours', in Commission Internationale d'Histoire des Movements Sociaux et des Structures Sociales, *Les migrations internationales de la fin du XVIIIème siècle à nos jours,* Editions du CNRS, Paris, pp. 161-74.

Eder, K. (1992), *Framing and Communicating Environmental Issues. A Discourse Analysis of Environmentalism,* European University Institute, Florence.

Esser, K. (1980), *Aspekte der Wanderungssoziologie. Assimilation und Integration von Wanderern, ethnischen Gruppen und Minderheiten. Eine handlungstheoretische Analyse,* Luchterhand, Darmstadt/Neuwied.

Faist, Th. (1994), 'How to Define a Foreigner? The Symbolic Politics of Immigration in German Partisan Discourse, 1978-1992', *West European Politics,* 17 (2), pp. 50-71.

Faist, Th. (1995), *Social Citizenship for Whom? Young Turks in Germany and Mexican American in the United States,* Avebury, Aldershot.

Faist, Th. (2000), 'Jenseits von Nation und Post-Nation. Transatlantische Räume und Doppelte Staatsbürgerschaft', *Zeitschrift für Internationale Beziehungen,* 7 (1), pp. 109-44.

Favell, A. (1998), *Philosophies of Integration : Immigration and the Idea of Citizenship in France and Britain,* Macmillan, Basingstoke.

Favell, A. (2000), 'Integration Policy and Integration Research in Europe: A Review and Critique', in A. Aleinikoff/D. Klusmeyer (eds.), *Citizenship: Comparisons and Perspectives,* Brookings Institute, Washington, DC, pp. 349-99.

Fijalkowski, J. (1993), 'Aggressive Nationalism, Immigration Pressure and Asylum Policy Disputes in Contemporary Germany', *International Migration Review,* 27 (4), pp. 850-69.

Gamson, W.A. and Modigliani, A. (1987), 'The Changing Culture of Affirmative Action', *Research in Political Sociology,* 3, pp. 137-77.

Gamson, W.A. (1988), 'Political Discourse and Collective Action', *International Social Movement Research,* vol. 1, pp. 219-44.

Goffman, E. (1974), *Frame Analysis – an Essay on the Organization of Experience,* Harper and Row, New York.

Granotier, B. (1976), *Les travailleurs immigrés en France,* François Maspéro, Paris.

Griotteray, A. (1984), *Les immigrés: le choc,* Plon, Paris.

Guiraudon, V. (1996), 'The Reaffirmation of the Republican Model of Integration: Ten Years of Identity Politics in France, *French Politics and Society,* 14 (2), pp. 47-57.

Habermas, J. (1981), *Theorie des kommunikativen Handelns,* 2 vols., Suhrkamp, Frankfurt a.M.

Heckmann, F. (1981), *Die Bundesrepublik: Ein Einwanderungsland? Zur Soziologie der Gastarbeiterbevölkerung als Einwandererminorität,* Klett-Cotta, Stuttgart.

Heinelt, H. (1993), 'Immigration and the Welfare State in Germany', *German Politics,* 2 (1), pp. 78-96.

Heinelt, H. und Lohmann, A. (1992) Immigranten im Wohlfahrtsstaat - am Beispiel der Rechtspositionen und Lebensverhältnisse von Aussiedlern, Leske & Budrich, Opladen.

Hoffmann-Nowotny, H.-J. (1970), *Migration. Ein Beitrag zu einer soziologischen Erklärung,* Enke, Stuttgart.

Hoffmann-Nowotny, H.-J. (1973), *Soziologie des Fremdarbeiterproblems. Eine theoretische und empirische Analyse am Beispiel der Schweiz,* Enke, Stuttgart.

Hoffmann-Nowotny, H.-J. (1992), *Chancen und Risiken multikultureller Einwanderungs-gesellschaften,* Schweizerischer Wissenschaftsrat, Bern.

Hoffmann-Nowotny, H.-J. and Hondrich, K.O. (1982), 'Zur Funktionsweise sozialer Systeme – Versuch eines Resumés und einer theoretischen Integration', in H.-J. Hoffmann-Novotny and K.O. Hondrich (eds.), Ausländer in der *Bundesrepublik Deutschland und der Schweiz. Segregation und Integration: Eine vergleichende Untersuchung,* Campus, Frankfurt and New York, pp. 569-635.

Kontos, M. (1994), 'Ethnische Kolonien und Multikulturelle Gesellschaft', in G. Böhme et al. (eds.), Migration und Ausländerfeindlichkeit, Wissenschaftliche Buchgesellschaft, Darmstadt, pp. 67-83.

Kurthen, H. and Minkenberg, M. (1995), 'Germany in Transition: immigration, racism and the extreme right', *Nations and Nationalism,* 1 (2), pp. 175-96.

Lapeyronnie, D. (1993), *L'individu et les minorités. La France et la Grande-Bretagne face à leurs immigrés,* Presses Universitaires de France, Paris.

Lloyd, C. (1995), 'International Comparisons in the Field of Ethnic Relations', in A. Hargreaves and J. Leaman, *Racism, Ethnicity and Politics in Contemporary Europe,* Edvard Elgar, Aldershot.

Long, M. (1988), *Etre Français aujourd'hui et demain.* Rapport de la Commission de la Nationalité présenté par M. Marceau Long au Premier Ministre, La Documentation Française, Paris.

Manfrass, K. (1991), *Türken in der Bundesrepublik, Nordafrikaner in Frankreich: Ausländerproblematik im deutsch-französischen Vergleich,* Bouvier, Bonn.

Miles, R. (1994), 'Explaining Racism in Contemporary Europe: Problems and Perspectives', in A. Rattansi and S. Westwood, *Racism, Modernity and Identity,* Polity Press, Oxford, pp. 189-221.

Nair, S. (1992), *Le regard des vainqueurs. Les enjeux français de l'immigration,* Grasset, Paris.

Noiriel, G. (1988), *Le creuset français. Histoire de l'immigration XIXe-XXe siècle,* Seuil, Paris.

Potter, J. (1996): *Representing Reality: Discourse, Rhetoric and Social Construction,* Sage, London.

Przeworski, A. and Teune, H. (1970), *The Logic of Comparative Social Inquiry,* Wiley-Interscience, New York.

Räthzel, N. (1995), 'Nation et nationalité en Allemagne au regard des nouveaux processus migratoires', in C. Neveu (ed.), *Nations, frontières et immigration en Europe,* L'Harmattan, Paris.

Schnapper, D. (1994), 'The Debate on Immigration and the Crisis of National Identity, *West European Politics,* 17 (2), pp. 127-39.

Schnapper, D. (1998), *La relation à l'autre. Au coeur de la pensée sociologique,* Gallimard, Paris.

Shapiro, I. (1982), 'Realism in the History of Ideas', *History of Political Theory,* 3 (3), pp. 525-78.

Silverman, M. (1992), *Deconstructing the Nation. Immigration, Racism and Citizenship in Modern France,* Routledge, London and New York.

SOPEMI (1999), *Trends in International Migration,* OECD, Paris.

Soysal, Y.N. (1994), *Limits of Citizenship,* The University of Chicago Press, Chicago.

Stasi, B. (1984), *L'immigration: une chance pour la France,* Laffont, Paris.

Stichweh, R. (1998), 'Migration, nationale Wohlfahrtsstaaten und die Entstehung der Weltgesellschaft', in: Bommes and Halfmann (eds.), *Migration in nationalen Wohlfahrtsstaaten,* pp. 49-62.

Targuieff, P.-A. (1987), *La force du préjugé: essai sur le racisme et ses doubles,* La Découverte, Paris.

Targuieff, P.-A. (ed.) (1991a), *Face au racisme, volume 1: les moyens d'agir,* La Découverte, Paris.

Targuieff, P.-A. (1991b), 'Introduction: La lutte contre le racisme, par-delà illusions et désillusions', in: Targuieff (ed.), *Face au racisme,* vol. 1, pp. 11-43.

Weil, P. (1991), 'Immigration and the Rise of Racism in France: The Contradictions in Mitterrand's Policies', *Politics and Society,* 9 (3-4), pp. 82-100.

Weil, P. (1995a), *La France et ses Étrangers,* 2nd ed., Folio, Paris.

Weil, P. (1995b), 'Die Französische Politik der Einwanderung, der Integration und der Staatsbürgerschaft', in CiRAC/CFi/DGAP/IFRi (eds.), *Handeln für Europa, Deutsch-Französische Zusammenarbeit in einer veränderten Welt,* Leske und Budrich, Opladen.

Weil, P. (1996), 'Nationalities and Citizenships. The Lessons of the French Experience for Germany and Europe, in D. Cesarini and M. Fulbrook (eds.), *Citizenship and Migration in Europe,* Routledge, London.

Wihtol de Wenden, C. (1988), *Les immigrés et la politique,* Presses de la Fondation Nationale des Sciences Politiques, Paris.

Wihtol de Wenden, C. (1994a), 'Frankreich', in H. Heinelt (ed.), *Zuwanderungspolitik in Europa. Nationale Politiken. Gemeinsamkeiten und Unterschiede,* Leske und Budrich, Opladen.

Wihtol de Wenden, C. (1994b), 'Immigrants as Political Actors in France', *West European Politics,* 17 (2), pp. 91-109.

Wihtol de Wenden, C. (1998), 'Einwanderung im Wohlfahrtsstaat: das Beispiel Frankreich', in Bommes and Halfmann (eds.), *Migration in nationalen Wohlfahrtsstaaten,* pp. 233-8.

Chapter 11

Migration Research and European Integration: The Construction and Institutionalization of Problems of Europe

Andrew Geddes

Introduction

Free movement, immigration and asylum were drawn to the very centre of the European Union (EU) by the Treaty of Amsterdam (1997) and subsequent developments such as the Tampere summit meeting of heads of government in October 1999. At Tampere the heads of government expressed the desire to create common migration and asylum policies within what has been rather grandiosely entitled 'an area of freedom, justice and security'. Simultaneously, efforts to consolidate and strengthen the single European market have seen attempts to stimulate intra-EU migration as a component part of the 'Lisbon agenda' for economic reform and its bold intention for Europe to be the world's leading knowledge based economy by 2010.

The ways in which free movement, immigration and asylum have become central to the 'European project' has prompted a flurry of analyses examining the immigration control and (less often) the immigrant integration implications of European co-operation and integration in these areas. This chapter surveys the development of these responsibilities and demonstrates the developing relationship between academic research, European integration and the construction and institutionalization of 'problems of Europe'. By this I mean research projects funded by European institutions that as part of their attempt to create 'European added value' focus on areas where European integration is seen to have been inadequate, failed, or in need of reform. The chapter develops its analysis by, first, outlining the development of EU responsibilities in this area. Second, it cautions against flights of fancy that adopt inappropriate yardsticks and read too much into European integration as a potentially progressive arena for attainment of migrant inclusion. And third, it assesses the connections between EU institutions and academic researchers seeking to analyse 'problems of Europe' that have rapidly ascended academic research agendas throughout the 1990s because of the various deficits – of democracy, rights, participation, mobility and inclusion – that have been identified as plaguing the EU's quest for legitimacy. These deficits have, for example, impinged on the development of academic research that addresses the problems of European-ized social exclusion, within which a burgeoning sub-field is migrant social exclusion. This increased attention paid to migrant exclusion and the assumption that Europe can become a force for inclusion can be seen as a function of the free movement, immigration and asylum policy responsibilities of the EU and the more general development of an EU 'social dimension'. As a result, it has become com-monplace to see analyses of European migration policy and politics that identify EU-level capacity to exacerbate or to rectify migrant exclusion. Put another way, on the one hand to build the exclusionary 'European fortress' or, on the other, to construct some kind of progressive alternative in the form of 'people's Europe' capable of greater inclusiveness. This chapter's focus is the connection between the development of EU responsibility for migration-related issues and the development of academic research agendas that focus on EU's role. The aim is to demonstrate how the EU's institutional context for the management of migration related issues connects with a range of ideas and practices associated with both *liberalization* and *securitization* and the associated construction of 'problems of Europe'. The sources of power associated with European integration can then provide new opportunities for academic research.

The Europeanization of Migration

There are no *a priori* grounds for supposing that European integration marks a re-run of processes of nation state formation in, for instance, some kind of para-digmatic Marshallian integrative form (as discussed in the chapter by Adrian Favell). To paraphrase Renan, the EU does not have its church, its army or its schools as agents of socialization. Rather it has its single market and the forms of economic, legal, political and social power connected with it in a 'regulatory' or 'post-modern' state without a centre (in a legal, political or geographical sense, see Caporaso, 1996).

Discussions of migration policy are, therefore, nested in a particular European-level institutional setting – to use the language of Bourdieu, a new political field at European level – that bears strong relation to national settings, but cannot be analysed wholly in such terms (Favell, 1998; Favell and Geddes, 1999a). Conse-quently, not only does the Europeanization of migration impact upon our understanding of contemporary European immigration (regulation) and immigrant (inclusion) policies, it also provides new structures and incentives for researchers seeking to probe these 'problems of Europe'. The apparent necessity for European conferences on migration to include analysis of the EU dimension has contributed to the identification of problems of European integration – of a 'democratic deficit' or of 'social exclusion', for instance – to which more often than not the solution can be closer European integration. The identification of European problems can beget

European responses. Indeed, it is not unusual to encounter analyses that identify the EU's accumulation of repressive state-like functions in the areas of immigration and asylum but that also address the EU as a possible source of funding for further research to counteract these worrying tendencies. To put it flippantly, the EU can then fund research into the question of exactly what kind of repressive state it is becoming. More seriously, perhaps what it also indicates is the motivations of institutional actors at EU level, such as the European Commission, that have an interest in developing research agendas and research opportunities linked to problems of European integration to which the answer can be enhanced European level responsibilities to tackle these problems. The identification of problems of European integration can enhance the perceived relevance of the European dimension and contribute to arguments for closer integration and more power for supranational institutions (the European Commission, the European Court of Justice and the European Parliament). When the motivations of EU level actors are taken into account, then it is far from beyond the realm of possibility that EU funding could be secured for research into the exclusionary effects of European integration. Indeed, the identification of 'problems of Europe' and the supranational funding available for such research has become a key opportunity for academics with an interest in migration and European integration. European integration now presents a series of opportunities for academics and academic networks, particularly because of the Europeanization of discussion of social inclusion/exclusion. These are made manifest by the large amounts of funding made available for collaborative projects within the Commission-funded Fifth and Sixth Framework projects. In turn, this also raises some interesting questions about what could be called the political science of the political science of migration. In practical terms, it is abundantly evident that library shelves groan under the weight of tomes on European integration and new journals spring up to meet the demands of this growing area of specialism. Jean Monnet's legacy on university life in Europe is formidable, as many academics who have benefited at one time or another from EU *largesse* in his name need little reminding. In more substantive terms, European integration has important implications for how we understand the key components of migration policy and politics: the attempts to control immigration and the inclusion/exclusion of immigrants and their descendants that results from these.

Academic research in Europe has become increasingly geared to 'problems of Europe' with the effect that such research is increasingly *structured by* and possesses the potential to *structure* debates about European integration.[1] This is not to claim that the future of Europe is being mapped by academic conferences determining the component parts of the EU's 'social dimension'. Rather, it is to suggest that European integration impacts upon the structure of incentives for academic researchers and provides new incentives to analyse the Europeanized problems of inclusion and exclusion. The EU migration context is not neutral: a nascent area of cooperation and integration onto which can be sketched a model of a more inclusive or integrated Europe. Far from it, EU migration policy has been deeply imbued with patterns of security-related co-operation that developed since at least the mid-1970s. This is not to say that migrant social inclusion is far from being a dead letter at EU level, as the directive outlawing direct and indirect discrimination passed in record time in 2000 indicates (Geddes, 2000).

Immigration and asylum have been largely determined in the intergovernmental Council of Ministers with unanimity as the decisional *modus operandi*. Free movement and 'social inclusion' have been quite extensively supranationalized with the effect that the Commission, the European Court of Justice and the European Parliament have wielded legal and political power. Yet, even in these arenas where ideas about inclusion, rights and participation acquire greater salience, they have done so in an elite oriented and elite dominated environment suffused by a technocratic ethos. In practical terms, this means that the deployment of expertise in elite level consultation and decision-making processes often characterizes the development of EU ideas and practices. This provides an opportunity for academic research to have an audience at EU level and, in some circumstances, to be co-opted into these procedures. It is, though, important to relate these consultation processes to the location of decisional capacity. The Council holds the upper hand in immigration and asylum policy and has shown itself to be unenthusiastic about the extension of EU competencies that impinge on national immigration control, immigrant inclusion and asylum policies (although the Amsterdam Treaty does genuinely create the possibility for supranationalization in these areas, see Geddes, 2000).

In the wake of the planned abolition of internal frontiers between member states by the 1986 Single European Act (albeit not yet fully attained despite the 1992 target date), immigration and asylum policy became matters of common interest. Cooperation between states bred new forms of interaction between state and non-state officials and agents with the potential for these iterative processes to become reinforcing over time and perhaps spawn deeper integration (Koslowski, 1998). But, crucially, immigration and asylum have yet to become the basis for a common EU policy in the sense that these issues are resolved at EU level with supranational institutions fully involved. It must also be said that many of these developments have occurred in a way that appears rather baffling to the non-EU expert. The development of cooperation and integration on migration policy is quite complex. This means that it can be useful to step back and specify the sources of power associated with European integration, their relation to migration policy, and the location of capacity to act.

The following landmarks in EU free movement, immigration and asylum policy co-operation and integration can be identified:

–   The Treaty of Rome (1957) setting up the European Economic Community (the Common Market, as it was more commonly known).
–   The Single European Act (1986) which sought movement from a common market to a single market within which people, services, goods and capital would be secured by European legislation that would be binding on the member states and override national laws.

–   The development of informal and ad hoc intergovernmental cooperation on immigration and asylum policy (1986-1993) which bracketed immigration and asylum with security threats to member states and built upon internal security cooperation between member states that was initiated in the 1970s.

–   The Maastricht Treaty on European Union (1992) which created an inter-governmental pillar for 'Justice and Home Affairs' as part of the newly created European Union. Immigration and asylum were thus brought closer to the Union as a result of the pillar, but were not included within the remit of 'Community' decision-making. The Council (composed of national ministers) held sway while the Commission, European Court of Justice and European Parliament were largely excluded. Maastricht also created the 'Social Chapter' that sought enhanced EU competencies to tackle social exclusion, although its relevance to migrants was small. This applied whether or not migrants were citizens of the member state in which they resided. For instance, the Social Chapter made no provision for tackling race, ethnicity or religious based discrimination or establishing Europeanized rights of denizenship that would allow legally resident immigrants to access rights of free movement that had been extended to EU citizens.

–   The Amsterdam Treaty (1997) which created a new Treaty Title dealing with free movement, immigration and asylum. This moved immigration and asylum from Maastricht's 'pillar' to within the remit of Community decision-making. That said, the continued possibility for use of national vetoes in the Council of Ministers maintained the strong intergovernmental element until at least 2004 and hinders development of supranational responsibilities. Amsterdam also introduced provisions in Article 13 to counter race, ethnicity and religion based discrimination which was turned into a 2000 directive outlawing direct and indirect discrimination.

–   The October 1999 Tampere summit which called for the creation of a common migration and asylum policy.

–   Agreement in June 2000 on two directives based on Article 13 of the Amster-dam Treaty which sought to combat discrimination on the grounds of race, ethnic origin and religion.

The effects have been that free movement for EU citizens has become supra-nationalized and is backed by EU institutions and EU law that is linked to the importance ascribed to free movement as a core EU aspiration. Yet the limits of supranationalization are highlighted by the control oriented and security dominated immigration and asylum framework from which supranational institutions (the Commission, European Court of Justice and European Parliament) have been largely excluded. The result has been a strengthening of executive authority over securitized immigration and asylum policy as a result of the establishment of patterns of intergovernmental co-operation on these issues that are largely divorced from democratic or judicial oversight and accountability at either national or supranational level. Moreover, non-EU nationals (third country nationals, of whom there are around 11.5 million resident in EU member states) are formally excluded from this supranationalized free movement framework because of the emphasis on prior possession of the nationality of a member state before EU rights can be accessed (in contra-distinction to civil, social and (less frequently) political rights acquired as a result of residence ('denizenship', Hammar, 1990) in member states).

The distinct and unique characteristic of the EU is its ability to turn treaties between states into laws that bind those states:[2] *constitutionalization* combined with the scope for subsequent *institutionalization* arising from new forms of political action when policy responsibilities become established. The result is the development of a European order that becomes less like anarchy and more like a hierarchy within which previously international politics is 'domestified' through supranational arrangements (Stone-Sweet and Sandholtz, 1998). The legal effect is that a triangular relationship can be established as a result of European integration between individuals, EU member states and EU institutions within which individuals are empowered by being allowed to also access legal redress at EU level through the European Court of Justice (Guild, 1998). This triangular relationship limits the competence and discretion of member states in areas where European integration has occurred. But these constraints on member states' powers are connected to the particular purposes of the EU: the building of a single market and its consequences (which have been closely linked to notions and practices of security as well as a limited social dimension). Institutionalization also implies scope for refocused political activity with altered patterns of political action that focus on Europeanized competencies. The creation of Europeanized policy contexts then raises the question of which forms of political action and which kinds of actors are privileged within these new institutional contexts.

The context for academic research on the problems of Europe is related to these processes of constitutionalization and institutionalization and the ways in which they create new patterns of governance. Indeed, 'new governance' has become a central term in analysis of European integration with important implications for how we conceptualize EU migrant social inclusion/exclusion. Typically, analyses of new governance focus on the establishment of regulatory capacity at EU level for management of private-public relations (Majone, 1996). The EU is characterized as 'a unique system of non-hierarchical, regulatory and deliberative governance' (Hix, 1998, p. 38). Multilevelness also imparts a degree of complexity derived from deliberation and co-operation between various levels of state and non-state officials. Governance perspectives emphasize the provision of guidance, steering, control and management (Kooiman, 1993) within a polycentric rather than state-centric system (Jahtenfuchs, 1995, p. 115) and have been described as 'governance without government' (Rosenau and Czempiel, 1992) or, because of the complexity and the uncertainty surrounding outcomes, 'the post-modern state' (Caporaso, 1996).

These new patterns of governance imply an EU-level articulation between the single market programme's liberalization and new forms of population control made manifest by security cooperation between member states, which includes immigration and asylum within its remit. It has been argued that the 'securitization' of migration rests on links between market relations embodied within the free movement framework and the control of population in a situation where micro-level power relations are viewed as determining the system of power relations that form the basis of capitalist class relations. Of particular importance are the modern technologies of surveillance, discipline and punishment. Attention is then directed towards the practices of security agencies and the implementation and effects of new technologies of population control. From this perspective it makes less sense to see security concerns as a knock-on effect of single market integration. Rather, processes of securitization and the control of population are the foundation stones of liberalization with the effect that migration becomes a part of the security issue marked by the intensification of co-operation between security agencies (Huysmans, 1995; Bigo, 1996, 1998). Migration becomes a security problem, which tends to rather crowd-out the way that migration issues are actually more broadly spread across a range of issue areas – labor markets, social rights to name two – and cannot be wholly subsumed by the discourse and practices of security. That said, securitization perspectives are particularly valuable because of the reflexivity they induce: they 'make politicians, activists and academics aware that they make a choice when they treat something as a security issue' (Wæver, 1996, p. 108).

A key methodological implication for research into European integration can be extracted from these features of the EU framework. New patterns of EU-level governance – and the articulation between liberalization and security therein – cannot be analysed by relying entirely upon the familiar reference points of comparative political analysis or international relations. The EU is 'not a 're-run' of the processes and policies that earlier made the national state' (Schmitter, 1996, p. 14). New governance perspectives and their inherent 'multi-levelness' derived from the distribution of power and authority across levels of governance (incorporating state and non-state agents) and through market mechanisms challenge a vocabulary of political analysis that takes the state as its point of reference. As Schmitter (1996, p. 132) notes: 'Our language for discussing politics – especially stable, itera-tive, "normal" politics – is indelibly impregnated with assumptions about the state. Whenever we refer to the number, location, authority, status, membership, capacity, identity, type or significance of political units we employ concepts that implicitly refer to a universe featuring sovereign states'. The internationalization of the state (Cox, 1987) inherent within the European project – to which European integration is both a response and a contributing factor – means that state power becomes something to be explained rather than something that explains European level developments. The effect is that states remain key actors but are not the only actors.

The implications for migrant inclusion can now be sketched in relation to the characteristics of the EU policy context. It would be incoherent to suppose that economic integration could be attained without some consideration of a social dimension (Meehan, 1993). This has largely centred on securing the transferability of social entitlements for EU citizens exercising their right of free movement and protection from racist or ethnic-based discrimination when doing so. It has not been linked to the building of some kind of European welfare state to replace national welfare states (Bommes and Geddes, 2001).

Over time the claims made by pro-migrant groups at EU level have become linked to this social dimension. There has been a particular eagerness to stress the potential economic contribution of legally resident migrants and the benefits that they can offer to the attainment of economic objectives if, for example, mobility rights are extended to legally resident third country nationals. The EU's migrant inclusion agenda is as a result strongly related to the sources of legal and political power associated with this social dimension and involves:

–   The establishment of a 'Resident's Charter' that Europeanizes the right of denizenship by extending to legally resident third country nationals rights of free movement and thereby extends the principle of denizenship to supra-national level. In 2003 the EU established a directive on the rights of long-term residents which extends to TCNs with five years continuous residence in a member state the right to move from one member state to another without encountering the procedures for new immigrants.
–   EU level action against discrimination on grounds of race, ethnicity or religion. Treaty provision was made in Amsterdam (2000) with two directives in June 2000.
–   Asylum procedures that are judged fair, humane and just in accordance with the provisions of international legal standards. This has been the most partic-ular bone of contention with fierce debate within the EU about the relationship between the developing EU framework and international legal standards.

The kinds of political action that have occurred at EU level in relation to this migrant inclusion agenda accord closely with elite patterns of European integration that have a strong technocratic ethos and which have privileged elite patterns of political activity. The EU has not tended to become an arena for new forms of contentious politics.[3] In fact, interest co-option is far more likely to occur where relevant interest groups are drawn into policy-making circles by EU institutions (Geddes, 2000). This occurs because EU institutions are often relatively small and can rely on the kinds of information and expertise that outside groups and experts can bring in the form of, for instance, specific recommendations or the 'voices' of civil society. Consultation with outside groups such as NGOs and academics/ academic networks can add a veneer of legitimacy to decision-making processes that are seen by many as relatively detached from the kinds of democratic oversight that can occur in national political systems. The co-option of interest groups can also contribute to the development of pro-European integration alliances as 'more Europe' is the solution to the problems of incomplete or ineffective integration. Most pro-migrant NGOs operating at EU level tend to call for more not less European integration. They want to see more power for the European Commission, the Court of Justice and the European Parliament because they see power for these institutions as a corrective to lowest common denominator Council of Ministers-based decision-making. It is not unusual for lobby groups supported by academic networks to advance these kinds of claims and then to be funded by EU institutions, i.e., the institutions they seek to influence (before its suspension, the Commission-sponsored European Union Migrant's Forum was the best example of this, Danese, 1998). This prompts the development of pro-integration alliances that emerge in response to the opportunities created by the particular sources of power associated with European integration (AGIT, 1999).

Understanding 'Problems of Europe'

The Europeanization of migration has been reflected in a number of recent studies (Wrench and Solomos, 1992; Miles and Thränhardt, 1995; King, 1993; Cesarini and Fulbrook, 1996; Baldwin-Edwards and Schain, 1994; Favell and Geddes, 1999). Two problems recur in much of this work. First, it is fairly commonplace for studies to counterpose the 'exclusionary' tendencies of 'fortress Europe' and its culturally and racially exclusive 'European identity' with an alternative liberating, 'inclusionary' multicultural agenda that is being pushed from below by ethnic mobilization around pro-migrant or anti-racist ideas. A good example of this is the debate about European citizenship (established by the Maastricht Treaty). EU citizenship is a rather under-nourished entity, but the emptiness of 'European citizenship' provisions is often identified as an example of a 'democratic deficit' – and the problem of legitimacy – that could be remedied by an improved EU level 'recognition' of cultural and racial diversity. The weakness of this kind of approach is that it rarely deals with the actual political dynamics that lie behind such Euro-rhetoric or the very limited institutionalized resources available for a mobilization of this kind. The European project's focus on market-making has drawn migration into the web of interdependence, but in relation to the legal, political and social sources of power within this regulatory 'state without a centre' rather than the national integrating state that has been the focus of the bulk of migration research. It has been argued that the maintenance of a nation state structured field of opportunities and constraints, in which a mix of élite partisanship, bottom-up mobilization, conflict over ethnic difference, and progressive ideas of citizenship, welfare-based justice and equality, provide the sources of social power necessary to challenge the existing exclusionary social order means that implicitly or explicitly nearly all scholars in the field are still working within this progressive *integrationist* paradigm (Favell and Geddes, 1999a). The problem is that to transfer this model of multicultural change to 'Europe' does not reflect *extant* legal, political and institutional context and the possible dynamics of change it might lead to. Opportunities and constraints can arise in places where the European integration process creates new spaces that facilitate the development of autonomous action by certain political groups privileged and enabled by the EU's institutional configuration and that tailor their strategies accordingly.

Second, research into ethnic mobilization in Europe has tended to focus on the mobilization of difference as the basis for the building of some kind of inclusive EU. This would lead us to expect that ethnic groups that have successfully pushed for improved recognition within the multicultural state - an often cited example being Islamic organizations in Europe – are said to have done so by mobilizing cultural, racial or religious 'identity' as a collective force (Soysal, 1994). But Soysal's work is grounded in a form of sociological institutionalism that tells us that ethnicity is only a successful mobilizing force under certain institutional conditions. Consequently it is necessary to examine the conditions under which EU institutions may induce, encourage and inculcate 'ethnic' mobilization oriented towards EU migration policy responsibilities. Few scholars have engaged with this new EU field of political action, and those who have explicitly looked for transnational ethnic mobilization in the new European context and made both of the two errors identified above. Kastoryano (1999) reads an emerging transnational multicultural state into the European integration process and then connects it with a range of successful transnational 'ethnic' mobilizations that actually have very little grounding in actual institutional developments at the European level. The result is that a strongly normative understanding of the constructive potential of 'European citizenship' does the explanatory work even though it has a limited basis in EU law. EU institutions and patterns of cooperation are seen to create the potential for new 'ethnic' based mobilizations that address claims to European level institutions rather than traditional national ones (Ireland, 1991; Soysal, 1993). As the previous sections of this chapter have sought to demonstrate, the risk is to overestimate the EU's capacity while also assuming that it is naturally progressive in its leanings on immigrant or ethnic politics. Such arguments also misrepresent the degree to which the genuine new opportunities that do exist can or have been seized by ethnic groups themselves, conceived romantically in social movements terms.

If analysis of Europeanized migration is related to the sources of legal, political and social power associated with the EU and the European project then a weakness within academic analyses of the development of European responsibilities emerges. Much work is too easily distracted by normative rhetoric that reads into the process competencies and capacities that are not necessarily possessed and which may bear little relation to EU level sources of power. This strikes a cautionary note before the chapter's next section, which explores the development of Europeanized research agendas informed by 'problems of European integration' and geared towards funding opportunities provided by EU institutions.

Institutionalizing 'Problems of Europe'

The EU itself has instigated new patterns of transnational activity and academic norms[4] that structure and are structured by relations between academics' research agendas, academic networks and European institutions and suggest that academic research can play a part in the construction and institutionalization of migration-related 'problems of Europe'. If new opportunities have been created then it would be possible to say that the EU has become more than an ephemeral forum for transnational exchange that is residual to national academic contexts and to enquire as to the extent to which national academic contexts have been Europeanized? This Europeanization would imply that not only has the EU acquired the capacity to sustain itself and its activities, but that it possesses the potential to create feedback effects into national structures. The result would be a form of Europeanization – with effects on institutions, policies and collective identities – of academic life that reflects the establishment of new policy competencies at EU level with feedback into teaching and research. This feedback effect also raises issues about the 'goodness of fit' of national academic contexts, which, as these are actually well entrenched at national level, offer scope for reconfiguration at the margins rather than transformation. Despite the array of new opportunities for Europeanized work, actual opportunities remain relatively restricted to small numbers of Euro-academics while national contexts retain their salience. Although these contexts are being reconfigured at the margins, they do possess capacity to resist Europeanization of well-entrenched national structures because, despite a burgeoning EU dimension, resources for university systems remain essentially nationally based. Of course, international academic collaboration and the cross-border diffusion of ideas are not new. It would be absurd to suggest otherwise. What is new, is their association with distinct Europeanized sources of supranational power with their own institutional context and the capacity to feedback into domestic structures.

Considerable academic attention has been devoted to Europeanized dimensions of immigration control and to Europeanized issues of migrant inclusion and exclusion. What is interesting about social inclusion/exclusion is the speed with which they have entered the vernacular of policymakers and academics. This demonstrates the ability of the EU to act as a forum for exchange of ideas and practices: in this case, French ideas and terminology associated with social inclusion/exclusion and an integrative ethos associated with a republican synthesis; then to give these ideas and practices a supranational meaning capable of feeding back into domestic structures in other EU member states. In the UK, for instance, a 'social exclusion' unit was established after Labour's 1997 general election victory within the Prime Minister's office. Indeed, in the case of social inclusion/exclusion the cross-border diffusion of ideas has been facilitated by the existence of an EU context that can to some extent 'disguise' the origin of ideas. Much of the domestic UK discussion linked this unit to British response to EU activity in these areas, rather than to French ideas and practices. This suggests scope for cross border diffusion of policy ideas, lesson learning and policy transfer that can use the EU policy context to partially deconstruct the national origins of policy frames and reconstruct them in terms of the discourses and practices associated with European integration.

Of particular interest are the ways in which social inclusion/exclusion have become constructed as problems of Europe. During 1999, academics across Europe have been busily engaged in formulating proposals for the European Commission funded Fifth and Sixth framework research programmes and establishing the networks of pan-European academics that facilitate access to these funds. The category of targeted socio-economic research was introduced as part of the 1993 13.1 million euro Framework IV programme. Social inclusion/exclusion was also an important part of the 1998-2002 Framework Five programme that committed 14.96 million euros to the EU's research priorities. There is a clear assumption that social and economic problems possess a European dimension and that European paths to social inclusion need to be found.

The Commission has become a key organization in any discussion of European-ized research opportunities because once the Council has adopted legislation then responsibility for implementation and management passes to the Commission. If we view the Commission as an instrumental actor then we can also discuss its relation to discussion of inclusion/exclusion. A key task for the Commission is that it is charged by Treaty with promoting closer European integration. It can also seek to act as a 'purposeful opportunist' where opportunities for integration present themselves (Cram, 1994). In this respect the existence of social exclusion and the pursuit of social inclusion can be viewed as instrumental resources for the Commis-sion because the existence of phenomena deemed indicative of social exclusion can help secure it a role as an actor with capacity to address Europeanized problems of exclusion. A potential problem is that it is far from clear what 'social inclusion' actually means. But, for purposeful opportunists like the units within the Commission with 'social inclusion' responsibilities, these kinds of problems also present opportunities. It is not so important that the meaning of social inclusion is indistinct because this presents further opportunities that can be exploited as a quest for the 'meaning of inclusion' occurs. It is also highly unlikely that concerted academic research will make the meaning any clearer. In fact, concerted academic research in various networks informed by different theoretical, empirical and methodological perspectives could further muddy the waters. It is, however, in the very absence of substantive meaning that resources for institutionalization can be identified. Consequently, it is not so important that the Commission has a commitment to combating social exclusion, although it is fairly clear that there is commitment within the relevant Commission units. What is important is that it has a positive view about its own potential role as a motor of European integration, despite the many constraints it faces when actually trying to serve as an engine of integration. Moreover, given the kinds of expert knowledge privileged by European integration, the inducement, inculcation and encouragement of academic research and academic networks that focus on these problems of Europe is rational in the context of the motivations of Commission units and academics with an interest in problems of Europe.

These kinds of opportunities do only present themselves to a relatively small number of Euro-academics hooked up with the relevant networks. For most academics, problems of Europe are not top of their priorities. Even though there is evidence that European social space has been open to some transnationalization, political space does seem to remain quite largely territorially configured. Systems of higher education, for example, bear closer relation to territorially configured political space than to transnationalized social space. This implies that European opportunities are open to a relatively small number of academics able to transcend national settings by accessing resources available at EU level. In addition to this, there are one or two Euro-institutions, but these are small and often serve as venues for academics and researchers who have their roots in national systems and then return to national systems. Academics who do successfully access Euro-research opportunities such as through the Framework Five programme and development of Euro-networks will necessarily keep a foot in both camps because their academic careers will tend to rely on the national systems within which they operate. This could be construed as ironic given the transnationalization of knowledge industries, but European higher education remains territorially configured. Moreover, the capacity of the EU to shape national contexts will be limited by resource constraints. The EU is not a lurking leviathan. Rather it has acquired the capacity to act at the margins with regards to the teaching and research of European integration. This then possesses the capacity to impact on the structure of opportunities for those academics that are well placed to benefit from this developing European dimension and the institutionalization of 'problems of Europe'.

Conclusion

In this chapter I have sought to outline the development of EU migration responsibilities, temper some of the flights of fancy about the EU's potential and link the EU context to forms of academic work that address problems of European integration. Clearly, the EU impinges on academic research agendas that address issues associated with migration policy because of the development of an institutionalized policy context and the associated new patterns of governance that have developed. A note of caution was also struck because it is necessary to be realistic about the EU as a form of institutionalized state-like power. The EU's powers are circumscribed, which makes it necessary to carefully delineate its capacities and the sources of power that configure them while noting that the forms of legal, social and political power associated with European integration mean that certain forms of action and certain actors are likely to be privileged at EU level. In particular, a prevailing technocratic ethos privileges expert knowledge that provides opportunities for academics able to match their research agendas with Europeanized issues of social inclusion/exclusion, which is good news for those academics well placed to seek to access these resources. The building of a European research area and the key roles of the European Commission funded research programmes can be viewed from the perspective of a happy confluence between idealism and instrumentalism. It is clear that units within the Commission are committed to 'social inclusion'; but they are also committed to the Europeanization of these problems.

These considerations of the scope for the construction and problems of Europe also raised the question of whether the Europeanization of an academic context promises to be more than an ephemeral form of transnational political exchange. Can the EU acquire the capacity to become institutionalized as an autonomous form of supranational state power and authority able to sustain itself? European integration does possess just such an institutionalizing capacity with the potential to feedback into domestic contexts and reconfigure national frameworks in particular areas of legal, political and social life in the member states. It is, though, important to locate an institutionalizing dynamics in relation to the sources of power underpinning European integration, which arise from the articulation between liberalization and securitization. It is also important not to exaggerate this scope for institutionalization and to pretend that the EU can do things that it cannot. This reflects on academic research that, via counter-factual normative reasoning, reads into the European project capacities and capabilities that it may not actually possess. In terms of its organizational implications, it also demonstrates that academic work in EU member states remains embedded at national level and the opportunities for Euro-research are open to only relatively small numbers of academics, most of whom retain strong links with their respective national systems. Even though we can point to the construction and institutionalization of 'problems of Europe' there remain conceptual and organizational limits to Europeanization and to the construction and institutionalization of problems of Europe that impinge on EU level migrant social inclusion/exclusion.

Notes

1 Institutions are not conceptualized as static constraints on political action. Rather, the interplay between structure and agency means that reflexivity becomes important, in the sense that: 'Institutions do not merely reflect the preferences and power of the units constituting them; the institutions themselves shape those preferences and that power. Institutions are thus *constitutive* of actors, as well as vice versa' (Keohane, 1989, p. 161, emphasis in original). *Structuration* perspectives emphasize interplay between structure and agency (Giddens, 1979), with emphasis placed not on institutions as 'static edifices' but as processes of structuration within which agency and structure become entwined. 'Structuration implies a process of continuing interaction between agent and structure, in which structures which are generally constraining can also change and be changed in certain conditions' (Cerny, 1990, p. xi).

2 The effect is to render 'the international system a bit less like anarchy, a bit more like a constitutionalized domestic polity' (Caporaso, 1996, p. 35). On the role of the ECJ see Mancini (1991); Mattli and Slaughter (1996).

3 Defined by Tarrow (1998) as 'a collective challenge, based on common purposes and social solidarities, in sustained interaction with élites, opponents and authorities'.

4 Norms can be defined as operating 'like rules that define the identity of an actor, thus having "constitutive effects" that specify what actions will cause relevant others to recognize a particular identity' (Katzenstein, 1966, p. 5).

References

Action Group on Immigration (AGIT) (1999), *Efficient, Effective and Encompassing Approaches to a European Union Immigration and Asylum Policy,* AGIT, Amsterdam.

Baldwin-Edwards, M. and Schain, M. (eds.) (1994), *The Politics of Immigration in Western Europe,* Frank Cass, London.

Bigo, D. (1996), *Polices en Réseaux, l'expérience Européene,* Presses de la Fondation Nationales des Sciences Politiques, Paris.

Bigo, D. (1998), 'Immigration at the Securitarian Crossroads'. Paper Presented to the Conference 'Dilemmas of Immigration Control in a Globalizing World', European University Institute, Florence, 11-12 June 1998.

Bommes, M., and Geddes, A. (2001), *Immigration and Welfare: Challenging the Borders of the Welfare State,* Routledge, London.

Caporaso, J. (1996), 'The European Union and Forms of State: Westphalian, Regulatory or Post-Modern?', *Journal of Common Market Studies,* 34 (1), pp. 29-52.

Cerny, P. (1990), *The Changing Architecture of Politics: Structure, Agency and the Future of the State,* Sage, London.

Cesarini, D. and Fulbrook, M. (eds.) (1996), *Citizenship, Nationality and Migration in Europe,* Routledge, London.

Cox, R. (1987), *Production, Power and World Order: Social Forces in the Making of History,* Columbia UP, New York.

Cram, L. (1994), 'The European Commission as a Multi-Organization: Social Policy and IT Policy in the EU', *Journal of European Public Policy,* 1 (2), pp. 195-217.

Danese, G. (1998), 'Transnational Collective Action in Europe: The Case of Migrants in Italy and Spain', *Journal of Ethnic and Migration Studies,* 24 (4), pp. 715-34.

Favell, A. (1998), 'The European Citizenship Agenda: Emergence, Transformation and Effects of a New Political Field'. Paper Presented at the 11th Conference of Europeanists, Baltimore, 26 February-1 March.

Favell, A. and Geddes, A. (1999), 'European Integration, Immigration and the Nation State. Transnationalising Collective Action'. Working Paper 99/32, Robert Schuman Centre, European University Institute, Florence, Italy.

Geddes, A. (2000), 'Lobbying for Migrant Inclusion: New Opportunities for Transnational Advocacy?', *Journal of European Public Policy,* 7 (4), pp.632-49.

Giddens, A. (1979), *Central Problems of Social Theory: Action, Structure and Contradiction in Social Analysis,* Macmillan, London.

Guild, E. (1998), 'Competence, Discretion and Third Country Nationals: The European Union's Legal Struggle with Migration', *Journal of Ethnic and Migration Studies,* 24 (4), pp. 613-26.

Hammar, T. (1990), *Democracy and the Nation State: Aliens, Denizens and Citizens in a World of International Migration,* Avebury, Aldershot.

Hix, S. (1998), 'The Study of the European Union II: The "New Governance Agenda and Its Rival"', *Journal of European Public Policy,* 5 (1), pp. 38-65.

Huysmans, J. (1995), 'Migrants as a Security Problem: Dangers of "Securitizing Social Issues"', in R. Miles and D. Thränhardt (eds.), *Migration and European Integration; The Dynamics of Inclusion and Exclusion,* Pinter, London, pp. 53-72.

Ireland, P. (1991), 'Facing the True "Fortress Europe": Immigrants and Politics in the EC', *Journal of Common Market Studies,* 24 (5), pp. 246-71.

Jahtenfuchs, M. (1995), 'Theoretical Perspectives on European Governance', *European Law Journal,* 1, pp. 115-23.

Journal of Ethnic and Migration Studies, European Integration and New Forms of Citizenship, October 1998 (edited by A. Favell).

Kastoryano, R. (1999), 'Transnational Participation and Citizenship: Immigrants Inside the European Union', *Transnational Communities on-line working paper series,* WPTC-98-12, <http://www.transcomm.oxford.ac.uk>.

Katzenstein, P. (1966), *Norms and National Security,* Columbia UP, New York.

Keohane, R. (1989), 'International Institutions: Two Approaches', in R. Keohane (ed.), *International Institutions and State Power: Essays in International Relations Theory,* Westview Press, Boulder, CO, pp. 158-79.

King, R. (ed.) (1993), *The New Geography of European Migrations,* Belhaven Press, London.

Kooiman, J. (ed.) (1993), *Modern Governance: New Government-Society Interactions,* Sage, London.

Koslowski, R. (1998), 'EU Migration Regimes: Established and Emergent', in C. Joppke (ed.), *Challenge to the Nation State: Immigration in Western Europe and the United States,* Oxford UP, Oxford, pp. 153-88.

Mancini, F. (1991), 'The Making of a Constitution for Europe', in R. Keohane and S. Hoffmann (eds.), *The New European Community: Decision-Making and Institutional Change,* Westview Press, Bolder, CO.

Majone, G. (1996), *Regulating Europe,* Routledge, London.

Mattli, W. and Slaughter, A.-M. (1996), *Constructing the EU Legal System from the Ground up: The Role of Individual Litigants and National Courts,* Harvard Law School, Cambridge.

Meehan, E. (1993), *Citizenship and the European Community,* Sage, London.

Miles, R. and Thränhardt, D. (eds.) (1995), *Migration and European Integration,* Pinter, London.

Rosenau, J. and Czempiel, E-O. (1992), *Governance Without Government: Order and Change in World Politics,* Cambridge UP, Cambridge.

Schmitter, P. (1996), 'Examining the Present Euro-Polity with the Help of Past Theories', in G. Marks, F. Scharpf, P. Schmitter, and W. Streeck (eds.), *Governance in the European Union,* Sage, London, pp. 1-14.

Soysal, Y.N. (1993), 'Immigration and the Emerging European Polity', in S. Anderson and K. Eliassen, *Making Policy in Europe: The Europification of National Policy Making,* Sage, London, pp. 136-57.

Soysal, Y.N. (1994), *Limits of Citizenship: Migrants and Post-National Membership in Europe,* University of Chicago Press, Chicago.

Stone-Sweet, A. and Sandholtz, W. (eds.) (1998), *European Integration and Supranational Governance,* Oxford UP, Oxford.

Tarrow, S. (1998), *Power in Movement. Social Movements and Contentious Politics,* 2nd ed., Cambridge UP, Cambridge.

Wæver, O. (1996), 'European Security Identities', *Journal of Common Market Studies,* 34 (1), pp. 103-32.

Wrench, J. and Solomos, J. (eds.) (1992), *Racism and Migration in Western Europe,* Berg, Oxford.

Conclusion

Michael Bommes and Ewa Morawska

The *spiritus movens* of this volume has been our belief that because of the central role of international migration in present-day societal transformations worldwide, it should play a pivotal role in the multidisciplinary study of contemporary societies similar to that played in different historical circumstances during the founding period of American sociology. As a base concept-reference 'bridging' several disciplines, international migration may serve, we argue, not only to reconceptualize accustomed representations of society and its actors in terms of territorially bounded nation-states as the sole creators and executors of laws and policies and national cultures as the exclusive focuses of citizens' identities and loyalties, but also to construct new theoretical frameworks for the investigation of contemporary societal processes in these disciplines.

This collection of eleven essays by international migration specialists from Europe and the United States representing eight disciplines is one step towards meeting the challenge of making international migration a key analytic tool in the investigation of contemporary societies. Contributors agree that foundations for this task should be laid by a collective critical reflection on accepted theoretical concepts and epistemological premises, taken-for-granted concerns and agendas (and, thus, also non-issues) and contextual entanglements of migration research as pursued in different disciplines.

Within the general framework of the project prepared by participants during a year-long seminar at the European University Institute in Florence, the contributors to this volume were free to choose the particular focus of their reflections. Given disciplinary differences in formulating and investigating research questions and individual scholars' preferences and temperaments, these reflections address a variety of issues and represent diverse approaches. Revealing this variety of agendas and modes of analysis in migration research, which in standard multidisciplinary volumes usually remains hidden in the background, is an important contribution to the effort to make international migration a guidepost concept for the study of contemporary societies. But the essays presented here reveal also some common positions shared by international migration specialists across disciplines despite differences in particular focuses and strategies of their research. Such common positions, one theoretical and three epistemological can be treated as launching a platform for multidisciplinary collaboration in this field of study.

As an enduring, constitutive component of macro- and micro-level societal processes in the contemporary world, international migration should become an integral element of empirical research and theoretical models explaining different aspects of contemporary societies. This premise has informed all contributions to this volume: those that highlight tacit premises of and implicit omissions in the key concepts and methodological approaches in different fields of the social sciences, and those that demonstrate how the study of international migration reflects discipline-specific modes of constructing the object of investigation, the limitations of these strategies and the challenges of crossing these disciplinary boundaries. Plurality or multidisciplinarity of theoretical approaches and methodological strategies in migration research is natural and intellectually healthy for the advancement of this field of scholarly investigation. Collaborative interdisciplinary work, viewed as the preferred strategy to effect this advancement, should produce 'polyglots' capable of translating concepts, problem agendas, and modes of analysis between different disciplinary studies and, thus, opening the path to deal with blind spots and taken-for-granted concerns and modes of analysis ingrained in a particular disciplinary perspective, rather than seek simply to aggregate or fuse, melting pot-like, knowledge from several disciplines that study this phenomenon. For such polyglot skills to develop among migration scholars and, thus, for meaningful interdisciplinary collaboration to ensue, all participants must continue self-reflexive examination and reveal for colleagues' inspection the usually tacit, backstage presuppositions informing the conceptualization, execution, and representation of their research.

In their critical inquiries into particular aspects of international migration research assembled in this volume scholar-representatives of different disciplines have addressed four general themes: firmly established epistemological premises, repertoires of theoretical concepts and interpretive frameworks informing the study of international migration and its preferred research methods; the place and contributions of international migration research as a subfield of different disciplines in the latter's mainstream problem agendas, dominant theories, and research; theoretical and methodological premises and dilemmas of interdisciplinary research on international migration; and interdependency between the scholarly study of international migration and the various social and political contexts in which it is embedded. These scrutinies reveal important issues in need of further self-reflexive, multidisciplinary examination in order to enhance the status of international migration in the study of contemporary societies.

From among the issues addressed in this volume (and many more await reassessment), reexamined against local evidence should be the notions of overpopulation and population pressure customarily used in historical and social science analyses as one of the macrostructural mechanisms triggering international migration. The social (economic, political, cultural) processes through which the population factor, itself a long-term effect of societal structures and human action, 'translates back' into these actions and societal structures also await investigation.

Sustained mass transnational migrations in contemporary societies expose and call for reexamination of the imprecise, vague meaning of the key concept in the social sciences, namely, social integration, that lies at the foundations of sociology and neighbouring disciplines and has informed mainstream theories and research in these fields. Related to it, the idea of the nation-state as the research agenda-setting concept in political science and political sociology also needs further scrutiny, particularly its usefulness for the analysis of contemporary civic-political institutions. The contributors to this volume have expressed three different opinions about this matter: that the nation-state has been displaced by worldwide transnational migrations and other globalizing processes; that it still performs important control and integration functions; and that its role depends on past and present circumstances.

The conceptual equivalents 'from below' of the nationalism versus postnationalism positions in political science research on international migration have been the notions of assimilation and transnationalism that inform studies of sociologists, anthropologists, and historians. Both these concepts have been ascribed different meanings not only in particular disciplinary studies but also by different researchers within the same field, and both need self-reflexive scrutiny and clarification in order to become 'legible' to all users and 'translatable' between disciplines and approaches. A thoughtful examination of the relationship between (im)migrants' assimilation and their transnational identities and involvements is also in order.

Because in current migration research the phenomena of assimilation and transnationalism are either presumed to be mutually exclusive or, if both are reported, theoretical and empirical grounds of their coexistence are unelaborated, we should investigate patterns of this convergence (or divergence) in different combinations contingent on historical, that is, time- and place-variant constellations of factors: the economic and geopolitical positions and interests of sender and receiver countries, their civic-juridical systems and national cultures, and the political, socioeconomic, and racial makeup of particular immigrant groups and their relations with native-born residents/institutions of host countries.

Further conversation among students of international migration 'from above' and 'from below' would be facilitated by the conceptual separation of the implicitly fused notions of society and the nation-state. Such distinction allows for the recognition of the latter's enduring importance for processes of assimilation without presupposing that it constitutes the exclusive frame of reference for understanding social engagements and collective identity-building processes associated with them.

The habituated identification of society and the nation-state underlies also the concept of language as commonly applied in the social sciences. The phenomenon of multilingualism in many immigration countries, a result of transnational migration reveals not only the historical specificity of the project of national homogenization but also its inscription into the basic concepts of the social sciences informed – contrary to the empirical reality of past and present – by the implicit premise of the 'naturalness' of monolingual communication and the deviancy of multilingual situations. The 'linguistic effects' of sustained transnational migration call for a reexamination of these presuppositions that underlie the concepts of language in different disciplines. Linguistic transformation means a transformation of sociocultural structures of immigration countries that cannot be assumed to be transitory as in the perspective tacitly subscribing to the nation-state project.

The issue of gender, misconceived as 'women's studies' and marginalized in migration research (as in most disciplines), certainly calls for further scrutiny – not by gender historians, sociologists, and so on, but by 'mainstream' migration scholars in all these disciplines – of tacit representations that cause this persistent misconception and the resulting marginalization, and of the ways to correct this situation.

Another area awaiting a focused multidisciplinary, self-reflexive conversation is delineated by the methodological strategies of migration research and, especially, the underlying concepts of a 'good science'. Although the contributors to this volume have in different ways addressed this issue while examining the place of migration research in their disciplines or in cross-disciplinary comparisons of the problem agendas and research strategies in this field of study, they have not scrutinized the premises and implications of their own epistemological standpoints against different approaches. Thus, two sets of 'undebated' propositions have been counterposed: the study of international migration as (1) a theoretical versus a (merely) descriptive science and (2) a 'pure' science disengaged from political, ideological, and other societal causes versus a multiple and context-entangled science.

If the preference would be, as postulated here, for a catholic coexistence of plural approaches in the study of international migration, then the purpose of further multidisciplinary reflexive work in this area should not be to search for ways of fusing these different positions, but to seek instead the clarification of terms and to reveal for scrutiny their epistemological underpinnings.

Thus, it would be useful to reexamine the standard counterposition of the terms theoretical and descriptive questioned in recent historical-sociological studies that argue for a more flexible, pluralized understanding of theoretical analyses. A parallel reconsideration is also needed of the epistemological foundations, connotations, and implications for research of the notions of the neutral (objective) versus engaged social science of international migration and the relationship of the former concept and the past and present contextual embeddedness of migration research discussed in several chapters in this volume. John Hall's recent assessment of strengths and weaknesses of different generalizing and particularizing strategies of social science inquiry (Hall, J.R. 1999, Cultures of Inquiry. From Epistemology to Discourse in Sociohistorical Research, Cambridge UP, New York; see also Morawska in this volume), informed by the belief that all inquiries combine in different constellations four constitutive elements – value discourse, narrative, theory, and, overlapping, explanation/interpretation – might serve as a good starting point for such multidisciplinary discussion.

To date, the 'obviousness' of international migration as a subject of scientific investigation has been the basis on which migration research has claimed its importance and scholarly significance. The term international migration has referred to a field of social problems usually treated as evidently 'given'. Contributions to this volume make it as evidently clear: that there is no direct access to social reality

– in this case, the transnational movement of people and its consequences for sender and receiver societies – and a reflexive effort to take stock should precede any claims to scholarly relevance.

The main idea informing this volume and the main purpose of further exercises recommended here in multidisciplinary, self-reflexive scrutiny of our distinct and shared epistemological positions and their implications for research and theory of international migrations is to help migration scholars from different disciplines understand each other's 'languages' so that they can enrich and enhance their own work, contributing in this way to a better, more encompassing understanding of the transformations of contemporary societies.

Index